Road to a More Intelligent World

Pengfei Sun

Road to a More Intelligent World

Revolutionizing Industries with Digital Transformation

Pengfei Sun
Global Public Sector
Huawei ICT BG
ShenZhen, China

ISBN 978-981-96-5128-3   ISBN 978-981-96-5129-0 (eBook)
https://doi.org/10.1007/978-981-96-5129-0

Jointly published with Posts & Telecom Press

The print edition is not for sale in Mainland China. Customers from Mainland China please order the print book from: Posts & Telecom Press

© Posts & Telecom Press Co.,Ltd. 2025

This work is subject to copyright. All rights are solely and exclusively licensed by the Publisher, whether the whole or part of the material is concerned, specifically the rights of reprinting, reuse of illustrations, recitation, broadcasting, reproduction on microfilms or in any other physical way, and transmission or information storage and retrieval, electronic adaptation, computer software, or by similar or dissimilar methodology now known or hereafter developed.
The use of general descriptive names, registered names, trademarks, service marks, etc. in this publication does not imply, even in the absence of a specific statement, that such names are exempt from the relevant protective laws and regulations and therefore free for general use.
The publishers, the authors, and the editors are safe to assume that the advice and information in this book are believed to be true and accurate at the date of publication. Neither the publishers nor the authors or the editors give a warranty, express or implied, with respect to the material contained herein or for any errors or omissions that may have been made. The publishers remain neutral with regard to jurisdictional claims in published maps and institutional affiliations.

This Springer imprint is published by the registered company Springer Nature Singapore Pte Ltd.
The registered company address is: 152 Beach Road, #21-01/04 Gateway East, Singapore 189721, Singapore

If disposing of this product, please recycle the paper.

Foreword

The high-tech industry is in the midst of a technological overhaul, with diversified technologies like artificial intelligence (AI), information technology (IT), biotechnology, and new materials pushed to the forefront of innovation. Multi-field technologies are aggregated, integrated, and iterated to drive global scientific and technological progress, making new applications and business models possible with far-reaching potential to benefit humanity.

Innovation is the intrinsic driving force behind the sustainable development of the high-tech industry. Every technological breakthrough has brought enormous value to society. Cross-industry convergence is the new norm for industry development, where the cross-application of technologies and mutual penetration of industries have given rise to emerging industries and business forms. Digital transformation is fueling the DNA of every enterprise. Data gradually becomes a new factor of production, helping inform business decision with new insights.

In the coming years, the main direction of high-tech development will be centered on emerging technologies. 5G and future communications technologies, AI, edge computing, biotechnology, blockchain, Internet of Things (IoT), and virtual reality (VR) will change the way we live and work while contributing to economic growth.

5G and AI have become the key drivers of scientific research and industrial transformation. Many countries have been actively developing 5G and AI for their digital strategies, such as the release of national development strategies and plans, policy support, implementation strategies, large capital investments, and initiatives spanning industry, universities, and research institutes. These approaches are taken to promote scientific and technological innovation and industrial upgrade, to gain a competitive edge in scientific and technological development, and to take the initiative in the global technological competition. The ultimate goal behind these efforts is to enhance the comprehensive national strength, extend the industry and value chains, accelerate the transformation of traditional industries from digital to intelligent, and drive the intelligent upgrade of national industries to move toward the mid- and high-end in the value chain.

This book gives an overview of the development of mobile communications technologies in China over the past years, from China being a follower in 2G to a pacesetter in 5G. It also explores the road to large-scale 5G implementation and the future trends of 5G development. 5G is playing an increasingly important role in society. Far beyond being a communications technology, it is the primary driving force to digital transformation in industries and the catalyst for a prosperous digital economy.

Recent years have seen rapid developments in social economy and technologies such as big data, mobile Internet, supercomputer, brain science, and sensor network. Over this period, AI has gone through three major stages: perceptual intelligence, perceptual enhancement, and cognitive intelligence. Along the development, AI presents new potential for cross-domain integration, deep learning, man-machine collaboration, and autonomous operation.

As digital transformation is gaining pace globally, the new-generation information technologies are increasingly integrated with the real economy. Around the world, countries are refining their innovation strategies, investing in digital infrastructure and industry chain, and promoting digital applications on key fields of the digital economy, with the aim to upgrade traditional sectors.

Against this backdrop, China has released a host of strategies and policies that aim to prioritize the sustainable industrial development. For example, 5G and AI have become strategic emerging industries, in which the government will constantly strive to innovate, to further integrate the digital economy with the real economy. What is more, China's telecom equipment vendors have made great strides in the R&D in 5G technologies, helping push China to become a global leader in 5G. China is also home to some of the most active research communities with the largest amount of data in the AI field, which significantly empowers the development of AI technologies.

Looking ahead, breakthroughs must be made to adapt 5G and AI technologies to a wider range of fields. China needs to increase investment in research on fundamental theories and core technologies, among others, and improve the innovation capabilities as well. China also needs to strengthen basic research and strive for key technology breakthroughs, enhance independent innovation capabilities, integrate resources worldwide, and promote collaborative innovation. In the meantime, it is necessary to improve the industry chain support system, form industrial clusters, and build a reliable closed-loop industry ecosystem, to reduce production costs and further improve competitiveness.

In summary, to ensure sustainable development of 5G and AI, China needs to take an overall view of the social environment and technological progress both at home and abroad, enhance innovation and R&D capabilities, and improve the industry ecosystem. In addition, China needs to strengthen its talent development system and enhance public awareness and recognition of the importance of 5G and AI. Only in this way can we substantially promote the sustainable development of 5G and AI and eventually make greater contributions to the progress of human society.

Chinese Academy of Engineering Zhang Ping
Beijing, China
Beijing University of Posts and Telecommunications
Beijing, China
January 2025

Editorial Board

- **Consultant:** Zhang Ping, Academician of the Chinese Academy of Engineering
- **Editor-in-Chief:** Sun Pengfei
- **Members:**

Zhang Lei	Xi Renjun	Yang Xinhua
Zhang Huijuan	Liang Xiaozeng	Huang Shuhua
Luo Jingrui	Liao Yunfa	Gao Qinghao
Zuo Yun	Wu Cheng	Wang Lei
Liu Ying	Tan Ziwei	

Preface

5G and artificial intelligence (AI) are currently the most popular technology sectors, and their integration has become a prominent trend in technology development.

For China, mobile communications is one of the few world-leading fields that are of fundamental and strategic importance to the economic and social development. China's mobile communications industry, which is worth over CNY1 trillion, has been steadily growing in size and strength since its early days. From being a follower in 2G to a strong competitor in 3G, and a forerunner in 4G, China has achieved major breakthroughs in the core mobile communications technologies. The overall level of the industry is significantly higher, with explosive growth in information consumption and vigorous development in the digital economy. China is steadily progressing to be a leader in 5G coverage, technology, and adoption.

With the widespread and deep integration of information and communications technologies (ICTs) into all sectors of the manufacturing industry, promoting new industrialization, 5.5G entered commercial use in 2024, marking a substantial step toward advanced operational capabilities and cost-effective networks. As the next step in evolution, 5.5G delivers tenfold network speeds, millisecond-level latency, and precise positioning to the centimeter, which enable AI to implement efficient and stable data transmission and processing in diversified scenarios. Meanwhile, the ever-improving intelligent computing allows AI to process more complex tasks and better adapt to the changing real environment, improving the accuracy and reliability and thereby better meeting the requirements in intelligent application scenarios. What is more, computing power infrastructure is continuously improving, which is paving the way for AI development and continuously empowers large AI models.

AI is empowering all aspects of society with diverse and intuitive applications and types and has fostered a highly collaborative industry system in a range of fields like industrial manufacturing, healthcare, education and training, and smart home. In such a system, enterprises and institutes are making every endeavor to promote the development of large AI models and upgrade the industry chain, which, as a result, will promote high-quality development of the entire industry.

Currently, the deep integration of 5G and AI can be seen in many fields, such as manufacturing, port, education, healthcare, and electric power, pushing these fields beyond digital to intelligent. Despite its clear advantages, this transformation raises new challenges. One main challenge is how to ensure privacy protection and data security management. Data security and privacy protection stand out as a fundamental requirement as large AI models are adopted in more and more fields. Another challenge is the immature ecosystem, which requires strengthened R&D and cooperation across industries for improvement. Last but not least, the relevant laws, regulations, and supervision mechanisms are yet to be improved to cover the full scope of operations. These issues must be addressed to ensure that AI and 5G create more value for society.

Shenzhen, China　　　　　　　　　　　　　　　　　　　　　　　　　Pengfei Sun
January 2025

Acknowledgments

This book is the result of collective efforts by experts, scholars, and enterprises across multiple industries and disciplines. We thank all contributors for their incredible work and support, without which this book would not have been possible. We would also like to extend our gratitude to the translators, proofreaders, editors, and technical support personnel who exhibited a high level of professionalism while translating this book into English. They are:

Translators: Chen Gong, Chen Mengyuan, Chen Xiexia, Du Yanjun, Feng Qiangqiang, Huang Juying, Huang Xiao, Ji Chenyang, Jin Yi, Liu Yong, Qian Ying, Wang Lili, Wang Xueying, Wang Ying, Wang Yuyuan, Xu Yu, Yang Xiaojing, and Zhang YuXuan

Proofreaders: Zhang Li, Li Xiaochun, Su Qin, Qu Hua, Liu Peng, Zhang Weiyu, Chen Xiahuan, Tan Chuan, Ji Xiangjia, and Han Qiang

Editors: Daniel Mark Curran, Ekaterina Roumenova Christova, Gavin Wills, Jimmy Xue Jing Ding, Kyle Melieste, Megan Mary Young, Peter Peiyu Zhao, and Samuel Luke Winfield-D'Arcy

Technical support personnel: Hou Junyan and Xie Congming

Contents

Part I   5G Large-Scale Replication

1   5G Drives New Developments in Global Digital Transformation   3
    1.1   Communications Technologies Lead Continuous
        Social Progress   3
    1.2   The World is Embracing a New Wave of Digital
        Transformation   5
    1.3   Digital Transformation Brings Big Opportunities   7
    1.4   5G Unlocks the Potential of Industry Transformation   9

2   5G Development Around the Globe   13
    2.1   5G Development in China   14
        2.1.1   5G Commercial Adoption in China   14
        2.1.2   5G Promotion Policies in China   17
        2.1.3   5G Application in China   18
    2.2   5G Development in South Korea   19
        2.2.1   5G Commercial Adoption in South Korea   19
        2.2.2   5G Promotion Policies in South Korea   19
        2.2.3   5G Application in South Korea   21
    2.3   5G Development in the USA   22
        2.3.1   5G Commercial Adoption in the USA   22
        2.3.2   5G Promotion Policies in the USA   24
        2.3.3   5G Application in the USA   25
    2.4   5G Development in Japan   26
        2.4.1   5G Commercial Adoption in Japan   26
        2.4.2   5G Promotion Policies in Japan   27
        2.4.3   5G Application in Japan   28
    2.5   5G Development in Germany   29
        2.5.1   5G Commercial Adoption in Germany   29
        2.5.2   5G Promotion Policies in Germany   30
        2.5.3   5G Application in Germany   31
    References   32

3 Challenges, Phases, and Trends of 5G Large-Scale Replication ... 33
- 3.1 Key Challenges of 5G Large-Scale Replication ... 33
  - 3.1.1 Challenges with 5G Network Construction ... 34
  - 3.1.2 Insufficient Convergence of 5G Technologies into Industry Services ... 35
  - 3.1.3 Insufficient Industry Supply Capabilities ... 35
  - 3.1.4 Lack of Standards for Industry Converged Applications ... 36
  - 3.1.5 5G Industrial Ecosystems Need to Be Strengthened ... 37
- 3.2 Phases of 5G Large-Scale Replication ... 38
  - 3.2.1 Foundations ... 38
  - 3.2.2 Phases and Key Factors ... 40
  - 3.2.3 Significance and Values ... 45
- 3.3 Trends of 5G Large-Scale Replication and 5.5G ... 46
  - 3.3.1 5G Applications Are Revolutionizing Future Society and Daily Life ... 46
  - 3.3.2 5.5G Empowers a New Future for Communications ... 48
- References ... 51

Part II A New Phase in AI Development

4 Introduction to AI ... 55
- 4.1 Definition of AI ... 55
- 4.2 History and Development of AI ... 56
  - 4.2.1 Phase I: Computational Reasoning-Driven AI (1950s to 1970s) ... 57
  - 4.2.2 Phase II: Knowledge-Driven AI (1970s to Early 1990s) ... 57
  - 4.2.3 Phase III: Data-Driven AI (1990s to Early 2000s) ... 58
  - 4.2.4 Phase IV: Computing Power-Driven AI (2020 to Present) ... 58
- 4.3 Applicable Scenarios of AI ... 59
- 4.4 National AI Strategies ... 61
  - 4.4.1 US: Maintaining Its Globally Leading Position by Taking Collective Measures ... 62
  - 4.4.2 China: Promoting Sustainable Industrial Development Through Diversified Policies ... 63
  - 4.4.3 Japan: Building "Society 5.0" with AI ... 64
  - 4.4.4 South Korea: Strengthening Its AI Power Through Policies ... 65
  - 4.4.5 Germany: Building the German Brand Through "Industry 4.0" ... 65
  - 4.4.6 UK: Increasing Investment in Innovation to Promote Achievement Transfer ... 66
- References ... 67

5	**Typical AI Technologies**		69
	5.1 Machine Learning		69
		5.1.1 Supervised Learning	72
		5.1.2 Unsupervised Learning	73
		5.1.3 Reinforcement Learning	74
		5.1.4 Deep Learning	76
		5.1.5 Multi-Task Learning	78
	5.2 Natural Language Processing		79
		5.2.1 Language Model	81
		5.2.2 Word Vector	83
		5.2.3 Machine Translation	84
		5.2.4 Text Classification	86
	5.3 Computer Vision		87
		5.3.1 Image Processing	88
		5.3.2 Object Detection	89
		5.3.3 Image Recognition	90
		5.3.4 Video Analysis	91
	5.4 Multimodal Technology		91
		5.4.1 Feature Representation	92
		5.4.2 Modality Fusion	93
	References		94
6	**Significant Developments in AI**		95
	6.1 Horizontal Expansion of the AI Industry		95
		6.1.1 AI Industry Overview	95
		6.1.2 AI Industry Trends	96
	6.2 AI Chip Iteration for Underlying Technologies		99
		6.2.1 NVIDIA	104
		6.2.2 AMD	105
		6.2.3 Intel	108
		6.2.4 Huawei HiSilicon	109
		6.2.5 Cambricon	109
	6.3 AI Cloud Platforms for Innovative Services		111
		6.3.1 Microsoft	112
		6.3.2 Amazon	114
		6.3.3 Huawei Cloud	114
		6.3.4 Alibaba Cloud	116
		6.3.5 Baidu AI Cloud	116
	6.4 AI Frameworks Empowering Engineering Capabilities		117
		6.4.1 AI Frameworks: Accelerating the Growth and Engineering of the AI Industry	118
		6.4.2 Training Platforms: Driving AI Engineering by Scalable Distributed Training	121
		6.4.3 MLOps: Streamlining the Last Mile of AI Engineering	123
	6.5 Computing Power Breakthroughs for Rapid AI Development		127

		6.5.1	Evolution of AI Computing from Rough Use to Sophisticated Collaboration	127
		6.5.2	Cloud-Edge-Device Collaboration Promoting Development of Ubiquitous Computing Power	129
		6.5.3	Intelligent Computing Power and Digital Twins	130
		6.5.4	Multi-Technology Collaboration Accelerating Advanced Computing	131
	6.6	Algorithm Updates Boosting AI Development		135
		6.6.1	New Algorithms Like AutoML Simplifying AI Development	135
		6.6.2	Rapid Development of Model-Centric Open-Source Communities	137
	6.7	Diversified Data Services Adding Value to AI		137
	6.8	Innovative Unicorns Enabling AI Applications		140
		6.8.1	Adept AI: Offering Artificial General Intelligence (AGI) Tools	141
		6.8.2	Cohere: Offering Tailored ToB AI Services	142
		6.8.3	Jasper: Offering Integrated AI Marketing Tools	144
		6.8.4	DiDi: Integrating AI into Autonomous Driving	145
		6.8.5	Dataa Robotics: Empowering Humanoid Robots with Cloud Brain	146
	References			148
7	**Dawn of the Large Model Era**			149
	7.1	History and Features of Large Models		149
		7.1.1	Parameter Size Jumps: Fast Iteration in Three Phases	149
		7.1.2	Collaboration of Large and Small Models for On-Device Model Deployment	152
		7.1.3	Synergy of Large Models and AI	154
		7.1.4	Faster Iteration and Development Trends of Large Models	156
	7.2	Typical Applications of Large Models		157
		7.2.1	NLP Models	158
		7.2.2	CV Models	164
		7.2.3	Multimodal Models	169
	7.3	Computing Power as the Foundation of Large Models		175
		7.3.1	General-Purpose Computing Power for Meeting the Requirements of Most Common Users	176
		7.3.2	Intelligent Computing Power Suitable for Simple Logic and Compute-Intensive Concurrent Tasks	176
		7.3.3	High-Performance Computing Cluster for Special Applications	178
	7.4	Large Models Empowering Generative AI		179
		7.4.1	Large Models Transforming Content Generation	179
		7.4.2	Generative AI Forming New Business Models	182

	7.5	A Myriad of Models and Modalities	184
		7.5.1 OpenAI's ChatGPT	184
		7.5.2 Google's Gemini	186
		7.5.3 Meta's LLaMA	187
		7.5.4 Huawei's Pangu Models	188
		7.5.5 Baidu's ERNIE Bot	189
	References		190
8	**AItoB Entering the Stage of Large-Scale Exploration**		191
	8.1	AI Combined with Industries for Diversified Implementations	191
	8.2	Large Models Becoming "Meta-Capability Engine" of the Intelligent Revolution	192
	8.3	Prospects of General AI	194
	References		195
9	**Challenges of Adopting AI in ToB Scenarios**		197
	9.1	Multifaceted Challenges of Large Model Engineering	197
	9.2	Intelligentization Unbalanced Between Industries	198
	9.3	Looming Risks of AI	198
	9.4	Immature AI Ecosystem	199
	References		200

Part III 5G + AI: Expediting Intelligent Industry Transformation

10	**Industries Evolving from Digital to Intelligent**		203
	10.1	Connotation of Digital Transformation	203
	10.2	Evolution from Digital to Intelligent	205
	10.3	Typical Course of Digitalization and Intelligent Development	206
		10.3.1 US: Consolidating Global Competitiveness in the Digital Economy Using Technological Advantages	206
		10.3.2 EU: Leading the Development of Digital Governance Rules to Form a Unified Digital Market	207
		10.3.3 UK: Adhering to a Digital Government Construction Strategy for Digital Transformation of All Industries	209
		10.3.4 Japan: Using Industry-Government-Academia Collaboration and the "Connected Industries" Initiative to Realize a Super-Smart Society	210
		10.3.5 South Korea: Focusing on Standards System Establishment and Releasing the New Growth 4.0 Strategy Roadmap	211
		10.3.6 China: Using Industry and Market Advantages for Efficient Markets and Public Services	212
	References		214

11 Collaborative Development Between 5G and AI: Accelerating Intelligent Industry Upgrade 215
11.1 Relationship Between 5G and AI.......................... 215
11.2 5G's Requirements for AI 216
11.3 AI's Requirements for 5G 216
11.4 Convergence of 5G and AI.............................. 217
References.. 217

12 Convergence of 5G and AI: Enabling Industry Intelligence........ 219
12.1 5G-Native Technology Optimization: Enhanced Network Endogenous Capabilities 219
    12.1.1 5G Private Network: Customized Network 220
    12.1.2 5G Network Slicing: Flexible Networking........... 221
12.2 5G + AICDE: Building Integrated Service Capabilities 222
    12.2.1 5G + AI: Comprehensive Sensing 223
    12.2.2 5G + IoT: Full Interconnection.................... 224
    12.2.3 5G + Cloud Computing: Cloud-Network Convergence...................................... 225
    12.2.4 5G + Big Data: Intelligent Decision-Making.......... 226
    12.2.5 5G + MEC: Edge-Cloud Synergy................... 227
References.. 227

13 Key Industry Practices 229
13.1 Government 229
    13.1.1 Overview of Digitalization and Intelligent Development in the Industry 229
    13.1.2 Trends of Digitalization and Intelligent Development in the Industry 231
    13.1.3 Requirements for Digitalization and Intelligent Development in the Industry 232
    13.1.4 5G + AI Technology Convergence Analysis........... 233
    13.1.5 Typical Solutions for Digitalization and Intelligent Development in Government 236
    13.1.6 Path for Large-Scale Replication and Promotion....... 238
13.2 Emergencies... 239
    13.2.1 Overview of Digitalization and Intelligent Development in the Industry 239
    13.2.2 Trends of Digitalization and Intelligent Development in the Industry 241
    13.2.3 Requirements for Digitalization and Intelligent Development in the Industry 242
    13.2.4 5G + AI Technology Convergence Analysis........... 243
    13.2.5 Typical Solutions for Digitalization and Intelligent Development in Emergencies...................... 245
    13.2.6 Path for Large-Scale Replication and Promotion....... 247

13.3	Meteorology		248
	13.3.1	Overview of Digitalization and Intelligent Development in the Industry	248
	13.3.2	Trends of Digitalization and Intelligent Development in the Industry	249
	13.3.3	Requirements for Digitalization and Intelligent Development in the Industry	251
	13.3.4	5G + AI Technology Convergence Analysis	252
	13.3.5	Typical Solutions for Digitalization and Intelligent Development in Meteorology	254
	13.3.6	Path for Large-Scale Replication and Promotion	257
13.4	Agriculture		257
	13.4.1	Overview of Digitalization and Intelligent Development in the Industry	257
	13.4.2	Trends of Digitalization and Intelligent Development in the Industry	259
	13.4.3	Requirements for Digitalization and Intelligent Development in the Industry	259
	13.4.4	5G + AI Technology Convergence Analysis	260
	13.4.5	Typical Solutions for Digitalization and Intelligent Development in Agriculture	262
	13.4.6	Path for Large-Scale Replication and Promotion	265
13.5	Culture and Tourism		266
	13.5.1	Overview of Digitalization and Intelligent Development in the Industry	266
	13.5.2	Trends of Digitalization and Intelligent Development in the Industry	267
	13.5.3	Requirements for Digitalization and Intelligent Development in the Industry	269
	13.5.4	5G + AI Technology Convergence Analysis	270
	13.5.5	Typical Solutions for Digitalization and Intelligent Development in Culture and Tourism	272
	13.5.6	Path for Large-Scale Replication and Promotion	275
13.6	Education		276
	13.6.1	Overview of Digitalization and Intelligent Development in the Industry	276
	13.6.2	Trends of Digitalization and Intelligent Development in the Industry	277
	13.6.3	Requirements for Digitalization and Intelligent Development in the Industry	278
	13.6.4	5G + AI Technology Convergence Analysis	280
	13.6.5	Typical Solutions for Digitalization and Intelligent Development in Education	282
	13.6.6	Path for Large-Scale Replication and Promotion	285

13.7	Healthcare		286
	13.7.1	Overview of Digitalization and Intelligent Development in the Industry	286
	13.7.2	Trends of Digitalization and Intelligent Development in the Industry	287
	13.7.3	Requirements for Digitalization and Intelligent Development in the Industry	289
	13.7.4	5G + AI Technology Convergence Analysis	290
	13.7.5	Typical Solutions for Digitalization and Intelligent Development in Healthcare	293
	13.7.6	Path for Large-Scale Replication and Promotion	295
13.8	Manufacturing		296
	13.8.1	Overview of Digitalization and Intelligent Development in the Industry	296
	13.8.2	Trends of Digitalization and Intelligent Development in the Industry	297
	13.8.3	Requirements for Digitalization and Intelligent Development in the Industry	298
	13.8.4	5G + AI Technology Convergence Analysis	300
	13.8.5	Typical Solutions for Digitalization and Intelligent Development in Manufacturing	304
	13.8.6	Path for Large-Scale Replication and Promotion	306
13.9	Ports		307
	13.9.1	Overview of Digitalization and Intelligent Development in the Industry	307
	13.9.2	Trends of Digitalization and Intelligent Development in the Industry	309
	13.9.3	Requirements for Digitalization and Intelligent Development in the Industry	310
	13.9.4	5G + AI Technology Convergence Analysis	311
	13.9.5	Typical Solutions for Digitalization and Intelligent Development in Ports	314
	13.9.6	Path for Large-Scale Replication and Promotion	316
13.10	Electric Power		317
	13.10.1	Overview of Digitalization and Intelligent Development in the Industry	317
	13.10.2	Trends of Digitalization and Intelligent Development in the Industry	318
	13.10.3	Requirements for Digitalization and Intelligent Development in the Industry	320
	13.10.4	5G + AI Technology Convergence Analysis	321
	13.10.5	Typical Solutions for Digitalization and Intelligent Development in Electric Power	326
	13.10.6	Path for Large-Scale Replication and Promotion	328
References			329

14	**Trends and Prospects**		331
	14.1	NaaS in 5.5G	331
	14.2	Upgrade from Cloud-Network Convergence to Computing-Network Convergence	334
	14.3	New Opportunities and Possibilities: Using Data to Create Value	336
	14.4	In-Depth Development of Innovative Digital Applications for Multiple Fields	339
	14.5	AI Big Models: Driving the Emergence of New Business Forms	340
	References		341

Abbreviations

5G AIA	5G applications industry array
5GtoB	5G to business
5GtoC	5G to consumer
AaaS	Analytics as a service
AC/DC	Alternating/direct current
AE	Auto-encoder
AGI	Artificial general intelligence
AGV	Automated guided vehicle
AI	Artificial intelligence
AIDD	AI-driven drug design
AIGC	Artificial intelligence generated content
AII	Alliance of industrial Internet
AIR	AI industry research
AMP	Advanced manufacturing partnership
API	Application programming interface
AR	Augmented reality
ARHT	AR holographic technology
ASIC	Adapter's application-specific integrated circuit
ASR	Automatic speech recognition
AT&T	American Telephone and Telegraph
AVSR	Audiovisual speech recognition
AWS	Amazon Web Services
BAAI	Beijing Academy of Artificial Intelligence
BDS	BeiDou navigation satellite system
BERT	Bidirectional encoder representations from transformers
BIM	Building information modeling
BIS	Bureau of Industry and Security
BLEU	Bilingual evaluation understudy
BMBF	Federal Ministry of Education and Research
BMDV	Federal Ministry for Digital and Transport
BOM	Bill of materials

CAD	Computer-aided design
CAGR	Compound annual growth rate
CAICT	China Academy of Information and Communications Technology
CANN	Compute architecture for neural network
CASP	Critical assessment of protein structure prediction
CATV	Cable TV
CBRS	Citizen broadband radio service
CCSA	China Communications Standards Association
CDMA	Code division multiple access
CESI	China Electronics Standardization Institute
CG	Computer graphics
CGN	China General Nuclear Power Corporation
ChatGPT	Chat generative pre-trained transformer
CHSCs	Community healthcare service centers
CIM	City information modeling
CLIP	Contrastive language-image pre-training
CNN	Convolutional neural network
CPC	Communist Party of China
CPE	Customer-premises equipment
CPU	Central processing unit
CSG	China Southern Power Grid
CSS	Cloud search service
CT	Communication technology
CUDA	Compute unified device architecture
CV	Computer vision
CVPR	Computer vision and pattern recognition
CvT	Convolutional vision transformer
DARPA	Defense Advanced Research Projects Agency
DB	Deutsche Bahn
DBM	Deep Boltzmann machine
DBN	Deep belief network
DBSCAN	Density-based spatial clustering of applications with noise
DDPG	Deep deterministic policy gradient
DESI	Digital Economy and Society Index
DGC	Data Lake Governance Center
DINO	Self-distillation with no labels
DL	Deep learning
DLI	Data Lake insight
DMA	Digital Market Act
DNN	Deep neural network
DOCA	Dynamics, quantum chemistry, and astrophysics
DoD	Department of Defense
DOE	Department of Energy
DOF	Degrees of Freedom
DOU	Data of usage

Abbreviations

DPA	Data Protection Act
DPU	Data processing unit
DPX	Dynamic programming X
DQN	Deep Q-learning network
DRAM	Dynamic random access memory
DSA	Domain-specific architecture
DWS	Data warehouse service
ECC	Error checking and correcting
ECG	Electrocardiogram
EGH	Emergency general hospital
EI	Enterprise intelligence
eIDAS	Electronic identification and trust services
ELMo	Embeddings from language models
eMBB	Enhanced mobile broadband
ePD	ePrivacy directive
ePR	ePrivacy regulation
ERI	Electronics resurgence initiative
ESG	Environmental, social, and governance
EU	European Union
FCC	Federal Communications Commission
FLOPS	Floating-point operations per second
FPGA	Field-programmable gate array
FWA	Fixed wireless access
GAN	Generative adversarial network
GDP	Gross domestic product
GDPR	General data protection regulation
GE	General Electric
GES	Graph engine service
GINT	Gigabit innovation track
GIS	Geographic information system
GMM	Gaussian mixture model
GNN	Graph neural network
GPGPU	General-purpose GPU
GPS	Global positioning system
GPT	General-purpose technology
GPU	Graphics processing unit
GQA	Grouped query attention
GSA	Global Mobile Suppliers Association
GSMA	GSM Association
GTI	Global TD-LTE Initiative
HCI	Human-computer interaction
HD	High definition
HELM	Holistic evaluation of language models
HPA	Hamburg Port Authority
HPC	High-performance computing

IaaS	Infrastructure as a service
IBM	International Business Machines Corporation
ICA	Independent component analysis
ICT	Information and communications technology
ICU	Intensive care unit
IDC	International data corporation
IGV	Intelligent guided vehicle
IIoT	Industrial IoT
IMS	Intelligent manufacturing system
IMU	Inertial measurement unit
IoE	Internet of Everything
IoP	Internet of People
IoT	Internet of Things
IoV	Internet of Vehicles
IP	Intellectual property
ISA	Instruction set architecture
ISAC	Integrated sensing and communication
ISO	International Organization for Standardization
IT	Information technology
ITOS	Intelligent terminal operating system
ITU	ITU Radiocommunication Sector
IUR	Industry-university-research
JUMP	Joint University Microelectronics Program
KNN	K-nearest neighbors
KOSMO	Korea Smart Manufacturing Office
KPI	Key performance indicator
KT	Korea Telecom
KTX	Korea Train eXpress
LAN	Local area network
LBP	Local binary pattern
LCK	League of Legends Champions Korea
LFW	Labeled Faces in the Wild
LiCO	Lenovo intelligent computing orchestration
LLM	Large language model
LoRA	Low-rank adaptation
LSTM	Long short-term memory
LTE	Long-term evolution
MaaS	Model as a service
MEC	Multi-access edge computing
MEM	Ministry of Emergency Management
MGI	McKinsey Global Institute
MIIT	Ministry of Industry and Information Technology
MIMO	Multiple-input multiple-output
MIPS	Microprocessor without interlocked pipeline stages
MIT	Massachusetts Institute of Technology

ML	Machine learning
MLB	Major league baseball
MLOps	ML operations
MMLU	Massive multitask language understanding
mMTC	Massive machine-type communications
MoE	Mixture of experts
MoLORA	Mixture of low-rank adaptation
MOOC	Massive open online course
MoV	Mixture of vectors
MR	Mixed reality
MRI	Magnetic resonance imaging
MRS	MapReduce service
MSIP	Ministry of Science, ICT and Future Planning
MSIT	Ministry of Science and ICT
MSMEs	Micro, small, and medium-sized enterprises
MTO	Make-to-order
MUM	Multitask unified model
MWC	Mobile world congress
NaaS	Network as a service
NAS	Neural architecture search
NBA	National Basketball Association
NDRC	National Development and Reform Commission
NE	Network element
NFV	Network functions virtualization
NHC	National Health Commission
NIC	Network Interface Card
NLG	Natural language generation
NLP	Natural language processing
NLU	Natural language understanding
NNMI	Network for manufacturing innovation
NPU	Neural processing unit
NR	New radio
NSA	Non-standalone
NSF	National Science Foundation
NSI	Network slice instance
NTN	Non-terrestrial network
O&M	Operations and maintenance
OCR	Optical character recognition
ONS	Office for National Statistics
OOE	Out of episode
OS	Operation system
OSTP	Office of Science and Technology Policy
OT	Operational technology
PaaS	Platform as a service
PAI	Platform for AI

PAL	Priority access license
PC	Personal computer
PCA	Principal component analysis
PDA	Personal digital assistant
PIPA	Personal Information Protection Act
PIPC	Personal Information Protection Commission
PLC	Programmable logic controller
PMU	Phasor measurement unit
PPO	Proximal policy optimization
PRC	People's Republic of China
PTC	Parametric Technology Corporation
PVT	Pyramid vision transformer
QoS	Quality of service
R&D	Research and development
RAG	Retrieval-augmented generation
RAM	Random access memory
RAN	Radio access network
RAS	Reliability, availability, and serviceability
RAT	Radio access technology
RBM	Restricted Boltzmann machine
RFID	Radio frequency identification
RGB	Red-green-blue
RISC	Reduced instruction set computer
RLHF	Reinforcement learning from human feedback
RNN	Recurrent neural network
RPA	Robotic process automation
RTG	Rubber-tired gantry
SA	Standalone
SaaS	Software as a service
SAM	Segment anything model
SAR	Synthetic aperture radar
SARSA	State-action-reward-state-action
SAS	Serial attached SCSI
SASAC	State-owned Assets Supervision and Administration Commission
SC	Sparse coding
SCA	Smart compliant actuator
SDN	Software-defined networking
SEC	Smart education of China
SEO	Search engine optimization
SGCC	State Grid Corporation of China
SIFT	Scale-invariant feature transform
SK Telecom	South Korea Telecom
SKU	Stock keeping unit
SLA	Service level agreement
SLAM	Simultaneous localization and mapping

SME	Small- and medium-sized enterprise
SMS	Short message service
SoC	System-on-a-chip
SOM	Self-organizing map
SRAM	Static random access memory
SVM	Support vector machine
TDIA	Telecommunication Development Industry Alliance
TDMA	Time division multiple access
TDP	Thermal design power
TF-IDF	Term frequency-inverse document frequency
TFLOPS	teraFLOPS
TFP	Total factor productivity
TNT	Transformer iN transformer
ToB	To business
ToC	To consumer
ToF	Time-of-flight
ToG	To government
TOPS	Trillion operations per second
TPU	Tensor processing unit
TSN	Time-sensitive networking
UAV	Unmanned aerial vehicle
UE	User equipment
UFO	Unified feature optimization
UGC	User-generated content
UHD	Ultrahigh definition
UHV	Ultrahigh voltage
UI	User interface
UPF	User plane function
URLLC	Ultrareliable low-latency communication
VGG	Visual geometry group
ViT	Vision transformer
VLAN	Virtual local area network
VPU	Video processing unit
VR	Virtual reality
VSLAM	Visual SLAM
WAIC	World Artificial Intelligence Conference
WAN	Wide area network
WAP	Wireless application protocol
WDM	Wavelength division multiplexing
WRC	World Robot Conference
YoY	Year-on-year

List of Figures

Fig. 1.1	Comparison between 5G and 4G network capabilities	5
Fig. 1.2	Overview of digital transformation	6
Fig. 1.3	5G-driven development of digital economy and society	10
Fig. 1.4	5G-enabled entire industry chain	11
Fig. 2.1	Global 5G population coverage	14
Fig. 2.2	5GtoC applications and content	16
Fig. 2.3	China's development in its mobile communications industry	16
Fig. 2.4	5G RedCap features and its typical applications	17
Fig. 3.1	5G industry application development phases. (Source: China Academy of Information and Communications Technology (CAICT))	41
Fig. 3.2	Key factors for large-scale 5GtoB development. (Source: CAICT)	43
Fig. 3.3	Color palette for large-scale application development in key fields. (Source: CAICT)	44
Fig. 3.4	A quadrant chart for 5G application development in key industries. (Source: CAICT)	44
Fig. 3.5	Phases of key industries in the large-scale development of 5G industry applications. (Source: CAICT)	45
Fig. 3.6	Key technologies related to candidate projects in the fourth "Zhanfang Cup". (Source: CAICT)	47
Fig. 3.7	Evolution from 5G to 5.5G and then 6G	49
Fig. 3.8	Typical applications and their deployment requirements	50
Fig. 3.9	Typical 6G application scenarios	51
Fig. 4.1	Four development phases and major events of AI	56
Fig. 5.1	Deployment stages of AI technologies	70
Fig. 5.2	Machine learning process	70
Fig. 5.3	Market shares of China's machine learning platforms in 2022. (Source: IDC China, 2023)	71
Fig. 5.4	Sector distribution of machine learning applications in China, 2022	71

Fig. 5.5	Supervised learning function	72
Fig. 5.6	Unsupervised learning function	74
Fig. 5.7	Basic reinforcement learning framework	75
Fig. 5.8	Multi-task learning and single-task learning	79
Fig. 5.9	Relationship between NLP and AI	80
Fig. 5.10	Categorization of basic NLP models	81
Fig. 5.11	Neural network language models	82
Fig. 5.12	Word vector calculation	84
Fig. 5.13	Text classification process	86
Fig. 5.14	Market shares of computer vision in China, 2022. (Source: IDC China, 2023)	88
Fig. 5.15	AI video analysis diagram	91
Fig. 6.1	AI industry chain	96
Fig. 6.2	Market revenue and growth of the global AI industry	97
Fig. 6.3	Key factors and vendors in the AI industry	97
Fig. 6.4	Major vendors of AI chips worldwide	101
Fig. 6.5	US data center AI chip market share in 2022	101
Fig. 6.6	AI chip market size in China	103
Fig. 6.7	Product share in China's AI chip market	103
Fig. 6.8	Delivery share of AI chip vendors in China	103
Fig. 6.9	GPU memory comparison	107
Fig. 6.10	Primary buyers of AMD Instinct MI300X	107
Fig. 6.11	Global AI platform software market revenue	112
Fig. 6.12	AI engineering technology panorama	118
Fig. 6.13	Evolution of AI framework technologies	119
Fig. 6.14	Core technology system of an AI framework	120
Fig. 6.15	Technical principle analysis	123
Fig. 6.16	Core technology system of AI engineering	124
Fig. 6.17	MLOps tool categories	126
Fig. 6.18	Technological system of digital twin	130
Fig. 6.19	AutoML workflow	136
Fig. 6.20	Number of AI data service providers in different countries	138
Fig. 6.21	Global distribution of AI enterprises by country	140
Fig. 6.22	Architecture of the T-Few fine-tuning algorithm	143
Fig. 6.23	T-Few fine-tuning process	143
Fig. 6.24	HELM	144
Fig. 6.25	Multimodal content generation supported by Jasper	145
Fig. 6.26	What makes Jasper better suited for marketing than ChatGPT	145
Fig. 6.27	AI capabilities integrated into DiDi's autonomous driving system	146
Fig. 6.28	Cloud brain of Dataa's robots	147
Fig. 7.1	Three phases in the development of large models	150
Fig. 7.2	Large language models (with more than ten billion parameters) released since 2019	152
Fig. 7.3	Feature comparison between large and small models	153

Fig. 7.4	Relationship between AI and large models	154
Fig. 7.5	Large models as a catalyst for inclusive and accessible AI	155
Fig. 7.6	Large models as an engine and a bridge	156
Fig. 7.7	Development of the three types of large models	158
Fig. 7.8	ViT model architecture	165
Fig. 7.9	Architecture upgrade of the open-source ViT model	166
Fig. 7.10	ImageBind model	170
Fig. 7.11	Visual ChatGPT framework	171
Fig. 7.12	CLIP cross-modal feature comparison and learning architecture	172
Fig. 7.13	Huawei Ascend AI industry ecosystem	177
Fig. 7.14	Gartner top 10 strategic technology trends for 2024	180
Fig. 7.15	Three cutting-edge capabilities that enable AIGC	180
Fig. 7.16	Generative AI application fields and models	183
Fig. 7.17	Distribution of major large models by country	184
Fig. 7.18	Framework for China's large model industry	185
Fig. 7.19	ChatGPT model training	185
Fig. 7.20	Principles of RLHF-based model training	186
Fig. 7.21	Derivatives of LLaMA	187
Fig. 7.22	Pangu models 3.0	188
Fig. 7.23	Architecture of ERNIE Bot	190
Fig. 8.1	Future development trends of general AI	194
Fig. 10.1	Digital transformation from different perspectives	204
Fig. 10.2	Evolution from informatization to digitalization and intelligence	205
Fig. 12.1	Convergence development path for 5G and other technologies	220
Fig. 12.2	Relationship between 5G and related technologies	223
Fig. 13.1	Triangular model of 5G + *X* large-scale application	230
Fig. 13.2	Intelligent dispatch center for the "Smart Baiyun" platform	237
Fig. 13.3	Intelligent emergency management architecture	240
Fig. 13.4	5G + smart firefighting solution at Guangdong Fire Department	246
Fig. 13.5	Development history of weather forecasting	248
Fig. 13.6	Chongqing "Yutian" intelligent disaster prevention solution	255
Fig. 13.7	Setup of the AI weather forecasting solution	256
Fig. 13.8	Digital agricultural park solutions	263
Fig. 13.9	5G smart agriculture solutions offered by Beijing Tongfang LEGENDSILICON Tech. Co., Ltd	264
Fig. 13.10	China Mobile Shanghai's 5G + smart culture and tourism solution	273
Fig. 13.11	5G cloud XR solution for cultural relics digitalization	274
Fig. 13.12	Phases of large-scale 5G application in culture and tourism	275
Fig. 13.13	Architecture of the 5G smart education solution	283
Fig. 13.14	5G + smart campus solution	284
Fig. 13.15	Phases of large-scale 5G application in education	285

Fig. 13.16	National emergency rescue system	294
Fig. 13.17	H3C 5G telemedicine solution.	295
Fig. 13.18	5G smart factory solution architecture.	305
Fig. 13.19	Phases of large-scale 5G application in manufacturing.	306
Fig. 13.20	Core production process of container wharves	308
Fig. 13.21	5G + smart port solution at the Port of Tianjin	314
Fig. 13.22	5G network architecture of the Port of Tangshan	315
Fig. 13.23	5G + smart grid solution of State Grid	326
Fig. 13.24	Overall architecture of the 5G virtual private network for Qinshan Nuclear Power Plant	327
Fig. 13.25	Phases of large-scale 5G application in electric power	328
Fig. 14.1	5.5G network capabilities	332
Fig. 14.2	5G-to-6G evolution roadmap.	333
Fig. 14.3	Diversified computing power requirements.	335
Fig. 14.4	Computing-network convergence capability evolution	335
Fig. 14.5	Major data circulation modes	337
Fig. 14.6	Trends in the application of data in industries.	338

List of Tables

Table 2.1	Deployment of commercial 5G SA networks	15
Table 5.1	Common supervised learning algorithms	73
Table 5.2	Common unsupervised learning algorithms	75
Table 5.3	Common reinforcement learning algorithms	76
Table 5.4	Typical deep learning algorithms	77
Table 6.1	Comparison of different chip types	100
Table 6.2	China's policies for the AI chip industry	102
Table 6.3	NVIDIA's main products	104
Table 6.4	NVIDIA's hardware and software products	106
Table 6.5	Comparison between the major GPU products of AMD and NVIDIA	108
Table 6.6	Comparison between the Huawei Ascend series processors and NVIDIA GPUs	110
Table 6.7	Main Cambricon products	111
Table 6.8	Services from the world's biggest AI cloud platform vendors in Q4 2022	113
Table 6.9	AI engineering products of global enterprises	126
Table 6.10	Evolution of advanced computing	132
Table 6.11	Well-known AI data service providers	139
Table 6.12	Technical specifications of Cloud Ginger 2.0	147
Table 7.1	MMLU	159
Table 7.2	MT-Bench and Arena Elo	160
Table 7.3	Overview of open-source foundation models	161
Table 13.1	Requirements of electric power communications for 5G networks	317
Table 13.2	Satellite technology applications in major electric power services	322
Table 13.3	Application of AI in major electric power services	323

Part I
5G Large-Scale Replication

Chapter 1
5G Drives New Developments in Global Digital Transformation

1.1 Communications Technologies Lead Continuous Social Progress

Information exchange is fundamental to the existence and development of human society. The means of storing and passing on information has been continuously evolving alongside improvements in productivity, in response to the growing demand for immediate access to information. Communication technologies have developed from pigeon delivery in ancient times, to telegraph and telephone in the modern era, and to mobile communication today, profoundly changing our lifestyles, production modes, and social contact modes. It is no wonder that studies on scientific development, technological progress, production innovation, and economic growth defined information communication as a general purpose technology (GPT)—a technology that has revolutionary impact on the progress of society, along with materials, transportation, and power supply systems.

In ancient times, people used to exchange information through verbal communication and body gestures. Written words, bamboo slips, and paper books were later invented in response to the demand for information recording. Afterwards, beacon fires, horses, and pigeons, among others, were creatively used as means of communication to enhance the efficiency of nation, army, and societal management. In about 1045, ceramic movable type printing was created by Bi Sheng, a Chinese inventor, and in 1450, Johannes Gutenberg in Germany invented metal movable type printing. These technological innovations hugely accelerated the spread of knowledge. The latter invention in particular ushered in a massive wave of printing in Europe. Being set against the backdrop of the Renaissance, this invention helped make information easily accessible and break up the church's monopoly on knowledge, which further laid the foundation for the Industrial Revolution.

During the first Industrial Revolution, modes of transportation such as ships and railways developed rapidly, extending people's connections and the scope of trade.

This in turn gave rise to the need for real-time communication, which could not be met by the previous communication methods such as letters. In 1835, Samuel F.B. Morse, a US painter and inventor, developed the world's first wired telegraph system, marking the beginning of the electronic communication era. The year of 1876 witnessed the world's first telephone invented by US inventor Alexander Graham Bell. In 1878, he successfully made a call from Boston to New York, which were 300 km apart. It was the first long-distance telephone call in human history. Telegraph and telephone technologies transformed the way information was transmitted because instead of relying on human- and object-based physical means, people were able to use electronic communication, which shattered the existing temporal and spatial barriers. In conjunction with the advances in transportation, these innovations changed the ways of production and trade, and contributed significantly to global economic integration and industrial development.

The advent of the ARPANET in 1969 revolutionized communication for another time. Internet technologies, along with computer technologies, software technologies, digital communication technologies, etc., have taken human society from the industrial age to a brand-new information age. The Internet has made it more convenient to transmit large amounts of information over long distances, substantially changing the mode of information dissemination. It has further made global collaborative production a reality, and in turn spurred the third wave of globalization, which is reshaping the world economy and the social and geopolitical landscape.

Since their inception in the 1960s and 1970s, mobile communications technologies have evolved from 1G to 5G. The 1G network was first commercially used in 1983, enabling voice communication using analog signals. In 1991, 2G was developed, which featured a narrowband digital cellular system running on either time division multiple access (TDMA) or code division multiple access (CDMA). The 2000s saw the advent of 3G smartphones, and since then services have shifted from being voice-dominated to data-dominated. The year of 2008 is seen as the beginning of the 4G era, for that is the time when the ITU Radiocommunication Sector (ITU-R) released standards for developing and managing 4G network, including a peak data rate of 100 Mbit/s for high-speed mobility and 1 Gbit/s for low-speed mobility or in stationary modes. In 2020, 5G standards were formulated, marking the beginning of 5G. Along the development, communication technologies have found ways to integrate with Internet technologies, helping popularize the Internet, empower new mobile Internet products, business forms, and models such as smartphones, mobile payment, mobile commerce, and the sharing economy. Figure 1.1 shows a comparison between 5G and 4G network capabilities.

With the integration of IT technologies, 5G networks feature flexible and efficient network functions and intelligent configuration. Network Functions Virtualization (NFV) and software-defined networking (SDN) decompose, abstract, and reconstruct functions of network elements (NEs). 5G networks are transferred into a flat IT-based platform, consisting of the access, control, and forwarding planes. The 5G network platform can configure network resources and functions based on specific requirements of virtual operators, services, users, or even certain service data flows. The platform is also able to customize and orchestrate

1.2 The World is Embracing a New Wave of Digital Transformation

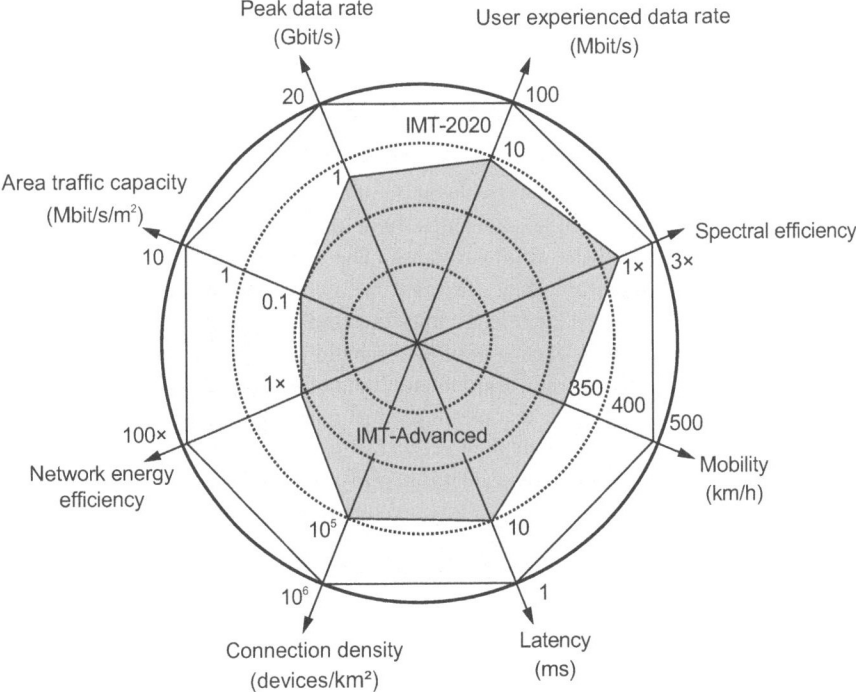

Fig. 1.1 Comparison between 5G and 4G network capabilities

corresponding network components to form various "network slices," to fit the demands of Internet of Things (IoT) and many other diverse applications. The centralized control plane offers data-powered intelligent network functions, resource allocation, and operation management. Such capabilities are built upon real-time perception, analysis, and decision-making using information such as geographical location, user preference, terminal status, and network dynamics.

1.2 The World is Embracing a New Wave of Digital Transformation

The global economy is gradually shifting from old economic engines to new ones, as the revolution of science and technology has been the catalyst for another wave of industrial revolution. Next-generation information and communications technologies (ICTs) are promoting the digital transformation of economies, societies, production methods, and people's daily lives all around the world. Digitalization, connectivity, and intelligence are becoming the most outstanding features of the new information era.

With the focus on boosting total factor productivity (TFP), the previous industrial revolutions centered on innovation and application of tangible technologies, such as steam and electric power, along with transformation in management and organizational restructuring. By contrast, the current era is characterized by accelerated overproduction and highly unstable demand fluctuations because demands are increasingly personalized, diversified, and dynamic. In this new phase of development, success is no longer defined by the scale of economy, the abundance of materials, or the strength of social relationships, but rather innovativeness, adaptability, swiftness, resilience, and the ability to learn. The inflexibility nature of material investments means that alone they are often not enough to secure a competitive edge. Data, information, and knowledge must be strategically explored. Powered by digital technologies, digital transformation can build data-driven loops for optimization through in-depth integration and interaction between the digital space and the physical world. This will drive reconfiguration of material investment and restructuring of organizational management, and as a result, will inspire more agility, vitality, and resilience across the industry. Digital transformation has forged a new path to developing long-term competitive advantage in the current uncertain climate. Figure 1.2 illustrates an overview of digital transformation.

Digital transformation offers accelerated development across enterprises, industries, and economies. Digital technologies were first used in the 1950s and 1960s in industries to improve efficiency, and their application in the service industry originated in the 1990s. In those times, however, the applications were mostly stand-alone, in non-critical processes, and for transaction purposes, limited by the low-level demands and underdeveloped technical systems, among other factors. Presently, new ICTs, such as mobile communication, IoT, big data, cloud computing, and artificial intelligence (AI), are rapidly developing while constantly converging with each other, creating new paths for industrial and economic digital transformation. These technologies will greatly reduce the costs of digital transformation and eliminate the technical barriers and will eventually accelerate digital transformation on a larger scale and in greater depth. Since the outbreak of the COVID-19 pandemic, digital transformation has gone from being a "nice-to-have" to a "must-have." The next 10–15 years will witness a remarkable acceleration of

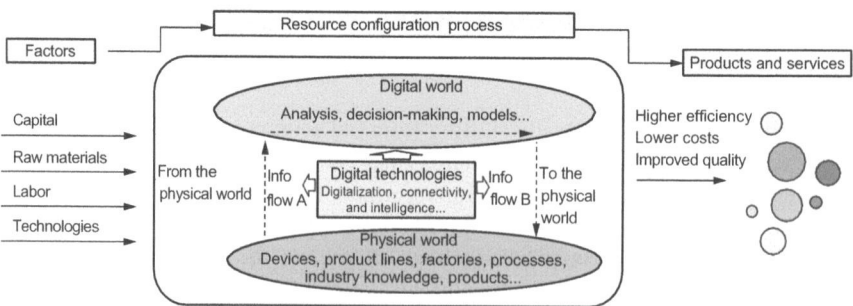

Fig. 1.2 Overview of digital transformation

digital transformation across society. Whether an enterprise seizes the landmark opportunity of digital transformation will determine its future comprehensive strengths and competitive position. This is also true for a country.

For this reason, countries around the world are placing great importance on digital transformation, with hopes to build a strategic digitalization framework and formulate policies aligned with digital transformation, in order to expedite digital transformation, boost the digital economy, and promote sustainable and comprehensive economic development. China is among the most proactive in this regard, having listed accelerating digitalization-based development as a strategic national priority in the *Outline of the People's Republic of China 14th Five-Year Plan (2021–2025) for National Economic and Social Development and Long-Range Objectives for 2035* (hereinafter the *Outline of the 14th Five-Year Plan (2021–2025)*). On October 18, 2021, President Xi Jinping called for grasping the trend and law of digital economic development and pushing forward the sound development of the digital economy in the country. President Xi Jinping stressed that China should give full rein to China's vast data troves and rich range of fields of application in order to firmly embed digital technology in the real economy, enable the upgrading and transformation of traditional industry, foster new industries, new business forms and models, and build up the strength, quality, and size of China's digital economy. He explained that this should be done while keeping in mind the larger strategic picture of national rejuvenation and the once-in-a-century changes occurring in the world and giving full consideration to China's domestic and international imperatives and China's development and security needs. In short, digital transformation is now a global consensus and a general trend.

1.3 Digital Transformation Brings Big Opportunities

Digital transformation is rapidly becoming a stable development strategy in a variety of industries, and this is a fitting indication of the potential scale of 5G to business (5GtoB) development. China's digital economy, growing at a compound annual growth rate (CAGR) of over 10%, is projected to be worth CNY65 trillion in 2025, accounting for over 50% of the country's gross domestic product (GDP). Therefore, to achieve fast-paced 5GtoB expansion, it is critical to take an accurate pulse of the new missions of, new expectations for, and new trends in digital transformation, and plan accordingly.

Let's start with the new missions of digital transformation. As the global digital economy booms, a new round of technological revolution and industrial transformation featuring digitalization, connectivity, and intelligence will change the global pattern of innovation and reshape the global economy. Many countries around the world, in an attempt to dominate the new round of development, are proactively seizing the opportunities offered by digital technological innovations and attaching importance to digitalization in their economic development and technological innovations. The ability to adapt to and lead digital development will be pertinent to the future of a country.

Digital transformation provides essential support for the new development blueprint. China's economic development, driven by new momentum from the evolving digital economy, has shifted from speed and scale to high quality. Digital development accelerates the formation of a "dual circulation" development pattern, in which China's domestic and international markets support and reinforce each other, which will help China more effectively respond to the increasingly complex international environment and maintain its economic security and stability. Digital development is fundamental to providing better-quality public services, which will lead to a narrowed digital divide. Leveraging modern information technologies and progressive governance is key to boosting the efficiency of governance and fostering a stronger sense of fulfillment in hundreds of millions of people when sharing the digital development achievements.

In terms of the new expectations for digital transformation, China has prioritized digitalization in its journey to building a digital economy and society. This is reflected in many of its national strategic plans, including the *Outline of the 14th Five-Year Plan (2021–2025)*. The plan has a dedicated section titled "Accelerate digitalization-based development and construct a digital China," in which the government proposes that China systematically deploys and unleashes the potential of data elements, accelerates the shaping of a digital economy, digital society, and digital government, and drives overall changes in production methods, lifestyles, and governance with digital transformation.

Initiatives have been taken to implement the strategies outlined in the plan. The Ministry of Industry and Information Technology (MIIT) of China has launched the *Integrated Computing Network*, *"Set Sail" Action Plan for 5G Applications*, *Dual Gigabit Network Coordinated Development*, and *East-to-West Computing channeling* initiatives. The State-owned Assets Supervision and Administration Commission (SASAC) of the State Council has outlined the steps to take in order for state-owned enterprises to take a lead in digital transformation. The National Development and Reform Commission (NDRC) has put in place the *Cloud-based Big Data and AI initiative* to promote the digital transformation of micro-, small-, and medium-sized enterprises (MSMEs). Local authorities have introduced policies to boost the digital economy. Nearly 200 cities have set up digital economy management offices, developed data resource systems, and built data infrastructure to promote the overall development of the digital economy.

Then, the new trends in digital transformation. It is now historically significant time when China has triumphed on a new journey towards the second centenary goal of fully building a modern socialist country. The next 10–15 years will be a strategic period for China's digital transformation, for which the new trends of digital transformation must be accurately analyzed.

Data is at the center of high-quality economic development. Data is a new, replicable, and shareable factor of production, and is thus a fundamental resource that embodies great potential value and strategic importance. The *Guideline on Improving the Market-based Allocation Mechanism of Production Factors* proposes data as a critical factor of production for the very first time. As the digital economy advances, data elements will be rapidly marketized. This means that in the course of digital transformation, focus should be placed on stimulating the efficiency of data elements, exploring the value of data, revitalizing data assets, and magnifying the effect of data on quality improvement, efficiency, and service innovation.

Digital infrastructure empowers economic and social digital transformation at an unprecedented speed. New technologies such as 5G, industrial Internet, and AI are exerting an even more significant impact when used together in creative ways, giving rise to new use cases, business models, and business forms. The systematic deployment and moderately advanced construction of new types of digital infrastructure can lay a new cornerstone for economic and social development, while highlighting the pioneering role of digital infrastructure and driving digital transformation forward in all fields.

Digital industrialization is trending towards a comprehensive digital ecosystem. The digital industry, featuring 5G, e-manufacturing, software, Internet, IoT, big data, and AI, among others, will develop even rapidly. Digital technologies will be more widely used by industries for digital penetration, integration, and restructuring. This will gradually lead to the formation of a digital ecosystem featuring diverse resources, industry convergence, advanced technologies, and quality services. Industrial digitalization will evolve to be AI-driven, differentiated in scenarios, and managed on platforms. Digital technologies such as 5G, big data, cloud computing, and AI will drive industries to become more specialized in terms of digital production, and will fuel producer services with more specialization while pushing them towards the higher end of the value chain. The innovations and applications of digital technologies will lead digital transformation into a new phase which is Internet of Everything (IoE)-enabled, data-driven, platform-based, software-defined, and intelligence-led.

Digitalization has become an industry consensus. It is seen as the inevitable path to transformation for enterprises. Using digital technologies as means of production can boost the quality and efficiency of traditional modes of production. Using them as management tools can enable business decision-making to be powered by data, computing, and algorithms for service innovation, capability development, governance, and value creation in enterprises.

1.4 5G Unlocks the Potential of Industry Transformation

The year of 2019 saw the commercial adoption of 5G technologies around the globe. The coincidence of the mobile communication technology revolution with the new round of industrial revolution is of historic significance. 5G will lay a new foundation for economic and social development in the new round of industrial revolution, and create new ways, methods, and paths for the digital transformation of industries, which will unleash productivity and improve standards of living,

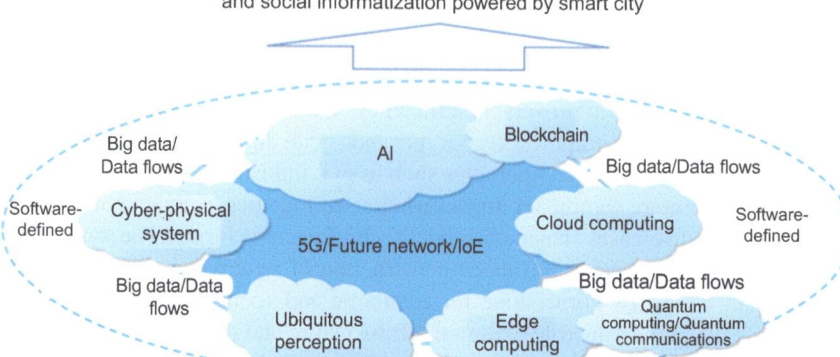

Fig. 1.3 5G-driven development of digital economy and society

catalyzing a new round of industrial revolution. Figure 1.3 illustrates how 5G drives the development of digital economy and society.

5G provides key technical support for data integration in various industries. Effective data collection is a prerequisite for the digitalization, connectivity, and intelligentization of any industry. 5G can provide connectivity for devices anytime and anywhere. With its unique features of massive connectivity, low latency, and high bandwidth, 5G can adequately meet the requirements of real-time transmission and distribution of tremendous amounts of production, service, and management data among various devices. When used in tandem with other technologies such as big data and AI, normalization, identification, processing, computing, and retrieval of data can be realized. 5G is becoming a key element bridging the digital and physical worlds. Figure 1.4 illustrates how 5G enables the entire industry chain.

5G paves the path for unmanned, intelligent production, as the only route leading to future industrial upgrade and advancement is building digital, manpower-saving, and intelligent enterprises. 5G can provide multifaceted support for enterprises in the innovation of their production modes. Firstly, 5G supports multi-channel and high-speed video transfer, and thus can enable high-precision, real-time monitoring, analysis, and control of production processes, when combined with computer vision (CV) technologies. Secondly, 5G is a key force in the fulfillment of cost-effective, long-distance, and large-scale remote control of mobile devices. Featuring high transmission rates and high reliability, 5G can ensure secure connections between remotely controlled devices and the console while reducing installation, commissioning, and maintenance costs. Thirdly, 5G increases production flexibility. By enabling production equipment to be wirelessly connected via the cloud, 5G can help realize timely updates and flexible adjustments of equipment functions. Fourthly, 5G facilitates unmanned inspections and remote monitoring, enabling enterprises to perform real-time monitoring in new and effective ways.

1.4 5G Unlocks the Potential of Industry Transformation

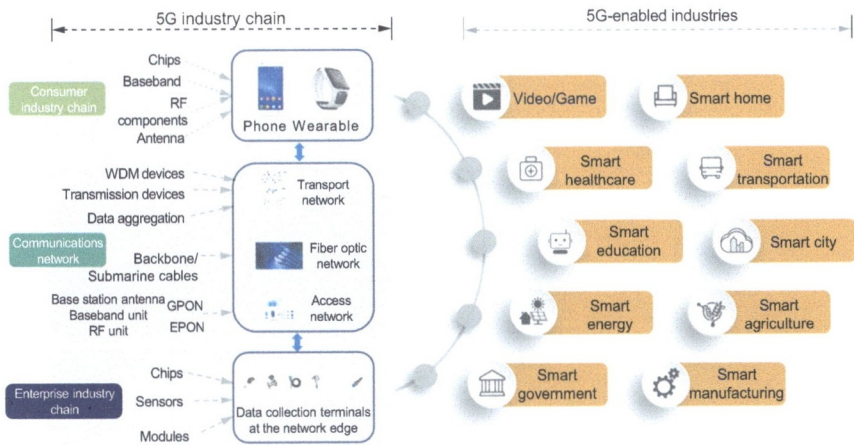

Fig. 1.4 5G-enabled entire industry chain

5G opens up new space for the development of products and services. In the production field, 5G will be deeply integrated with technologies such as edge computing, cloud computing, and AI to nurture remotely controllable or automated products and solutions, such as 5G UAVs, 5G engineering vehicles, 5G + unmanned agricultural machinery, and 5G + autonomous driving. With regard to people's lives, 5G will promote the development of consumer-oriented devices and applications with three of its capabilities: cloud-edge-device integration, multi-device collaboration, and extensive connectivity. 5G's cloud-edge-device integration capability will bolster technologies such as ultra-high-definition (UHD), virtual reality (VR), and augmented reality (AR), which are expected to lead people into a new immersive virtual world and revolutionize people's lives, entertainment, and education. And "5G + extensive connectivity" will hopefully lead to the realization of new use cases like smart home and smart fitness.

Looking ahead, 5G will be adopted even more widely in all aspects of society, gradually reshaping the development model of traditional industries. 5G will also nurture new demands, new services, and new business models, fully unlocking the potential of digital transformation and stimulating new momentum for economic and social transformation.

Chapter 2
5G Development Around the Globe

5G is gaining momentum globally. According to the Global mobile Suppliers Association (GSA), 294 operators in 109 countries and regions had launched 5G services, either mobile or fixed wireless access, as of November 2023 [1]. Many of the emerging 5G markets are in developing areas, indicating that 5G is a truly global phenomenon. Since 2023, 11 additional countries and regions have made commercial 5G newly accessible, including six in Africa. Of the 29 newly launched 5G networks, 14 are in Africa. Unsurprisingly, global 5G population coverage has increased year by year as well. As of September 2023, 5G networks had covered 36.9% of the world's population, a year-on-year increase of 6.4%. Notably, 5G population coverage had surpassed 50% in 60 countries and regions, or 58% of 5G-available countries and regions, and even 90% in 29 countries and regions. Globally, this figure is projected to exceed 50% by 2026 [2], as shown in Fig. 2.1.

Non-standalone (NSA) is still a majority, as only 112 operators in 53 countries and regions, or 20.6% of 544 5G-available operators [1], had invested in standalone (SA) networks by the end of September 2023, as illustrated in Table 2.1, according to GSA as well.

5G to consumer (5GtoC) applications are in their early stages [3], still lacking broad appeal, except terminal promotion, tariff plan differentiation, and immersive entertainment towards a small proportion of users. Extended reality (XR), high-definition (HD), and immersive experience are the buzzwords, and related services include 4K streaming, gaming, interactive live streaming for sports and performances, virtual reality (VR), and augmented reality (AR). Figure 2.2 shows the main 5GtoC applications and content.

Since 2022, 5G has been branching out into the industrial Internet, cultural and sporting events, healthcare, and smart transportation. Elsewhere, 5G industry applications are not mature, still in extensive verification and demonstration.

5G is crucial to economic and social development, and governments have positioned 5G as a key part in their strategic plans and projects. For example, they have stepped up efforts to create favorable environments for 5G application innovations

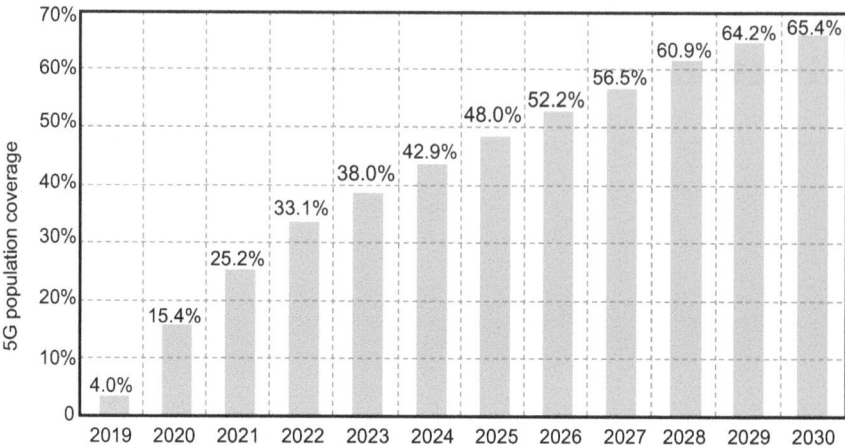

Fig. 2.1 Global 5G population coverage

in ways suited to their local conditions, promote 5G adoption in vertical industries, and foster 5G application ecosystems, hoping to inject strong momentum into the digital transformation of the economy and society.

South Korea has made a top-level strategic plan to accelerate 5G application. The USA has released the *5G FAST Plan*, for comprehensive strategic arrangements for 5G development. In Europe, policies and projects has been earmarked to integrate 5G into vertical industries. In its "Society 5.0" plan, Japan is encouraging the large-scale convergence of 5G with other technologies in key sectors. China is a major pioneer of 5G commercial adoption. Since June 2019 when 5G licenses were issued, China has seen rapid 5G adoption across industries, and a system favoring further 5G to business (5GtoB) growth has taken shape. This enables a positive 5G business cycle and signals an increased momentum in innovations and ecosystems.

2.1 5G Development in China

2.1.1 5G Commercial Adoption in China

China has achieved major breakthroughs in mobile communications—a market worthy of over CNY1 trillion—fueling a huge scale of information consumption and supporting a flourishing digital economy. This offers a strong foundation for China to promote commercial 5G, which formally started on October 31, 2019, well earlier than other major 5G players. Now, China excels in 5G coverage, technology, and adoption [4]. Figure 2.3 shows a brief summary of China's development in its mobile communications industry.

2.1　5G Development in China

Table 2.1 Deployment of commercial 5G SA networks

Region	2020	2021	2022	2023 (Till Sep.)
Oceania		Australia: TPG	Australia: Optus	
Africa				Nigeria: Mafab
America	USA: T-Mobile	Canada: Rogers	Brazil: Claro Brasil	Brazil: Brisanet
		Canada: Bell (Bell Canada Enterprises or BCE)	Brazil: Telefonica	USA: UScellular
		Canada: Xplornet	Brazil: TIM	USA: Comcast Corp
			USA: Verizon	USA: AT&T
Europe	Switzerland: Sunrise	Germany: Vodafone	Austria: Three Austria	Denmark: TDC
	Switzerland: Swisscom	Germany: O_2 (Telefonica)	Bulgaria: A1 Bulgaria	Spain: Orange
	Switzerland: Salt	Finland: DNA	Germany: Deutsche Telekom	Spain: Telefonica
	Spain: Vodafone	Italy: Linkem	Finland: Telia	UK: Vodafone
			Latvia: Tele2	
Asia	Thailand: AIS	Philippines: PLDT	Bahrain: STC (VIVA)	UAE: Etisalat
	China: China Telecom	South Korea: KT	Philippines: Globe Telecom	
	China: China Unicom	Kuwait: STC (VIVA)	Kuwait: Zain	
	China: China Mobile	Japan: NTT DOCOMO	Japan: KDDI	
	China: China Mobile Hong Kong	Japan: SoftBank	Saudi Arabia: Zain	
		Japan: Rakuten Mobile	China: China Broadnet	
		Singapore: M1	India: Reliance Jio	
		Singapore: Singtel		
		Singapore: StarHub		

Five years later, there are 3.377 million 5G base stations and 23.02 million gigabit network ports in China, bringing 5G connections to 805 million people across this country and over 80% of villages. Now, 47% of data traffic is on 5G networks, and 5G has expanded to 71 categories of the national economy, including manufacturing, mining, electric power, ports, and healthcare, with 94,000 use cases practiced and more than 29,000 5G virtual private networks. This contributes to digitalization and empowers the information and communications sector. In 2023, the telecommunications sector saw revenue up 6.2% year-on-year and a business volume rise of 16.8% year-on-year.

5G standards continue to evolve. In December 2021, 3GPP Release 18 was approved, focusing on coverage and uplink capacity enhancements, deterministic networks, passive Internet of Things (IoT), as well as XR and media support.

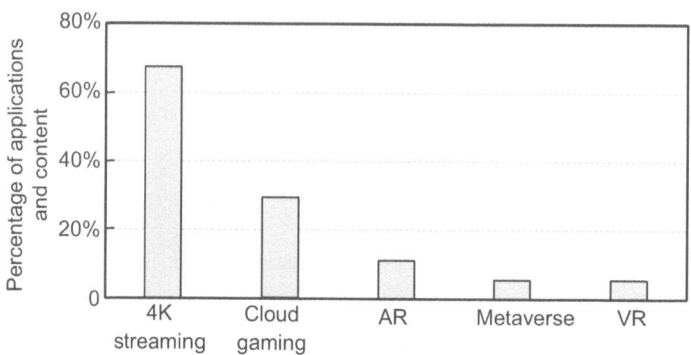

Fig. 2.2 5GtoC applications and content

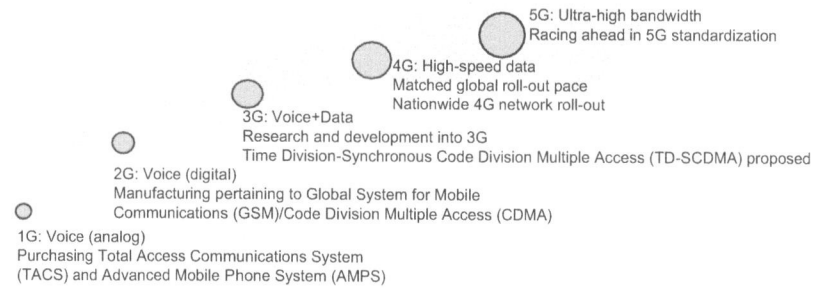

Fig. 2.3 China's development in its mobile communications industry

Scheduled to be finalized in H2 2024, 3GPP Release 18 marks the evolution of 5G to 5G-Advanced (5G-A) (hereinafter referred to as 5.5G) to enable ubiquitous 10 Gbit/s, 100 billion smart connections, and green networks. 3GPP Release 19 and Release 20 are planned to further evolve 5.5G.

In August 2023, the Ministry of Industry and Information Technology (MIIT) of China proposed to scale up the uptake of reduced capability or RedCap (a technology that 5G introduces to reduce adoption costs), with the objective of achieving development goals relating to products, business models, and security by 2025. Figure 2.4 shows 5G RedCap features and its typical applications.

As 5G has been increasingly adopted in industries, five application chains have been formed: the device chain, network chain, platform chain, application solution chain, and security chain. The device chain has new products with distinctive industry features, and its challenges include costs, technical bottlenecks, and market fragmentation. The network chain has some new converged and lightweight devices, while customization, operations and maintenance (O&M), and scalability are still challenges. The platform chain introduces the operations platform and the edge platform, but a universal, multi-purpose platform necessary to cultivate a 5G application ecosystem is still lacking. The application solution chain encompasses

2.1 5G Development in China

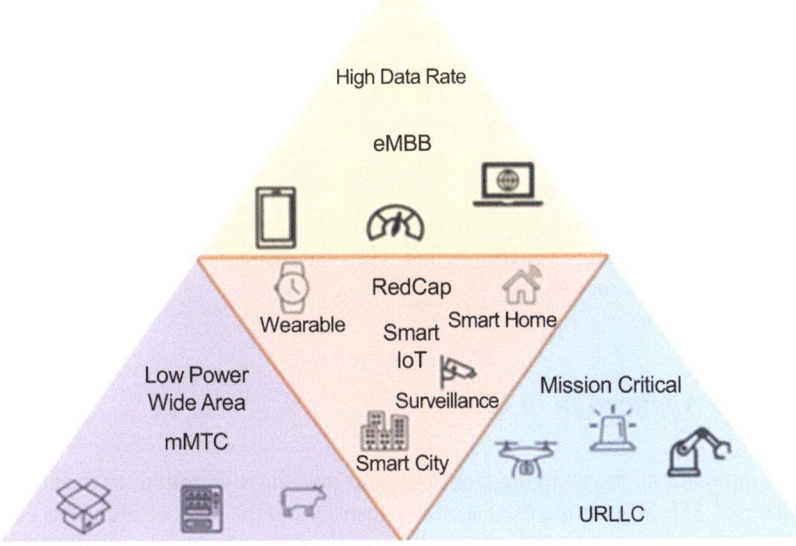

Fig. 2.4 5G RedCap features and its typical applications

applications featuring the convergence of 5G into industries, and innovation is required to nurture more convergence use cases. For the security chain, which now also covers industry security, technology and product design enhancements are necessary for cross-industry 5G security.

2.1.2 5G Promotion Policies in China

China's 14th Five-Year Plan (2021–2025) proposes to accelerate the rollout of 5G and boost 5G user penetration to 56% by 2025. It has identified ten key sectors, covering smart transportation, smart energy, smart manufacturing, smart agriculture and water conservation, smart education, smart healthcare, and smart cultural tourism.

China has further prioritized 5G development in its planning for the information and communications industry, while strengthening policy support for network construction, use case creation, industrial development, and more.

In the *"Set Sail" Action Plan for 5G Applications (2021–2023)* issued by the MIIT, 32 tasks were identified to increase the adoption of 5G in the consumer (ToC), business (ToB), and government (ToG) sectors. The 15 key areas for 5GtoB include information consumption, industrial manufacturing, energy, transportation, agriculture, healthcare, education, cultural tourism, and smart city. This plan also involves sharing experiences and achievements in 5G adoption and collecting use cases in conjunction with other departments. It also encourages local governments to work with the telecom industry to accelerate 5G deployment.

In January 2023, China unveiled policies and measures towards 5G and gigabit optical networks, industrial Internet, standards systems, application systems, and industrial virtual private networks. In May 2023, China unveiled further action plans aimed at coordinating dual-gigabit implementation in terms of 5G site and equipment room resources and indoor mobile networks. These plans detail strategies for sharing network infrastructure, such as poles, pipes, equipment rooms, optical cables, and base station transmission lines, while also promoting 5G network sharing and cross-operator roaming.

Local governments have been offering various policy support for 5G development and creating favorable environments. They have released tailored action plans for 5G network construction.

2.1.3 5G Application in China

5GtoB applications are evolving from trial use into massive rollout to develop on the fast track [5]. 5G is being used across industries and the number of 5G use cases has grown by leaps and bounds. According to the China Academy of Information and Communications Technology (CAICT), the sixth "Zhanfang Cup" 5G Application Competition held in 2023 received over 45,000 5G application projects from across China, an increase of 60% over 2022, many related to smart city, industrial Internet, smart healthcare, smart education, public safety, and cultural tourism.

In 2023, over 60% of projects were ready for "commercial implementation" and "scalability," a marked increase over 2022. Over 6300 projects demonstrated "scalability," a 60% increase from nearly 4000 projects in 2022.

Basic telecom service providers have established industry-specific teams tasked with providing end-to-end solutions. These solutions aim at enriching industry-specific products, enhancing core digitalization capabilities, and helping 5G expand from large enterprises to small- and medium-sized enterprises (SMEs), including 2149 medical institutions, 6948 factories, 691 mining enterprises, and 547 energy companies. 5G has enabled them to enhance quality, efficiency, and security at reduced costs and to achieve green development. Notably, 5G has been adopted in 71 out of the 97 categories of China's national economy, such as manufacturing, mining, electric power, ports, and healthcare. China is also intensifying its efforts to explore 5G adoption in water conservation, construction, and textile. In manufacturing, 5G has expanded to core services, such as research and development (R&D) as well as design, production and manufacturing, O&M, and product services. 20 typical scenarios have been created, such as machine vision-aided quality inspection and onsite assembly assistance. In the electric power industry, 5G has expanded from transmission-related unattended inspection to all scenarios across generation, transmission, transformation, distribution, and consumption. 5G has reached 92% of China's 25 major coastal ports, as well as 95% and 85% of top 20 coal producers and steelmakers, respectively. The scaled 5G adoption has led to 5G DICT (data, information, and communications technology) contracts worth over CNY100 billion for telecom service providers. This demonstrates that the benefits of 5G as an enabler have become apparent.

2.2 5G Development in South Korea

2.2.1 5G Commercial Adoption in South Korea

South Korea has led the way in commercializing 5G, first tried 5G at the PyeongChang Winter Olympics in early 2018. In June 2018, South Korea auctioned the 3.5 GHz and 28 GHz bands, and on December 1, 2018, its three operators, South Korea Telecom (SK Telecom), Korea Telecom (KT), and LG U+, launched enterprise 5G. By April 3, 2019, 5G services had reached 17 cities.

According to Omdia, an analytics and advisory company, by the end of June 2023, the total number of 5G subscribers exceeded 30 million for the first time, a 25% increase from 2022, signaling a steady growth in 5G subscribers since 2019. Data from South Korea's Ministry of Science and ICT (MSIT) revealed that 5G users made up 38% of the total 80.2 million subscribers. SK Telecom recorded the highest number at 14.7 million, followed by KT and LG U+ with 9.3 million and 6.7 million, respectively. In total, about 115,000 3.5 GHz 5G base stations were installed in 85 cities.

The 5G and 4G co-networking contributed to a rapid 5G uptake. As the 5G user base expanded, 4G connections became slower. As 4G base stations were not duly maintained, users in rural areas also suffered during the rapid promotion of 5G. Now, the operators have started to build 5G SA networks, to better serve consumers and verticals. Their limited investment could mean quite a while for large-scale 5G SA adoption.

5G applications, particularly consumer ones, were given a high priority from an early stage. SK Telecom, KT, and LG U+ have channeled their efforts into cultivating quality content, such as VR, AR, cloud gaming, and 4K HD video, and launched sports and idols services to spur 5G traffic. In terms of data of usage (DOU) per connection, in January 2023, 5G averaged a monthly DOU of 26.8 GB per connection, 3.6 times the 4G level.

2.2.2 5G Promotion Policies in South Korea

South Korea is among the first countries to have mapped out a national strategy for 5G, encompassing coordinated arrangements, heavy investment, rigorous R&D, joint construction and sharing, and tax concessions. These measures allowed South Korea to commercialize 5G 1 year ahead of schedule. After its initial 5G commercialization, South Korea released a second strategy to beef up its 5G ecosystems with other leading technologies. The policies included accelerating 5G network deployment, enhancing service quality, and expanding 5G into more industries.

In December 2013, the Ministry of Science, ICT and Future Planning (MSIP)[1] of South Korea held a hearing on "Creative 5G Mobile Strategy," announcing its ambition to start launching commercial 5G services in 2020. It estimated that by 2026,

---

[1] Ministry of Science, ICT and Future Planning (MSIP) was renamed Ministry of Science and ICT (MSIT) in 2017.

the 5G equipment and consumption market would be worth KRW476 trillion and KRW94 trillion, respectively. In 2013–2020, it invested KRW500 billion into R&D, standardization, infrastructure, and others and put 5G industry-university-research (IUR) collaboration into operation to promote 5G.

In April 2018, the MSIT unveiled a package of measures to put 5G into commercial use in advance, allowing telecom operators to use government-managed infrastructure, such as street lamps and transportation facilities, through legislation, for the purpose of constructing 5G networks. The operators pledged to share their infrastructure for initial 5G deployment, such as pipes and utility poles, and to jointly build new infrastructure, such as sandpoint wells and pipes.

Riding the initial wave of 5G commercialization, the MSIT released a 5G+ strategy in April 2019 to promote the convergence of 5G with various services and industries and to establish South Korea as a leader in the global market. This strategy pledged over KRW30 trillion of public and private investment to build the world's best 5G ecosystem by 2022, creating 600,000 quality jobs, and generating KRW180 trillion in gross domestic product (GDP) and USD73 billion of exports out of 5G by 2026.

In April 2020, the "5G+ Strategy Committee"—chaired by the Minister of the Ministry of Science and ICT—announced that the government's commitment of KRW650 billion for strategic 5G+ industries and services. The government vowed to launch 5G+ projects, including 200 5G smart factories, digital healthcare to lay the foundation of an intelligent emergency healthcare system, smart city, vehicle-to-everything (V2X) infrastructure (accreditation and testbed), vehicle-to-cloud infrastructure and autonomous driving, and XR (an umbrella of VR, AR, and mixed reality (MR)) in public services, industry, science and technology, etc.

In late January 2021, South Korea came up with new plans to promote its 5G+ strategy. Naming 2021 as the first year of nurturing a world-leading 5G+ ecosystem, this plan further introduced attractive measures to cultivate new sectors based on leading 5G networks, and to break down legal and institutional barriers for enterprises to adopt 5G services in their business activities. The four core missions are as follows:

1. Nationwide top-notch 5G services. To achieve nationwide 5G coverage by 2022, the MSIT adopted a string of measures, including deploying 5G networks in key urban and rural areas, such as key administrative buildings, subway and Korea Train Express (KTX) stations, and 4000 multi-purpose facilities across 85 cities; facilitating roaming and network sharing in rural areas among the three telecom operators; increasing the maximum tax credit for 5G investment from 2% in 2020 to 3%; strengthening quality assessment; and reducing registration and licensing taxes by 50%.
2. 5G-enabled services and equipment. South Korea planned to fund KRW165.5 billion in 2021 to support the innovation, verification, and commercialization of 5G in major core service areas. Other measures include exploring 5G and multi-access edge computing (MEC) in the public service domain over dedicated networks to offer new services. In addition, end-to-end support (from module and device development to infrastructure construction and service activation, popularization, and development) would be strengthened to develop the equipment industry.

2.2 5G Development in South Korea   21

3. World-class 5G ecosystem. This was to be achieved by deepening collaboration with key markets and supporting enterprises in expanding internationally.
4. FutureProof foundation for sustained 5G development, achieved by allocating spectrum necessary for strategic 5G+ industries, enhancing management, talent development, etc.

In August 2021, the MSIT unveiled a new plan to promote 5G services in various sectors, with specific tasks and timetables. These targeted sectors mainly include distance education, industrial security, and disaster response, where both consumers and enterprises can directly feel and enjoy the benefits of 5G. This plan promotes the deployment of private 5G networks for various projects. By setting up quantitative goals with regard to use cases, engaged companies, and technical levels, this plan aims to scale up the adoption of 5G across verticals, even in international markets. The quantitative goals are as follows:

1. Locations where 5G+ services are adopted increase from 195 in 2021 to 630 by 2023 and 3200 by 2026, with new use cases in public services up from 1 in 2021 to 5 in 2023 and 11 by 2026.
2. 5G-specialized companies increase from 94 in 2021 to 330 by 2023 and 1800 by 2026, with the 5G+ technical level up from 84.5% in 2021 to 88% by 2023 and 95% by 2026.

2.2.3   5G Application in South Korea

Due to a strong government push and sufficient market arrangements, a variety of killer applications, from HD videos to VR, AR, and cloud gaming, have been available for consumers in South Korea across the sectors where the country typically excels, such as entertainment, sports, gaming, etc.

VR and AR sports, performances, gaming, fitness, shopping, social networking, and library services created a huge sensation. SK Telecom offers three AR and VR services to enhance esports immersion: "Jump AR," "LCK VR Live Broadcasting" (LCK for League of Legends Champions Korea), and "VR Replay". "Jump AR" allows users to tour an esports stadium, League of Legends Park, on their mobile phones. "LCK VR Live Broadcasting" allows for a 360-degree view of esports games. "VR Replay" provides users with a 360-degree view of battle scenes from game characters' point of view. SK Telecom also has "Virtual Social World," a 5G VR social networking service. LG U+ has VR live streaming, AR user-generated content (UGC), AR navigation, and AR library and offers various new XR experiences from drama performances, shopping, and fitness to education and social networking. It has "MR + AI" services that create ubiquitous smart life experiences. Notably, its "U+ Idol Live" app allows fans to view live idol performances from various close-up angles, and its "U+ Pro Baseball" app allows fans to watch live baseball games from user-custom angles.

Cloud gaming is another big-wave application of 5G where its fast connections and low latency encourage users to pay. With this service, players can enjoy high-quality gaming experiences on a wide range of devices, with no need to invest in expensive gaming hardware. This greatly expands the 5G user base. Cloud gaming features in-depth collaboration between operators and gaming companies. KT has developed a 5G game streaming platform in collaboration with Ubitus, a cloud gaming company. SK Telecom has 5G-based cloud game streaming services, which are supported by Microsoft. LG U+ provides 5G users with cloud gaming services that are based on NVIDIA's GeForce NOW and has set up cloud gaming experience zones in 100 direct-sale stores.

The deveopment of a content ecosystem is a major focus for operators seeking to provide differentiated 5G services, such as live sports and exclusive VR/AR games, bundled with value-added content from content providers. For live streaming, a common approach is to partner with professional baseball, golf, and esports events to offer HD and multi-view streaming. Meanwhile, operators create quality content such as VR/AR products and cloud-based games, both independently and in collaboration with content producers. LG U+ has partnered with startup company Spatial, AR product developer Nreal, and Qualcomm to develop 5G-based AR solutions. SK Telecom has worked with Microsoft to launch Jump Studio, an MR capture studio, which uses volumetric video technology to produce MR content, such as 3D holographic videos, quickly and affordably. While enriching its own VR and AR content library, SK Telecom provides quality MR content to operators across Europe, the Americas, and Asia.

Global presence has also been pursued by South Korean operators by partnering with operators abroad to develop and distribute premium content. LG U+ has signed contracts with other operators to provide 5G content products and solutions, resulting in a total export volume of USD10 million. In addition, LG U+ has initiated the establishment of the Global XR Content Telco Alliance with partners.

Beyond the consumer market, pilots were implemented in factories, ports, healthcare, transportation, urban public security, and other sectors. To date, 5G has begun to be implemented in industrial Internet, healthcare, smart transportation, urban public security, and emergency response. The groundbreaking applications include "5G + AI" machine vision-aided quality inspection, digital teleconsultation, pathology and surgery teaching, remote robot control or unmanned aerial vehicles (UAVs) for emergency rescue and pandemic prevention, and 5G autonomous driving for in-campus material delivery.

2.3 5G Development in the USA

2.3.1 *5G Commercial Adoption in the USA*

Despite an early start, the 5G adoption in the USA showed high population coverage but low user penetration. In the early phase, as no mid-band spectrum was available, 5G networks were mostly on millimeter wave (mmWave) bands. Such

2.3 5G Development in the USA

high-band networks have several limitations, such as limited coverage and high deployment costs. From the end of 2019, low-band spectrum and spectrum sharing became available for nationwide 5G coverage. In March 2021, the Federal Communications Commission (FCC) completed the auction of 3.7–3.98 GHz C-band, followed by plans from major operators for C-band 5G.

Verizon Wireless, also known as Verizon, made fixed wireless accessible in four cities in the USA based on proprietary standards, starting on October 1, 2018. In April 2019, it launched 3GPP-compliant 5G mobile services on mmWave spectrum 28 GHz and low-band spectrum 850 MHz. Between January 2021 and June 2022, its 5G data usage grew by 249%. Verizon planned to cover at least 250 million people by 2024, with peak speeds of 4 Gbit/s in certain locations.

American Telephone and Telegraph, or AT&T, launched commercial 5G services in 12 cities in the USA at the end of 2018. Based on NSA 5G, the early services were mainly oriented to industry customers. AT&T's networks had covered 250 million people across the country by 2021, 6 months ahead of schedule. In 2022, it increased capital expenditure by 26.3% over 2021 to increase its 5G user base to 290 million and fiber broadband coverage to 38%. By working with AST SpaceMobile (a satellite provider) and Frontier (a fiber network provider) as well as with BlackRock Alternatives to form a fiber-centric joint venture, AT&T eliminated dead zones and expanded coverage. Its 5G networks continued to improve in both capacity and performance due to its efforts to accelerate mid-band and SA 5G deployments. By the end of 2022, more than 150 million people were on AT&T's mid-band 5G network—more than twice as expected. In the first quarter of 2023, AT&T completed 5G SA verification tests. In this period, AT&T's 5G download and upload speeds exhibited a 44.8% and 23.2% increase, respectively, in comparison to the same period in 2022, according to Opensignal, an analytics company.

T-Mobile launched 28 and 39 GHz commercial 5G services at the end of June 2019 and rolled out 600 MHz 5G networks for nationwide coverage at the end of 2019. T-Mobile acquired Sprint, which deployed 5G networks in 2.5 GHz, thereby making it an operator in possession of low-, mid-, and high-band 5G networks. On June 10, 2023, T-Mobile launched its 5G hotspot service as an affordable option for users needing 5G access. T-Mobile's 600 MHz 5G network has been operational nationwide, and an ultra-capacity 2.5 GHz 5G network offers ultra-high-speed connections in hundreds of cities.

2.3.2 5G Promotion Policies in the USA

The USA regards 5G as an industry priority. Its efforts in strategic planning, 5G R&D promotion, spectrum provisioning, and 5G security have laid a foundation for a world-leading 5G industry.

In October 2018, the FCC released the *5G FAST Plan* to promote 5G construction and strengthen the country's technical advantages in 5G. The Plan comprises a comprehensive package of strategies:

1. Make more spectrum available to the market, specifically by prioritizing mmWave auctioning, assigning mid-band spectrum, improving the use of low-band spectrum, and creating new opportunities for next-generation Wi-Fi in unlicensed spectrum.
2. Update infrastructure policies to clear the way for 5G development at all levels, with a focus on introducing new rules related to the small cells needed for 5G. The new rules are expected to reduce regulatory impediments to deploying the small-cell infrastructure and shorten the process for small cell site approval.
3. Modernize outdated regulations, including abolishing network neutrality, updating the rules governing the attachment of new network equipment to existing poles in order to reduce costs and expedite 5G backhaul deployment, promoting investment in next-generation networks and services, lifting regulations on data service tariffs to incentivize investment in fiber networks, and prohibiting the purchase of equipment and services from companies that pose a national security threat to the integrity of communications networks or the communications supply chain.

In October 2018, the federal government issued a memorandum, proposing that sufficient spectrum resources and effective spectrum management were critical to maximizing the economic driving effect of 5G networks and maintaining national security. Following the release of this memorandum, the FCC announced a plan to release more low-, mid-, and high-band spectrum for 5G networks, with high-band mmWave spectrum to be auctioned first. Low-band spectrum was meant for expanding network coverage, and high-band spectrum for increasing network capacity. In the initial phase of 5G development, mmWave bands were used for two reasons. First, sub-6 GHz mid-band spectrum had all been allocated to services such as radio stations, TV, satellite, and radar. Second, given the low optical fiber coverage, telecom operators used mmWave (which offers high speed and large capacity) as an alternative to fiber to ensure last-mile reachability. Since 2019, 24, 28, 37, 39, and 47 GHz have been auctioned, with a total of 5 GHz of 5G spectrum.

However, mmWave can hardly provide continuous coverage due to its short-range coverage and vulnerability to obstructions. As such, mmWave 5G networks are deployed only in specific urban areas for hotspot coverage, and low-band 5G networks for wide-scale coverage. However, low-band 5G spectrum resources are limited, and consequently the high bandwidth of 5G cannot be fully leveraged.

Realizing the shortcoming of mmWave 5G networks, the USA has taken corrective measures. In April 2019, the US Department of Defense (DoD) proposed that sharing sub-6 GHz spectrum be prioritized in the 5G spectrum planning to compensate for the insufficient coverage of high-band spectrum. At the end of 2019, the US Senate Committee on Commerce, Science, and Transportation passed a bill to put 280 MHz (in the 3.7–3.98 GHz portion) of spectrum in the 3.7–4.2 GHz C-band for 5G systems on public auction. In February 2020, the FCC decided to establish a nearly USD10 billion fund to support satellite companies' transition to new spectrum, clearing the way for the auction of these frequencies for 5G.

2.3 5G Development in the USA   25

Since 2020, the USA has stepped up auctions of mid-band 5G spectrum. 70 MHz of priority access licenses (PALs) in the 3.55–3.65 GHz Citizen Broadband Radio Service (CBRS) band was auctioned in August 2020; the 3.7–3.98 GHz C-band was auctioned in March 2021; 100 MHz in 3.45–3.55 GHz (originally used for military purposes) was put into commercial use in December 2022.

2.3.3 5G Application in the USA

To address the problem of insufficient optical fiber coverage, USA-based telecom operators have been deploying 5G fixed wireless access (FWA) as an alternative to optical fibers for last-mile coverage. This has helped provide better Internet services for households and enterprises while reducing cable deployment and maintenance costs. With the high data rates of mmWave 5G networks, telecom operators have made enhanced mobile wireless access available in hotspot areas, such as airports, stadiums, arenas, shopping centers, and campuses. Since October 2018, Verizon has provided mmWave 5G Internet services for households, and by July 2021, the services had expanded to over 40 cities. T-Mobile started to vigorously explore the 5G FWA market in 2021, with the aim of expanding its 5G Home Internet to 7–8 million households in 5 years.

Another trend is that cooperation is established between telecom operators and specialized companies, such as content and gaming companies, to provide VR, AR, HD video, and cloud gaming services. For example, AT&T cooperated with Inception to provide an immersive AR book-reading experience for children through Bookful, a 3D and AR reading app, bringing stories to life. It also teamed up with Facebook Reality Labs, a unit of Meta (formerly known as Facebook), to build collaborative video calling and AR experience on the Instagram and Messenger apps. AT&T and Verizon both cooperated with Google's cloud gaming platform, Stadia, to supercharge a seamless gaming experience using optical fibers and 5G networks.

Given the limited coverage provided by high-band spectrum, mmWave 5G networks are leveraged to cover densely populated areas. Stadiums and arenas, which are popular among Americans, feature high traffic volume and therefore are the main areas for 5G network deployment. In the early phase of 5G network construction, they were the only areas covered by 5G in some cities. As for 5G applications, they are centered on enhancing user experience, with the typical applications including high-speed mobile access, HD live streaming of sports events/performances, and VR/AR.

T-Mobile's Major League Baseball (MLB) AR app provides fans with an immersive AR experience. 5G-enabled cameras mounted on player hats and catcher masks place fans virtually on the field in real time, so that they can catch a glimpse of actions from the players' perspective, regardless of whether they are at the ballpark or at home.

Verizon has deployed 5G in more than 60 arenas and stadiums. Using 5G and MEC provided by Amazon Web Services (AWS), connectivity in these places has been improved, thereby enhancing user experience. Its ShotTracker system uses data from sensors mounted in the stadiums and worn by players to create an "indoor GPS," which captures the players' location and movement speed within the stadiums and delivers statistics in real time. Verizon launched an AR mobile game, allowing fans at the NFL Super Bowl to toss a football into the back of a pickup truck positioned in the middle of a field, all within a virtual environment.

Another example is the Stats Zone, an AR-enabled app, co-developed by AT&T, the Chicago Bulls, and Nexus Studios, an XR team. The app provides visual statistics of players and some customized content for fans, creating an enhanced viewing experience. In addition, AT&T, the official 5G wireless network partner of the National Basketball Association (NBA), provided fans with unique multi-dimensional views of concerts through its 5G Courtside Concert Series.

The USA is committed to building its strengths in 5G technologies and ensuring the security, reliability, and availability of 5G networks. To date, no government policies have been released with regard to the application of 5G. 5GtoB applications are still under exploration and technical verification, with tests covering applications in multiple sectors including industrial Internet, healthcare, V2X, and smart city. The mmWave 5G networks deployed in the early phase provide a solid network foundation and test environment for developing 5GtoB applications. The industry players, in close collaboration with each other and with the help of innovation-driven organizations such as innovation centers and incubators, are exploring digital technologies such as edge computing and advanced manufacturing, in order to build a sound ecosystem for 5GtoB applications. There are already 5GtoB applications implemented, though on a small scale, such as 4K video-aided security monitoring in factories, VR/AR-based employee training and positioning services, and "5G + VR/AR" remote diagnosis and emergency rescue services.

2.4 5G Development in Japan

2.4.1 5G Commercial Adoption in Japan

In March 2020, Japanese operators NTT DOCOMO, KDDI, and SoftBank launched commercial 5G services. Due to the COVID-19 pandemic, network verification was delayed and Rakuten Mobile consequently postponed the rollout of commercial 5G services from June 2020 to September 2020. To speed up 5G network deployment in rural areas of Japan, KDDI and SoftBank agreed to share base station assets. By the end of 2020, there were fewer than 10,000 5G base stations in Japan. Since 2021, operators have accelerated network deployment, with 15,500 new base stations deployed in 6 months. By the end of June 2023, a total of 150,000 5G base stations had been deployed in Japan. The number of base stations per 10,000 people was about 11.7, with networks covering 36% of the country's population.

Four Japanese network operators have obtained both 5G mid-band spectrum and mmWave spectrum. In the early stage of network construction, the mid-band spectrum (3.7 and 4.5 GHz) was mainly used for deploying networks and low-band spectrum was used for wide coverage. For example, in 2021, KDDI launched 700 MHz 5G services as a supplement to existing 5G services, thereby expanding 5G network coverage and improving indoor and outdoor mobile services. Rakuten Mobile announced a plan to use the newly granted 1.7 GHz band for 5G deployment in small- and medium-sized cities. mmWave (28 GHz) was mainly used to provide the capacity layer in hotspot areas. In September 2020, NTT DOCOMO launched mmWave services at a maximum downlink rate of 4.1 Gbit/s and a maximum upload rate of 480 Mbit/s. SoftBank launched 5G mmWave services in densely populated urban areas, reducing the total cost by up to 35% and providing higher data capacity for FWA and enterprise access.

2.4.2 5G Promotion Policies in Japan

The Japanese government has formulated a clear roadmap for 5G development and has been promoting technical tests, spectrum allocation, and commercial deployment. In September 2014, Japan established the Fifth Generation Mobile Communications Promotion Forum to strengthen industry-academia-government cooperation in areas such as 5G basic research, technology development, and standard formulation, and to further promote international cooperation. In 2016, the Japanese government released the *Japan's Radio Policy to Realize 5G in 2020*, aimed at guiding the adoption of 5G across industries. The Policy sets the goals of carrying out 5G radio access network (RAN), core network, and 5G application tests from the fiscal year 2017, allocating 5G spectrum in 2019, and putting 5G into commercial use during the Tokyo Olympic Games. Efforts have centered on strengthening the R&D in key technologies, improving the policy support for 5G, fostering industry-academia-government cooperation, and actively participating in international standardization activities.

At the end of June 2020, the Ministry of Internal Affairs and Communications (MIC) of Japan released the *Beyond 5G Promotion Strategy*: a document that sets the goals of accelerating 5G commercial deployment, rapidly promoting large-scale early-stage 5G deployment and application expansion in industrial and public fields, establishing 5G use cases with international and national influence within the next 5 years, and generating new value totaling JPY44 trillion by 2030. To achieve these strategic goals, a number of measures have been planned. For example, Japan's MIC has released the *Master Plan 2.0 on the Regional Development of ICT Infrastructure* to guide the promotion of 5G.

2.4.3 5G Application in Japan

Guided by the vision of building "Society 5.0," the Japanese government has been actively promoting the convergence of 5G with AI, IoT, and robotics, while also supporting large-scale early-stage deployment of 5G and application expansion in key fields. According to the *Information and Communications White Paper* released by the MIC of Japan on July 9, 2019, Japan will adopt 5G in major scenarios, including healthcare, remote education, UAV-based transportation, autonomous driving, agricultural and industrial production, and disaster relief by leveraging 5G features, such as ultra-high speed, multi-point access, and low latency.

From 2018 to 2019, the Japanese government supported more than 40 comprehensive 5G application test projects, involving entertainment services, disaster protection, tourism, healthcare, agriculture, and transportation. From 2020 onwards, the Japanese government focused on supporting 5G application in the following fields: industry, agriculture, healthcare, autonomous driving, and smart city. In 2021, the MIC of Japan invested JPY21.95 billion to build advanced communications infrastructure for remote office, remote education, and telehealth services, including helping 5G network construction in areas with unfavorable geographical conditions and supporting local enterprises in building local 5G systems.

Japanese operators mainly provide users with 5G home broadband and high-speed mobile access services, as well as content and entertainment services such as VR, AR, games, and HD videos. Similar to operators in other countries and regions, Japanese operators are also actively carrying out proof-of-concept tests for 5G-based live-sports event streaming.

In 2019, NTT DOCOMO launched a pre-commercial 5G service and provided dedicated smartphones compatible with 5G networks for attendees at the Rugby World Cup to help them view the game from multiple angles. The attendees enjoyed an engaging and completely immersive viewing experience. KDDI integrated 5G and other advanced technologies into the main stadium and fan communications systems of the Kyoto Sanga FC to improve the spectator experience. Rakuten Mobile cooperated with Vissel Kobe to use AR for displaying statistics and real-time tracking data and to provide low-latency and multi-angle video services on an mmWave 5G network at Noevir Stadium Kobe.

Japanese operators have consistently prioritized the development and adoption of HD video apps. NTT DOCOMO has developed a 5G-based 8K VR live streaming system. KDDI has completed 4K video transmission tests using 5G UAVs and is exploring the adoption of UAVs in public safety and surveillance services, agricultural monitoring, and disaster response.

XR is another important user-oriented application in Japan. KDDI, one of the initiators of the Global XR Content Telco Alliance (established in September 2020) cooperates extensively with partners to propel the adoption of VR in multiple scenarios. It offers "au XR Door," a smartphone app that enables users to explore XR environments through a door displayed on their smartphone screens without the need for VR glasses. The 360-degree VR space provides immersive experiences in gaming, accommodation booking, virtual tours, and virtual shopping with 8K video support. In 2021, KDDI leveraged its 5G network that extends to the summit of Mount Fuji to provide visitors with a real-time virtual tour of the summit. "au VISION STUDIO," established by KDDI, is oriented towards next-generation media and entertainment content and application. It provides users with a unique experience by using technologies such as 5G, XR, and MEC. To date, the virtual human "coh" has been created using an HD 3D model.

2.5 5G Development in Germany

2.5.1 5G Commercial Adoption in Germany

Germany is one of the first countries to have mapped out a 5G development program. Germany's first 5G spectrum auction was held in June 2019, with Deutsche Telekom, Vodafone, Telefonica Deutschland, and 1&1 AG all winning their bids. The Federal Network Agency of Germany—the regulatory authority responsible for spectrum allocation—also announced all licensed 5G operators would be obligated to provide 100 Mbit/s speeds to at least 98% of households across Germany by the end of 2022.

According to data from the Federal Network Agency of Germany, 5G mobile networks covered 89% of the country's territory as of July 2023. The number of 5G users have exceeded 38 million, with a user penetration rate of 32.3%. A total of 79,000 5G base stations have been deployed in Germany, resulting in a density of 9.5 base stations per 10,000 people. Deutsche Telekom's 5G networks have been accessible to 95% of households, with that figure expected to reach 99% by 2025. Its 4G coverage has reached 99% of households across Germany. The company has deployed over 80,000 5G antennas, including a total of 8200 3.6 GHz antennas. Deutsche Telekom's 5G SA is technically available in the 2.1 GHz band, and commercial use of 5G SA for residential customers will start as soon as applications are available. Vodafone's 5G networks have covered 90% of the country's population through 15,000 5G base stations and its 5G SA networks have covered 45% of the population.

In June 2023, the German national railway company Deutsche Bahn (also known as DB AG), Ericsson (network equipment supplier), O2 Telefonica (telecommunications provider), and Vantage Towers (tower operator) jointly launched the Gigabit Innovation Track (GINT) project. The project aims to establish an extensive 5G mobile communications infrastructure along train tracks in Germany, providing passengers with gigabit-level connections. The German Federal Ministry for Digital and Transport (BMDV) will provide approximately EUR6.4 million in funding to support the GINT project. The GINT partners aim to develop technical and financial solutions for high-performance and sustainable 5G mobile coverage along train tracks.

2.5.2 5G Promotion Policies in Germany

Great efforts are already underway in Germany to develop 5G networks and applications, including communications infrastructure construction, spectrum allocation, industry-specific standard rollout, R&D support, and township- and city-level showcases. Germany unveiled its national 5G strategies in 2017 with the goal of promoting joint construction and sharing of public facilities, as well as a substantial increase in fiber deployment. These strategies also aim to help Germany become a leading market for 5G applications. 5G is seen as a key economic driver for Germany, and therefore, 5G testing has been targeted at promoting commercial accessibility. This will facilitate the adoption of 5G in production, everyday life, and services. Germany aims to have full 5G connectivity by 2025 as part of its "Gigabit Society" goals. This means that 5G connectivity will be made available in both urban and rural areas, and specifically along federal highways, railway lines, major waterways, and other transportation systems. Germany also focuses its efforts on promoting innovative 5G applications, in order to fully leverage its 5G gigabit infrastructure, while also aiming to foster a diverse range of user-friendly applications. Startups as well as SMEs have been actively involved in the sustainable development of 5G.

Regarding spectrum allocation, the Federal Network Agency of Germany began its 5G spectrum licensing process in November 2019. Frequencies in the 3.7–3.8 GHz band have been allocated for local 5G networks, as these frequencies are particularly suited for a range of scenarios, including Industry 4.0, agriculture, and forestry. Interested applicants, either property owners or users, could apply for the frequencies. A number of prominent companies, including BMW, Bosch, Volkswagen, BASF, and Lufthansa, have applied to set up local 5G networks since spectrum licensing requests began being accepted.

Regarding private network construction, 5G, which is recognized as a key technology for the industrial Internet, has attracted attention from many large industrial enterprises amid the development of Industry 4.0 in Germany. In 2019, industry associations, including the German Association of the Automotive Industry and the Machinery and Equipment Manufacturers Association, submitted their requests for private 5G spectrum to the Federal Network Agency of Germany. The agency believes that the development of 5G technology will give rise to new business models, which will then necessitate the establishment of local wireless networks in specific locations. For this reason, the agency has set aside spectrum for local 5G networks before Germany's 5G spectrum auction and has scheduled the phased opening of mid-band (3.7–3.8 GHz) and mmWave spectrum for private 5G licenses. By March 2023, the Federal Network Agency of Germany had issued 304 mid-band spectrum licenses and 17 high-band spectrum licenses. The majority of spectrum holders are IT service companies, consulting companies, system integrators, research institutes, and industrial enterprises. Automakers are the most prevalent among industrial enterprises, and all of Germany's leading automakers have applied for local 5G licenses.

2.5 5G Development in Germany

The German government has also demonstrated its support for 5G and the construction of communications infrastructure by offering funding and coordination services.

One of its key programs funds research into 5G networks and applications. A total of EUR5 billion has been earmarked for the expansion of 5G standards and for new construction. This has been released as part of the German government's economic stimulus package, which was designed to mitigate the effects of the COVID-19 pandemic. Another key funding program will invest EUR1.1 billion into closing almost 5000 wireless coverage gaps currently identified across the country, which are especially prevalent in rural areas, by 2025. The German government is also funding research into scenario-specific applications, with nearly EUR80 million dedicated to research and development of 5G technology for the industrial Internet. The government's primary objective there is to support basic research projects that can be used to assess the impact of 5G technology and increase the societal acceptance of 5G. The fund's focus is on three research priorities: reliable wireless communications, industrial Internet, and tactile Internet.

In Germany, 5G research is conducted in a multitude of places. In addition to research and development centers that are directly financed by network operators and equipment manufacturers, almost all universities with IT faculties and numerous non-university research institutions are engaged in research into issues pertaining to 5G. Coordination between these research activities is critical for efficient resource allocation, and therefore, the German government has devised a series of measures to support this effort, including registering all relevant nationwide 5G research projects, specifying their respective areas of research; clustering research areas and linking-up the research establishments; and transferring research findings to all relevant stakeholders.

In addition to the aforementioned fields of action, 5G pilots are also being mapped out for towns and cities. One of the key measures taken by the Federal Government is to organize 5G competitions. Participating districts, cities, and municipalities will be required to address significant municipal and management challenges and to show in an initial outline how and by when these challenges can be addressed with 5G. Funding will be awarded to the most convincing project proposals, which will be subject to subsequent verification. A total of at least EUR2 million will be made available for these projects. Another key measure being taken is helping municipal applicants approach suitable industry partners and consortia during their initiatives. This measure will provide professional services and financing assistance for pilot projects.

2.5.3 5G Application in Germany

Germany has coordinated its efforts to achieve full 5G connectivity, promote 5G adoption across vertical industries, and facilitate innovation, in order to bring about a broad digital transformation and stimulate economic growth. Germany's initial 5G strategy identified a number of examples of the digital transformation that would be facilitated or centrally supported by 5G, spanning sectors as diverse as smart transportation, Industry 4.0, smart agriculture, smart grids, smart healthcare, and media and content.

BMW has already built a dedicated 5G network at its plant in Regensburg. This network supports interconnected and automated production processes, enabling seamless communication between robots and machines. This improves the flexibility and efficiency of production lines while maintaining data security.

Bosch rolled out its first 5G campus network at its Industry 4.0 demonstration plant in Stuttgart-Feuerbach at the end of 2020. This network, built in collaboration with Nokia, enables connectivity and effortless movements for all production environments, significantly enhancing overall production efficiency.

The Port of Hamburg, one of Europe's largest seaports, has been equipped with a dedicated 5G network to improve logistics and transportation operations. This network helps manage and coordinate the movements of containers, trucks, and ships. In addition, the Hamburg Port Authority (HPA) has initiated a "Smart Port Logistics" project and has earmarked EUR250 million for infrastructure investments. The Port of Hamburg has already deployed cutting-edge control systems, which have significantly improved operational efficiency. The improvements are largely due to the integration of sensor technology with analysis, forecasting and information systems. This exemplifies the potential for innovation in the logistics and energy sectors.

References

1. GSA. Evolution from LTE to 5G[R]. 2024.
2. China Academy of Information and Communications Technology. White Paper on Global Digital Economy (2023) [R] (in Chinese). 2024.
3. China Academy of Information and Communications Technology, China Telecom, China Mobile, et al. White Paper on 5G Application Innovation and Development [R] (in Chinese). 2023.
4. LI R, SHI Q, WAN X Y, et al. Current situation and prospect of 5G development in China [J] (in Chinese). Digital Communications World, 2022(4): 113–115.
5. China Academy of Information and Communications Technology. White Paper on China's 5G Development and Its Economic and Social Impacts (2023) [R] (in Chinese). 2023.

Chapter 3
Challenges, Phases, and Trends of 5G Large-Scale Replication

3.1 Key Challenges of 5G Large-Scale Replication

Currently, the digital economy is developing at an unprecedented rate, both in terms of scope and capabilities. By creating opportunities for technological and industrial revolution, digital transformation has become a national strategic focus for developing new competitive advantages. From a supply and demand perspective, digital transformation is expected to improve manufacturing and supply, so that enterprises are better able to meet diverse consumer requirements through the use of information and communications technologies (ICTs). When taking data elements and implementation into account, digital transformation encompasses the entire data management process, including data generation, transmission, analysis, and transaction. Throughout the process, a wide range of ICTs is required, specifically sensing technologies (involving sensors, devices, and more), connection technologies (involving mobile communications networks, wired broadband, satellite communication, IoT, cloud computing, and more), intelligent technologies (including AI, short for artificial intelligence, and big data), and trust-related technologies (including cyber security, information security, and blockchain). Recent years have seen accelerated innovation in technologies such as 5G, big data, cloud computing, AI, and blockchain. Individual technological breakthroughs are facilitating technological synergies and paving the way for collective evolution. These technologies are becoming the core engine of economic development rather than being just a fundamental driving force. Next-generation ICTs are gradually being used in various areas of economic and social development, and therefore are becoming a key force in reorganizing global resources, reshaping the global economic structure, and spurring changes in the global competitive landscape.

5G is now at the forefront of next-generation ICTs due to its strong penetration and compelling power. It accelerates the convergence and iteration of various technologies, and benefits both the consumer and production fronts, promoting chain evolution and generating a multiplier effect during industry transformation. 5G needs to cope with societal expectations which are significantly different from those expected of previous generations of mobile communications technologies. 1G, 2G, 3G, and 4G networks mainly deal with connections between people whose main expectations on networks are a continuous and consistent communications experience. Therefore, these networks share similar characteristics and the devices running on them take on similar forms. 5G, however, focuses more on connections between devices, which come in different forms, computing capabilities, and computing purposes, and therefore the required network capabilities differ significantly from one another. 5G is expected to drive the development of industries, and enable massive connectivity. 5G is powerful enough to support diversified applications, of which enhanced Mobile Broadband (eMBB), Massive Machine-Type Communications (mMTC), and ultra-reliable low-latency communication (URLLC) are the three typical application scenarios. And after years of research, exploration, and pilot demonstration, the infocommunications industry has come to understand more deeply how 5G empowers a vast range of industries, being aware that it is important to carefully analyze the common requirements, basic services, and main scenarios, and to work out comprehensive solutions, develop the core capabilities, and monetize on them.

Industries have been focused on finding the best way to develop capabilities that match the requirements, apply 5G technologies in vertical industries, and realize large-scale 5G to business (5GtoB) application. This is also a challenge the ICT industry is eager to resolve.

5G has seen growing adoption across various industries, and the key sectors and typical application scenarios have stood out. However, there is still a long way to go before full-fledged application is achieved: many challenges need to be addressed in terms of network construction, service convergence, supply chain management, and ecosystem buildup.

3.1.1 Challenges with 5G Network Construction

5G networks are expected to provide different capabilities depending on industry requirements. For example, uplink 4K/8K video transmission is necessary in industrial machine-vision-based inspection and live broadcasting. The upload rates of 4K and 8K videos need to reach around 50 Mbit/s and 150–200 Mbit/s, respectively, for each of the four to six channels. The required uplink bandwidth is thus much higher than the downlink bandwidth. Therefore, special uplink and downlink slot configuration must be engineered and the corresponding technologies and network solutions must be studied. For industry enterprises, customizing private networks is costly, and charging by traffic may be unaffordable. Using public infrastructure is also not feasible because it is more costly and some functions are redundant. Operators have to bear high network construction and operation costs, and yet the profit model is not clear. Such high costs were common during the early stages of

5G commercial use. At present, most demonstration projects receive financial subsidies and earn revenue through intense publicity, which mitigates the investment risks to some extent. However, if there is not enough market or a clear profit model, a positive business loop will not be formed for 5G, and consequently, it will be impossible to drive investment in this area.

3.1.2 Insufficient Convergence of 5G Technologies into Industry Services

5G convergence is still in the initial stage, in that 5G has not found ways to carry core industry services. The production devices used in industries apply diversified protocols and interfaces, most of which are defined by vendors outside China. This makes the transformation required for converging 5G technologies into industry services costly and time-consuming. Additionally, the convergence of 5G technologies with certain technologies (such as industrial control technologies) is quite challenging. Till now, 5G technologies are mainly used for production supporting services and information management services. Most of the core production control services are still carried on traditional networks such as industrial Ethernet and field buses. As a result, a myriad of transport networks co-exist, making management more complex. There is thus an urgent need to carry out technological innovation and test verification in order to achieve a deeper convergence of 5G technologies into industry services.

5G convergence calls for transformation of multiple links in the industry chain, which requires further exploration. 5G technologies are expected to promote the development of intelligent devices. However, China's global market share in high-end devices (such as digitally controlled machines) is still small, and China enjoys little advantages in intelligent devices such as next-generation sensors, automated production lines, and industrial robots. 5G technologies will drive the cloudification of processing and computing functions, allowing for the traditional onsite treatment of programmable logic controller (PLC) devices to be carried out over the cloud. This area, however, is still under exploration. Furthermore, 5G security performance is not yet convincing enough in industrial use cases, and this also causes insufficient adoption of 5G in industrial production.

3.1.3 Insufficient Industry Supply Capabilities

As 5G converges into industry services, new components, particularly industry-specific 5G modules and chips, become part of the industry chain. However, the corresponding supply capabilities are still weak because of the required R&D investment is now rather high due to various reasons. As a result, such modules and chips are still highly priced and their mass production is hard to achieve. Another new component, which is equally important, is customized 5G virtual private networks. For the time being, the cost of deploying customized networks is high and operations and maintenance (O&M) is difficult. In summary, the empowering capabilities for the 5G industry need to be improved.

In addition, the 5G converged applications have posed higher requirements on 5G technologies. The requirements include enhancement on the conventional performance indicators, such as uplink bandwidth, delay, and reliability, as well as assurance of the new performance indicators, like delay variation, network time serving, and positioning. 5G, with its current level of technical standards and commercial devices, is not able to meet these requirements, which in turn has slowed down its convergence into industry services [1]. Therefore, extensive research has to be done into the 5G technologies, including 5G enhancement, 5G time serving, 5G positioning, 5G time-sensitive networking (TSN), and 5G local area network (LAN), and the related devices, in order to facilitate deeper convergence of 5G into industry services.

3.1.4 Lack of Standards for Industry Converged Applications

The public 5G standalone (SA) networks combined with edge computing can meet the requirements of most industrial use cases. The industry enterprises, however, have concerns about relying on public infrastructure for all of their production and development. The concerns focus on whether they have full control over the production and operation data, whether they can access network upgrade and maintenance services in time, and obtain the network costs over the entire lifecycle with precision, as well as whether they can be assured of a stable network performance. In addition, capital flow is a discouraging factor. According to a research on large-scale manufacturers in China, most enterprises hope to recoup their investment within three years. By contrast, the business models for 5G applications are still under exploration, and it is likely to take a long time for enterprises to realize economic benefits and achieve a complete return on investment. It is also worth noting that most players in the Chinese market are small- and medium-sized enterprises (SMEs), which face challenges including a weak foundation for informatization and digitalization, high costs of investment and financing, and high pressure on cash flow. Therefore, they are unlikely to become the main 5G investors in the short run.

The 5G Applications Industry Array (5G AIA) organized the formulation of the *General Technical Requirements for 5G Industry Virtual Private Networks*. This document defines the overall architecture, service capabilities, key devices, and key technologies of 5G industry virtual private networks. In response to the requirements for lower cost and joint O&M, the array is also driving the development of a series of network device standards, such as the customized user plane function (UPF) and service capability platforms. Research is also being conducted on

3.1 Key Challenges of 5G Large-Scale Replication

wireless Service Level Agreement (SLA) assurance and key 5G LAN technologies to meet the requirements for network performance assurance and integration with existing networks. Standards tailored for industries, including electric power, steel, and mining, are also in progress, with the goal of standardizing the industry requirements on 5G networks, the network architecture for 5G convergence into industries, and the key network capabilities to provide. Completion of these standards calls for coordination between ministries, industries, and sectors, which is not efficient yet. Given the variety of use cases 5G must be fitted into, the lack of standards aggravates the process of reaching consensus across industries on 5G terminals, modules, chips, security, and related tests and accreditation. All this has made the large-scale promotion of 5G applications a challenging task.

3.1.5 5G Industrial Ecosystems Need to be Strengthened

In contrast to the rapidly evolving ICTs, some of the information equipment in vertical industries can no longer meet the requirements of digital transformation. Deploying 5G networks requires replacing the assets on the current networks, resulting in sunk costs. If the enterprises choose to continue using communications devices such as Ethernet, field buses, and Wi-Fi, driven by short-term benefits, the investment in and deployment of 5G in vertical industries will be postponed. What is also worth mentioning is that the industry enterprises have already achieved enormous returns, established solid supply chains and partnerships, and have come to depend more on the established collaborations. This is also a constraint to the cultivation of 5G industry ecosystems.

Efforts are still needed to work out the models for the players in the 5G industry to collaborate. Telecom operators are actively embracing the opportunities 5G has brought to business (ToB) markets, but are confronted with a tricky situation with uncertainties, where equipment manufacturers, Internet enterprises, solution providers, and industrial application makers compete and collaborate with each other. The industry landscape is quite complex, with players trying to seize strategic heights in their own ways. There are a multitude of industry platforms, which are independent of each other, rendering high costs from repeated development. The industry also lacks a mature end-to-end (E2E) solution, covering from the network to security, modules/terminals, platforms, and software and hardware. Such a solution is expected to integrate the information technology (IT), communication technology (CT), and operational technology (OT), efficiently connect supply and demand, promote the transformation of 5G technologies into achievements, and eventually lead to the establishment of a 5G industry ecosystem featuring deep convergence.

3.2 Phases of 5G Large-Scale Replication

3.2.1 Foundations

The commercial use of 4G in China happened 3–4 years later than in the first batch of countries. That was time when the industry had achieved certain level of maturity, with numerous consumer-oriented applications already deployed. China was able to learn from these examples and launch large-scale commercial use of 4G applications without having to spend much effort on the exploration. However, in the 5G era, China cannot bypass the exploration phase since 5G is mainly oriented towards industry scenarios, with 70% to 80% of applications involving vehicle-to-everything (V2X) and industrial Internet. China is one of the first countries in the world to use 5G commercially, without precedents, lessons, and experiences to learn from when it comes to technology, industry development, and application. This is particularly true for converged applications targeted at the industry and the real economy as a whole. Therefore, extra caution must be taken to grasp the features of 5G, follow the rules regarding network construction, mobile communications technology evolution, standards formulation, and market development, in order to realize large-scale application of 5G in industries.

1. 5G Infrastructure Construction Outpaces 5G Application

    As is common with the previous generations of communication technologies, the construction of 5G infrastructure outpaces its application. High-quality 5G infrastructure is the foundation for the innovation of 5G applications, and the key to the success of these applications. If we look back at 3G and 4G, even the killer applications received doubts at the early stages of their commercial use. Innovation in mobile communications applications requires a solid network and a vibrant market. Network coverage and user penetration generally take 2–3 years or even longer before reaching the satisfactory level. For example, killer apps such as microblogs in the 3G era and short video apps in the 4G era all appeared 2–3 years after network rollout. The success of such killer apps opened up the market space and in turn attracted more resources (capital, talent, R&D, etc.) to innovation. Therefore, the principle of "building roads before vehicles" must be upheld to accelerate the innovation of 5G applications as the 5G technologies continue to mature and the network construction expands.
2. 5G International Standards are Introduced in Phases

    High rate, low latency, and massive connectivity are the defining features of 5G. The International Telecommunication Union (ITU) has defined three usage scenarios that align with these defining features, respectively: eMBB, URLLC, and mMTC. In the eMBB scenario, 5G delivers an exceptional experience for mobile Internet users, supporting consumer-oriented applications, such as ultra-high-definition (UHD) video, virtual reality (VR), and augmented reality (AR), as well as traffic-intensive and high-rate industrial applications, such as machine-vision-based inspection and real-time production monitoring. In the URLLC

3.2 Phases of 5G Large-Scale Replication

scenario, 5G enables industrial applications that require higher on latency and reliability, such as industrial control, telemedicine, and autonomous driving. In the mMTC scenario, 5G is designed to power applications that focus on sensing and data collection, such as smart city, safe city, smart home, and environmental monitoring.

LTE Release 8, issued in 2009, was the first set of specifications on 4G. It established the main framework and technical solution for 4G. Subsequent releases such as Release 9 and Release 10 enhanced the 4G performance. As for 5G, 3GPP issued the first full set of 5G standards, Release 15, in June 2018, which defined a wide range of basic functions, with a focus on eMBB services. Since then, the 5G standards have continued to upgrade. Release 15 defined the 5G network architecture featuring unified air interfaces and flexible configurations. It focuses on eMBB applications and supports some low-latency and high-reliability scenarios, laying an important foundation for 5G applications. Release 15 specifications are able to cover more than half of the 5G application scenarios, basically all 5G to consumer (5GtoC) scenarios and most 5GtoB scenarios. Release 16, released in July 2020, upgraded the 5G experience from being "usable" to being "easy to use." With a focus on URLLC, Release 16 meets the requirements of V2X and industrial Internet applications. As an enhancement to Release 15, Release 16 supports TSN services in a full range of low-latency and high-reliability scenarios, which has given rise to applications requiring low latency and high reliability, such as industrial Internet. Release 16 also defines the specifications for positioning of meter-level precision. Release 17, which was finalized in June 2022, puts emphasis on mMTC and supports medium- and high-speed massive connections. By then, a full set of standards for 5G capabilities was completed.

3. Standardization is a Prerequisite for 5G Industrialization, and Industrialization is the Basis for 5G Converged Application

   The industrialization of 5G standards is implemented in phases. At present, the majority of commercial 5G products are compliant with Release 15 or 16. Certain Release 16-compliant functions are already mature and require ongoing enhancements for various application scenarios. Each set of 5G standards has a specific focus on network performance and functions. 5G technology and industry development is a progressive process. Phased standardization leads to phased industrialization, which in turn results in phased 5G converged application.

   Currently, the industry can consider prioritizing the improvement of the following two types of functions:

   (a) Functions that are related to 5G basic capability enhancement, including network slicing enhancement, network intelligence, multiple-input multiple-output (MIMO) enhancement, user equipment (UE) power saving enhancement, and interference suppression.
   (b) Functions that are urgently required in various vertical industry application scenarios. Examples are functions commonly used on 5G private networks,

such as large uplink bandwidth, 5G LAN, high-precision positioning, and URLLC.

4. Function Selection and Development Pace of Subsequent 5G Releases Depend on Market Conditions

    Based on experiences with the previous mobile communications standards, both technology roadmaps and market requirements can be critical factors into function selection of technical specifications. Generally, 3GPP issues a release every 1.5–2 years, and 1–1.5 years later, most network devices and chips are put into commercial use. But after Release 15 was issued, products were designed with selective functions from Releases 16 and 17 based on market and customer requirements, which may not follow the pace of standard release. Standard releases can be categorized into major releases (like Release 15) and minor releases (like Releases 16 and 17). Release 18 is expected to be a major release that opens the 5.5G era.

5. 5G Industry Application Development Needs to Keep Pace with Each Industry's Digital Transformation

    Currently, 5G industry applications in China are mostly deployed across the secondary and tertiary sectors (mainly the service industry), where the level of digitalization is relatively high. According to the McKinsey Global Institute (MGI) Industry Digitization Index, the tertiary sector (which includes media, entertainment, public utilities, and healthcare) has taken the lead in digitalization, and the secondary sector (which includes high-end manufacturing, oil and gas, and ore smelting) follows with only a narrow gap, while the primary sector is quite a distance away. This is reflected by the candidate projects submitted for the sixth "Zhanfang Cup" 5G Application Competition, a competition hosted by China's Ministry of Industry and Information Technology (MIIT), held in 2023. The proportion of projects related to inclusive and convenient social services was higher than that in 2022 since the application of 5G in healthcare, education, cultural tourism, and public security can better meet people's increasing life requirements. Apart from mature 5G applications such as smart city and industrial manufacturing, innovative applications in fields such as water conservation, ocean, food, medicine, textile, and rail transportation are also being developed. This has led to the emergence of candidate projects in more industries, with over 1000 projects in each of these fields, promoting innovation in 5G applications in these areas.

3.2.2 Phases and Key Factors

1. Industry Application Development Rules

    The development of 5G applications cannot be achieved overnight. Gradual introduction from technologies, standards, to industries is a must. 5G technical standards are not mature enough for commercial use at any one time. Instead,

3.2 Phases of 5G Large-Scale Replication

they are re-introduced and improved with each release. The functions and performance quality of each iteration of the 5G standards are limited. These iterations together form a phased 5G application development path. Research has been conducted on 5G applications in leading tertiary industries (including healthcare, entertainment, city management, education, transportation, and emergency security) and secondary industries (including steel, industrial manufacturing, metallurgy and mining, and electric power). Considering the development cycles of 5G and other new technologies, the level of digitalization, and the development of 5G applications in each industry, 5G industry application development is divided into four phases: the warm-up phase, the startup phase, the growth phase, and the scale development phase. Figure 3.1 provides a more detailed illustration of these phases.

Warm-up phase: During this phase, 5G standard formulation and R&D are in progress. Requirement analysis and scenario-specific technical discussions are held in industries. The key to this phase is to complete the commercialization of 5G technical standards as soon as possible and realize preliminary cooperation between the 5G industry and other industries in order to pave the way for future development. Take Release 15 as an example. After the release was issued, the 5G industry, driven by technologies, started to carry out preliminary cooperation with other industries and perform R&D of Release 15-compliant products.

Startup phase: In the second phase, industry leaders start in-depth cooperation with 5G. In particular, they jointly explore 5G application scenarios and product requirements, perform large-scale scenario adaptation, and launch small-scale pilot projects. The 5G converged application industry chain starts to take shape, and the upstream and downstream parts of the industry chain begin to cooperate with each other. The key to this phase is to establish industry

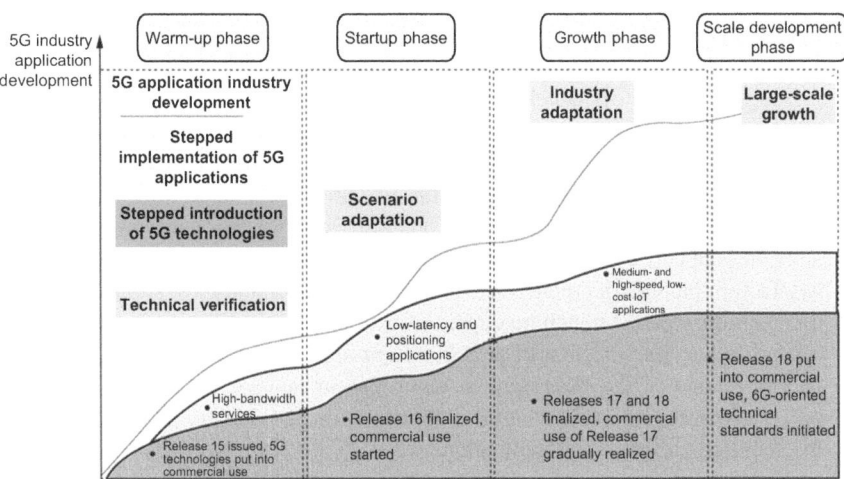

Fig. 3.1 5G industry application development phases. (Source: China Academy of Information and Communications Technology (CAICT))

cooperation platforms (such as competitions, alliances, and cross-industry associations) under government guidance. Small-scale 5G application pilot projects should also be promoted in various industries to discover the real industry requirements and eliminate requirement uncertainties.

Growth phase: Solutions and products for 5G industry application are launched in small batches and continuously optimized to adapt to various industries. Once they have fully adapted to the industries, customized industry requirements can be met, and the application business models gradually become clear enough for small-scale deployment. The key to this phase is to promote and accelerate in-depth cross-industry cooperation at the government level, eliminate industry barriers, and start publicity and promotion in various industries based on typical application showcases with industry influence.

Scale development phase: In this phase, obstacles to 5G convergence into various industries are gradually eliminated and the cost of applications is sharply reduced. Key products and mature solutions are launched in batches and replicated on a large scale. Their application scope is extended from leading enterprises to SMEs, significantly enabling key industries to reap the benefits. 5G has become a critical part in the digital transformation of leading industries in terms of enablement and profitability. The key to this phase is to give full play to the market, develop replicable and low-cost products and solutions based on the digital level of various industries and enterprises, and achieve fast and high-quality delivery to accelerate the popularization of 5G industry applications and extend the application scope.

2. Current Phase and Key Factor Analysis

   In general, China has made notable improvements in the breadth and depth of 5G application practices and technological innovations. However, the application standards, business models, and industry ecosystems are not mature enough. 5G applications are still being piloted mainly in top enterprises and have not been applied on a large scale. While some leading industries have entered the growth phase, some potential industries are still in the startup phase.

   Large-scale 5GtoB development is affected by many key factors (as illustrated in Fig. 3.2), which can be classified into demand-side factors, supply-side factors, and factors related to the development environment. From a demand-side perspective, the digital level of the industry, acceptance of new technologies, clarity of scenario requirements, visibility of application effectiveness, and activeness of core enterprises are all key factors. From a supply-side perspective, key factors include the relative advantages of 5G technologies, support level of the 5G industry, cost matching degree of applications, conditions in application-related industries, and maturity of common application solutions. In addition, factors related to the development environment involve the business models, policy environment, and promotion channels for 5G industry applications, and the standardization of 5G applications.

   Based on the analysis of these factors in key fields such as manufacturing, healthcare, energy, and cultural tourism, the color palette for large-scale

3.2 Phases of 5G Large-Scale Replication

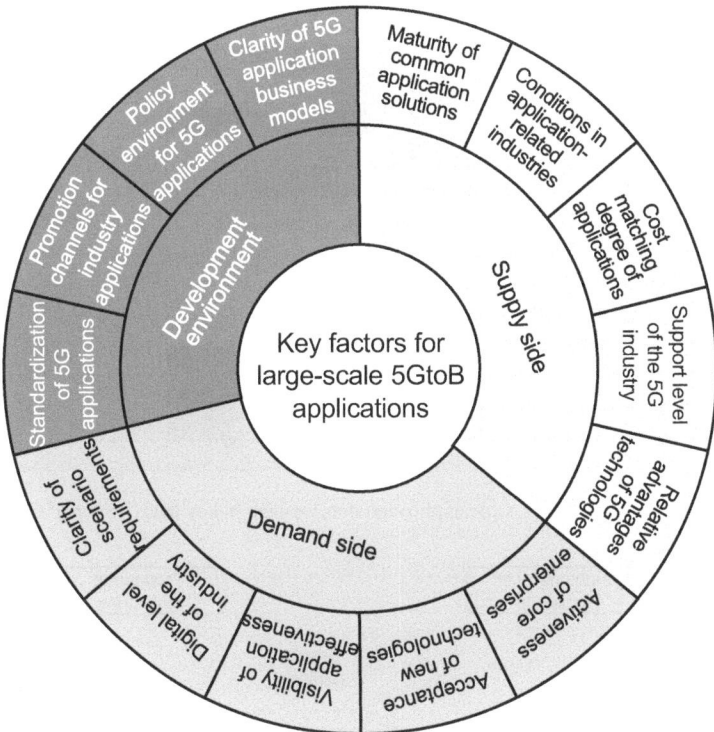

Fig. 3.2 Key factors for large-scale 5GtoB development. (Source: CAICT)

application development can be represented in Fig. 3.3. A deeper color represents a higher factor level.

Based on the digitalization level and 5G application maturity in various industries, the overall development of 5G applications in these industries, and the analysis of applications in key fields, industries can be categorized into four types: pioneering, having potential, to-be-explored, and to-be-cultivated. Figure 3.4 illustrates industries with different 5G application levels. Pioneering industries are highly digitalized and have clear requirements for 5G. 5G has made some achievements in the digital transformation of these industries, guiding the development of other industries through large-scale replication and promotion. Industries with potential have low digitalization levels, but industry enterprises are willing to invest in 5G applications. There is potential for the development of industry converged applications. Industries that ought to be explored have relatively high digitalization levels and a solid digital foundation. However, industry requirements for 5G are not clear and need to be explored further. Developing 5G converged applications in these industries is challenging. Industries which should be cultivated have low digitalization levels and the requirements for 5G in these industries are also unclear.

Key Factors for Large-Scale Development		Manufacturing	Energy	Healthcare	Cultural Tourism	Education	V2X	Agriculture
Demand side	Clarity of scenario requirements							
	Digital level of the industry							
	Visibility of application effectiveness							
	Acceptance of new technologies							
	Activeness of core enterprises							
Supply side	Relative advantages of 5G technologies							
	Support level of the 5G industry							
	Cost matching degree of applications							
	Conditions in application-related industries							
	Maturity of common application solutions							
Development environment	Clarity of 5G application business models							
	Policy environment for 5G applications							
	Promotion channels for industry applications							
	Standardization of 5G applications							

Fig. 3.3 Color palette for large-scale application development in key fields. (Source: CAICT)

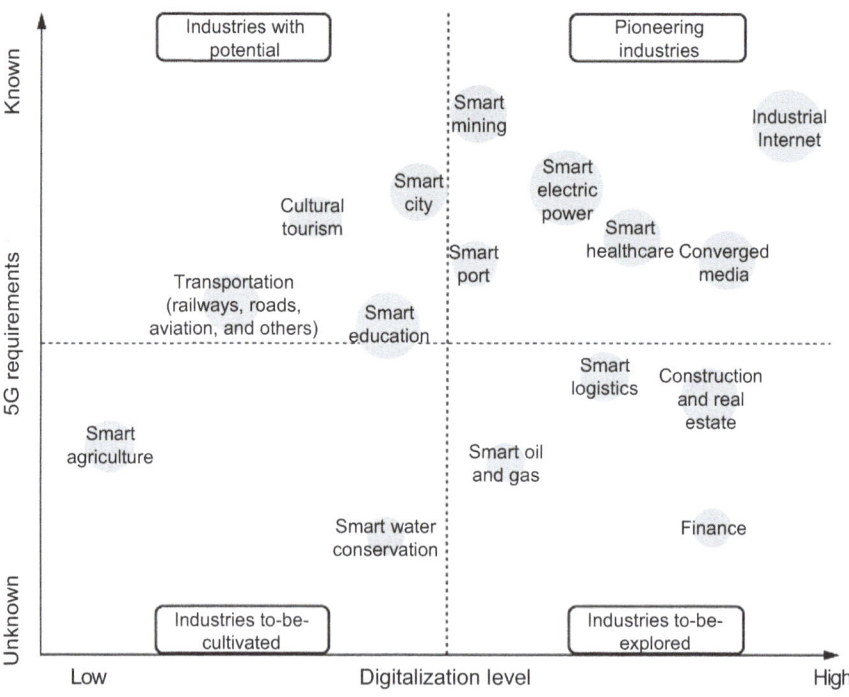

Fig. 3.4 A quadrant chart for 5G application development in key industries. (Source: CAICT)

According to the overall development rules of 5G applications, pioneering industries in China, such as industrial Internet, electric power, and healthcare, have entered the growth phase. 5G application products and solutions are continuously adapting to these industries and engaged in business exploration. In

3.2 Phases of 5G Large-Scale Replication

potential industries, such as cultural tourism and transportation, industry requirements and application scenarios are being identified for product and solution development and scenario adaptation. Most industries are currently in the startup phase. Industries to be cultivated and explored, such as education (partially to be cultivated), agriculture (partially in the warm-up phase), and water conservation, are gradually developing towards the startup phase through active technology verification. According to the phases of key industries in the large-scale development of 5G industry applications (illustrated in Fig. 3.5), it can be concluded that the convergence of 5G and industries is a gradual process which encompasses pilot demonstration, large-scale promotion, and finally large-scale application. It is important to understand the complexity and difficulty of this process.

3.2.3 Significance and Values

As the Chinese saying goes, the last leg of a journey marks the halfway point. Now is the time for 5G. 5G is not just a communication technology. It is the foundation of a new and thriving digital economy, and it enables the digital transformation of various industries. CAICT predicts that by 2025, 5G will drive network construction investment of about CNY1.2 trillion, information consumption of CNY8 trillion, and economic growth of CNY293 million.

The use of 5G in industries has a huge potential for development and a multiplier effect. Its large-scale replication not only promotes digital industrialization, but also greatly improves industry digitalization in China. Digital industrialization refers to the production and use of information, and it involves technology innovation in the production and supply of information products and services. It is associated with

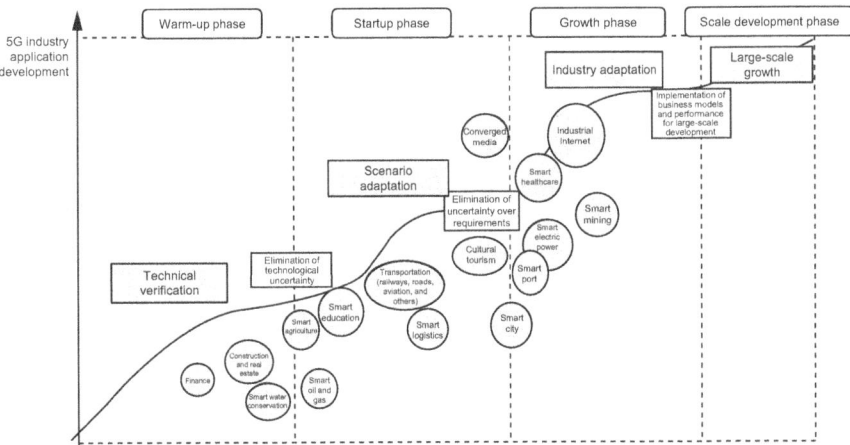

Fig. 3.5 Phases of key industries in the large-scale development of 5G industry applications. (Source: CAICT)

information industry departments and new models in information technology services. 5G industry applications empower industries, reshape industry development models, and create new value. With the evolution and industrialization of 5G standards, the technological spillover effect of 5G is expected to be far greater than that of previous generations of mobile communications technologies, leading to more application scenarios and business models. By connecting resources across the entire industry and value chain, data flows will drive information flows and promote the restructuring of capital, material, talent, and technology flows, which in turn will drive the transformation of business models and organizational forms, reshape industry development models, and inject vitality into digital industrialization. Industry digitalization is the application of information technologies in traditional industry departments, and it is reflected in the increased output, improved quality, and enhanced efficiency that soon follows. The increased output contributes significantly to the total digital economy. 5G applications differ from previous generations of mobile communications technologies in that they are distributed based on the 80–20 rule and will be used mainly in vertical industries. It is estimated that every one unit of investment in the 5G industry in China will generate six units of economic output. This significant spillover effect leads to more robust drivers and promotes reforms of quality and efficiency in industry development. Facing informatization requirements in all sectors of society, 5G is not only a new set of opportunities for the mobile communications industry, but also a new field waiting to be explored. Promoting the large-scale development of 5G industry applications will have a profound impact on all industries and ultimately build a new digital economy.

To achieve this ambitious goal, the key to 5G industry application development lies in innovation, transformation, and ecosystem construction. Further work is required to facilitate digital transformation in vertical industries through technological innovation, and this in turn will accelerate convergence through an open ecosystem.

3.3 Trends of 5G Large-Scale Replication and 5.5G

3.3.1 5G Applications are Revolutionizing Future Society and Daily Life

5G is a powerful driver of information and communication development. Projects presented at the fourth "Zhanfang Cup" held in 2021 (shown in Fig. 3.6) demonstrated that some key technologies, including positioning, big data, edge computing, cloud computing, virtual private network (network slicing), and AI, have usage rates exceeding 40%. Compared with the previous three competitions, technologies related to positioning, virtual private network (network slicing), uplink enhancement, and 5G LAN are gaining significantly more attention in many projects across

3.3 Trends of 5G Large-Scale Replication and 5.5G

	2018 (Usage/Ranking)	2019	2020	2021
Positioning	N/A	N/A	N/A	58%/1 ↑
Big data	18%/3	44%/2 ↑	52%/2 =	52%/2 =
Edge computing	20%/1	33%/4 ↓	43%/3 ↑	52%/2 ↑
Cloud computing	20%/1	38%/3 ↓	40%/4 ↓	51%/4 =
Virtual private network (network slicing)	N/A	N/A	19%/5 ↑	47%/5 =
AI	13%/4	55%/1 ↑	55%/1 =	46%/6 ↓
Uplink enhancement	N/A	N/A	N/A	38%/7
5G LAN	N/A	N/A	N/A	12%/8

Fig. 3.6 Key technologies related to candidate projects in the fourth "Zhanfang Cup". (Source: CAICT)

different industries. Continuous improvement in key technical capabilities has led to more comprehensive 5G solutions and brought smoother convergence of 5G into industries. Combining 5G with technologies and industries such as AI, IoT, big data, cloud computing, and HD video will promote breakthroughs in the development of products like autonomous driving, smart robots, and VR/AR, while also accelerating innovation in application scenarios such as smart factory, smart city, smart transportation, and smart healthcare. However, none of these technologies or industries are yet mature enough, and the corresponding industry applications are still developing and evolving.

5G collaborates with other next-generation information technologies for mutual promotion, paving the way for the future development of industry applications. Connectivity technologies, represented by 5G, are combining with cloud, intelligence, and computing to boost the development of industry applications and the creation of more diverse applications and services. With the maturity and integration of 5G and other next-generation information technologies, coordinated development is a must for both technologies and industries. 5G + XtoB is the future and systematic innovation must be realized to enable digital transformation in various industries.

Currently, the formulation and implementation of 5G industry application standards are accelerating in China. Industry standardization organizations and alliances, led by the China Communications Standards Association (CCSA) and Alliance of Industrial Internet (AII), are working together to develop these standards, while leading enterprises such as the State Grid Corporation of China (SGCC), China Petroleum and Chemical Corporation (Sinopec), and China Southern Power Grid (CSG) are promoting the implementation of these standards. For instance, CAICT is actively promoting the development of 5G standards in healthcare under the guidance of the MIIT and the National Health Commission of China. Together, they have formulated three national standards, including one that defines communication specifications for medical imaging equipment. Industry leaders, such as Sinopec and SGCC, are pioneering the implementation of 5G application standards in the petrochemical and electric power fields, following instructions from standardization organizations and alliances such as CCSA and 5G AIA. This constant promotion of standardization will enable 5G to better support social and economic development.

Connectivity technologies, particularly 5G, have become a key factor in bringing about industry transformation and upgrade in the future. The main goal of connectivity technologies is to provide intelligent connectivity that boasts ubiquitous gigabit, a deterministic experience, and hyper automation. In the future 5G + XtoB form, X can represent one of the next-generation information technologies such as cloud, computing/storage, or intelligence. Cloud and computing/storage will serve as the foundation of the digital world, as they provide powerful computing support. AI, as a new engine, will provide true intelligence for enterprises. AI algorithms and models, once integrated with intelligence requirements, will help enterprises reduce costs and improve quality and efficiency. These technologies are also intended to work together. Specifically, connectivity and computing will coordinate with each other through intelligence; intelligent connectivity will transmit data for computing; and computing will provide support for intelligent connectivity. The convergence of 5G with key technologies such as cloud, intelligence, and big data, provides connection assurance for industry applications and makes connections among people, among things, and among people and things easier and faster. This convergence also expands the reach of ICTs from the consumption field to the production field and from the virtual economy to the real economy, ushers in a new Internet of Everything (IoE) era, and creates a new digital economy.

3.3.2 5.5G Empowers a New Future for Communications

The integration of 5G with the economy and society is growing increasingly closer due to its commercial use and the exploration of converged applications. At the same time, various applications place higher requirements on communications networks. This is why 5.5G is needed. 5.5G was officially named 5G-Advanced (5G-A) (hereinafter referred to as 5.5G) by 3GPP in April 2021 and is planned to be specified by 3GPP Releases 18, 19, and 20. The next 3–5 years will be critical for 5.5G development in terms of service scenarios, network technologies, industry progress, and deployment rate. 5.5G is expected to define new goals and capabilities for 5G development, provide better services to users, and promote the generation of greater social and economic value through 5G. Additionally, 5.5G will act as a bridge between 5G and 6G. During the evolution from 5G to 5.5G and then 6G, as illustrated in Fig. 3.7, 5G network capabilities will continuously develop while 6G-oriented technologies are explored and prepared.

5.5G evolution is already an industry consensus, and during this evolution it is expected that support capabilities for broadband services and network operation efficiency will be improved and new use cases and network intelligence will be developed. Network design must be based on the evolution direction, and support capabilities for emerging services must meet application requirements. Both

3.3 Trends of 5G Large-Scale Replication and 5.5G

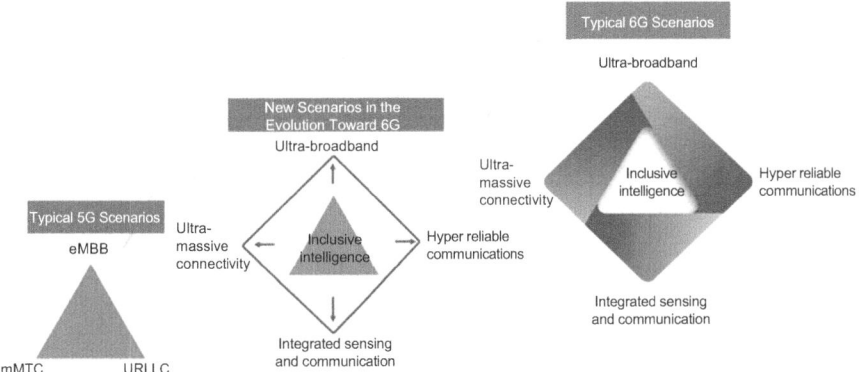

Fig. 3.7 Evolution from 5G to 5.5G and then 6G

network and terminal evolution must also be considered. To effectively meet these requirements, 5.5G evolution will cover the following three areas:

1. Improvements in broadband capabilities and efficiency to satisfy industry development and network application requirements. While 5G technologies greatly enhance key capability indicators such as data transmission rate, latency, and reliability, 5G traffic keeps surging due to the wide development of applications and increase in user penetration. Requirements for the performance of high-rate, low-latency applications, such as AR, VR, and telemedicine, are becoming increasingly strict. To allow a large number of 5G users to enjoy such applications simultaneously, network capacity needs to be improved. Therefore, 5.5G technologies must aim to improve network coverage, enhance aspects of network performance such as uplink spectral efficiency, multiplexing capability, power consumption efficiency, and service latency, and meet the requirements of services with higher data rates, such as HD video calling and extended reality (XR) gaming.

   There are several methods available for enhancing broadband capabilities. First, spectral efficiency can be increased through application research into technologies related to multi-antenna enhancement and large uplink bandwidth. Second, service capabilities can be improved to support more broadband services, such as millimeter wave (mmWave) services, and improve terminal capabilities. Potential key technologies include enhancements in XR, computer graphics (CG), out-of-episode outlier exposure, and UE power saving. Third, the flexibility and efficiency of system deployment can be improved through enhancements in network energy saving, mobility, and coverage performance. Finally, non-terrestrial communication can be enhanced through the development of functions for non-terrestrial networks (NTNs) in transparent mode, research and standardization based on signal regeneration, and research into air-ground integrated networks.

Typical Application	Expected Connection	Connection Rate	Capability	Technical Requirement
XR and machine vision	1x	≥ X00 Mbit/s	V2X, sensing, low latency/high reliability, large uplink bandwidth, and high-accuracy positioning	NR eMBB
Video surveillance, wearables, and industrial sensors	2x	≤ X00 Mbit/s	Large uplink bandwidth, network time serving, high-accuracy positioning, low latency/high reliability, and intercommunication with LAN/TSN	RedCap
Sharing economy, smart finance, and smart home	4x	≤ X0 Mbit/s	Low power consumption, high-accuracy positioning, and low cost	eMTC
Location tracking, smart city, and instrument connection	8x	≤ X00 kbit/s	Small data packets, low power consumption, and extremely low cost	NB-IoT

Fig. 3.8 Typical applications and their deployment requirements

2. Refined design for vertical industries. Vertical industries place high requirements on 5G network capabilities, such as large uplink bandwidth, low latency, and high indoor capacity. To better support vertical industries with 5G, the complexity of lightweight UEs must be further reduced. 5G applications should be extended to markets that require lower costs, less energy consumption, and slower data rates. In addition, diverse IoT terminals with improved positioning accuracy and relay need to be supported, including those for new IoT, low-power-consumption positioning, and industrial scenarios. Figure 3.8 shows typical applications and their deployment requirements.
3. Evolution of innovative technologies and applications. 6G is expected to go live around 2035. This technology will be widely used in inclusive intelligence, integrated sensing and communication, and other scenarios, as shown in Fig. 3.9, ultimately helping society realize the incredible vision of "intelligent connection of everything and digital twins." The exploration of new technical fields comes with the accumulation of technical knowledge that will be applicable to 6G, including AI and 5G integration, duplex evolution, XR enhancement, intelligent relay, network energy saving, and low-power UE wake-up signals and receivers. As AI and 5G integration deepens, 5.5G is expected to focus more on 5G-related big data, computing power, and AI algorithms, and enhance 5G network performance through the introduction of new methods and tools. During this integration and enhancement, data, algorithms, and simulation methods will be studied further, thus laying the foundation for 6G research [2].

The evolution from 5G to 5.5G will also be key to meeting the complex and comprehensive user requirements brought about by diversified 5G services. For example, in the face of various terminals, numerous network elements, and increasing network complexity, a wireless network that is flexible, adaptive, and intelligent is essential. The integration of powerful AI technologies can enhance the efficiency and intelligence of 5G, meaning networks can intelligently support applications and provide more high-quality and diverse services.

Fig. 3.9 Typical 6G application scenarios

Researches into 5.5G technical specifications and standards can be divided into two stages: improving the performance of existing characteristics and exploring new technical fields. Improving the performance of existing characteristics aims to achieve high-quality system performance, which is necessary for upgrading industry applications and addressing the common issues of system applications. Exploring new technical fields will focus on optimizing the structure of industries and shaping the long-term development landscape.

In summary, 5.5G aims to deliver ubiquitous 10 Gbps experience, support hundreds of billions of smart connections, and enable ultra-energy-efficient green businesses. This makes 5.5G essential not only in terms of national strategies and industry upgrades over the next five years but also as a transformative catalyst for 6G.

References

1. GONG D, WANG X M, CAO L. Global 5G commercial development and trend prospect [J] (in Chinese). Information and Communications Technology and Policy, 2020(12): 7–10.
2. LIANG B J. Thoughts on 5G-A/6G simultaneous development [J] (in Chinese). Information and Communications Technologies, 2023, 17(6): 4–10.

Part II
A New Phase in AI Development

Chapter 4
Introduction to AI

4.1 Definition of AI

In 1956, artificial intelligence (AI) was first proposed by a group of young scientists led by John McCarthy, Marvin Minsky, and Nathaniel Rochester after discussion on issues related to machine-simulated intelligence. It was the first time that AI had been described as something that "can in principle be so precisely described that a machine can be made to simulate it." This marked the birth of AI as a field of research.

However, there is no universally accepted definition of AI, which is a cutting-edge interdisciplinary field. In 2018, China Electronics Standardization Institute (CESI) published a white paper on AI standardization and defined AI as theories, methods, technologies, and application systems that use a digital computer or computer-controlled machine to simulate, extend, or enhance human intelligence, perceive the environment, and acquire knowledge to find the best results [1]. According to the European Commission's *White Paper on Artificial Intelligence* released in 2020, "AI is a collection of technologies that combine data, algorithms and computing power." In 2021, the Commission issued a proposal for AI regulations, called the AI Act. This proposal considers a technology AI if it involves an AI system and a certain level of standardization. Standardization means that specific inputs (such as data) can be interpreted using preset or other instructions, but this interpretation is limited to developers and is aligned mainly with their goals.

Generally speaking, AI uses a machine to simulate human thinking and awareness and implements important functions such as cognition, recognition, analysis, and decision-making. Due to its simulation of human intelligence, AI is also a topic in behavioral science involving computer simulation of human intelligence.

AI is usually classified into weak AI, strong AI, and super AI based on its development stage and the technologies involved. Weak AI often uses deep learning for basic information collection and processing and cannot generate results without human intervention. It is a separate auxiliary tool designed to serve humans' specific purposes. Strong AI is a theoretical form of AI that possesses general intelligence on par with humans, giving it a high level of autonomy. That means, though designed and created by humans, it can adapt to environmental changes and make its own decisions. Super AI is a hypothetical type of AI that is self-aware and exceeds human intelligence. Nowadays, weak AI technologies are well-developed, and regular AI products fall into this category. These products are used for applications such as facial recognition, speech recognition, speech translation, smart cars, smart homes, and smart writing. Chat Generative Pre-trained Transformer (ChatGPT) is somehow thought of as strong AI because it can conduct a natural and smooth conversation very much like a human does. But actually it is not. ChatGPT cannot perceive the context of the questions you ask, nor can it understand your intent. However, the emergence of ChatGPT is widely considered a milestone in general AI development towards strong AI.

It is clear that AI is a future-oriented strategic technology that will continue to be a powerful engine for a new round of scientific and technological revolution and industrial transformation. In recent years, AI-related technologies have been evolving with modern information technologies, accelerating AI industrialization and commercialization. This not only makes industries more intelligent, but also provides a propellant for a high-quality development of a country's economy. That's why many countries are committed to exploring possible ways of integrating AI into industry development.

4.2 History and Development of AI

AI was not discovered overnight but developed gradually like an upward spiral with progressive achievements through decades of improvements. Over the years, AI development has been driven by different technologies, which can be used to divide the history of AI into four phases, as shown in Fig. 4.1. Namely, computational reasoning-, knowledge-, data-, and computing power-driven AI.

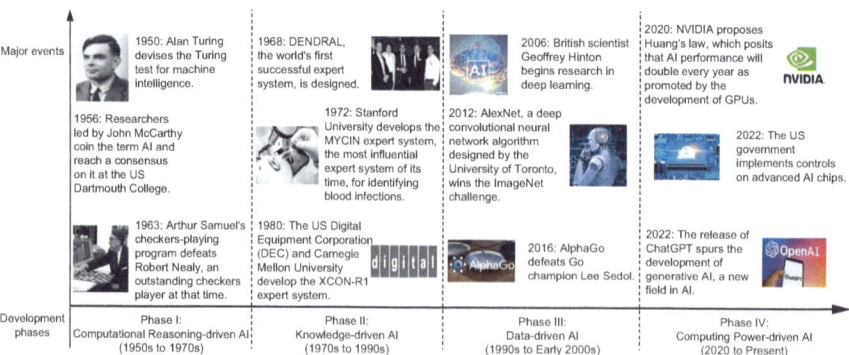

Fig. 4.1 Four development phases and major events of AI

4.2.1 Phase I: Computational Reasoning-Driven AI (1950s to 1970s)

AI-related research dates back to 1950, the year when the famous mathematician and logicist Alan Turing proposed and tried to answer the question "Can machines think?" in his paper *Computing Machinery and Intelligence*. According to Turing, the best strategy for a machine in an imitation game is not to imitate "the behaviour of a man" but "try to provide answers that would naturally be given by a man [2]." This laid the foundation for the renowned Turing test. Then in 1956, the Dartmouth Summer Research Project on Artificial Intelligence took place in the USA, in which researchers have reached a consensus on the concept of AI. That's why 1956 is regarded as the beginning of AI. One of the mainstream research topics in this phase was "Reasoning is no more than search."

Researchers tried to compile laws of human thinking and use computers for simulation. For example, for the checkers-playing program developed by Arthur Samuel, a computer would search for the best move for winning the game from all possible moves generated by calculation. In 1963, this program won a match against Robert Nealey, an outstanding American checkers player at that time. This phase can be regarded as the first prime period of AI growth. However, due to factors such as insufficient computing capability, high computing complexity, and difficulties in implementing logical reasoning, engineers tended to fail in their attempts to develop some practical products. As a result, the development of AI stalled.

4.2.2 Phase II: Knowledge-Driven AI (1970s to Early 1990s)

As AI technologies continued to develop, researchers found that computational reasoning was not enough to achieve industry intelligentization. The 1970s saw the emergence of knowledge-driven AI, led by expert systems. The focus of AI development in this phase shifted from theoretical research to practical application, and researchers sought breakthroughs in fields that required specialized knowledge. One of the most notable developments was DENDRAL, the world's first successful expert system developed in 1968. Its automated process could help chemists identify the molecular structure of substances based on readings from chemical instruments. The continual improvement and commercialization of DENDRAL made people realize that a knowledge-based computer system can be as useful as a human expert in a specialized field. This meant that AI had begun representing knowledge.

However, these expert systems had drawbacks. While an expert system focuses on a specialized field, the knowledge it requires often comes from manual summary and inputs. The number of reasoning decisions a system can make is directly proportional to the number of knowledge inputs it receives. Expert systems were built by compiling and imparting human knowledge to a computer. As you can imagine, specialized expert systems cannot be used in fields outside their field of application.

In the late 1980s, knowledge-driven AI entered a winter of development. The situation did not improve until breakthroughs were made in neural network technology.

4.2.3 Phase III: Data-Driven AI (1990s to Early 2000s)

As technologies such as the Internet, cloud computing, and big data matured, neural networks became a key technology for AI. AI has since ushered in a phase of rapid development. A neural network can be used for machine learning (i.e., letting a machine learn by itself using data from the neural network, without relying on manual inputs). This was a lesson learned from the failures in developing computational reasoning- and knowledge-driven AI. In 2006, British scientist Geoffrey Hinton and his students published a paper titled *Reducing the Dimensionality of Data with Neural Networks*. The paper unleashed a wave of research in deep learning [3]. With neural networks composed of multiple complex processing unit layers, deep learning algorithms achieve significant performance while learning from larger datasets to provide complex outputs such as speech and image recognition results. In 2012, AlexNet, a deep convolutional neural network algorithm designed by the University of Toronto, won the ImageNet challenge. This marked the beginning of the deep learning revolution in the industry. In 2014, DeepFace and DeepID emerged. The facial recognition accuracy of DeepID reached 99.15% on the Labeled Faces in the Wild (LFW) dataset, almost surpassing that of humans. In March 2016, AlphaGo defeated Go champion Lee Sedol, another milestone in the AI industry.

4.2.4 Phase IV: Computing Power-Driven AI (2020 to Present)

A debate over whether Moore's law was still valid in 2020 and beyond arose with the continued development of AI. Against this backdrop, NVIDIA, a core service provider of AI computing power, came up with Huang's law on computing power. It was observed that the AI processing capability of NVIDIA's graphics processing units (GPUs) has increased by 1000 times in the decade starting from the late 2000s, with AI performance doubling each year as promoted by the development of GPUs. On this basis, a new Moore's law was proposed by Sam Altman, CEO of OpenAI (a leading company of AI 2.0). Altman stated that the number of global AI computations would double every 18 months. As the iteration of models speeds up significantly, the cost will be greatly reduced.

As early as the 1980s, the academia designed competent algorithm models for AI chips to meet "brute-force computing" needs of applications. However, such models were unable to realize their intrinsic value at that time, nor could they in recent years. This was mainly due to insufficient hardware capabilities for providing enough computing power for the training or reasoning process of deep neural networks. Led by the new Moore's law, computing power has become a key driving force for AI development. To maintain the US leading position in computing power, the Bureau of Industry and Security (BIS) of the US Department of Commerce implemented new export controls against the People's Republic of China (PRC) in October 2022. These new rules restricted the export of US-origin advanced computing chips and semiconductor manufacturing items.

The main conclusion that can be drawn from these developments is that computing power is the core element of productivity and value creation in the current phase of AI development. High-performance computing has nourished AI development. The emergence of large AI models represented by ChatGPT opened a new chapter for artificial intelligence-generated content (AIGC), or generative AI. AI is no longer something designed only for a small number of experts. With the implementation of AI models such as ChatGPT-4 and Midjourney V5, open-source application programming interfaces (APIs), and AI tools from top Internet companies are seeing widespread use. The evolving GPT-5 and GPT-6 demonstrate that large models are getting better and better at reasoning, logic, creation, and interaction for more complex and versatile tasks. The outlook for these models is promising. With the Transformer architecture, generative AI is able to create new data similar to that used for training, mimicking the human creation process. In this way, humans are no longer merely enablers of AI, but AI has become a potential collaborator with us. Generative AI, with its revolutionary potential in AI development has drawn unprecedented attention and sparked creativity worldwide.

4.3 Applicable Scenarios of AI

Recent years have witnessed the next-generation scientific and technological revolution and industrial transformation, from the development of big data and innovative theoretical algorithms to the improvements being made in computing capability and the evolution of network infrastructure. These changes have brought us into a new phase of AI development where AI is being integrated both into everyday life through our clothing, food, housing, and transportation as well as into various economic and social sectors including healthcare and education. AI will reshape all sorts of economic activities from production and distribution to exchange and consumption, and promote technological advancement, industry upgrade, economic transformation, and social progress.

AI applications already span all stages of industrial production, like robotic welding, intelligent assembly, intelligent inspection, and warehousing and logistics. These are backed up by the advantages in efficiency, stability, reliability, and repeatability that AI can unlock, as well as the AI's ability to reduce human involvement in labor-intensive and dangerous tasks. For example, technologies developed by SenseTime, a leading AI software company, shorten the iteration period in detection tasks of dry coating cracks for lithium batteries and welding defects for power batteries by 90%. SenseTime also enables accurate identification of defects with a false detection rate of less than 0.5%. Another example is AI-powered fan inspection, which improves the inspection efficiency by up to ten times and eliminates the need for electric power technicians to operate in dangerous places in the field. Since human workers have always had clear physiological limits that hinder production, AI-powered robots have created new opportunities and can be regarded as a landmark milestone in the history of industrial development. These robots are able to complete many tasks that would otherwise require manual work but may have adverse effects on human bodies.

AI is also playing an important role in the financial sector. For example, mobile payment, mobile banking, peer-to-peer (P2P) platforms, and e-commerce platforms are involved in an increasingly large percent of daily transactions. The efficiency and quality of financial services significantly improve, thanks to information technologies such as big data, cloud computing, computer network applications, and blockchain. Big data-based credit investigation, supply and demand analysis, and supply chain financing are just a few areas that have benefited from AI, thanks to its ability to leverage massive amounts of accurate information, more personalized and targeted risk locating models, more scientific and rigorous investment decision-making processes, fairer and more transparent credit intermediary roles, and so on.

In governance, AI's powerful information processing capability has also transformed the quality and efficiency of government services. AI enables more efficient archive collection, sorting, and transfer processes, provides more accurate information for decision-making, and facilitates more reasonable macroeconomic regulation and control. This allows governments to provide more diverse services to the public, satisfying their demands in an efficient way. For example, the facilities for providing government services in China are equipped with a number of applications that assist in government service support, including intelligent consultation and guidance, automatic monitoring, self-service information query, and data collection and processing. This helps alleviate the pressure placed on manpower in dealing with numerous service requests.

In the field of healthcare, AI software has become an essential part of healthcare devices, and multimodal data has promoted the development of AI-powered healthcare applications. These applications so far have primarily been in medical imaging, drug discovery, disease prediction, and health management. Following the release of GPT-4, some healthcare enterprises are working on optimizing healthcare service applications with GPT models, or seeking opportunities to collaborate with AI companies for empowering AI-based healthcare services. AI applications are also now being used in more complex healthcare scenarios such as preliminary analysis and evaluation of health status that can be performed before one sees a doctor. Other examples include assistance in patient information processing for improving service quality and precise guidance for patients in hospitals. It also reduces the amount of medical resources needed to serve each patient and makes healthcare services more easily accessible. For example, AstraZeneca, a pharmaceutical and biotechnology company, has developed a new deep learning algorithm for whole-sample slide scanning using digital pathology. It can accurately identify many cancers including those with low- or even negative-expressed indicators that cannot be identified by the human eyes. This helps ensure timely treatment and targeted therapy.

In the field of education, AI technologies are used for application analysis through principal component analysis (PCA), local binary pattern (LBP), and other algorithms including metric learning. By doing so, technologies such as speech recognition and big data are now put into use for education. AI has become a key means for both teachers and students to improve their experiences. It can be used to accurately evaluate the quality of class delivery and provide unique suggestions for teaching and learning. AI can also tailor study strategies for students and make one-on-one teaching easier. More personalized machine-based teaching allows for more appropriate teaching methods and strategies for each individual and helps students better identify their own areas of improvement for knowledge acquisition from classes.

AI has also achieved great success in the consumer field, such as gaming, entertainment, e-commerce, and social networking. In particular, large AI models represented by ChatGPT have set off a wave of AIGC-based commercial applications. For example, ChatGPT can be used to upgrade and reconstruct information query tools (like search engines), develop text generation tools to assist humans for improving office efficiency, and provide expert-level consulting and coaching services for humans. New applications such as digital humans and virtual assistants are also expected to soon arrive, providing an even wider range of personalized services for people's everyday life in education, healthcare, nursing, and many other areas.

Finally, the integration of AI into scientific research has transformed the conventional deductive reasoning approach. Since AI is capable of analyzing massive amounts of data, researchers can use it to identify associated information based on high-dimensional data, which facilitates research. Take AlphaFold2, a DeepMind-developed AI system for predicting a protein's 3D structure, as an example. It has a prediction accuracy comparable to experimental techniques such as cryo-electron microscopy, which helped it rank first in Critical Assessment of protein Structure Prediction (CASP) in 2020. Now, AI-integrated research is being applied to many more fields, including mechanics, chemistry, materials, biology, and even engineering. AI is expected to find its place in more versatile and complex applications.

4.4 National AI Strategies

AI has a huge impact on the economic growth of a country and is therefore crucial for national development. To improve their scientific and technological competitiveness, countries around the world have been trying to seize new opportunities that have emerged alongside the development of AI. One of such attempts is to formulate AI-related national development strategies and plans.

4.4.1 US: Maintaining Its Globally Leading Position by Taking Collective Measures

To maintain its globally leading position in technology, the USA has formulated an all-round framework for AI-related strategic planning and organizational construction. In the second half of 2016, the US government released three globally influential reports related to AI development: *Preparing for the Future of Artificial Intelligence*, *The National Artificial Intelligence Research and Development Strategic Plan*, and *Artificial Intelligence, Automation, and the Economy*. These reports provided suggestions on AI development for the federal government and associated organizations, discussed AI R&D issues, and analyzed AI's impacts on the economy [4–6].

In May 2018, the White House hosted the Summit on Artificial Intelligence, during which it proposed methods to maintain the US lead in the age of AI through joint efforts from the government, industry, and academia. The Select Committee on Artificial Intelligence was founded at the summit. Its function is to prioritize AI R&D issues, oversee-related investments, and promote AI R&D and its application through public-private and other forms of multi-party collaboration. The *National Cyber Strategy* and *National Strategy for U.S. Leadership in Advanced Manufacturing* released in the second half of 2018 also confirmed the priority position of AI-related issues. The US National Science Foundation (NSF) has also invested in AI research in a number of newly announced scientific research projects.

In February 2019, the Trump Administration launched the *American Artificial Intelligence Initiative* via executive order to stimulate investment and development in AI. The Initiative focused on raising AI R&D investment, unleashing data and computing resources of the federal government, and setting technical standards on AI governance. In June 2019, the White House released the *National AI R&D Strategic Plan: 2019 Update*, in which it set priorities for federal investment in AI R&D. The updates also called for the government to collaborate with academia, industry, international allies, and other non-federal entities, as part of an eighth strategy in addition to the existing strategies in order to promote long-term R&D investment and accelerate AI development.

In March 2020, the US Senate and House of Representatives voted to approve the *National Artificial Intelligence Initiative Act of 2020*, which includes a number of federal AI policies, including the American AI Initiative, and outlines relevant measures to be taken. In May 2020, the *Endless Frontier Act* proposed the investment of USD100 billion in the R&D of ten key technologies, including chips and AI, over the next 5 years. In August 2020, the US Office of Science and Technology Policy (OSTP), NSF, and Department of Energy (DOE) announced that they would provide more than USD1 billion to new research institutes focusing on AI and quantum computing.

In February 2022, the US House of Representatives reviewed and approved the *America Creating Opportunities for Manufacturing Pre-Eminence in Technology and Economic Strength Act of 2022* (also known as the *America COMPETES Act of*

2022). The Act authorizes the government to allocate more than USD250 billion in subsidies to essential fields of the USA and aims to help boost the national chip industry through reinvestment, improve competitiveness in semiconductors, and help the USA become less dependent on the supply chain of other countries. The ultimate goal of the Act is to help the USA maintain its leading position in technology. In recent years, the US federal government, together with its affiliated institutions, has also implemented multiple organizational reforms with the goal of removing institutional barriers to AI development and promoting collaboration in AI development both within and between institutions.

4.4.2 China: Promoting Sustainable Industrial Development Through Diversified Policies

In light of the new technological revolution and industrial transformation, the Central Committee of Communist Party of China (CPC) and the State Council of China have made a major strategic decision to develop AI to help accelerate the process of China becoming an innovative and powerful country on the world stage in the fields of science and technology. In July 2015, the State Council of China released the *Guiding Opinions of the State Council on Vigorously Advancing the "Internet Plus" Action*, which was the first time that AI development was included as part of China's major tasks.

The *Next-Generation Artificial Intelligence Development Plan* released by the State Council of China in 2017 clarified the basic principles, strategic objectives, and main tasks and marked the beginning of AI development in China. This plan set an ambitious three-milestone timeline for developing AI technologies and applications: (1) to reach the world's cutting-edge by 2020; (2) to achieve a world-leading level by 2025; (3) to become a major global center for AI innovation by 2030 [7]. In October 2017, the 19th CPC National Congress report mentioned the need for deep integration of the Internet, big data, AI, and the real economy.

In March 2019, AI appeared for the third time in a row in the annual report on the work of the Chinese government. In August 2019, the Chinese Ministry of Science and Technology issued the work guidelines for constructing national open and innovative platforms as well as pilot zones for the innovation and development of next-generation AI. By doing so, AI development can be led by the established pilot zones and pioneer enterprise platforms equipped with cutting-edge AI technologies, which adapts to the application scenarios and arising demands in the Chinese market.

In 2021, the *Outline for the 14th Five-Year Plan for Economic and Social Development and Long-Range Objectives Through the Year 2035* proposed to boost emerging industries, such as next-generation AI, in order to help tackle challenges at the frontier of scientific and technological revolution. In August 2022, the *Guiding Opinions on Accelerating Scenario Innovation and Promoting High-quality Economic Development with High-level Application of Artificial Intelligence* was released. Leveraging its massive amounts of data and unified national market, China has been actively exploring and extending the application scenarios of AI by designing scenario-specific systems, unleashing the potential of scenario-specific applications, and improving the scenario innovation ecosystem. With these initiatives, AI can make a big difference in promoting the high-quality development of the real economy.

4.4.3 Japan: Building "Society 5.0" with AI

In the 2015 revision of the *Japan Revitalization Strategy*, the Japanese government proposed a strategic plan for Internet of Things (IoT), big data, and AI technologies. The 2016 revision of the *Japan Revitalization Strategy* proposed technological innovations to help usher in the fourth industrial revolution, or "Industry 4.0," and stipulated the pivotal role AI technologies will play in helping Japan increase its Gross Domestic Product (GDP) from JPY500 trillion to JPY600 trillion. In Japan's fifth *Science and Technology Basic Plan* released in October 2016, AI is identified as one of the key technologies requiring efforts to be made in. The plan also promoted strategic AI R&D through collaboration between relevant government departments during the period from 2016 to 2020. The biggest highlight of the plan was the concept of "Society 5.0," which appeared for the first time. The concept assumes that in a super-smart society, people will live alongside robots and AI, which will help improve people's quality of life. AI technologies are undoubtedly crucial for implementing "Society 5.0."

In 2017, Japan formulated the *AI Technology Strategy* and an industrialization roadmap in which it provided guidelines for AI development. According to Japan's *AI Strategy 2019* released in June 2019, a number of strategic objectives were set to develop human resources, improve industrial competitiveness, establish technological infrastructure, and promote internationalization. With the importance of improving AI R&D systems highlighted in this document, the Japanese government would focus on funding universities and top R&D institutions so that they can lead Japan's AI R&D efforts.

The *AI Strategy 2021* released in June 2021 continued to prioritize fields such as healthcare, agriculture, and infrastructure for AI application, and targeted measures were taken to improve the transparency of technology application. This strategy focuses on developing key AI R&D projects from four dimensions: basic theories and technologies, devices and design, reliable and high-quality development, and system elements. This cannot be achieved without great efforts in both basic and integrated R&D. In April 2022, Japan released the *AI Strategy 2022*, in which it set five strategic goals relating to talent development, industrial competitiveness, technological systems, international cooperation, and dealing with imminent crises. In August 2023, Japan's Ministry of Education, Culture, Sports, Science and Technology announced that it would start to provide economic support for top young researchers engaged in developing technologies such as AI from 2024. It also stated its plan to develop AIGC-based foundation models for relevant research from 2024.

4.4 National AI Strategies

4.4.4 South Korea: Strengthening Its AI Power Through Policies

In 2019, the government of South Korea released the *National Strategy for AI* to promote the development of the AI industry. With the goal of helping South Korea transform from a world leader in IT to a world leader in AI, this strategy outlined South Korea's plan to strengthen its AI power and ultimately become a global forerunner in AI by 2030. According to projections, economic benefits worth KRW455 trillion were expected to be generated in the AI field by 2030 if recommended measures were taken. This strategy also proposed the construction of a world-leading AI ecosystem, the development of advanced AI applications, and the implementations of people-centered AI technologies. In terms of the construction of an AI ecosystem and AI R&D, the South Korean government strived to fully open public data by 2021, complete construction of the AI complex in Gwangju by 2024, and invest around KRW1 trillion in the R&D of next-generation AI chips that integrate storage and computing capabilities by 2029.

In October 2020, the South Korean government released the *Support Plan for AI Semiconductor Industry Promotion*, which detailed the government's plan to create a powerful AI semiconductor industry in South Korea by 2030. It hoped to develop the AI semiconductor industry in South Korea so that it was as successful as South Korea's dynamic random access memory (DRAM) industry.

In September 2023, the Ministry of Science and ICT of South Korea reviewed and approved a future-oriented and AI-based digital media plan, setting strategic objectives of accelerating digital transformation based on AI and ensuring the global competitiveness of the media and content industries. According to this plan, the South Korean government would invest KRW909 billion in developing AI for everyday life in order to improve competitiveness in this field. At the end of October 2023, the Ministry of Science and ICT of South Korea reviewed and voted on a task-oriented strategic roadmap in the AI and cutting-edge biological sectors and set four key technological objectives in the AI sector, including efficient learning and AI infrastructure construction, advanced modeling and decision-making, industry utilization and AI innovation, as well as trustworthy and safe AI.

4.4.5 Germany: Building the German Brand Through "Industry 4.0"

The "Industry 4.0" strategy proposed by the German federal government in 2013 already included AI-related content. Since 2018, the German federal government has emphasized the importance of AI R&D and application. In September 2018, the German federal government issued the *High-Tech Strategy 2025*, which listed 12 missions to be completed. Among them was the mission to promote AI applications and make Germany one of the world's leading centers of AI research, development, and application. The strategy also proposed various measures for AI development, for example, the formulation of AI strategies and the establishment of institutions including an AI competitiveness center, a committee on data ethics, and a joint Franco-German AI center [8].

In November 2018, the German government proposed an AI strategy at a cabinet meeting, which earmarked EUR3 billion in funding to promote AI development by 2025. The strategy also aimed to make Germany a world-leading center of AI research, with special focus on the ability to widely and quickly convert research results into applications and the adoption of a modern management paradigm. Urgent actions were needed to achieve this goal, including: (1) providing funding for R&D and innovative transformation in key AI-related fields; (2) preferentially increasing salaries of German AI experts; (3) cooperating with France to build an AI competitiveness center as soon as possible and achieving interconnectivity; (4) establishing a European AI innovation cluster; (5) setting up specialized competitiveness centers; (6) strengthening the construction of AI infrastructure. It was estimated that the German federal government would invest a total of EUR3 billion to help "AI made in Germany" become an international brand recognized for high quality by the end of 2025.

In December 2020, the German government approved a new AI strategy, proposing to increase funding in AI from EUR3 billion to EUR5 billion by 2025 and focusing efforts on five key areas: specialized experts, research, technology transfer and application, regulatory framework, and social recognition. These new key areas of focus aim to tackle emerging challenges under topics such as sustainable development, environmental and climate protection, epidemic prevention, as well as international and European networks. In addition, the new strategy proposed to further leverage Germany's leading advantages in Industry 4.0, accelerate the application and transformation of AI in the industrial field, and establish the "AI made in Germany" brand.

In August 2023, the Federal Ministry of Education and Research (BMBF) of Germany released the *Artificial Intelligence Action Plan 2023*, which called for urgent actions in 11 specific areas, including but not limited to: strengthening the research base, coming up with a new research agenda, strengthening AI infrastructure, improving AI-related competencies, extending AI application scenarios, and promoting multidisciplinary research. These efforts will constitute the essence of Germany's future science and technology policies and promote further AI development. The BMBF also announced that more than EUR1.6 billion would be invested in AI during the current term of office of the German federal parliament.

4.4.6 UK: Increasing Investment in Innovation to Promote Achievement Transfer

In 2017, the UK proposed the *Industrial Strategy: building a Britain fit for the future* for the next 10 years, listing "AI and data" as the top of the four Grand Challenges emerging in technological revolution and industrial development. In April 2018, the

AI Sector Deal was released following negotiations between the UK government and the industry and academia. According to the *AI Sector Deal*, the UK government and the industry would invest a total of GBP1 billion to support AI development, with the former investing GBP700 million and the latter GBP300 million, respectively. Subsequently, a dedicated AI Council was established to coordinate and supervise the implementation of the *AI Sector Deal*. In addition, the cross-department Office for AI was set up to formulate AI strategies, develop frameworks for the UK government's AI procurement, and guide relevant departments to implement AI solutions.

In January 2021, the UK AI Council released the *AI Roadmap*, providing 16 recommendations for the government to develop its national AI strategy. This report was divided into four parts, corresponding to the four fundamentals of UK AI development: (1) research, development, and innovation; (2) skills and diversity; (3) data, infrastructure, and public trust; (4) national, cross-sector adoption. It also proposed several measures, including: continuing to increase investment in AI, improving infrastructure, building high-level educational and research institutions, attracting and cultivating top technical experts, improving public trust, and strengthening cross-sector application of AI.

In September 2021, the UK government released the *National AI Strategy* in order to lay a foundation for AI development in the next 10 years. In June 2022, the UK Department of Defense released the *Defence Artificial Intelligence Strategy*, in which it promoted the use of AI in the defense sector in order to improve decision-making and efficiency, create new competencies, and enhance overall strength. In terms of financial support, the UK's national defense budget will provide an additional GBP24 billion for developing AI technologies in a 4-year period. In September 2023, the UK government announced that it would spend GBP900 million on building the Isambard-3 supercomputer in order to promote AI research and innovation.

References

1. CESI. AI standardization white paper (2018) [R] (in Chinese). 2018.
2. TURING A M. Computing machinery and intelligence [J]. Mind, 1950, 59(236): 433-460.
3. HINTON G E, SALAKHUTDINOV R R. Reducing the dimensionality of data with neural networks [J]. Science, 2006, 313(5786): 504-507.
4. National Science and Technology Council. Preparing for the future of artificial intelligence [R]. 2016.
5. National Science and Technology Council. National artificial intelligence research and development strategic plan [R]. 2016.
6. Executive Office of the President. Artificial intelligence, automation, and the economy [R]. 2016.
7. State Council. Next-generation artificial intelligence development plan [2017] No. 35 [R] (in Chinese). 2017.
8. SUN H L. Progress in the implementation of the high-tech strategy 2025 in Germany [J] (in Chinese). Science and Technology China, 2020(1): 102-104.

Chapter 5
Typical AI Technologies

Artificial intelligence (AI) technology research mainly studies how to make machines function like humans in many capacities such as learning, thinking, reasoning, and planning. The development of different technologies like big data, mobile Internet, supercomputing, brain science, and sensor networking as well as the social economy has created three main stages of AI development: the perceptual intelligence stage, the perceptual enhancement stage, and the cognitive intelligence stage. Each new development stage adds new features to AI like interdisciplinary fusion, deep learning, man-machine collaboration, and autonomous manipulation. See Fig. 5.1.

5.1 Machine Learning

Machine learning is the process where a computer learns from a large amount of data using algorithms to identify relationships and patterns in datasets, which can then be used by humans in practical applications. Typical machine learning algorithms include deep learning, artificial neural networks, and decision trees. Currently, the deep learning algorithms that are widely used can automatically summarize and extract important features from immense volumes of data. This ability also allows for multi-layer feature extraction and description, as well as feature restoration, to achieve the goal of deep learning. The journey of AI evolving from perceptual intelligence to cognitive intelligence is defined by breakthroughs in neural networks. This evolution enables machines to be fed with data with the help of nonlinear network structures and to learn and integrate essential features from smaller amounts of sample data. In general, machine learning technologies mainly include supervised learning, unsupervised learning, reinforcement learning, deep learning, and multi-task learning [1].

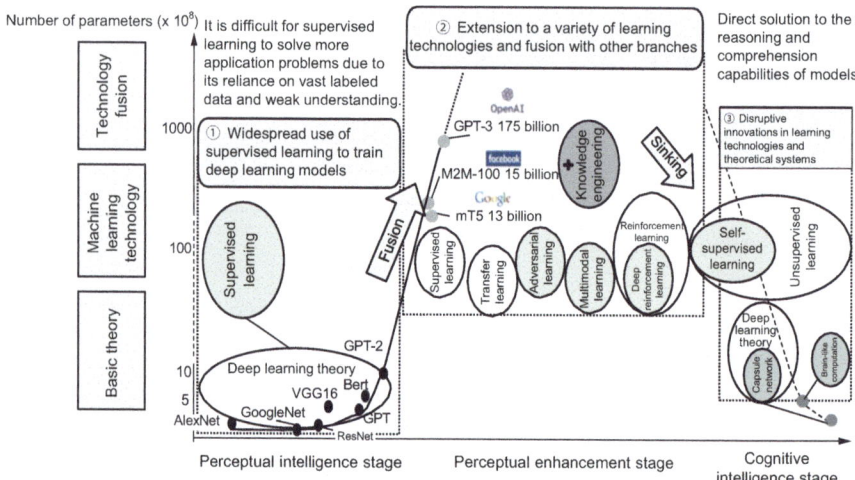

Fig. 5.1 Deployment stages of AI technologies

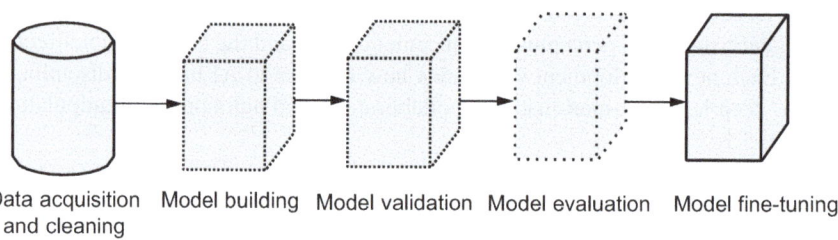

Fig. 5.2 Machine learning process

The machine learning process roughly consists of five steps, as shown in Fig. 5.2. The process starts with data acquisition and cleaning. In this step, the collected data is cleaned and divided into three parts: a training dataset, a validation dataset, and a test dataset. The second step is to construct a reasonable feature model by referring to the training dataset. The third step is to validate the model. In this step, the constructed feature model is validated and its trustworthiness is verified by using the validation dataset. The fourth step is to evaluate the model. In this step, the validated feature model is evaluated and tested by using the test dataset, and then the evaluated feature model is used to make predictions from new inputs. The fifth step is to fine-tune the model. In this step, the algorithm performance is improved by a range of methods like changing parameters, optimizing results, adjusting weights, and analyzing bad cases.

Today, machine learning applications are gaining traction in the healthcare, industrial production, retail, and finance sectors. The AI-driven drug discovery (AIDD) platform has become one popular area of investment under machine learning. According to the *China AI Software Market Shares, 2022* report published by the International Data Corporation (IDC), the market size of China's machine learning platforms reached CNY3.54 billion in 2022. Top players in the China's machine

5.1 Machine Learning

learning market seem to be benefiting significantly from their scale, with the top four occupying 68.9% of the market share (see Fig. 5.3) [2]. A range of challenges including technical barriers and implementation difficulties hinder other players who want to enter this market. Finance is also currently the leading sector in terms of machine learning applications. Research has found that, in 2022, 37.5% of machine learning applications in China serve the financial sector, whereas 12.1% serves the industrial production sector [3]. There is still great growth potential in machine learning applications for the industrial production sector (see Fig. 5.4).

Machine learning products are primarily platforms and focus on diagnostics, prediction, and decision-making purposes. Since 2015, machine learning platforms have transitioned from embedded modules in big data products to internal development tools that vendors can use to develop industry solutions; now, machine learning platforms are professional products that can be packaged and sold to industry customers separately. Data platform service providers, AI enterprises, Internet giants, and comprehensive solution developers are the major players in the machine learning market. AI enterprises have certain advantages when it comes to model

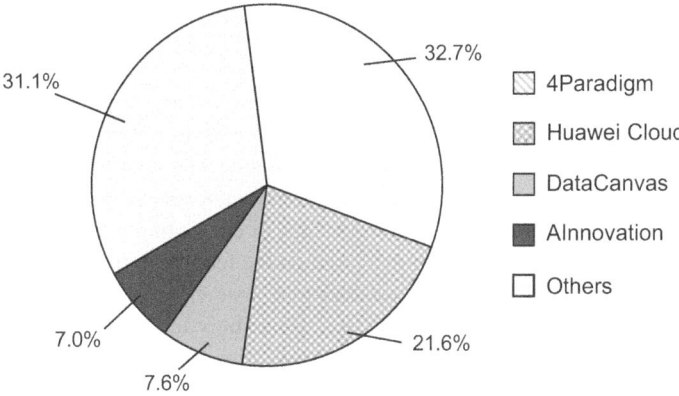

Fig. 5.3 Market shares of China's machine learning platforms in 2022. (Source: IDC China, 2023)

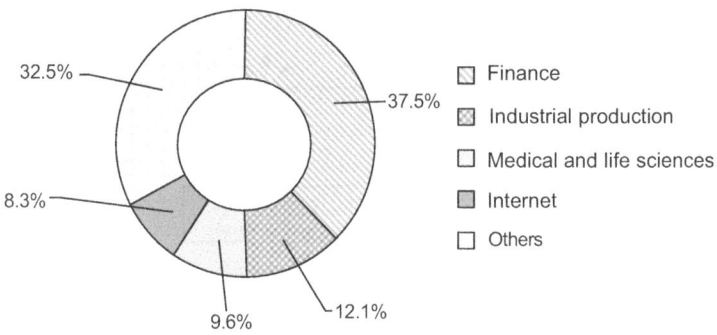

Fig. 5.4 Sector distribution of machine learning applications in China, 2022

development. They are positioned to consolidate the layout of intelligent decision-making and to backtrack and strengthen any weak links in data governance and data computing. Data platform service providers and Internet giants, on the other hand, have advantages in terms of data capabilities, which help them improve the "know-how" capabilities for industries during application development.

5.1.1 Supervised Learning

Supervised learning is the most common type of machine learning. Given target samples, a supervised learning algorithm computes the relationships between target samples and feature variables. Specifically, supervised learning uses labeled samples (inputs and expected outputs) to train algorithms to create an optimal model or function, and then uses this model or function to predict new unlabeled inputs and outputs. Figure 5.5 shows how supervised learning works. The output of a function can be a continuous value (referred to as regression) or a classification label (referred to as classification). Supervised learning algorithms can therefore be categorized into regression algorithms and classification algorithms, depending on whether the label distribution is continuous or discrete.

Regression refers to the prediction of continuous, specific values. Based on the analysis of inputs and outputs of known samples, regression fits a function that can be used to predict the outputs for new sample inputs. The machine learning algorithms test different prediction functions and obtain feedback by comparing the difference between the predicted and true values of each sample, and then continuously fine-tune the prediction functions based on the feedback. In this type of learning, the true values of the predicted variables play a supervisory role in the learning process by providing feedback. Regression algorithms include linear regression, nearest neighbor regression, and neural network regression. Classification, on the other hand, refers to the differentiation of samples into categories and is used for

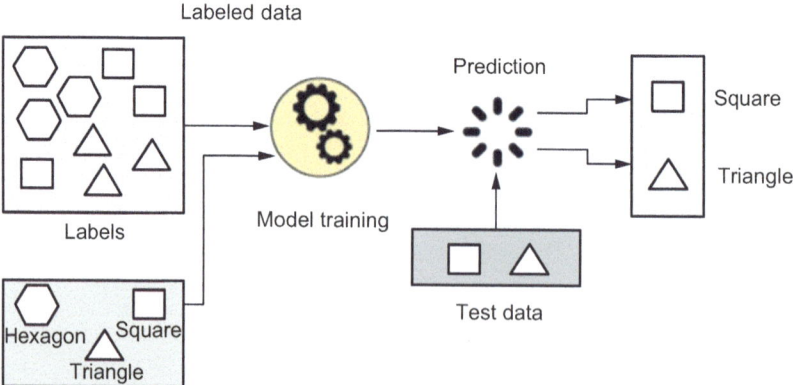

Fig. 5.5 Supervised learning function

discrete prediction. The training samples are categorized to generate a predictive model. After the machine learning process is complete, the machine predicts the type of new data based on the model.

Currently, common supervised learning methods include Naive Bayes classification, support vector machine (SVM), *k*-nearest neighbors (KNN) algorithm, linear regression, artificial neural network, least square, and decision tree (see Table 5.1). In practice, supervised learning is a very efficient way of learning and can be used for risk assessment, image classification, fraud detection, spam filtering, and other such scenarios. Supervised learning is currently being applied in fields like intelligent customer service, smart households, and image and speech recognition.

5.1.2 Unsupervised Learning

Unsupervised learning is another mainstream machine learning method. In unsupervised learning, there are no labels available for a specified dataset, with the data neither classified nor having target variables specified. Unsupervised learning

Table 5.1 Common supervised learning algorithms

Algorithm	Overview
Decision tree	It performs splitting based on feature values and makes predictions or classifications based on the final leaf nodes. It is easy to understand and interpret, can handle discrete and continuous features, and is suitable for classification and regression tasks
SVM	It is a binary classification algorithm based on margin maximization and performs classification by finding an optimal hyperplane in the feature space. It can deal with both linear and nonlinear problems and has strong generalization capabilities
Naive Bayes	It is a set of probabilistic classification algorithms based on the Bayes' theorem and the assumption of conditionally independent features. It performs classification by calculating posterior probabilities and assumes that features are independent of each other
KNN	It performs classification based on the distance between instances. It makes predictions based on the labels of the *k*-nearest neighbors and is suitable for classification and regression problems
Linear regression	It is used to predict the continuous variable outputs. It establishes a linear relationship between input features and outputs and finds the best-fit line by minimizing the error
Logistic regression	It is used for binary classification problems. It uses a logistic function (sigmoid function) to transform linear combinations of features into probabilities and then classifies the probabilities based on thresholds
Random forest	It is an ensemble learning method that performs classification or regression by combining multiple decision trees. It uses random feature selection and voting to improve accuracy and generalization of models
Gradient boosting	It is an ensemble learning method that works by iteratively training weak learners and using a weighted combination of weak learners to improve model performance. Common gradient boosting algorithms include the gradient boosting tree and XGBoost

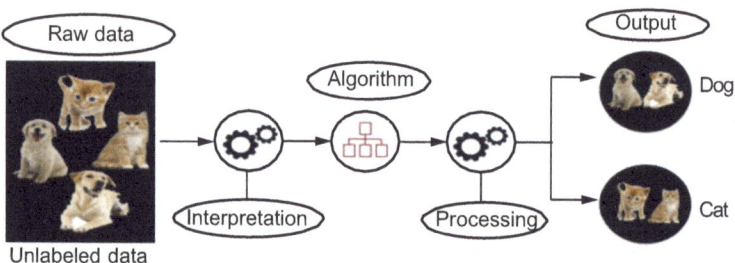

Fig. 5.6 Unsupervised learning function

cannot be directly applied to a regression or classification problem. The objective of unsupervised learning is to discover the underlying structure of a dataset, group the data according to similarities, and create a compressed representation of the dataset (see Fig. 5.6).

Unsupervised learning algorithms are tasked with identifying features on their own, and do this by clustering datasets into groups based on data similarities. Unsupervised learning uses unlabeled data as inputs to train the machine learning model. The trained model interprets the raw data to find hidden patterns from the data and then applies appropriate algorithms. Clustering and dimensionality reduction are the two dominant unsupervised learning methods. Table 5.2 lists common unsupervised learning algorithms. Compared with supervised learning, unsupervised learning is used for more complex tasks with easier access to unlabeled data, but is inherently more difficult to use and its outputs may be less accurate. Unsupervised learning is commonly used in fields like market segmentation and social network analysis.

5.1.3 Reinforcement Learning

Reinforcement learning, also known as reward-based learning, evaluative learning, or augmented learning, is one of the paradigms and primary methodologies of machine learning. Reinforcement learning aims to maximize the rewards for agents in complex, uncertain environments. The basic framework of reinforcement learning consists of two parts: agent and environment (see Fig. 5.7). The agent and environment continuously interact with each other during the reinforcement learning process. The agent learns to take an action, also known as a decision, based on a state that is acquired from the environment. The action is executed in the environment. Based on the outcome of the action, the environment determines the next state and provides feedback in the form of a reward for the agent. The agent works to maximize the rewards received from the environment.

Repeated experiments and delayed rewards are the two most important features of reinforcement learning. Reinforcement learning focuses on maximizing rewards

5.1 Machine Learning

Table 5.2 Common unsupervised learning algorithms

Algorithm	Overview
Clustering	It classifies data samples into groups or clusters and data samples with similar features are clustered together. Common clustering algorithms include k-means clustering, hierarchical clustering, and Density-based Spatial Clustering of Applications with Noise (DBSCAN)
Dimensionality reduction	It maps data from high-dimensional spaces to low-dimensional spaces for better visualization or faster computation. Common dimensionality reduction algorithms include principal component analysis and independent component analysis
Association rule mining	It discovers frequent itemsets and association rules in data and can reveal implicit relationships and correlations in data. Common association rule mining algorithms include Apriori and Frequent Pattern Growth (FP-Growth) algorithms
Anomaly detection	It identifies abnormal samples in data that deviate significantly from normal patterns, helping to detect potential problems or anomalies
Self-organizing map (SOM)	It is a type of neural network algorithm that maps multi-dimensional data onto a two- or three-dimensional topology. It is utilized for the visualization of data distribution and clustering
Gaussian mixture model (GMM)	It is a type of probabilistic model for modeling a combination of multiple Gaussian distributions. It can be used for clustering, density estimation, and generation of new samples
Independent component analysis (ICA)	It is an algorithm that separates mixed signals into independent components. It is often used in fields such as speech signal separation and electroencephalogram signal analysis

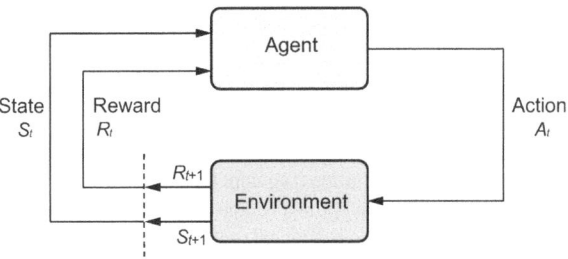

Fig. 5.7 Basic reinforcement learning framework

instead of trying to find hidden dataset structures. Using unsupervised learning to find hidden dataset structures can be useful for reinforcement learning tasks, but it does not fundamentally address the problem of maximizing rewards. In addition to the agent and environment, there are four basic elements in a reinforcement learning system: policy, reward, value, and environment (model). A policy defines how the agent behaves at a given state. A reward signal defines the objective of a reinforcement learning problem. A value function is a prediction of future rewards and specifies what is a good or bad state based on the analysis of the transitions between states. An environment (model) is a simulation of the environment, predicting how the environment will behave in the next step.

Reinforcement learning is a computational method used to understand and automate goal-directed learning and decision-making. It is distinguished by its emphasis on learning by an agent from direct interactions with the environment, without relying on supervision or a complete environment (model). Reinforcement learning can be viewed as the first effective method to learn from interactions with an environment to achieve long-term goals. Among all the forms of machine learning, reinforcement learning is considered the closest to how humans and other animals actually learn. Currently, common reinforcement learning algorithms include Q-learning, State-Action-Reward-State-Action (SARSA), Deep Deterministic Policy Gradient (DDPG), Advantage Actor-Critic (A2C), Proximal Policy Optimization (PPO), and Deep Q-learning Network (DQN) (see Table 5.3). Reinforcement learning has been used in a variety of fields such as gaming, robotics, and decision-making.

5.1.4 Deep Learning

Deep learning is one of the most popular cutting-edge technologies applied for AI in recent years. It is a machine learning method that uses artificial neural networks to simulate the connections and information transfers that occur between neurons in the human brain. Deep learning can be categorized into supervised learning and unsupervised learning. The former includes deep neural network (DNN), convolutional neural network (CNN), recurrent neural network (RNN), and so on. The latter

Table 5.3 Common reinforcement learning algorithms

Algorithm	Overview
Q-learning	It is a model-free, off-policy reinforcement learning algorithm, featuring simplicity and the ability to deal with large continuous state spaces. It iteratively updates the Q-value (an optimal action-value function) using the Bellman equation until convergence is attained or the maximum number of iterations is reached
SARSA	It is a model-free, on-policy reinforcement learning algorithm, featuring the ability to deal with problems with stochastic transition dynamics. It centers on updating the value function based on the Q-value of the current state and action
DDPG	It is a model-free, off-policy algorithm for continuous action spaces. It is a type of actor-critic algorithm, particularly useful for robotic control and other continuous control tasks
A2C	It is an on-policy actor-critic algorithm that updates the policy using the advantage function. The algorithm is simple to implement and can handle both discrete and continuous action spaces
PPO	It is an on-policy algorithm that updates the policy using trust region optimization. It is particularly useful in environments with high-dimensional observations and continuous action spaces
DQN	It is a model-free, off-policy algorithm that uses a neural network to approximate the Q-function. It is particularly useful for Atari games and other similar problems

includes deep belief network (DBN), restricted Boltzmann machine (RBM), autoencoder (AE), and so on. Table 5.4 lists typical deep learning algorithms.

Neural networks are representative algorithms for deep learning. They imitate the behavioral features of animals' neural networks and perform distributed parallel information processing. Based on system complexity, neural networks process information by adjusting the interconnection relationships between a large number of internal nodes. In addition, neural networks are capable of self-driven learning and adaptation.

Deep learning has demonstrated powerful prediction, classification, clustering and other capabilities, and has been widely used in the fields like computer vision, natural language processing (NLP), and speech recognition. Deep learning has also achieved outstanding results in image recognition. In 2012, AlexNet (a type of CNN model) achieved remarkable success in ImageNet, marking a significant milestone in image recognition applications of deep learning. After AlexNet, a series of CNN models including ResNet and Inception emerged, which continuously improved the accuracy and efficiency of image recognition. Deep learning is also widely used in

Table 5.4 Typical deep learning algorithms

Algorithm	Overview
DNN	It is an artificial neural network architecture composed of multiple layers of nonlinear transformation units and can be trained to learn the mappings between inputs and outputs
CNN	It is a type of feedforward neural network consisting of one or more convolutional layers, a pooling layer, and a fully connected layer on top. It excels in image processing
RNN	It is a type of neural network used for processing sequential data and uses a specific form of memory to simulate temporal dynamics. The output of an RNN at a given time point depends not only on inputs for that time point but also on previous inputs, making the RNN behave like it "remembers" the historical context
Generative adversarial network (GAN)	It uses random noise as inputs and generates outputs, which are samples from the training set distribution
DBN	It is a multi-layered neural network that allows for multiple times of information transfer and feedback within the network. It is capable of handling complex problems and learning abstract features
RBM	It is a two-layered neural network with full connectivity between adjacent layers and no connectivity within a layer. It can effectively extract data features and pre-train traditional feedforward neural networks, significantly improving the discriminative capabilities of networks
Sparse coding (SC)	It is an algorithm that establishes a descriptive function of input data through training and learning, and it works to find a set of super-complete basis vectors for representing input data. It is an effective method to reconstruct input data by discovering structures and patterns hidden in the input data
AE	It is a special type of artificial neural network that learns effective features from data, mostly used for the dimensionality reduction and feature extraction of high-dimensional data

NLP. For instance, RNNs can be used for a variety of tasks, including speech sentiment analysis, machine translation, and natural language generation. Long short-term memory (LSTM) networks are also popular deep learning models that are widely used in tasks such as speech recognition and text classification. In addition, pre-trained models (such as BERT, short for Bidirectional Encoder Representations from Transformers) have provided significant gains across NLP tasks. As deep learning technologies advance, they have become integrated to a wide range of industries, from healthcare and financial risk control, to smart transportation and beyond.

Complex deep learning models often consume vast amounts of storage space and computational resources, making them difficult to apply in resource-constrained environments like edge- or device-computing environments. As such, the industry tends towards technologies that require less memory and computation overhead. Lightweight deep learning is considered essential in such scenarios. Future research in lightweight deep learning is expected to pursue more compact and efficient neural network structure designs, large model pruning (i.e., sections of large model structures are "trimmed"), and network parameter quantizing to minimize computation. Google's MobileNet and Megvii's ShuffleNet are good examples of this kind of compact model, and Baidu's lightweight PaddleOCR model that is downsized to 2.8 MB has gained its popularity since it was open-sourced on the GitHub platform.

5.1.5 Multi-Task Learning

Multi-task learning is a training paradigm for machine learning. It involves training a single model to simultaneously perform multiple related tasks based on shared representations. By sharing representations between related tasks, multi-task learning improves data efficiency and potentially enables faster learning for related or downstream tasks. This helps compensate for deep learning's weaknesses in large-scale data requirements and computational demand. Multi-task learning enables a single model to solve different tasks. Figure 5.8 shows the comparison between multi-task learning and single-task learning.

Multi-task learning, first, has a collection of related tasks that can serve as mutual sources for each other to improve the performance of the learning. Specifically, the machine learning model is trained with data from multiple tasks in parallel, and one task can benefit from the useful information contained in the training signals of other tasks, thereby improving overall performance. Second, the multi-task learning model exhibits a regularization effect, meaning that the model learns well from not only one task but also other tasks. The model tends to learn the features that perform well on multiple tasks. Third, multi-task learning allows partial sharing of the algorithm structure, reducing its memory footprint and speeding up its inference with minimization of repeated computations.

Existing multi-task learning methods are categorized into hard parameter sharing and soft parameter sharing. Hard parameter sharing is a method to share parameters

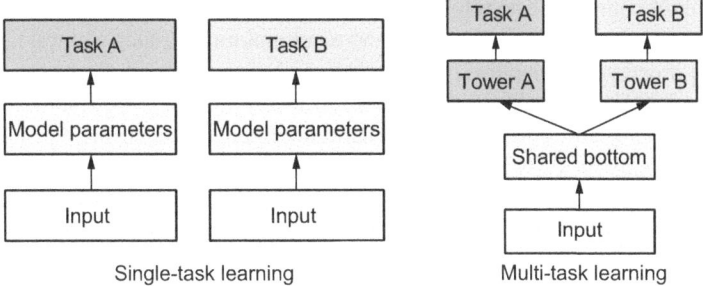

Fig. 5.8 Multi-task learning and single-task learning

between multiple tasks in the main part of the model, while keeping task-specific output structures. With hard parameter sharing, the model learns shared features between multiple tasks to reduce the risk of overfitting to a single task. In other words, hard parameter sharing is the practice of sharing model weights between different tasks, so that each model weight is trained to jointly minimize multiple loss functions. Soft parameter sharing is a method where each task has its own model with certain constraints imposed on the relationships between the model-specific parameters. In soft parameter sharing, different tasks have their own task-specific models with separate weights, but the distance between the parameters of these task-specific models is added to the joint objective function. Current research into multi-task learning is exploring how to transfer shared parameters fused with unshared parameters from the bottom layer to the top layer.

Multi-task learning stands out, thanks to its ability to solve multiple tasks by using a single model. In addition, multi-task learning exploits the differences between tasks to enhance generalization capabilities and prevent overfitting to a single task. Multi-task learning can also be used for knowledge migration to improve the performance of the main task. Currently, multi-task learning is widely used in the computer vision field that focuses on target recognition, detection, and segmentation. Take facial recognition as an example. Facial landmark detection is not an independent problem, and the prediction of facial landmarks is affected by different but subtly related factors, such as occlusion and pose changes. Multi-task learning improves the accuracy of facial landmark detection by combining facial landmark detection and some different but subtly related tasks, such as head pose estimation and facial attribute inference.

5.2 Natural Language Processing

Natural language processing (NLP) is one of the key technologies in the field of human-computer interaction. NLP typically refers to the conversion of a natural human language into a data format that a computer can process, as well as the conversion of computer data into a natural human language. NLP makes communication and interaction between humans and machines much easier. Natural language data to be processed is usually speech or text, and processing involves certain technologies related to areas like information retrieval, information extraction, and so on [4]. The sparse and smooth nature of natural language data means it is necessary to perform syntax analysis and text generation for human language.

NLP spans three disciplines: computer science, AI, and linguistics. Figure 5.9 shows the relationship between NLP and AI. NLP has come a long way in enabling computer systems to understand natural languages, evolving from reliance on imitative learning (like imitating birds flapping wings to take off) to the utilization of statistical approaches based on powerful mathematical theories. Today, NLP is continuing to grow, supported by the constant optimization of various models and the evolution of computers. The purpose of NLP is to enable computers to understand a natural language, rather than feeding an obscure computer language into a system for data processing. Generally, NLP techniques mainly include language model, word vector, machine translation, and text classification.

Regarding the overall process, NLP encompasses natural language understanding (NLU) and natural language generation (NLG). NLU focuses on comprehending the meanings of text inputs, including word- and structure-level meanings, while NLG uses a three-phase system in its approach. In phase 1, NLG determines what goal to achieve. In phase 2, NLG plans how to achieve the goal, including evaluating the situation and available communicative resources. In phase 3, NLG implements the plan as text. NLP can be divided into two categories covering six models. In one category, a model receives sound inputs and provides outputs as text, another sound, or a class. In the other category, a model receives text inputs and provides outputs as sound, another piece of text, or a class. Figure 5.10 shows the categorization of basic NLP models.

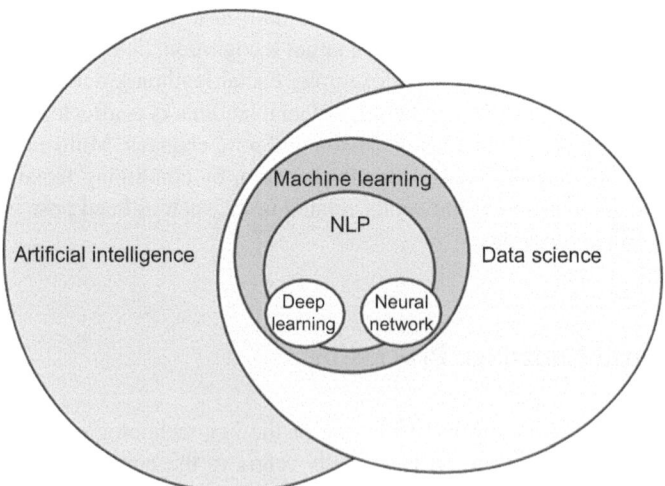

Fig. 5.9 Relationship between NLP and AI

5.2 Natural Language Processing

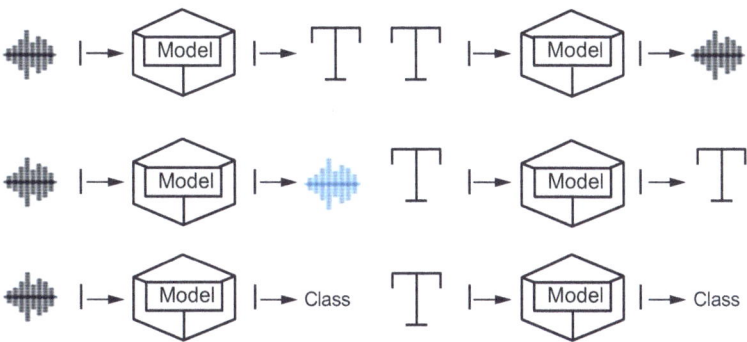

Fig. 5.10 Categorization of basic NLP models

NLP acts as the cornerstone of semantic intelligence and has grown rapidly in recent years. Statistics indicate that the global NLP market size reached USD24.86 billion in 2022. As an important part of the NLP market, China's growth rate exceeds the global average, with its NLP market size reaching CNY17.59 billion in 2022 [5]. The continuously optimized industrial environment and broad market prospects in the NLP field in China have provided good development space for NLP vendors. In China, NLP applications have been widely used in numerous fields. In the financial field, NLP applications have been used for risk alerting, contract analysis, knowledge base construction, and so on. In the Internet field, they have been employed for search optimization, recommendation engines, text reviews, and much more. Meanwhile, in the government/public security field, NLP applications have been used in areas like opinion polling, investigations, and intelligence analysis. In the enterprise service field, they have been used for machine translation, information retrieval, text generation, patent processing, robotic process automation (RPA), and more. In the future, upstream and downstream enterprises in the NLP industry chain, focusing on the development and application of large language models, will seize development opportunities created by advances in the pre-trained large model technologies and paradigms as well as the commercialization of large language models.

5.2.1 Language Model

A language model transforms a natural language into a sequence of words, based on which the language model predicts the probability of the next word. As the core element of an NLP system, language models are able to compute the joint probabilities of word sequences and generate vector representations of words. Today, language models are being widely used in many fields.

The evolution of language models can be divided into two major phases. The first phase is statistical language modeling, done on the basis of statistics. This phase uses traditional language modeling methods that primarily utilize information such as context-related feature information. With increases in computing power, language modeling has entered the second phase, which involves neural network language modeling. This phase may be further divided into two sub-phases based on the nature of models. The earlier of these sub-phases focuses on designing neural network structures, while the latter adopts pre-trained language modeling, which means a model is trained on an immense corpus of language content, fine-tuned, and then applied to downstream tasks. With the introduction of generative models into large language models, neural network language models can generate new texts similar to training data by learning the probabilistic distribution of word sequences. This represents a breakthrough in NLP tasks. Figure 5.11 depicts neural network language models.

Today, high-quality datasets have become an important means to improve language model performance. Enterprises and research institutes have built high-quality datasets to significantly improve model performance. For instance, OpenAI released Whisper, a new speech system based on high-quality datasets. Compared with other models, Whisper cuts error rates by 50% in zero-sample tasks such as language identification, phrase-level timestamping, and multilingual speech transcription. Whisper is already approaching human levels of accuracy for the English language. In another instance, Tencent and Northwestern Polytechnical University jointly released a pre-trained Chinese speech model based on WenetSpeech, a multi-domain transcribed Chinese speech dataset consisting of over 10,000 h of speech data, promoting research into Chinese speech recognition tasks.

In addition, enterprises in the intelligent speech sector have been developing application-oriented technical schemes with lower training costs but higher reasoning efficiency. In one example of such efforts, iFLYTEK proposed speech

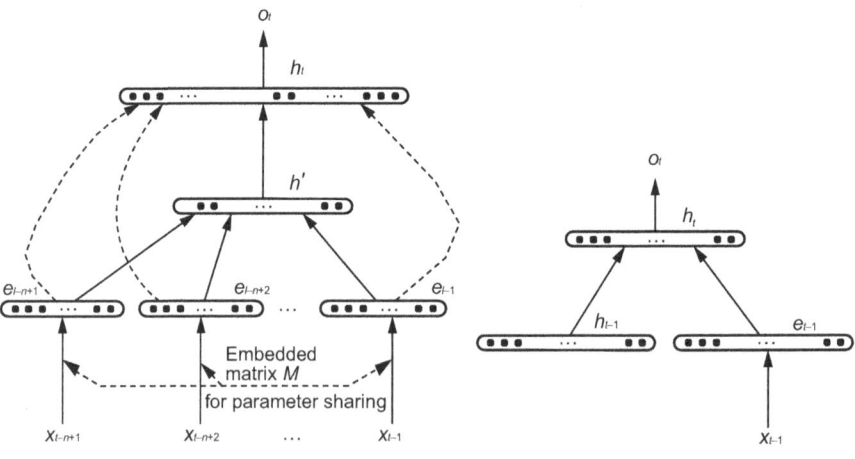

Fig. 5.11 Neural network language models

5.2 Natural Language Processing

technology based on small samples. This technology is able to clone timbre merely by fine-tuning one sentence in a speech synthesis task, and enables 100 h of speech data to achieve the same speech-recognition effect that would usually take 10,000 h of speech data in a speech recognition task. In another instance, Kuaishou built a streaming acoustic model integrated with hardware-optimization techniques. This model reduces latency by 40%, without sacrificing precision in application scenarios such as voice searches, voice inputs, and real-time subtitles, thus meeting service needs.

Speech synthesis is a critical technology within intelligent speech interaction. Enterprises are attempting to improve the synthesis effect and optimize the interaction experience by making breakthroughs in timbre replication. For instance, ByteDance-owned Volcano Engine developed an automatic, efficient, and lightweight timbre customization solution. This solution requires only 0.3% of the data volume of a traditional approach to achieve timbre cloning, with studio-quality-level timbre space modeling. Another example is Amazon's voice assistant, Alexa, which can mimic any human's voice from less than 1 min of recorded audio, a technique which will be applied to smart speakers.

Speech recognition has already entered large-scale commercial use, with the recognition effect constantly being improved to meet the needs of segmented scenarios. Multiple enterprise-level automatic speech recognition (ASR) models based entirely on neural networks have been successfully put into practical applications, such as the voice assistant Alexa and AssemblyAI, an API platform that specializes in speech transcription and comprehension. Enterprises are also improving their model performance based on segmented scenarios. In the financial field, for instance, VoiceAI launched the anti-fraud platform VoiceDNA based on the voiceprint recognition technique. This technique offers customer identity confirmation and suspicious voiceprint retrieval with a recognition accuracy rate of 95%. VoiceDNA has been applied to the service environment of Industrial and Commercial Bank of China. In the transportation field, as another example, Alibaba Cloud released a solution that achieves accurate voice interaction in environments where noise exceeds 90 dB and also increases the computing speed by more than 30%. Furthermore, the Beijing Subway launched a voice ticketing system for the Capital Airport Line and Daxing Airport Line, and continuously works to improve voice recognition performance. With voice ticketing, each ticket purchase takes an average of just 1.6 s.

5.2.2 Word Vector

NLP uses words as the basic unit. Word vector, also known as word embedding, is the collective name for a set of language modeling and feature learning techniques in NLP. Words or phrases from a vocabulary are mapped to vectors of real numbers, and these vectors can then indicate the semantic relationships between words. Conceptually, word vectors involve mathematical embeddings, from a multi-dimensional space per word to a continuous vector space with lower dimensions.

84   5 Typical AI Technologies

Word vectors are proven to boost the performance of NLP tasks such as text classification, syntax analysis, and sentiment analysis.

In NLP tasks, discrete representation and distributed representation are both commonly used for word vector representation. Discrete representation treats each word as a long vector, of which the dimension is the vocabulary size. Distributed representation transforms a word into a fixed-length (specifiable) vector that is dense and semantically related to other vectors. Herein, "semantically related" means that words with similar distributions have the same semantics. The meaning of any word can thus be represented by its surrounding words. Figure 5.12 depicts the word vector calculation.

As research advances, word vectors will be applied in more fields, not just NLP. Word vectors are typically obtained from statistical methods (such as co-occurrence matrix or singular value decomposition) or language models. A representative technique for word vectors, for example, is Google's Word2Vec. Word2Vec performs well in capturing similarities and analogies between words through the skip-gram model and continuous bag-of-words model as well as by using two approximate training methods, namely, negative sampling and hierarchical softmax.

5.2.3 Machine Translation

Machine translation is an automated process of translating one natural language into another by using computer algorithms. As a composite and marginalized discipline, machine translation was born out of blooming computer science techniques, supported by modern linguistics, statistics, and theories such as probability theory. At present, machine translation is mainly categorized into rule-based machine translation, corpus-based machine translation, and hybrid machine translation, depending on intelligent algorithms and the method used to process linguistic knowledge.

The characteristics of machine translation are outlined as follows:

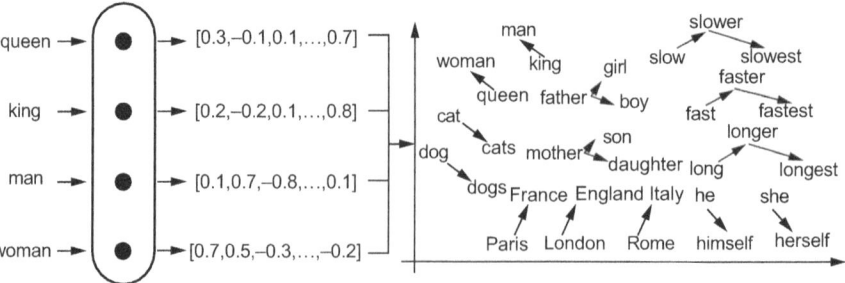

Fig. 5.12 Word vector calculation

5.2 Natural Language Processing

1. Data preparation. Machine translation requires immense amounts of supervisory data from "inputs-correct outputs" matches. For example, speech-to-text machine translation requires labeled data from source-language speech and target-language text.
2. Modeling. Most models adopt an encoder-decoder architecture, where an encoder is used to encode source-language semantics and a decoder is used to generate target-language text.
3. Training. Models are trained with an emphasis on generating the target language rather than gaining a semantic understanding based on the source-language text during generation.
4. Evaluation and optimization. Almost all existing machine translation models rely on automatic quality evaluation metrics (such as BLEU, short for bilingual evaluation understudy) for the evaluation and optimization of machine-translated outputs.
5. Application. Most applications of machine translation are static use cases, where there is no other interaction between users and models except that models receive the texts to be translated from users and generate the translation results as outputs.

In recent decades, the mainstream methods of machine translation have migrated from rule-based and statistical machine translation to neural machine translation. End-to-end neural machine translation is a brand-new machine translation technique, which relies on a partitioning strategy and multi-coding mechanism to solve the issue of traditional artificial neural networks being sensitive to sentence length. This technique can ensure that semantic information is not lost when translating a long sentence, through a shortened length and simplified structure of translation. Existing neural machine translation methods typically employ an encoder-decoder framework (represented by the Transformer model) to learn mappings from source-language sentences to target-language sentences based on training data from a large-scale bilingual corpus.

Machine translation meets today's needs of multilingual translations among countries around the world, with record turnaround times at lower costs. The machine translation platforms launched by AI industry giants such as Google Translate, Baidu Translate, and Sogou Translate dominate the machine translation industry, by virtue of their efficiency and accuracy of translation. As machine translation has been evolving and become increasingly tailored to specific scenarios and needs based on large models, machine translation has gradually expanded its area of use to speech translation, image translation, video translation, multi-language translation, and low-resource minority-language translation.

5.2.4 Text Classification

Text classification is a fundamental task of NLP. It is designed to automatically determine text categories based on text content in a given classification system. Typically, supervised learning methods are used to train text classification models. Early on, most of the text classification methods are based on statistical learning paradigms, such as Naive Bayes, KNN, and SVM. These methods, despite significantly outperforming simple rule-based methods in both accuracy and stability, require extensive efforts in feature engineering.

In contrast, deep learning methods can automate the construction of text representations containing rich semantics, bypassing the manual process of designing rules and features. As such, since 2010, deep neural networks (such as RNN, CNN, and GNN) have gradually replaced statistical learning methods to become the dominant methods of text classification. GNN is short for graph neural network.

A text classification task is typically accomplished in two phases: the training phase and the testing phase. The training phase aims to train a text classification model based on the training set data, while the testing phase aims to predict the class of new data using the model trained during the training phase. Each phase involves three steps: preprocessing, feature dimensionality reduction, and classifier training, as shown in Fig. 5.13. Preprocessing transforms textual data into a format that can then be fed into a computer model. This step involves partitioning words, removing stop words, representing text, and the like. Feature dimensionality reduction increases the speed and accuracy of processing high-dimensional textual data. The approaches frequently used during this step include term frequency-inverse document frequency (TF-IDF), chi-square statistics, and so on.

Unsupervised pre-training technologies have bloomed in recent years. As a result, the pre-trained models represented by Embeddings from Language Models (ELMo), Generative Pre-trained Transformers (GPT), and Bidirectional Encoder Representations from Transformers (BERT) have all achieved high-quality text semantic modeling based on massive text corpora, thus greatly improving the performance of text classification tasks. Text classification has been widely used across various fields such as public opinion monitoring, spam filtering, news classification, commodity classification, and sentiment analysis. For instance, in news classification applications, text classification can be employed to assign articles to different

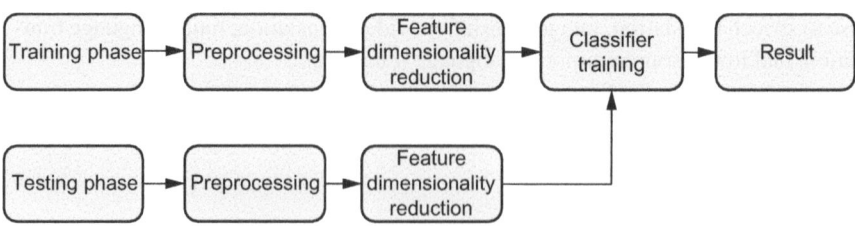

Fig. 5.13 Text classification process

subject areas; in e-commerce website applications, text classification can be used to assign commodities to different categories.

5.3 Computer Vision

Computer vision, also known as machine vision, is a discipline that enables machines to learn how to "see." It is an important application of deep learning technology and has been widely used in a range of scenarios including public security, industrial quality inspection, and autonomous driving. Computer vision aims to simulate the human visual system. More specifically, computer vision enables a machine to identify an object in a picture or video taken by a camera, detect the object's location, and track the object. This allows computer vision to understand and describe the scenario or story in the picture or video.

Computer vision is designed to build artificial systems that can "sense" information from images or videos. As Internet technology continues to advance, data volume is experiencing massive growth and increasingly rich datasets are emerging. In addition, computing power is constantly growing, owing to improvements in hardware capabilities. Researchers have been applying new models and algorithms to the field of computer vision, giving rise to high-precision models with numerous structures. Meanwhile, computer vision has become able to deal with a vast array of tasks, including classification, detection, segmentation, scenario description, image generation, style transformation, and even video processing techniques and 3D vision. Today, common computer vision tasks include image processing, object detection, image recognition, and video analysis.

Overall, computer vision has progressed through three main stages. It started with traditional feature extraction, relying on manually designed operators (e.g., scale-invariant feature transform, abbreviated as SIFT), then advanced to CNNs that enabled innovations for image processing, and made its latest move into the "large model era" driven by vision transformers (ViTs) that employed a multi-attention mechanism. According to *China AI Software Market Shares, 2022* published by IDC, the market size of China's computer vision industry reached CNY12.30 billion in 2022. SenseTime remained top of the market share list from 2018 through to 2022, followed by Hikvision, AInnovation, Megvii, CloudWalk, and AthenaEyes (see Fig. 5.14) [2]. It is worth noting that cloud service vendors have grown into an important part of the computer vision market in China. Although not on the list, cloud service vendors have also seen a rapidly expanding market size. In addition to top vendors, those that deliver cloud-edge-device solutions and focus on industry application scenarios (such as quality control and inspection) are a significant part of the computer vision market. Computer vision deserves to be the highlight of AI with promising incremental growth prospects, whether in terms of its popularity in the capital market sector, market size, or scenario generalization.

The sectors in which computer vision is applied vary greatly. Some sectors, like pan-security (public security, transportation, and community buildings) and finance,

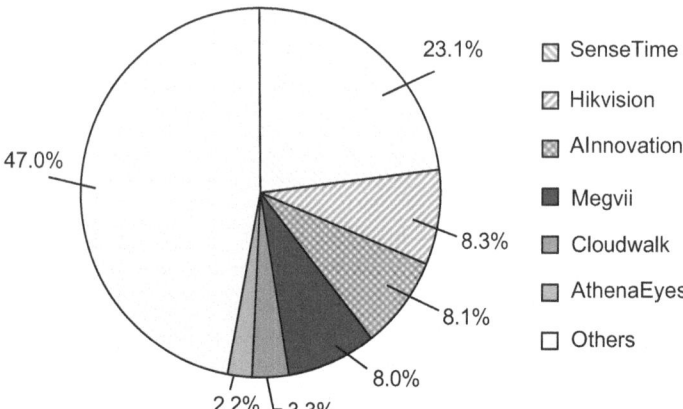

Fig. 5.14 Market shares of computer vision in China, 2022. (Source: IDC China, 2023)

have seen supportive policies released by Chinese authorities or large and continuous investments in computer vision. Some other sectors with strategic significance, like healthcare, energy, and industry, have great growth potential for computer vision but are subject to long review and approval periods or prudent decision-making; the market need for computer vision cannot be satisfied quickly enough in such sectors. Other sectors, like retailing and agriculture, have frequent long-tail requirements or low digitalization levels and are sensitive to prices. Meanwhile, other sectors still, like robotics and autonomous driving, emphasize the fusion and application of technologies [6]. In a word, each of these sectors varies in terms of vendors, business models, implementation bottlenecks, and competition strategies, but all are engaged in the same core pursuit: revenue growth and business continuity.

From the perspective of application capabilities, generated videos and images have seen significant improvements in fineness, smoothness, and fidelity. The virtual-real boundary has now disappeared, with rendered objects and environments now being perfect replicas of those in the real world, undetectable to human eyes. In the future, computer vision has the potential to change the development patterns of various industries, such as film and television, animation, gaming and entertainment, news broadcasting, as well as virtual customer services.

5.3.1 Image Processing

Image processing refers to the use of AI to mimic the human visual system in order to recognize and process images and other multi-dimensional data information [7]. A digital image processing task is typically divided into three steps. Step one is to improve image clarity, that is, the visual quality. Step two is to identify and extract certain feature values or feature information of images. Step three is to transform,

5.3 Computer Vision   89

encode, and compress image data, plus other processing operations, so that image data can be propagated, stored, and analyzed in a digital format.

Image processing techniques mainly include image description and image segmentation. Generally, image description adopts two-dimensional shape description, including boundary description and region description. Image segmentation aims to extract the meaningful parts of an image, such as edges, regions, and shapes, for further image data analysis and processing. Image denoising is an effective approach for improving image quality, while image enhancement and image restoration can significantly improve the visual effect of an image. Image compression aims to reduce the time it takes for image transmission and processing, in addition to effectively minimizing the memory required for storing images. Encoding is one of the most mature and frequently used compression techniques. The information above summarizes the main image processing approaches and techniques in computer-based image processing.

Deep learning has made significant breakthroughs in image recognition, marked by the milestone AlexNet (a high-precision image recognition network) proposed by Geoffrey Hinton in 2012. Today, image processing is an important field of research in deep learning, and almost all deep learning frameworks support image processing tools. Image processing has also been applied to a number of fields such as earth resource exploration, weather forecasting, traffic monitoring, industrial inspection, law enforcement, man-machine interaction, film and television, and entertainment. The gaming industry is a great example. In March 2022, Unity released a 4K-resolution promo video with real-time AI rendering. During the video, the finest details of the eyes, hair, and skin of the portrayed digital human were almost identical to those of a real human. In addition to significant enhancements to video/image generation and refinement capabilities, the three-dimensional processing capabilities of models continue to improve.

5.3.2 Object Detection

Object detection is an indispensable computer vision technique that works to locate objects within images and assign them to specific classes. A range of tasks, such as image segmentation, object tracking, and key point detection, typically rely on object detection. Object detection can help robots accomplish certain routine tasks, such as parts sorting by industrial robotic arms. In addition, object detection can serve as the basis for accomplishing complex computer vision tasks such as navigation and scenario comprehension.

Object detection is categorized into traditional detection algorithms and deep neural network methods. Traditional detection algorithms use a sliding-window approach to determine object locations, involving detection window selection, feature design, and classifier design. In contrast, deep neural network methods have significantly improved object-detection performance. Specifically, the performance of traditional detection algorithms notably improves as data volumes increase at the early stages of data training, but this improvement becomes increasingly insignificant as data volumes continue to grow at the later stages. This drawback of traditional detection algorithms is laid bare in the case of vast amounts of data trainings. In contrast, the performance of deep neural network methods constantly steps up alongside the number of data trainings, not exhibiting a saturation type curve.

Today, object detection is widely used in a variety of fields such as intelligent security, smart transportation, robotics, smart households, and medical diagnosis. Taking autonomous driving as an example, object detection serves as a fundamental technique for environment perception, which is the core of autonomous driving. Supported by object detection, the autonomous driving system can better understand various environment-specific scenarios, such as detection of obstacle types, road signs and markings, pedestrians and vehicles, and the semantic classification of traffic signals and other data.

5.3.3 Image Recognition

Image recognition involves the use of computers to process, analyze, and understand images, aiming to recognize targets and objects in various patterns from the images. Image recognition is designed to enable computers to process large amounts of physical information in place of humans. The image recognition process is divided into information acquisition, preprocessing, feature extraction and selection, classifier design, and classification decision. Information acquisition refers to the conversion of information, such as light or sound into electrical information, through sensors. Preprocessing refers to operations such as denoising, smoothing, and transforming within image processing to enhance an image's most important features. Feature extraction and selection refers to the process of extracting features from an image and selecting useful ones for the purpose of pattern recognition. Feature extraction and selection is one of the most critical techniques in image recognition. Classifier design involves formulating a set of training-based recognition rules for feature classification, realizing high image recognition efficiency. Classification decision involves assigning recognized objects to specific classes within the feature space, thus helping determine the exact class to which the studied objects belong.

Today, image recognition is already being applied in many fields such as public security, biology, manufacturing, agriculture, transportation, and healthcare. Examples include facial recognition and fingerprint recognition in public security; seed recognition and food quality detection in agriculture; license plate recognition in transportation; electrocardiograph recognition in healthcare; unmanned shelves, smart retail cabinets, and mobile payment in unattended retailing.

5.3.4 Video Analysis

Video analysis uses cutting-edge technology to digitally analyze video clips and identify critical events and suspicious activities with improved detection accuracy and classification capabilities. Driven by AI and deep learning, intelligent video software detects and extracts objects from videos, identifies these objects based on trained deep neural networks, and then classifies each object. Following this, intelligent video analysis is enabled, which includes functions such as searching, filtering, alerting, data aggregation, and visualization, for a comprehensive analysis of objects, attributes, behaviors, and events. Figure 5.15 shows the AI video analysis diagram.

Evolving technologies and market needs have made intelligent video analysis more powerful and popular. Intelligent video analysis mainly involves four parts: moving object detection, object tracking, object classification, and behavioral understanding. It has been widely applied to better suit security and civilian needs, including perimeter alert and intrusion detection, object movement direction detection, human behavior analysis, object disappearance/emergence detection, human traffic statistics, vehicle identification, flame detection, and so on.

5.4 Multimodal Technology

Multimodal technology aims to collaboratively process and comprehend multi-source modal information, which comes with a mixture of modalities, including texts, images, speeches, and gestures. Every source or form of information can be referred to as a modality. Different modalities can complement each other, thus providing better capabilities to comprehend and process objects than any one modality can individually. The key techniques of multimodal technology mainly include feature representation, modal fusion, and multi-task learning [8].

According to an IDC survey in 2022, about 94% of data generated globally and nearly 77% of data stored is unstructured data. This means the governance and analysis of multimodal data in enterprises will become a key trend in the future.

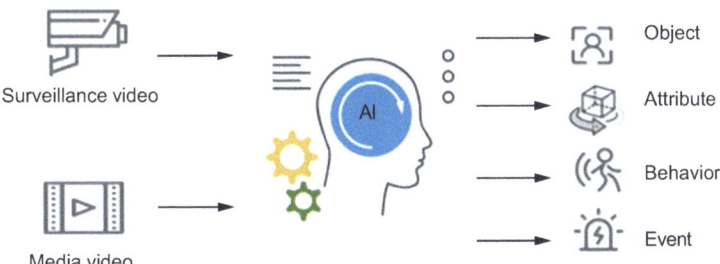

Fig. 5.15 AI video analysis diagram

Currently, the development of multimodal technology is being driven by three powers. The first of these is the evolution of AI model algorithms and large models, which acts as the major technical driving force. Second, digital transformation is accelerating across various industries, meaning the needs for AI solutions are growing rapidly. Third, multimodal data has exploded due to the popularity of applications such as the Internet of Things (IoT), social media, and online shopping; such data is therefore now serving as a key resource for AI development.

As an innovative approach to human-machine interaction, multimodal technology integrates multisource modal information that includes images, speeches, texts and more, and is becoming increasingly prominent. The current progress of multimodal technology has demonstrated its enormous potential in multiple fields such as intelligent customer service, autonomous driving, and medical diagnosis. In these fields, multimodal technology improves system richness and accuracy, optimizes user experience, and boosts the generalization capability of models.

5.4.1 Feature Representation

Feature representations concern how to summarize information from multiple modalities, aiming to solve challenges such as how to combine data of different modalities, how to deal with the different levels of noise contained in different modalities, and how to deal with missing data. Feature representations can be grouped into two categories: joint representations and coordinated representations. Joint representations project the various single-modal information into the same feature space. In contrast, coordinated representations separately project the information of each modality but coordinate the projected information of all modalities with a constraint enforced on the coordinated spaces. The simplest example of joint representations is a concatenation of single-modal features. Beyond that, more complex approaches include neural networks, probabilistic graphical models, and sequence models.

Neural networks are a common approach and have been widely used to represent single-modal features from visual, auditory, and textual sources. This approach is increasingly used in multimodal applications. When neural networks are used to construct a multimodal feature representation, the data of each modality passes through several separate neural network layers, and then passes through one or more hidden layers to project the modality to a joint space. In this way, the joint feature representation is obtained. Next, the joint feature representation either passes through multiple hidden layers or is directly used for final prediction. A Deep Boltzmann Machine (DBM) is the most popular feature representation method based on probabilistic graphical models. Similar to a neural network, a DBM is composed of a stack of RBMs. The advantage of DBM is that it can be trained completely unsupervised. Furthermore, DBM can effectively handle missing data. Its disadvantage lies in enormous computation costs. Sequence models are primarily used for variable-length sequences, such as sentences or video/audio streams.

5.4 Multimodal Technology

Sequence models mainly use RNNs and their variants, such as LSTM networks. In early research, RNNs are used to construct multimodal feature representations, which are then applied to Audiovisual Speech Recognition (AVSR) for emotion recognition and human behavior analysis.

In coordinated representations, individual modalities are projected into separate but coordinated spaces and the projection is independent for each modality, with a constraint enforced on these coordinated spaces to bring them into a multimodal space. Coordinated representations mainly use similarity models and structured coordinated space models. Similarity models aim to minimize the distance between different modalities in a coordinated space. For example, a similarity model is designed to make the distance between the word "vehicle" and the vehicle image features less than the distance between the word "aircraft" and the vehicle image features. In contrast, a structured coordinated space model enforces additional constraints on the basis of similarities between modalities. Such constraints vary depending on tasks.

5.4.2 Modality Fusion

Modality fusion is an integration process where the information of different unimodal data (such as images, texts, and audios) extracted from a range of sensors or data sources is integrated into a single multimodal representation. Modality fusion is used for task classification or regression, aiming to improve the accuracy and efficiency of tasks. The modality fusion methods can be roughly divided into two categories: model-independent fusion methods and model-based fusion methods.

Model-independent fusion methods can be classified into three categories: early fusion, late fusion, and hybrid fusion. An early fusion method merges the unimodal features after initial extraction. The most common application of early fusion is to simply concatenate individual features into a joint representation. An early fusion method exploits the correlations and interactions between the low-level features of individual modalities, and the training process of early fusion is easier as only single-model training is needed. In contrast, in a late fusion method, a model is separately trained for each modality, after which all of the trained modality-specific models are combined into one with a fusion mechanism. Common late fusion methods include the averaging method, voting method, weighting method based on channel noise and signal variance, trained fusion model, and so on. A late fusion method performs modality-specific model training and thus brings about better modeling for different unimodal data, achieving higher flexibility. In addition, model training with a late fusion method is generally robust against unimodal data missing. Hybrid fusion combines the advantages of both early and late fusion methods and, further, comes with higher training difficulty. In deep learning, hybrid fusion is most typically used, as different models exhibit high flexibility and uncertainty.

Model-related fusion methods are designed to achieve multimodal fusion from the perspective of implementations and models. There are three common methods: multi-kernel learning, image model, and neural network. The multi-kernel learning method enables SVMs to use different kernels that are specific to the forms or views of data, so that the optimal kernel function can be found for each modality. The image model method mainly performs image segmentation, stitching, and prediction to fuse the shallow or deep layers of a model, thereby achieving the ultimate fusion of modalities. The advantage of this method lies in the easy utilization of the spatial and temporal structures of data and the integration of expert knowledge into models, enhancing their interpretability. The neural network method has been heavily used in multimodal tasks. By piecing together models, the neural network method can achieve better performance than the preceding two methods. Furthermore, neural networks perform well in image captioning tasks and can learn autonomously from large amounts of data. However, the interpretability becomes challenging as network modalities increase.

Modality fusion technology has a wide range of application fields, including computer vision, NLP, and intelligent interactive systems. Taking motion detection assistance as an example, modality fusion can improve the accuracy of recognition and understanding of a user's status and behavior by utilizing the advantages of different information sources, thus providing the user with more accurate motion guidance and evaluation. In addition, by integrating multiple information sources, the system can gain a more comprehensive understanding of the user's individual needs and preferences, thus providing the user with more personalized and accurate services and suggestions.

References

1. YANG X J, ZHANG F D, HU C B. Review of Machine Learning Research [J] (in Chinese). Science & Technology, Economy, and Market, 2021(10): 40–42.
2. IDC. China AI Software Market Shares, 2022 [R] (in Chinese). 2022.
3. iResearch. AI-related Report: 2022 China Artificial Intelligence Industry Research Report [R] (in Chinese). 2022.
4. WANG D. Analysis and Research of Natural Language Processing Technology [J] (in Chinese). Science and Technology Innovation Herald, 2020(7): 141–142.
5. CCID Consulting. 2022-2023 China NLP Market Research Annual Report [R] (in Chinese). 2023.
6. SONG Y L. Research on Computer Vision Technology and Application [J] (in Chinese). Telecom World, 2021, 28(8): 195–196.
7. MA M. On the Development and Application of Artificial Intelligence Technology [J] (in Chinese). Technology Innovation and Application, 2023, 13(8): 173–176.
8. IDC. China Multimodal Technology and Application Scenario Trend Outlook [R] (in Chinese). 2023.

Chapter 6
Significant Developments in AI

Artificial intelligence (AI) has entered a new phase of development after decades of evolution. With the aid of deep learning (DL), large-scale computing, and big data, AI is becoming more popular, integrated, and intelligent. It has ultimate potential, with far-reaching impacts on economic and social development.

6.1 Horizontal Expansion of the AI Industry

6.1.1 AI Industry Overview

Fueled by technological advancements, market demand, and policy support, the AI industry has experienced steady growth globally and played a vital role in improving efficiency, optimizing decision-making, providing personalized services, and boosting economic growth. Figure 6.1 shows the AI industry chain, which consists of three layers: base layer, technology layer, and application layer. The base and technology layers provide the technical computing platforms, resources, and algorithms that are essential for developing the application layer.

The base layer, used for data collection and computation, is the foundation for AI development. Specifically, the base layer comprises basic software/hardware platforms (such as intelligent chips, intelligent software, servers, and storage devices) and supporting technologies and products (such as cloud and edge computing, Internet of Things (IoT), big data, and smart sensors). For example, smart sensors and big data are responsible for collecting data, while intelligent chips and cloud computing perform computations.

The technology layer is the core of AI industry development. It performs data mining, learning, and intelligent processing to interconnect the base and application layers. This layer involves general-purpose technologies (such as machine learning (ML), knowledge graph, brain-like intelligent computing, frameworks, and

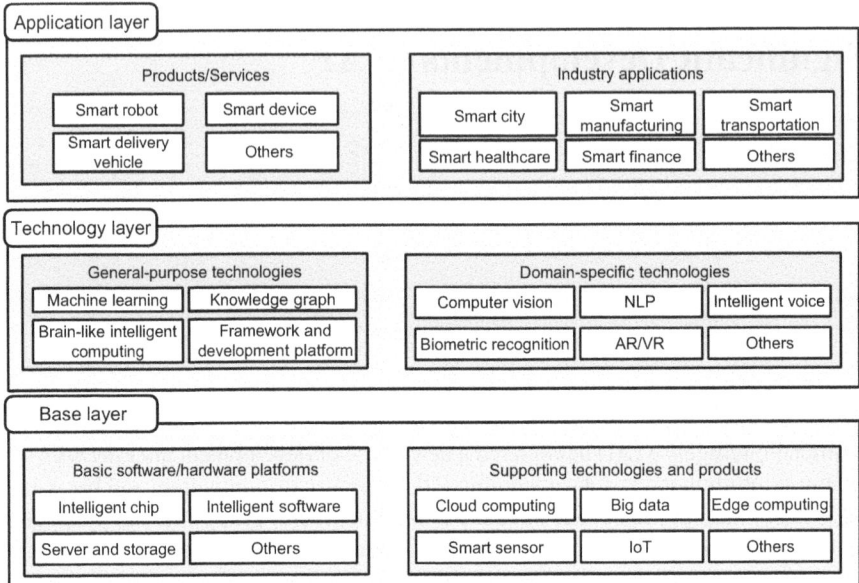

Fig. 6.1 AI industry chain

development platforms) and domain-specific technologies (such as computer vision, natural language processing (NLP), intelligent voice, and biometric recognition). Among these, computer vision is the most prominent field of technical development for AI enterprises, as it is a core technology for AI.

The application layer builds upon the base and technology layers to commercialize AI technologies and integrate them with various industries. It involves products or services (such as smart robots, smart devices, and smart delivery vehicles) and industry applications (such as smart city, smart manufacturing, smart transportation, smart healthcare, and smart finance).

6.1.2 AI Industry Trends

The AI industry is booming with a global market revenue of USD513.2 billion in 2023, marking a year-on-year (YoY) growth of 20.7%, as shown in Fig. 6.2. This is projected to hit USD894.1 billion by 2026. AI software remains the dominant force, accounting for almost 90% of the market revenue. In 2023, the AI software market reached USD448.8 billion (20.4% YoY growth), with the Americas region recorded as the largest market share at USD288.6 billion or 64.3%; by contrast, the Asia-Pacific region has a smaller market size, reaching only USD55 billion [1].

According to research, the US leads the world in production of core AI technologies such as chips and frameworks, with NVIDIA in particular dominating the

6.1 Horizontal Expansion of the AI Industry

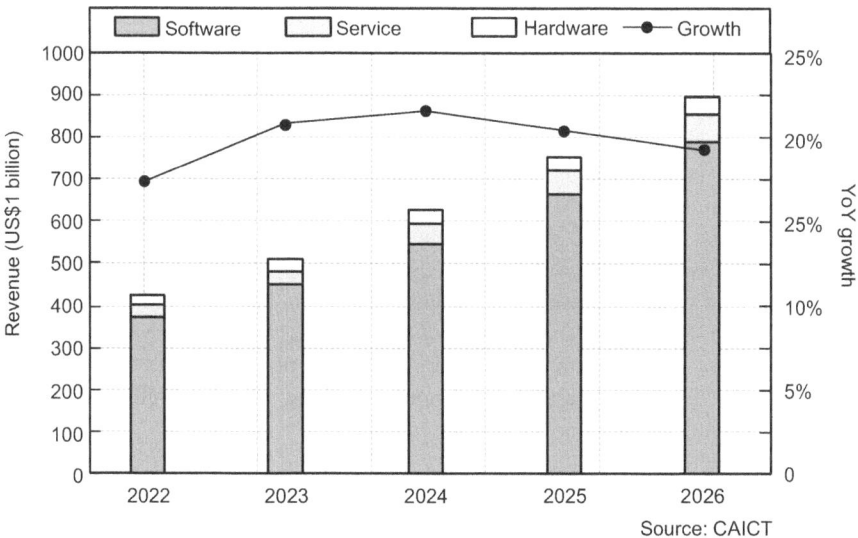

Fig. 6.2 Market revenue and growth of the global AI industry

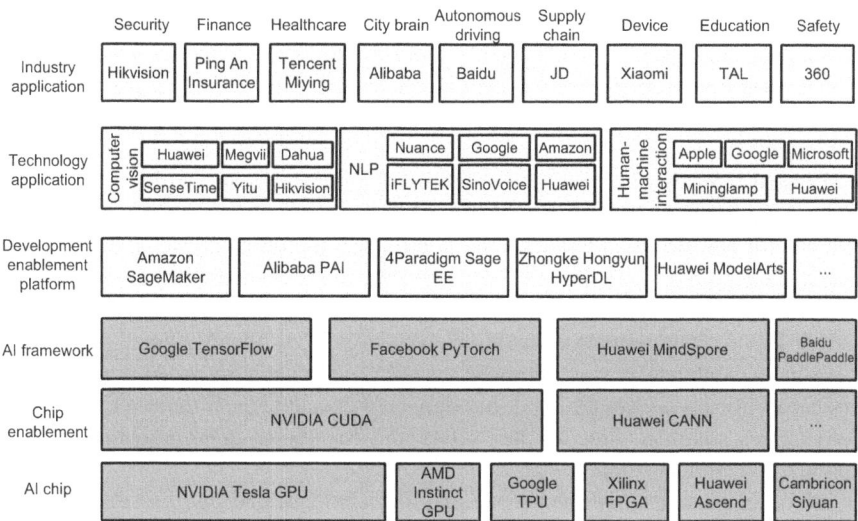

Fig. 6.3 Key factors and vendors in the AI industry

graphics processing unit (GPU) chip market. The US has a strong foothold in the AI industry, but this dominance is being challenged by intense competition from China. Figure 6.3 shows the key factors and vendors in the AI industry. The chip industry chain in China is maturing, where innovation is built on collaboration. For example, Huawei's Ascend AI chips have already adapted to over 100 foundation models in China and are gradually replacing NVIDIA's AI chips. Huawei's Ascend AI chips now provide computing power that rivals NVIDIA's high-end chip A100 and are helping to establish China's computing power [2].

China is at the forefront of the world's boom in AI applications, with a large market size and high penetration rate in sectors such as security, manufacturing, finance, retail, and education. Despite these successes, there is still significant room for expansion in government, healthcare, agriculture, and entertainment sectors where AI is not mature. AI applications include smart robots, smart driving, unmanned aerial vehicles (UAVs), augmented reality (AR), virtual reality (VR), big data and data services, as well as various vertical applications that incorporate AI. By the end of 2023, the core AI industry in China has reached a remarkable scale of CNY578.7 billion, supported by a thriving ecosystem of 4482 enterprises. The AI industry chain covers chips, algorithms, data, platforms, and applications, both upstream and downstream, continuously making breakthroughs in various segments.

Industry trends indicate the AI industry is expanding horizontally, with the following overall changes:

Diverse and custom computing requirements are defining new specialized computing chips. For example, the NVIDIA BlueField-3 data processing unit (DPU) provides robust computing and a broad range of programmable acceleration engines in the I/O path, to enable cloud-native supercomputing, multi-tenancy, and security accelerations with software-defined hardware-accelerated information technology (IT) infrastructures. Also, the NVIDIA ConnectX-6 Dx offloads open vSwitch data path forwarding from the host's central processing unit (CPU) to the adapter's application-specific integrated circuit (ASIC), enabling extreme performance and scalability.

Vertical industry platforms and specialized applications are on the rise. This is best exemplified in healthcare. As the COVID-19 pandemic has increased the demand for new drugs and policies like centralized procurement and medical insurance have resulted in declining benefits, pharmaceutical enterprises are turning to AI to accelerate the research and development (R&D) of new drugs and reduce the risk of failure. The biotech company Galixir uses AI to identify small molecular preclinical candidates for autoimmune diseases, demonstrating its AI drug discovery capabilities in a closed loop. It has delivered excellent performance in pharmacodynamics, pharmacokinetics, and safety and has shown great potential in vitro and vivo preclinical studies.

AI development tools are becoming more sophisticated and can support the entire lifecycle of data forwarding and model development. In fact, the field is so competitive that the AI development tool category was added to the 2022 CB Insights AI 100 list. Nearly one-third of enterprises on the list are developing platforms and other tools to support management in each phase of the AI lifecycle, from data annotation and model development to model monitoring. This is making AI development more accessible to a broader range of businesses.

6.2 AI Chip Iteration for Underlying Technologies

In the AI industry, computing power serves as the foundation for data and algorithms, and it is primarily provided by various computing chips. AI chips are specifically designed to accelerate AI computations, whereas the "CPU + X" heterogeneous computing mode significantly enhances the computing efficiency of AI applications. X refers to AI chips, such as GPUs, field-programmable gate arrays (FPGAs), ASICs, and brain-like chips. Table 6.1 outlines the differences between various chip types, and Fig. 6.4 displays the major vendors of AI chips worldwide.

According to Gartner, the global market size for AI chips reached USD53.4 billion in 2023, an increase of 20.9% over 2022, and is forecast to hit USD67.1 billion (25.6% increase) by 2024. AI chips include GPUs, FPGAs, and ASICs such as video processing units (VPUs) and tensor processing units (TPUs). By 2027, AI chips revenue is expected to be more than double the 2023 market size, reaching USD119.4 billion. With the growing demand for AI chips in areas like intelligent security, unmanned driving, smartphones, smart retail, and smart robots, the number of global AI chips is increasing year by year. Statistics show the global count of AI chips is 14.33 million in 2022 (18.2% YoY growth) and 16.4 million in 2023 (14.4% YoY growth).

GPUs currently dominate the global AI chip market and are primarily used in computing and electronic devices such as data centers, computers, and servers. By 2023, the rapid development of large AI models caused GPU prices to skyrocket but contributed to AI chip revenue growth, including both GPUs and FPGAs. Statistics indicate the price of NVIDIA H100 increased by over 20% in H2 2023. It is projected that AI chip revenue growth will decrease to about 15% in 2024 and then remain stable.

The AI chip landscape is highly concentrated, dominated by European and American vendors like NVIDIA, AMD, Intel, and Google. NVIDIA is the dominant player in the GPU market, holding an 80% global market share, whereas AMD and Intel hold the majority of the remaining market share [3]. To break the monopoly in general-purpose AI chips, cloud service providers such as Google, Amazon Web Services (AWS), and Microsoft began to develop special-purpose chips like ASICs. According to Liftr Insights, in 2022, NVIDIA dominated the data center AI accelerator market with an 82% market share. Amazon and Xilinx held 8% and 4% market shares, respectively, while AMD, Intel, and Google each held a 2% share (see Fig. 6.5).

China has put a huge emphasis on the AI chip industry and released a series of supportive policies to stimulate its growth and success. These are briefly outlined in Table 6.2.

The explosive growth of China's AI chip market is showing significant influence globally. According to Deloitte, China's AI chip market was valued at CNY85 billion in 2022 and CNY120.6 billion in 2023, with a compound annual growth rate (CAGR) of 80% from 2018 to 2023 (see Fig. 6.6).

Table 6.1 Comparison of different chip types

Technical architecture	Custom design	Editability	Computing power	Price	Benefit	Drawback	Target use
GPU	General-purpose	Uneditable	Medium	High	It is widely used and well suited for large-scale parallel computing, with mature design and manufacturing processes	Its parallel computing cannot be fully utilized for inference tasks	Advanced and complex algorithms and general-purpose AI platforms
FPGA	Semi-custom	Easy to edit	High	Medium	Its chip architecture can be flexibly programed to adapt to algorithm iteration, resulting in high mean performance, low power consumption, and short development time	It is expensive for mass production, has limited peak computing capability, and involves complex hardware programming	Various specific industries
ASIC	Full-custom	Hard to edit	High	Low	It uses fixed algorithms to deliver superior performance and energy efficiency, resulting in high mean performance, low power consumption, and small size. It is the most cost-effective for mass production	It involves a substantial upfront investment, a long R&D phase, and high technical risks	Professional intelligent algorithm software tailored for individual cases
Brain-like chip	Brain-simulated	Uneditable	High	–	It has the lowest power consumption, high communication efficiency, and strong cognitive capability	It is not mature.	Various specific industries

6.2 AI Chip Iteration for Underlying Technologies

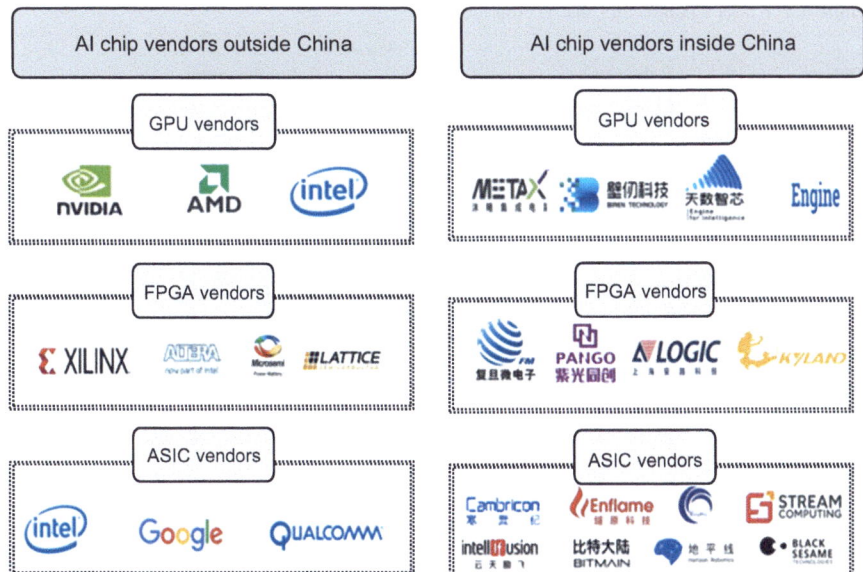

Fig. 6.4 Major vendors of AI chips worldwide

Fig. 6.5 US data center AI chip market share in 2022

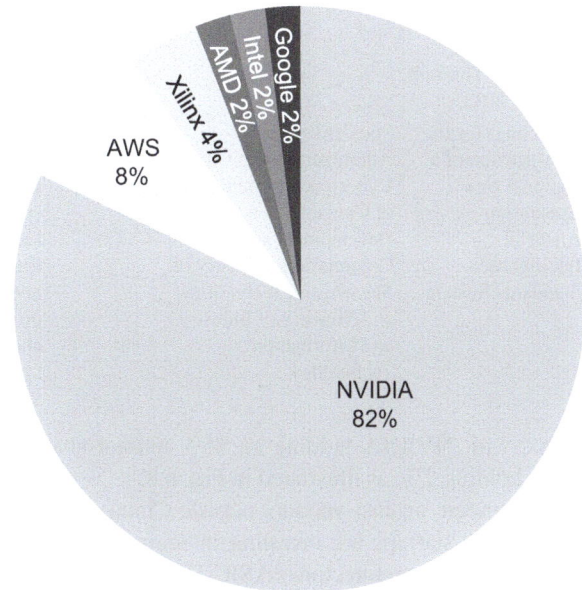

The Chinese market is primarily dominated by GPUs, which accounts for 86% of the market share in 2022, followed by neural processing units (NPUs) (12%), and ASICs (2%), as illustrated in Fig. 6.7. This market currently relies on imported AI chips. In 2022, approximately 1.09 million AI accelerator cards were delivered in

Table 6.2 China's policies for the AI chip industry

Policy	Released by	Released in	Related content
14th Five-Year Plan for Digital Economy Development	State Council of China	2022	Focus on strategic and future-oriented fields such as sensors, quantum information, network communications, integrated circuits, critical software, big data, AI, blockchain, and new materials, leverage China's strengths by pooling resources in the new nationwide system and ultra-large market, to improve R&D in digital technologies
14th Five-Year Plan for National Health	State Council of China	2022	Promote emerging IT elements such as AI chips, big data, 5G, blockchain, and IoT to enable intelligent healthcare, real-time health monitoring and evaluation, disease warning, and chronic disease screening
Outline of the 14th Five-Year Plan for Economic and Social Development and Long-Range Objectives Through the Year 2035	Fourth session of 13th National People's Congress	2021	The AI industry in China will focus on developing open-source algorithm platforms, innovating in key fields such as learning, inference, decision-making, and graphics, and concentrating on high-end chips during the 14th Five-Year Plan period
Guidelines for the Construction of a National New Generation Artificial Intelligence Standards System	Standardization Administration of China, Cyberspace Administration of China, National Development and Reform Commission, Ministry of Science and Technology, and Ministry of Industry and Information Technology	2020	By 2023, establish preliminary AI standards, prioritize standards for data, algorithms, systems, and services, while focusing on key sectors such as manufacturing, transportation, finance, security, home, elderly care, environmental protection, education, healthcare, and justice

China, with NVIDIA holding an 85% market share, Huawei holding 10%, and Baidu holding 2%, as illustrated in Fig. 6.8.

To compete against vendors outside China, Chinese Internet service providers and AI chip startups are investing in segmented product architectures like ASIC domain-specific architecture (ASIC-DSA) and general-purpose GPU (GPGPU). These innovations are key to the development strategy of "inference before training" and supported by initiatives like the Eastern Data and Western Computing, pushes for intelligent computing centers and next-gen data centers, as well as in-house development and investments by Internet service providers. In this strategy, ASIC-DSA-based AI chips will replace GPUs on the inference side thanks to their

6.2 AI Chip Iteration for Underlying Technologies

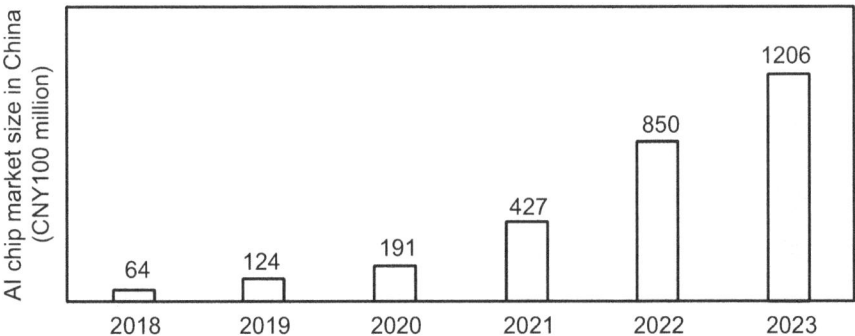

Fig. 6.6 AI chip market size in China

Fig. 6.7 Product share in China's AI chip market

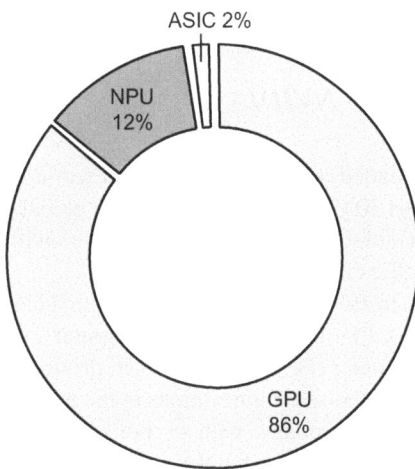

Fig. 6.8 Delivery share of AI chip vendors in China

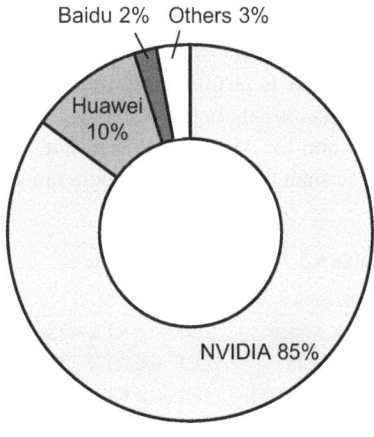

customizable ASICs and programmable DSA software that enable extreme performance for a wide range of workloads [4].

Internet service providers are leveraging focused R&D investment, strong technical skills, and internal testing environments to lead national product developments. Cloud AI chips represented by Baidu Kunlun and those from Huawei HiSilicon have been successfully integrated in tens of thousands of products, both for external and internal solutions. Chinese ASIC startups who have completed product iteration are forming partnerships with Internet short video platforms, pan-security vendors, or automobile enterprises, toward the goal of product verification, small-scale sales, or large-scale application. In addition, Chinese GPGPU vendors have gradually released their products throughout 2023. In general, AI chip vendors in China have launched their products and will focus on system clusters and software ecosystems, while continuously enhancing an independent and controllable base [5].

6.2.1 NVIDIA

Founded in 1993, NVIDIA is a world-renowned graphics card company. Over the past 30 years, it has grown into a global giant in the AI chip industry, designing and manufacturing computer processors with a market capitalization hitting trillions of dollars in 2023.

In 1999, NVIDIA became the first chip company to introduce GPUs to the world. Its GPU model redefined computer graphics, fueling the growth of the personal computer (PC) gaming market, driving the advancement of modern AI, and significantly boosting innovations in the metaverse. The company is now a full-stack computing company, with its portfolio expanded to cover CPUs, GPUs, and DPUs. Table 6.3 lists NVIDIA's main products catering to markets such as data center, gaming, professional visualization, and automotive. Their major customers include multinational companies like Microsoft, Google, Amazon, and Alibaba.

NVIDIA has four major business lines, with data center and gaming lines the primary drivers of growth. Its gaming business has been in gradual decline since 2022, due to terminal requirements. By contrast, the company's data center business has become its biggest revenue line. Experiencing excellent growth following high demand for AI computing power, the data center business has generated more revenue than the gaming business since the second quarter of 2023.

Table 6.3 NVIDIA's main products

Data center	Gaming	Professional visualization	Automotive
DGX system	GeForce RTX 40 series	Quadro series	DRIVE AGX series
Grace CPU	GeForce RTX 30 series	RTX series	Orin series
BlueField DPU	GeForce RTX 20 series	Quadro virtual	NVIDIA DRIVE
Hopper GPU	GeForce GTX 16 series	Workstation	–

6.2 AI Chip Iteration for Underlying Technologies

Table 6.4 provides an overview of the company's data center product system, covering both hardware and software. This system helps to establish NVIDIA's robust and competitive moat in the AI sector with a powerful GPU + CUDA software ecosystem. (CUDA stands for Compute Unified Device Architecture.)

In terms of hardware, NVIDIA's data center business focuses on CPUs, GPUs, and DPUs. It has developed three main product types using Grace CPU, BlueField DPU, and Hopper GPU architectures. The Hopper architecture advances the Tensor Core technology with the Transformer Engine, which can apply mixed FP8 and FP16 precisions to dramatically accelerate AI calculations for transformers. It also triples the floating-point operations per second (FLOPS) for TF32, FP64, FP16, and INT8 precisions over the prior generation. Then at COMPUTEX 2023, NVIDIA launched the DGX GH200 AI Supercomputer that empowers generative AI, recommender systems, and data analytics. The new architecture provides higher bandwidth than its predecessor, 5 times higher interconnect power efficiency than its competitors, and significantly larger GPU memory than previous generations, as shown in Fig. 6.9. The DGX GH200 provides nearly 500 times more memory than a single DGX A100 with 320 GB of memory, for the shared-memory-based GPU programming model that uses NVLink.

In terms of software, NVIDIA has developed a CUDA-centered software development platform and ecosystem. This enables developers to write programs that run on CUDA using languages such as C, C++, and Fortran, and use GPU parallel computing to accelerate complex computations. Since 2006, NVIDIA has been a strong supporter of the CUDA system in the AI industry, investing USD500 million in R&D each year despite having an annual revenue of only USD3 billion. Available for free for US universities and research institutions, CUDA has been continuously updated to rapidly advance AI and general-purpose computing. This sets NVIDIA apart from other GPU vendors who cannot match their superb architecture, encapsulation technology, and driver optimization capabilities. CUDA currently works with NVIDIA Tesla GPUs, creating significant barriers for other enterprises to break into this market in the short term.

6.2.2 AMD

Founded in 1969, AMD is a globally renowned semiconductor company. The company initially focused on its efforts on CPUs but, through continuous mergers and acquisitions, has since expanded its offerings to establish a complete chip layout of CPUs, GPUs, DPUs, and FPGAs. Now, AMD competes with Intel in the CPU market and NVIDIA in the GPU market and holds the second-largest market share for both CPUs and GPUs worldwide.

AMD is involved in the gaming, client, data center, and embedded segments, which contributed 29%, 26%, 25%, and 20% to the company's 2022 revenue, respectively. For the data center segment, it provides enterprise-grade EPYC server processors for cloud computing and high-performance computing (HPC), Instinct

Table 6.4 NVIDIA's hardware and software products

Hardware product		Software product
CPU	The Grace CPU is built on TSMC's 4 N process and features 72 Arm v9.0 cores. It uses an instruction set architecture (ISA) and a self-developed CPU core Performance: 2.3× faster for microservices and 2× faster in memory-intensive data processing than ×86 CPUs Mass production: H2 2023	CUDA was launched in 2006 and is a parallel computing platform and programming model for general computing on GPUs. It expands the use of GPUs beyond 3G gaming and image rendering to include compute-intensive applications such as scientific computing, big data processing, and ML
GPU	H100: TSMC's 4 N process (5 nm), 80 billion transistors, 1513/1979 TOPS (3× to 6× better than A100), 128 Gbit/s PCIe or 400/900 Gbit/s NVLink, 80 GB memory H800 (tailored to the Chinese market): 5 nm process, 1513/1979 TOPS, 128 Gbit/s PCIe or 450 Gbit/s NVLink, 80 GB memory A100: 7 nm process, 624 TOPS, 64 Gbit/s PCIe or 600 Gbit/s NVLink, 40/80 GB memory A800 (tailored to the Chinese market): 7 nm process, 624 TOPS, 64 Gbit/s PCIe or 400 Gbit/s NVLink, 40/80 GB memory V100: 12 nm process, 112/125/130 TOPS, 32 Gbit/s PCIe or 300 Gbit/s NVLink, 16/32 GB memory	CUDA is developer-friendly: (1) It is easy to install and supports many programming languages such as C, C++, Fortran, Java, and Python (2) It is highly compatible and can run on various operating systems (OSs) such as Windows, Linux, and MacOS (3) It is free of charge CUDA offers a wealth of development resources: (1) It has a strong community of professional developers and experts who provide support to other CUDA developers by sharing their experiences and answering questions (2) It offers a vast collection of code libraries that support various computing applications CUDA extensions increase the variety of users: (1) CUDA introduces university courses to expand the reach and application of CUDA from the ground up (2) CUDA establishes certification programs, research centers, and teaching centers (3) CUDA forms a robust partner network in various fields such as DL, image and NLP, foundation models, and scientific computing (including weather simulation, fluid dynamics, molecular dynamics, quantum chemistry, and astrophysics simulation) DOCA was launched in 2021 and is a software development platform that runs on DPUs. It enables high-performance, software-defined, and cloud-native DPU-accelerated services, which can be used to program the data center infrastructure and optimize the acceleration performance of data centers. DOCA is to DPUs what CUDA is to GPUs
DPU	DPUs are used to improve the efficiency of data infrastructure and offload workloads from CPUs, which are common bottlenecks due to low processing efficiency or processing failures BlueField-3: 400 Gbit/s, 32 GB DDR5 memory, 16 Arm A78 CPU cores, 10× the accelerated computing power and 4× the acceleration for cryptography of the previous generation	
Grace Hopper Superchip	The Grace Hopper Superchip combines the 72-core Grace CPU with the Hopper 100 GPU using the NVLink Switch technology. It features 96 GB of HBM3, 512 GB of LPDDR5X, and 200 billion transistors Performance: Up to 546 GB/s of CPU memory bandwidth, 3000 GB/s of GPU memory bandwidth, 900 GB/s of GPU-CPU bidirectional bandwidth, 900 GB/s of GPU-GPU bidirectional bandwidth	
DGX GH200 Supercomputer	The DGX GH200 Supercomputer combines 256 GH200 superchips and 144 TB of shared memory into one unit, providing 1 exaflop of performance (one quintillion FLOPS). Mass production: End of 2023	

6.2 AI Chip Iteration for Underlying Technologies

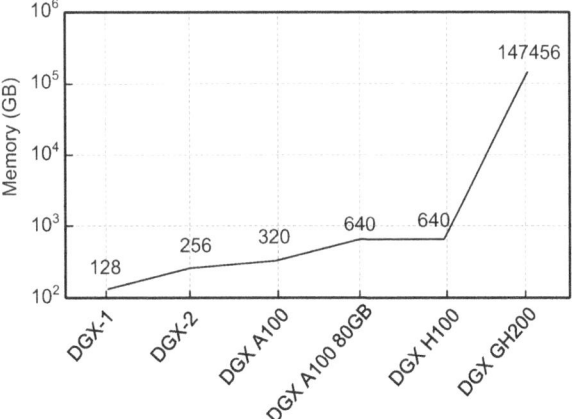

Fig. 6.9 GPU memory comparison

Fig. 6.10 Primary buyers of AMD Instinct MI300X

MI series GPU accelerators for HPC and AI, Xilinx AI, and Pensando DPUs. For the gaming segment, it provides semi-custom system-on-a-chip (SoC) solutions for game vendors, consumer-grade Radeon series graphics cards, and Radeon PRO series graphics cards for workstations. For the client segment, it provides Ryzen and Athlon processors for personal desktops and laptops, and Threadripper PRO and Ryzen PRO processors for workstations. For the embedded segment, it provides Ryzen and EPYC embedded processors, as well as Xilinx Alveo, Versal, and Zynq series products for healthcare, industrial, robotics, automotive, and computer vision fields, among others.

AI is a strategic priority for AMD, evident with the launch of the MI300 series accelerators in December 2023, which marked a milestone in its AI evolution. The MI300 series accelerators include MI300X and MI300A. The former is an advanced graphics processor designed for AI computing, while the latter combines graphics processing with a standard CPU for AI and scientific research purposes. The MI300X accelerators have been adopted by industry giants like Meta, Microsoft, and Oracle, as well as server providers like Dell, HP, Lenovo, and Supermicro (Fig. 6.10). Published results show that the MI300X offers up to nine times the AI computing power with different floating-point precisions and 2.4 times the HPC workload performance compared to NVIDIA's H100 SXM. Table 6.5 compares the major GPU products of AMD and NVIDIA.

Table 6.5 Comparison between the major GPU products of AMD and NVIDIA

	AMD			NVIDIA	
Product name	MI250X	MI300A	MI300X	H100 SXM	H200 SXM
Released	Nov 2021	Dec 2023	Dec 2023	Mar 2022	Nov 2023
AI computing power (peak TFLOPS)	INT8: 383 TOPS FP16: 383 BFLOAT16: 383	FP8: 1961.2 INT8: 1961.2 TOPS FP16: 980.6 BFLOAT16: 980.6 TF32 (Matrix): 490.3	FP8: 2614.9 INT8: 2614.9 TOPS FP16: 1307.4 BFLOAT16: 1307.4 TF32 (Matrix): 653.7	FP8: 1978.9 INT8: 1978.9 TOPS FP16: 989.4 BFLOAT16: 989.4 TF32 (Matrix): 494.7	FP8: 1978.9 INT8: 1978.9 TOPS FP16: 989.4 BFLOAT16: 989.4 TF32 (Matrix): 494.7
Maximum clock frequency (GHz)	1.7	2.1	2.1	1.98	1.98
Manufacturing process	TSMC 6 nm FinFET	TSMC 5 nm/6 nm FinFET	TSMC 5 nm/6 nm FinFET	TSMC 4 nm	TSMC 4 nm
Chip size (mm^2)	724	1017	1017	814	
Number of transistors (one billion)	58.2	146	153	80	80
Memory size (GB)	128 HBM2e	128 HBM2e	192 HBM2e	80 HBM2e	141 HBM2e
Memory bandwidth (TB/s)	3.3	5.3	5.3	3.3	4.8
Interconnect (Gbit/s)	100	≈800	896	900 (NVLink) 125 (PCIe Gen5)	900 (NVLink) 125 (PCIe Gen5)
Thermal design power (TDP) (W)	500	550–760	750	700	700
Stream processors	14,080	14,592	19,456	16,896	16,896
Texture mapping units	880	880	880	528	528
GPU architecture	CDNA 2	CDNA 3	CDNA 3	Hopper	Hopper

6.2.3 Intel

Intel has been a dominant player in the CPU market, with a staggering 90% market share in previous years, but the CPU market witnessed a steady decline following the evolution of GPUs and other alternative processors. To transform its brand, Intel acquired Altera, an FPGA manufacturer, and later Nervana, which helped fill gaps in its hardware platform products with talented personnel and technology and offer a springboard to develop next-gen AI chips.

The company continues to expand its product lines and invest in its own AI chip ecosystem, cumulating in its first cloud AI chip Nervana NNP-I in 2019, and then later the Gaudi 3 chip for generative AI software in December 2023. Once in mass production, Gaudi 3 will be in competition with NVIDIA's H100 and AMD's MI300X, giving Intel a foothold to enter and even dominate the AI chip market.

6.2.4 Huawei HiSilicon

Since Huawei announced its AI chip strategy at HUAWEI CONNECT 2018, the company has become a leading AI chip enterprise in China. Its flagship Ascend series chips are its secret weapon to enter all spaces from edge computing to HPC. In November 2018, Huawei unveiled its first powerful AI chip designed for edge computing—Ascend 310—which runs 8 teraFLOPS (TFLOPS) at FP16 and can effortlessly perform tasks like mobile device inference. This model was later leapfrogged by the Ascend 910 in 2019, an AI chip capable of 320 TFLOPS at FP16 and designed for cloud AI training. Then in 2023, Huawei launched the Ascend 910B chip, which uses advanced manufacturing processes and features higher performance and lower power consumption than previous models. Table 6.6 compares the Huawei Ascend series against NVIDIA A100 and H100 GPUs, indicating that the Ascend 910 is a strong competitor to NVIDIA A100, with comparable computing power.

6.2.5 Cambricon

Cambricon was founded in 2016 and went public in 2020. The majority of the company's R&D team are from the Chinese Academy of Sciences, including the CEO, Chen Tianshi, who was previously a researcher at the Institute of Computing Technology. Cambricon is dedicated to the R&D and technological innovation of AI chip products, with a focus on developing core processor chips for cloud servers, edge computing devices, and terminal devices. It offers a range of products, including cloud smart chips and acceleration cards, training products, edge smart chips and acceleration cards, terminal intelligent processor IP products, and software development platforms (see Table 6.7).

Cambricon is currently focusing on its cloud product line, specifically the Siyuan series products. The Siyuan 370 is its third-generation cloud product, which uses the 7 nm process and is its first AI chip to incorporate Chiplet technology, which enables a maximum computing power of 256 trillion operations per second (TOPS). Additionally, mass production for the new-generation Siyuan 590 is scheduled to begin in the first half of 2024. Targeted at cloud-based intelligent training, the

Table 6.6 Comparison between the Huawei Ascend series processors and NVIDIA GPUs

	Ascend 310	Ascend 910	Ascend 910B	A100 80GB PCIe	A100 80GB SXM	H100 PCIe	H100 SXM
Processor architecture	Da Vinci	Da Vinci	Da Vinci	Ampere	Ampere	Hopper	Hopper
INT8 (TOPS)	16	640	640	624/1248[a]	624/1248[a]	1513/3026[a]	1979/3958[a]
FP16 (TFLOPS)	8	320	376	312/624[a]	312/624[a]	756/1513[a]	989/1979[a]
Power consumption (W)	8	310	400	300	400	300–350	700
Process (nm)	12FFC	7	7	7	7	4	4
Target use	Inference	Inference and training	Inference and training	Inference and training	Inference and training	Inference and training	Inference and training

[a] Indicates that sparsification is used

Table 6.7 Main Cambricon products

Product line	Product type	Main product	Released
Cloud	Cloud smart chip and acceleration card	Siyuan 100 (MLU100) chip and cloud smart acceleration card	2018
Cloud	Cloud smart chip and acceleration card	Siyuan 270 (MLU270) chip and cloud smart acceleration card	2019
		Siyuan 290 (MLU290) chip and cloud smart acceleration card	2020
		Siyuan 370 (MLU370) chip and cloud smart acceleration card	2021–2022
	Training	Xuansi 1000 smart accelerator	2020
		Xuansi 1001 smart accelerator	2022
Edge	Edge smart chip and acceleration card	Siyuan 220 (MLU220) chip and edge smart acceleration card	2019
IP licensing and software	Terminal intelligent processor IP	Cambricon 1A processor	2016
		Cambricon 1H processor	2017
		Cambricon 1 M processor	2018
	Basic system software platform	Cambricon basic software development platform (applicable to all Cambricon chips and processors)	Continuous R&D to adapt to new chips

Siyuan 590 is expected to partially take market space from NVIDIA A100 in foundation model market for training and inference.

Cambricon's cloud products have been adopted by top Internet customers like Alibaba Cloud, engaged in detailed technical exchanges with top banks and other financial customers, and received recognition from leading server vendors. The rise of large AI models like ChatGPT is driving demand for higher levels of AI computing power, while the supply of AI chips is becoming more localized. As a leading AI chip company in China, Cambricon is perfectly placed to grow in the global market space, with advantages as a first-mover in product R&D, market expansion, and customer engagement.

6.3 AI Cloud Platforms for Innovative Services

AI cloud platforms integrate end-to-end (E2E) development and supporting tools designed to boost AI productivity. These platforms provide technical services and intelligent algorithms to improve and streamline AI model development, including data processing, algorithm development, model training, model management, and deployment inference [6].

AI platforms have become one of the most important ways to develop new applications and add value to existing E2E solutions. This evolution is one based on differentiated, scenario-specific demands, where AI platforms are tailored to vertical

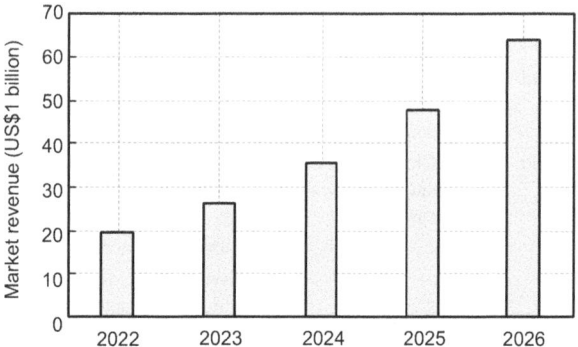

Fig. 6.11 Global AI platform software market revenue

industries like healthcare, transportation, and city management, for applications such as auxiliary medical diagnosis, lesion-directed screening, high-precision positioning, environmental sensing, and virtual simulation. One example is the CloudWalk human-machine collaborative platform. It uses high-precision algorithms to support functions like vehicle and abnormal behavior analysis for large-scale applications such as security management and port ship detection. Another option is the YITU city platform that runs smart applications like road analysis and traffic warning using real-time data backhaul on a centralized user interface (UI). These platforms are supported by advances in professional-grade capabilities that better identify and eliminate long-tail problems in water detection using synthetic aperture radar (SAR), rare disease diagnosis, and radiotherapy assistance.

According to the International Data Corporation (IDC), the global AI platform software market grew by 35% in 2023, reaching a market size of approximately USD26.4 billion, and is projected to generate a revenue of USD60 billion by 2026 (Fig. 6.11) of which USD28.3 billion will come from generative AI platforms and applications [7].

The world's leading cloud service providers like Alibaba Cloud, AWS, Baidu, Google, International Business Machines Corporation (IBM), Microsoft, and Tencent have all released a series of competitive AI cloud platforms that use low- or no-code development technologies and tailored software packages to simplify AI cloud deployment. These cloud platforms are equipped with the latest general-purpose AI models from different vendors to create distinctive competition. Table 6.8 provides an overview of the services offered by the worlds' biggest AI cloud platform vendors in Q4 2022.

6.3.1 Microsoft

Microsoft's cloud computing platform—Azure—draws on the company's vast expertise in AI and cloud computing, to develop a range of AI tools and services, including Azure Machine Learning, Cognitive Services, and AI Services. In

6.3 AI Cloud Platforms for Innovative Services

Table 6.8 Services from the world's biggest AI cloud platform vendors in Q4 2022

Vendor	Major AI cloud platform service	Service region
Alibaba Cloud	Pre-trained DAMO model invoking platform that enables intelligent customer service through human-machine interaction	China
AWS	Amazon SageMaker ML model, Amazon Kendra AI service, etc.	Global
Baidu	No-code development platform, open-source DL platform, Baidu Brain industry solution library, etc.	China
Google	Vertex AI model training platform, Document AI, healthcare AI platform, etc.	Global
IBM	Watson NLP AI platform, Maximo Visual Inspection, etc.	Global
Microsoft	Azure AI platform, including intelligent voice, translation, NLP, and OpenAI services	Global
Tencent	Tencent AI platform, including online modeling services	China

particular, Azure Cognitive Services is a set of pre-defined AI algorithms that cover vision, speech, language, decision, and Azure OpenAI services.

Launched in March 2023, Azure OpenAI is an exclusive platform developed in collaboration with OpenAI. It is powered by various pre-trained foundation models, including GPT, GPT-4, and DALL·E models, to offer enterprise-grade services and industry solutions. With Azure AI, enterprises can customize pre-trained models, build their own multimodal models, and develop intelligent applications for mainstream industries and service scenarios, such as retail, customer service, finance, manufacturing, finance, law, healthcare, and IT. For example, to help banks detect undesirable activities, KPMG created Magna, a risk analytics solution built on Azure AI's speech, language, and translation capabilities. Magna consolidates growing volumes of unstructured data from email, phone calls, and chats to identify potential risks quickly, reducing the time to issue an alert from 30 days down to 2 days. Separately, the KPMG global tax group uses Azure OpenAI Service as a foundational layer for building use cases on top of generative AI. They incorporate it into KPMG Digital Gateway, initially focused on helping enterprises more efficiently identify and classify tax data that can be applied to environmental, social, and governance (ESG) taxes. Azure OpenAI Service helps KPMG assess data relationships to pull and predict the right tax data and type, reducing risk factors and increasing confidence in making tax contributions public.

Microsoft is expanding partnerships to better support new customers and developers. The Azure AI platform now provides support for and access to sophisticated AI models from companies like Databricks, Hugging Face, and OpenAI, which are all backed by Azure AI's infrastructure and enterprise-grade safety, security, and privacy. Azure OpenAI Service is further integrating OpenAI models into other Azure AI services like cognitive search, vision, speech, and language.

6.3.2 Amazon

AWS is Amazon's flagship cloud computing platform built on the company's 20+ years of experience in AI and ML innovation. It provides over 200 fully featured services, including elastic computing, storage, database, and IoT, from data centers globally. Its success has been widely recognized, notably by the research firm Gartner who named AWS as a global leader in cloud computing for 12 consecutive years.

Amazon Elastic Compute Cloud (EC2) is a fundamental service on the AWS platform that offers access to GPU instances for ML training and graphics workloads, as well as the lowest cost per inference instances in the cloud. AWS has unveiled next-generation AWS-designed chips—AWS Graviton4 and AWS Trainium2—to accommodate a broader range of workloads, including ML training and generative AI applications. Trainium2 can be deployed in computing clusters of up to 100,000 chips, greatly reducing the model training time while doubling the energy efficiency.

Another service is Amazon SageMaker, which equips AI developers with a broad set of fully managed infrastructure, tools, and workflows to build, train, and deploy ML models for any use case. For example, the SageMaker Studio prepares data for model development, while the SageMaker Canvas provides a visual interface for business predictions.

Moreover, AWS launched a series of new services and capabilities for enterprise-grade generative AI, making it simpler and safer for enterprises to use generative AI in their operations. These offerings include Amazon Q, a new generative AI–powered assistant that re-imagines the future of work, Amazon Bedrock that provides more model options and new powerful capabilities, and five new Amazon SageMaker capabilities for scaling with models.

6.3.3 Huawei Cloud

Huawei Cloud is a leading cloud service brand that opens up Huawei's over 30 years of expertise in information and communications technology (ICT) infrastructure. It is committed to delivering reliable, secure, and sustainable cloud services, promoting inclusive AI that is affordable, user-friendly, and widely accepted, and cultivating fertile soil for the intelligent world. For large- and medium-sized enterprises, this means a streamlined path to cloud transformation, while for small- and medium-sized enterprises, it supports growth in the era of cloud infrastructure 2.0.

Huawei Cloud Enterprise Intelligence (EI) is an AI service that provides developers and enterprises with high-performance and efficient solutions for AI application development. It provides an open, reliable, and intelligent platform that uses AI and big data to enable enterprise application systems to view, listen, and speak based on industry scenarios and equips the systems with the ability to analyze and

6.3 AI Cloud Platforms for Innovative Services

understand images, videos, speeches, and texts. This makes AI and big data services more accessible to a wider range of enterprises, accelerating service development and benefiting the society.

As a general-purpose AI solution, Huawei Cloud EI services integrate innovative technologies such as cloud, big data, and AI with industry mechanisms and expert knowledge through a unified platform and architecture to deliver integrated and collaborative intelligent services, including ModelArts and FusionInsight.

- ModelArts is a one-stop AI development platform that enables developers of any skill level to rapidly build, train, and deploy models anywhere from the cloud to the edge. It provides full-lifecycle AI workflow management for both ML and DL, including massive data preprocessing, semi-automated data labeling, large-scale distributed training, and automated model building. The platform can be used in various AI application scenarios, such as computer vision, NLP, and audio and video analysis. It supports diverse data formats for a range of tasks such as image classification and segmentation, object detection, speech paragraph labeling, and text classification, as well as data processing and pre-labeling for autonomous driving, medical imaging, and remote sensing. ModelArts provides ML for service developers who are not experienced in algorithm development to develop algorithms. It automatically generates models based on transfer learning and neural architecture search (NAS), selects parameters for model training, and tunes models for rapid model training and deployment. For example, it can automatically generate models that meet developers' precision requirements without the need for coding, based on the labeled data and application scenarios such as image classification, object detection, predictive analytics, and sound classification. Models can be automatically optimized and generated based on the deployment environment and inference speed requirements.
- FusionInsight is an intelligent data lake that provides cloud-native big data solutions with converged lakes and warehouses for enterprises. As the data foundation for Huawei Cloud's data enablement solutions, it offers a suite of cloud services that are instrumental to a wide range of big data analytics scenarios, including MapReduce Service (MRS) for cloud-native data lakes, Data Warehouse Service (DWS), Cloud Search Service (CSS), Graph Engine Service (GES), Data Lake Insight (DLI), and Data Lake Governance Center (DGC). Scenarios include real-time analysis, offline analysis, interactive query, real-time retrieval, multimode analysis, data warehouse, data mart, data access, and data governance. This unleashes the true value of data, with one lake for one enterprise and one lake for one city.

To sum up, Huawei Cloud EI provides developers and enterprises with a wide range of functions and computing resources, as well as robust support for ML, vision processing, speech processing, and NLP, enabling them to efficiently develop and deploy more powerful AI applications and enhancing their competitiveness in the AI industry.

6.3.4 Alibaba Cloud

Alibaba Cloud offers a complete suit of more than 1600 AI cloud products and services covering language, vision, and ML. It particularly excels in pre-trained large language models (LLMs), digital humans, and sign language translation.

At the Apsara Conference 2021, Alibaba Cloud launched Alibaba AI, an integrated big data and AI product system, including the Platform for AI (PAI) for ML services and MaxCompute for cloud-native big data computing services. Whale Cloud, developed by PAI, is a distributed DL training framework that enables rapid iterative training of 100 billion pre-trained multimodal models.

In 2022, Alibaba Cloud introduced the industry's first "Model as a Service (MaaS)" concept, promoting a new model-centric AI development paradigm. It developed a cloud computing technology and service architecture that centers around AI models and made these capabilities available to foundation model start-ups and developers. With this concept, Alibaba Cloud launched ModelScope, an open-source community that offers various AI models for developers to download. This allows developers to access Alibaba Cloud's computing power and a one-stop large AI model training and inference platform. To date, ModelScope is home to over 2 million AI developers and more than 1000 AI models and has seen over 45 million model downloads.

At the Apsara Conference 2023, Alibaba Cloud launched Bailian, a one-stop platform for developing foundation model applications. This platform integrates mainstream high-quality foundation models from in and outside China and provides a range of services, including model selection, fine-tuning training, security suites, and model deployment, as well as full-link application development tools. This simplifies complex tasks such as underlying computing power deployment, model pre-training, and tool development. Thanks to this platform, developers can create a foundation model application in just 5 min and refine an enterprise-dedicated model in just a few hours. This frees up more time for developers to focus on application innovation.

6.3.5 Baidu AI Cloud

Baidu AI Cloud is a leading AI platform in China, with a customer base spanning thousands of enterprises across multiple industries, most notably including the State Grid Corporation of China (SGCC), China Life Insurance, and China Unicom. It has two core products: BML, a full-featured AI development platform, and EasyDL, a low-code AI development platform.

Baidu AI Cloud outperforms other cloud AI platforms in three aspects: (1) Its robust AI computing infrastructure is fueled by the Baige heterogeneous AI computing platform, which provides a stable and reliable system, high-performance training and inference services, and high-speed-network-based data exchange capability for AI clusters. It is compatible with mainstream chips and OSs and improves utilization of computing resources from different vendors and generations. Additionally, it uses a built-in performance-enhanced engine that can significantly reduce training time and inference costs. (2) Its powerful AI capabilities are best represented by the ERNIE models, which are embedded into its product portfolios with clear product roadmaps and provide leading foundation models for AI development. It optimizes both Baidu PaddlePaddle's DL framework and ERNIE foundation models to support efficient foundation model training and inference deployment. In addition, an active ecosystem is established based on both PaddlePaddle and ERNIE, successfully attracting AI developers for collaborative innovation. (3) It is a one-stop enterprise-grade platform that offers E2E management capabilities for AI development, including data management, model development, model training, model management, and inference services. Its scalable architecture can seamlessly interconnect with and adapt to enterprises' data middle-end, service middle-end, and service front-end applications, even in complex service environment, while ensuring enterprise-grade security and high-quality services.

In response to the global surge of large AI models, Baidu AI Cloud upgraded its AI platform portfolio by integrating key features designed for foundation model development and application. It also launched ModelBuilder, a "super factory" for foundation model services, in which differentiated services can be tailored for customers who want to directly invoke foundation model application programming interfaces (APIs), customize existing foundation models through secondary development, or develop native AI applications using foundation models. Specifically, it offers exclusive access to the powerful ERNIE 4.0 model and supports 44 mainstream foundation models, giving customers the ability to select, deploy, and use foundation models on demand. Since going online, ModelBuilder has nearly 10,000 active enterprises per month, with an ever-growing number of foundation model API requests.

6.4 AI Frameworks Empowering Engineering Capabilities

AI engineering is catching the widespread attention of people from all walks of life. In academia, the Software Engineering Institute of Carnegie Mellon University has begun a research program into AI engineering in recent years, and it has worked with universities and industries to undertake a national research program funded by US official institutions. World-renowned AI experts including Michael I. Jordan and Eric Poe Xing believe that AI engineering is a new form of engineering science and a trend of AI development from theoretical disciplines to engineering disciplines. In industries, Gartner listed AI engineering as one of the annual strategic technology trends for two consecutive years, and enterprises such as Alibaba Cloud regard AI engineering as an engine for turning AI into enterprise productivity.

Gartner pointed out in a report on strategic technology trends in 2022 that if enterprises expect transformative value from AI, they cannot just apply individual

AI technologies. Instead, they need to operationalize AI models in their business ecosystems, to quickly and continuously drive new service value, and the key to this is to apply AI engineering technologies. Figure 6.12 shows the panorama of AI engineering technologies.

6.4.1 AI Frameworks: Accelerating the Growth and Engineering of the AI Industry

AI frameworks are basic tools and infrastructure for developing AI, acting as OSs within the AI technology ecosystem. They provide the foundation for academic innovation and industrial commercialization of AI, enabling AI to move from theory to practical application and facilitating quick entry into the scenario-based AI application era. As the importance of AI frameworks becomes increasingly prominent, they have become one of the focuses of AI industry innovation and attracted attention from academia and industries.

1. AI framework connotation and development

    An AI framework is mandatory for designing, training, and verifying AI algorithm models. It consists of a set of standard APIs, feature libraries, and toolkits, integrating algorithm encapsulation, data invoking, and computing resource uti-

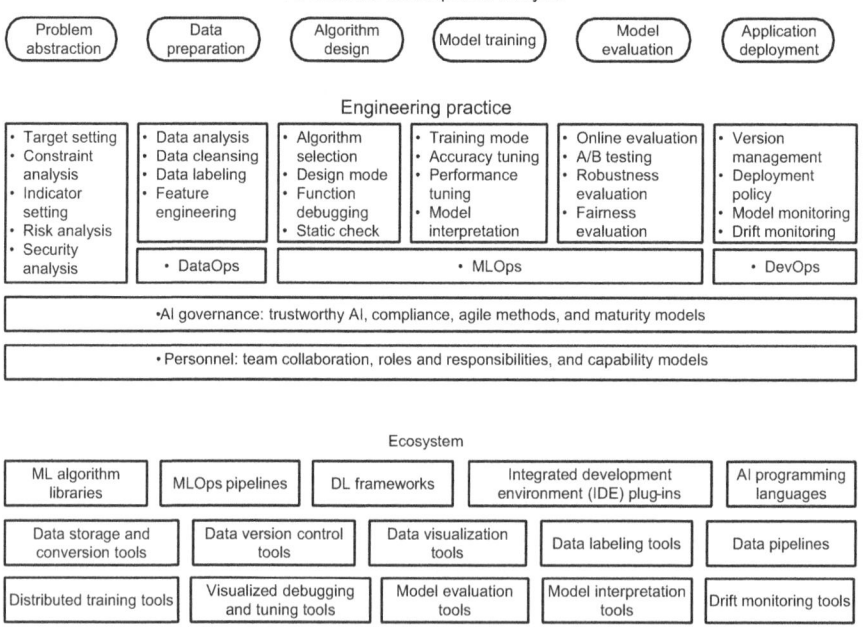

Fig. 6.12 AI engineering technology panorama

6.4 AI Frameworks Empowering Engineering Capabilities

lization and providing a development UI and an efficient execution platform for developers [8]. With an AI framework, developers can use mathematical operations to build neural network models. It converts complex mathematical expressions into computational graphs that can be recognized by computers, and automatically trains neural networks to obtain models for classification and regression in ML. This enables applications such as object classification and speech recognition.

Based on the history of AI development and the technical features of AI frameworks, there are generally four phases of AI framework development: the early phase (early 2000s), the growth phase (2012–2014), the stabilization phase (2015–2019), and the deepening phase (2020 and later). The development of AI frameworks is especially related to remarkable neural network technologies. Figure 6.13 illustrates the evolution of AI framework technologies.

- Early phase: Limited computing capabilities restricted the impact of neural network technologies during this phase. Traditional ML tools, serving as prototypes of AI frameworks, offered basic support, but the AI frameworks at this stage were incomplete, requiring developers to perform a significant amount of foundational work.
- Growth phase: In 2012, Alex Krizhevsky and others proposed a deep neural network architecture, that is, the famous AlexNet. The architecture achieved the best accuracy on the ImageNet dataset convincingly, and set off the deep neural network boom. Since then, the development of AI frameworks has grown rapidly. In this phase, the AI framework system was initially formed.
- Stabilization phase: In 2015, Kaiming He and others proposed ResNet, which broke through the boundary of image classification again, enabling the accuracy on ImageNet datasets to reach a record high. In this phase, DL became a new major technological trend. AI frameworks were booming. During the continuous development, various frameworks were evolving and were natu-

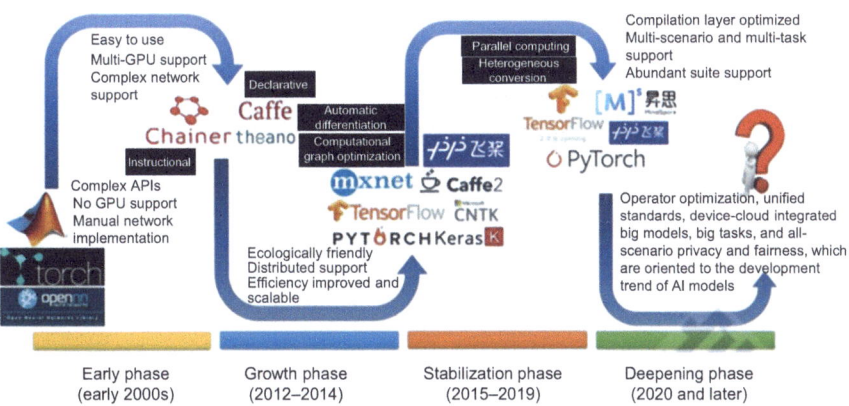

Fig. 6.13 Evolution of AI framework technologies

rally selected by developers. After fierce competition, two camps represented by TensorFlow and PyTorch were formed.
- Deepening phase: With the further development of AI, new trends are emerging. For example, the emergence of ultra-large-scale models poses higher requirements on AI frameworks, and AI frameworks need to maximize compilation optimization, better utilize and mobilize computing power, and fully utilize the potential of hardware resources.

2. Market landscape

Globally, international mainstream AI frameworks have formed a double oligopoly pattern represented by Google's TensorFlow and Meta's PyTorch. In China, the AI framework market landscape is developing toward diversification under the situation of double oligopoly. China has obvious advantages in AI applications. A large number of AI applications are built on international mainstream AI frameworks. In addition, the market share of AI frameworks launched by Chinese vendors in the past two years is steadily increasing. Since becoming open source, the MindSpore framework has received positive responses from developers in and outside China. It ranks number one among tens of millions of Gitee open-source projects and becomes the most active AI open-source framework in China. Meanwhile, the number of developers using Baidu's PaddlePaddle is also growing.

3. AI framework technologies

In terms of segments and orientations, the core technologies of mainstream AI frameworks can be classified into the base layer, component layer, and ecosystem layer. Figure 6.14 shows the core technology system of an AI framework.

The base layer implements the basic and core functions of an AI framework and consists of three sub-layers of programming, compilation optimization, and hardware enablement. The programming sub-layer provides developers with APIs for building AI models. The compilation optimization sub-layer optimizes the

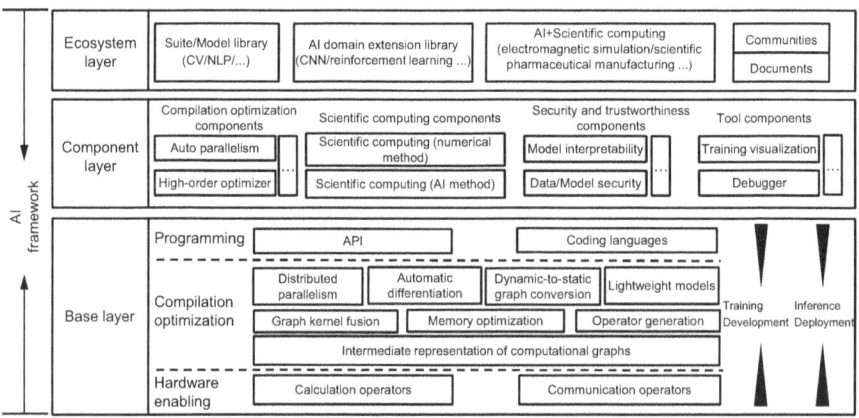

Fig. 6.14 Core technology system of an AI framework

compilation of AI models and schedules hardware resources for computing. The hardware enablement sub-layer helps developers shield the details of underlying hardware technologies. The component layer mainly provides configurable high-level functional components for the AI model lifecycle to optimize and improve the performance of segmented domains. This layer includes compilation optimization components, scientific computing components, security and trustworthiness components, and tool components. The ecosystem layer is oriented to application services and is used to support the application, maintenance, and improvement of various AI models developed based on the AI framework. This layer is visible to developers and application users and includes suites or model libraries, AI domain extension libraries, AI+scientific computing, documents, and communities.

6.4.2 Training Platforms: Driving AI Engineering by Scalable Distributed Training

1. Resource configuration

   Based on actual data fitting, the AI computing volume increases by at least tenfold annually, and the speed is far higher than that described in the Moore's Law, according to which the number of transistors on a single chip would double every 18 months. Therefore, the capability of adjusting task resources in DL training becomes particularly important. At present, with the increase of the cluster scale, the probability of machine failure at a given moment in a cluster is increasing. As the complexity of training models increases, the amount of training resources and the training time increase significantly, and the fault tolerance of tasks decreases. Moreover, the increasing cluster scale causes resources to become idle and not negligible, and there is a growing demand for flexible cluster resource configuration.

   Distributed training allows elastic configuration of underlying resources, improving system resource utilization. For example, Baidu's PaddlePaddle uses the general-purpose heterogeneous parameter server technology to enable task division, so that users can deploy distributed training tasks on heterogeneous hardware clusters. This allows for efficient utilization of chips with different computing power and provides a training capability that features high throughput and low resource consumption. However, there are also great obstacles to the application of distributed training. Modules that implement scalable control on various frameworks and adaptation of corresponding scheduling systems to implement scalable training involve a lot of workload. In addition, if different frameworks have their own scalable training solutions, integrating these framework-specific solutions into AI development platforms induces high maintenance costs.

   Scalable distributed training is a trend of AI development platform services that can reduce costs and improve efficiency for users. When users require a large number of computing resources, capacity is expanded to improve computing power and stability and reduce model training time. When users require a small number of computing resources, the underlying resource configuration is reduced to decrease the service fee caused by resource usage.

2. Algorithm upgrade

    Algorithms get AI and big data associated. Internet applications such as social media, positioning technologies, and search engines generate and store a large amount of data in real time. Based on massive data, AI continuously infers users' interests, preferences, and requirements to generate user profiles, realizing personalized and precise customization of digital culture from production and propagation to acceptance.

    Currently, AI training platforms have integrated or will integrate multiple AI technologies, such as computer vision, NLP, cross-media analysis and reasoning, intelligent adaptive learning, group intelligence, autonomous unmanned systems, and brain–computer interfaces.

    – Computer vision: Cameras and computers are used to identify, track, and measure objects and to perceive the environment in three dimensions.
    – NLP: Formal computing models are established to analyze, understand, and process natural languages.
    – Cross-media analysis and reasoning: This technology enables coordinated processing of composite-media objects that have mixed media forms, such as text, audio, video, and image.
    – Intelligent adaptive learning: This technology simulates the one-to-one teaching-learning process to provide tailored teaching capabilities for the learning system.
    – Group intelligence: This technology gathers opinions from many people to make decisions, reducing the risk of random choices by one person.
    – Autonomous unmanned systems: These systems use advanced technologies to perform or manage tasks without manual intervention.
    – Brain–computer interfaces: These interfaces establish a direct communication link between a human or animal brain and an external device to exchange information.

With the implementation of AI-based learning methods in fields such as finance, healthcare, and social networking, AI training algorithms will be continuously improved based on the feeding of a large amount of data. For example, in a paper of IEEE Conference on Computer Vision and Pattern Recognition (CVPR) 2021, a new type of convolutional layer called skip-convolutions was proposed. This type of convolution layer subtracts information in one frame of an image from that in the following frame of the image and performs convolution only on the changed parts. In image preprocessing technologies, a convolutional neural network (CNN) can be used as a feature extraction tool, and the powerful learning capability of CNN can enhance the robustness of feature extraction in AI models. The FrameExit network consisting of multiple cascaded classifiers can change the number of neurons used in the model based on the complexity of video

6.4 AI Frameworks Empowering Engineering Capabilities 123

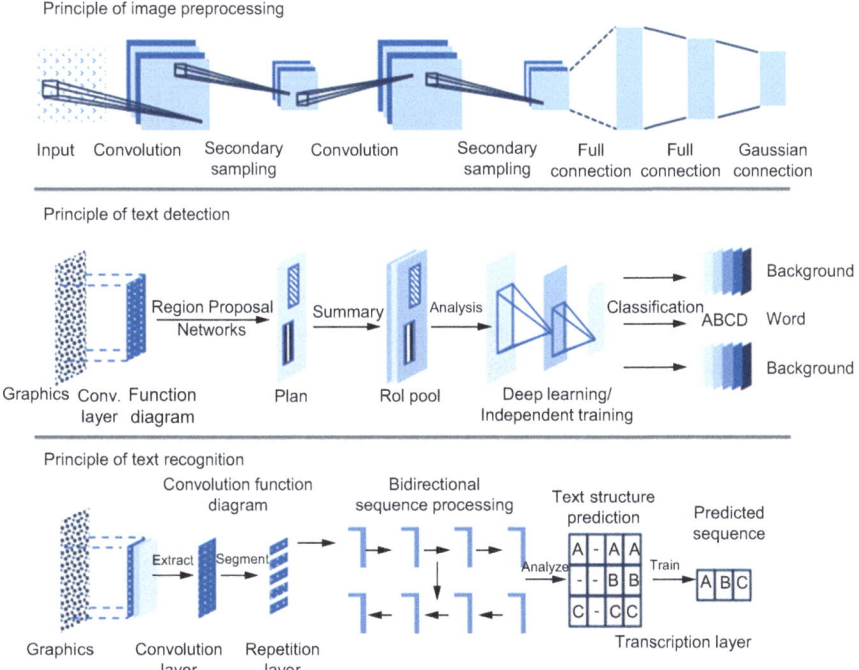

Fig. 6.15 Technical principle analysis

frames. Specifically, when the difference between two consecutive frames of a video is large, AI uses the entire model for calculation, and when the difference between them is small, AI uses only a part of the model for calculation [9]. Figure 6.15 shows the technical principle analysis.

6.4.3 MLOps: Streamlining the Last Mile of AI Engineering

AI engineering has three key processes: data handling (Data), ML model training and inference (Model), and application delivery and maintenance (Implementation). Correspondingly, Gartner believes that AI engineering includes three core technologies—data operations (DataOps), ML operations (MLOps), and development operations (DevOps), and the goal of AI engineering is to shorten the lifecycle of data analysis, ML, and application deployment and rollout through cross-functional collaboration, automation, and quick feedback. This enables AI models to quickly and continuously provide service value [10]. Figure 6.16 shows the core technology system of AI engineering.

DevOps is a combination of cultural philosophies, practices, and tools adopted by software development teams and operations and maintenance (O&M) teams to

Fig. 6.16 Core technology system of AI engineering

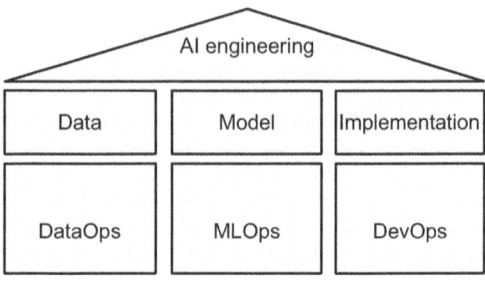

improve their ability to quickly deliver applications or services. DevOps is highly praised by teams that deliver microservices and cloud-native applications. DataOps is a technical practice that combines data processing and integration processes with automation and agile software engineering methods to improve the quality and speed of data analysis as well as team collaboration and to promote long-term improvement. MLOps is a practice of reliably and efficiently deploying and maintaining ML models in production environments. It is a key field in the AI industry. MLOps combines traditional DevOps concepts with ML to improve the deployment, monitoring, and management efficiency of ML models, accelerating the process of model rollout and continuous optimization.

As an important part of AI engineering, MLOps aims to solve problems such as difficult team collaboration, disordered management, and long delivery period during AI production, achieving high-quality, efficient, and sustainable AI production. Currently, MLOps is considered as a key to implementing ML models and has become an important development direction in the ML field. For the second year running, Gartner believes that MLOps is the last mile of AI engineering implementation.

1. MLOps system

    Simply speaking, MLOps is a toolkit for model development, training, deployment, O&M, and monitoring. With the wide application of ML models and the rapid development of AI and ML technologies, the deployment and maintenance of ML models were becoming complex and difficult and a more efficient and reliable method was required to manage and maintain these models. MLOps addresses this issue and covers the entire process of taking ML models from the lab environment to the production environment. It requires collaboration across teams, such as data scientists, algorithm engineers, O&M IT personnel, in phases including model training, verification, deployment, monitoring, and maintenance. MLOps not only improves the efficiency and quality of model training but also emphasizes the stability and performance of models after they are launched. It combines the best practices of ML engineering, software development, and O&M to improve the reliability and reproducibility of ML models in enterprise production environments.

    MLOps enables automatic model deployment and continuous integration, significantly simplifying the model rollout process and improving deployment

6.4 AI Frameworks Empowering Engineering Capabilities

efficiency. It also emphasizes model monitoring and maintenance to ensure continuous and stable model running in production environments. It can promptly detect abnormal model behavior and mitigate it by taking measures to adjust and optimize models, improving the management and O&M efficiency of ML models. In application, MLOps not only helps enterprises quickly apply models to production but also effectively reduces maintenance costs after models are launched, while improving model stability and reliability.

2. Expanding MLOps market

According to the 2022 research report of the intelligence and market research platform MarketsandMarkets, the MLOps market scale will increase from USD1.1 billion in 2022 to USD5.9 billion in 2027.

In recent years, the MLOps tool chain has become a star track in AI investment and financing, leading to the emergence of numerous startups that develop MLOps tools as their main products. For example, Weights & Biases, which focuses on DL visualization tools, received USD200 million in financing and the platform was valued at USD1 billion; Tecton, which focuses on providing ML platforms, received USD160 million in financing; OctoML, which focuses on multi-hardware adapted deployment of ML models, received USD133 million in financing and the platform was valued at USD850 million.

Driven by the capital market, MLOps tools continue to innovate. According to partial statistics, there are about 300 tools worldwide, which can be classified into two types: E2E MLOps tool platforms and specialized MLOps tools. A E2E MLOps tool platform provides support for the entire lifecycle of ML projects. Such platforms include Amazon SageMaker, Microsoft Azure, Google Cloud Platform, DataRobot, Algorithmia, Kubeflow, MLflow, Baidu AI Cloud's enterprise AI development platform, Alibaba Cloud's PAI, Huawei Cloud's MLOps platform, Tencent's Taiji ML platform, and DataCanvas APS. MLOps specialized tools provide more centralized support for specific steps, mainly including data processing, model building, and operation monitoring. Such specialized tools include the data sharing tool provided by Cloudera, data and model version management tool provided by DVC and DAGSHub, metadata management tool provided by Neptune.ai, the operation monitoring tool provided by Transwarp, the real-time feature processing tool provided by 4Paradigm, and the labeling tool provided by Testin. Figure 6.17 shows the classification of MLOps tools.

As a key tool for AI engineering, MLOps has become a key investment target of many vendors. Vendors such as Amazon, Microsoft, Google, Baidu, and Alibaba have invested in MLOps, covering data management, feature extraction, version control, and automatic training. At the same time, there are a number of startups focusing on specific functions of AI engineering, such as 4Paradigm and Transwarp. Table 6.9 lists the AI engineering products of global enterprises.

3. MLOps industry applications advancing steadily in diverse use cases

MLOps vendors and users benefit from the rapid development of the MLOps system at varying degrees. With the development of the tool market and industry applications, new tools are emerging and are widely used and implemented in IT, finance, telecom, and other industries.

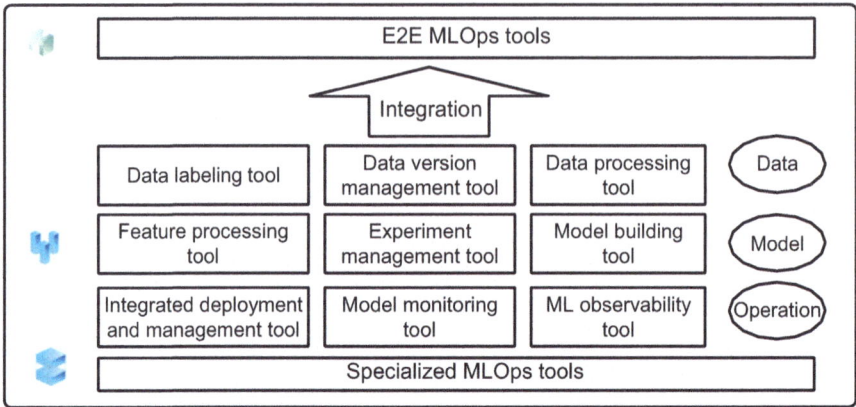

Fig. 6.17 MLOps tool categories

Table 6.9 AI engineering products of global enterprises

Enterprise	AI engineering product
Amazon	Amazon S3 (for data management), Amazon SageMaker (MLOps platform), AWS CodeCommit (for version control)
Microsoft	Azure Blob Storage (for data mining), Azure ML (MLOps platform), Azure DevOps (for version control)
Google	Vertex AI (MLOps platform)
IBM	IBM Wastson Studio (MLOps platform)
Baidu	EasyDL (MLOps platform), BML (MLOps platform)
Alibaba	Alibaba AI (AI engineering tool platform, including the MLOps platform)
4Paradigm	Sage AIOS (MLOps platform)
DataCanvas	DataCanvas APS (MLOps platform), DataCanvas RT (for data management)
Transwarp	Sophon MLOps (MLOps platform)

Outside China, MLOps is widely used and has achieved remarkable results. It is mainly used in scenarios such as service operation, product or service development, marketing, risk prediction, and supply chain management within an organization. The relevant industries include IT, finance, e-commerce, manufacturing, chemical, and healthcare. Take the IT industry as an example. After MLOps is used, a US IT company shortens the time for developing and deploying new AI services to 1/12 to 1/6 of the original time, almost halving the operation cost; a German IT company runs 10 times the number of experiments with the same workload through automatic orchestration and experiment tracking; the experiment reproduction time of an Israeli IT company is reduced by 50%; the number of ML products of a US transportation technology company is increased from zero to over 100 in three years.

In China, MLOps is in the stage of planning and construction, and there has been initial achievement in explorative implementation. IDC predicted in 2022 that 60% of Chinese enterprises would run their ML workflows through MLOps by 2024. Over the past three years, various industries in China have begun to explore MLOps solutions that suit their own characteristics. In the boom of digital intelligence transformation, industries with high digitalization levels, such as IT, finance, and telecom, are relatively leading, while other industries are progressing slowly [11].

6.5 Computing Power Breakthroughs for Rapid AI Development

Intelligent computing power enables AI as an infrastructure like networks and electric power, making AI capabilities available to a range of industries and fields. It can form an intelligent foundation to promote industrial digitalization and transformation. It can fuel new achievements in scientific research and technological fields such as biology, medicine, astronomy, and geography, or specific applications like smart driving and film rendering. On a wider level, people will experience the changes brought by intelligent computing power in daily life.

6.5.1 Evolution of AI Computing from Rough Use to Sophisticated Collaboration

Achievements in cross-layer joint optimization of software and hardware systems mean AI computing gains have exceeded the prediction of Moore's law. As advanced manufacturing has moved from the micron to the nanometer scale, more and more silicon circuits are being integrated into the same small space and this leads to ever-increasing heat generation, rendering the Moore's law that the processing capability doubles every two years inapplicable. Statistics from MLPerf show that AI training efficiency improved by 16–17 times within 18 months, manifesting the gains of software and hardware optimization. With system integrators, Internet giants, chip vendors, and others investing heavily in computing systems, algorithm frameworks, data formats, underlying chip architectures, and other fields, multi-disciplinary collaboration has catalyzed the development of sophisticated, large-scale, and flexible computing power and improved the capabilities to support AI computing.

Collaboration between industry-oriented mainstream software and hardware systems facilitates the application ecosystem development. In terms of computing systems, software iteration is tailored for application scenarios, while distributed heterogeneous computing can improve the distributed training performance of large models. In terms of hardware, NVIDIA released the computer vision and image acceleration library Computer Vision-Compute Unified Device Architecture (CV-CUDA), which supports pipeline processing with high efficiency 10 times that of a single GPU. It also launched tools for healthcare, autonomous driving, robotics, and metaverse to support vertical industries. Its NVLink-C2C supports interconnection between heterogeneous chips and delivers data transmission speeds seven times that of PCIe 5.0. In terms of software, Baidu's PaddlePaddle supports the heterogeneous multivariate distributed training function, which allows for training at multiple interconnected computing centers.

AI model optimization must prioritize both improved hardware utilization and lower computing load. In this regard, the bottom-layer computing is optimized to reduce the computing load of algorithms and improve performance. For example, Deepmind's AI system AlphaTensor uses an innovative matrix multiplication technique that increases the computing speed by 20% by reducing the number of multiplication operations.

Further, the bottom layer must be AI-native to uplift computing efficiency. To design a hardware architecture adaptive to AI computing algorithms, NVIDIA H100 introduces the Transformer engine, which uses 16-bit floating-point (FP16) precision and a new 8-bit floating-point data format to train larger networks at faster speeds. The underlying instruction set uses recursion and memory techniques, which can speed up healthcare service delivery and simulate workflows, while Dynamic Programming X (DPX) instructions increase the dynamic programming speed by 40 times. FP8 was jointly developed by Intel, Arm, and NVIDIA to allow a low-precision data format to be used in both training and inference to speed up AI training. In practice, this achieved a 4.5-fold acceleration of AI training on the Bidirectional Encoder Representations from Transformers (BERT) language model.

Intelligent computing power will be ubiquitous and combines elements of heterogeneity, software-hardware collaboration, energy efficiency, and cloud-edge-device collaboration. In terms of heterogeneity, CPUs, GPUs, XPUs represented by NPUs and DPUs, as well as ASICs and FPGAs have realized diversified computing power, and heterogeneous computing is growing rapidly as an increasing number of chip companies are adopting new architectures such as Arm, reduced instruction set computer (RISC)-V, and microprocessor without interlocked pipeline stages (MIPS) in addition to the traditional ×86 architecture. In terms of software-hardware collaboration, a design allowing efficient management of multiple types of resources is required, so that elastic expansion, cross-platform deployment, and multi-scenario compatibility of computing power can be achieved. An example is the DL compilation technology, which can be continuously optimized through software-hardware collaboration to improve the performance, openness, and usability of the operator library, mask the differences between underlying processors, and enable upward compatibility with more AI frameworks. Energy efficiency highlights the importance of seeking a balance between higher computing power and lower energy consumption for data centers and 5G facilities. This can be achieved by using more green energy, adopting innovative cooling technologies to reduce data center energy consumption, and managing IT devices comprehensively to improve computing power utilization [12].

6.5.2 Cloud-Edge-Device Collaboration Promoting Development of Ubiquitous Computing Power

With the large-scale development of industries such as 5G, IoT, and industrial Internet, centralized cloud computing can no longer meet requirements in terms of network latency, bandwidth cost, data security, and service agility. Edge computing and AI have reinforced each other and given rise to a new field of research—edge intelligence. Edge computing transfers computing resources from the cloud center to servers at the network edge, providing computing support for networked terminal devices. After computing power is transferred to devices and sensors, real-time processing and decision-making can be performed more quickly, reducing dependency on networks and protecting data privacy. AI technologies represented by DL enable each edge compute node to have computing and decision-making capabilities, allowing some complex intelligent applications to be processed at the local edge. This meets the requirements of agile connection, real-time services, data optimization, application intelligence, security and privacy protection, and others [13].

In edge intelligence, edge computing and AI benefit each other. Edge computing uses AI to maintain and manage edge devices and AI uses edge computing platforms to provide intelligent services. By computing and analyzing data on edge nodes, data transmission and processing delays are reduced to improve real-time performance of intelligent applications. At present, edge intelligence is pushing the development of applications such as smart transportation, smart manufacturing, and cloud gaming, accelerating the application of AI in industries and providing important guarantees for the comprehensive improvement of intelligence levels. In the future, edge intelligence will be widely used in many scenarios, such as public security, smart transportation, smart manufacturing, and intelligent driving. A large number of intelligent devices will be deployed on edge nodes, and the edge side will become the front line for data aggregation and processing on the entire network. The question remains how to cope with the impact of massive heterogeneous data in edge computing, calling for innovations in data filtering, classification, integration, storage, access, and security management will become hot topics in edge intelligence technology research.

Cloud-edge-device collaboration, based on edge intelligence, is a model that enables computing power to be appropriately deployed in the three-tier architecture of cloud data centers, edge computing nodes, and terminal devices. The cloud is responsible for unified management and large-scale centralized computing, the edge performs agile data access and real-time computing, and terminals realize ubiquitous sensing and local intelligence. With unified computing resource management and intelligent computing resource scheduling, low-latency and cost-controllable computing services can be realized to meet the varying computing needs of more industrial scenarios. A new distributed OS based on cloud-edge-device collaboration will become a basic platform for digital transformation of various industries, empowering digital transformation and intelligent upgrade of various industries. Such an OS integrates capabilities such as ubiquitous access, network management, cloud-edge-device synergy, unified scheduling, AI, data platform, component development, and ecosystem openness, hides differences between underlying heterogeneous resources, and interconnects with enterprises' internal service systems to provide unified application and operation management for service scenarios.

6.5.3 Intelligent Computing Power and Digital Twins

A digital twin is a digital representation of a physical object mapped in virtual space and is used to simulate the lifecycle of the object. The simulation is achieved using physical models, sensor updates, historical operational information, and other data and involves cross-disciplinary knowledge, multiple physical quantities, multiple dimensions, and varying probabilities. Theories and technologies of digital twins are relatively mature outside China, and digital twins have already been applied in many industrial fields. In China, digital twin development is in its infancy, and the research is still theoretical. The digital twin technology is collaborating with emerging technologies such as IoT, XR (AR, VR, and mixed reality (MR)), edge computing, cloud computing, 5G, big data, blockchain, and AI. Figure 6.18 shows the technological system of digital twin.

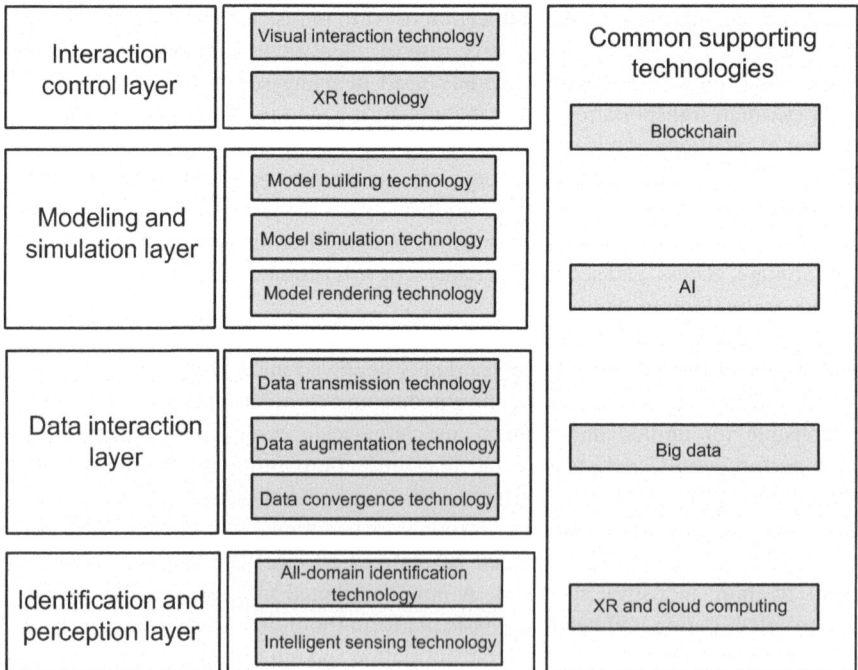

Fig. 6.18 Technological system of digital twin

Intelligent computing power supports modeling, simulation, and optimization of digital twins and streamlines their wide application in industries. With the help of technologies such as cloud computing, big data analytics, and ML, intelligent computing power can process and analyze large amounts of data and generate highly accurate digital twin models. In addition, intelligent computing power can realize real-time data synchronization and model updating, improving the performance and reliability of the digital twin system.

Intelligent computing power has enabled digital twins to be widely used in a range of fields. For example, in education, an immersive learning environment can be created based on Huawei AI computing power base to provide rich and real learning experience. The 3D digital twin metaverse technology makes abstract concepts tangible and provides students with intuitive and vivid learning materials. Chemistry experiments can be simulated in a virtual environment for students to observe the process and results of chemical reactions and improve experimental operation skills and scientific thinking. Another field is the city planning and traffic management. Intelligent computing power can be used to establish a digital twin model for a city to optimize traffic flow and environment layout. 3D modeling and simulations of urban roads, buildings, and green spaces can help assess the effects of different urban planning schemes. These simulations can provide more scientific and rational information for planners to streamline operations and improve sustainability. In healthcare, intelligent computing power can be used to create digital twin models for human bodies. These models can be used to perform highly accurate simulation and prediction of human physiological processes, as well as simulation of the movement, metabolism, and lesions of human organs, thereby providing assistance in medical research, surgery planning, diagnosis, and treatment. Doctors can use the 3D digital twin metaverse technology to simulate operations or surgeries before carrying them out in real life, helping doctors formulate more accurate plans and improving the operation or surgery success rate and treatment effect for patients.

6.5.4 Multi-Technology Collaboration Accelerating Advanced Computing

Cutting-edge computing technologies possess superior computing power in some fields, and some technological routes are quickly advancing toward industrialization. As computing technologies develop rapidly, heterogeneous computing has become the mainstream for intelligent computing. Against the backdrop where the prediction in the Moore's law slows down while revolutionary technologies are immature, innovations in various applications represented by large AI models are catalyzing a new wave of intelligent computing, redefining the computing industry's landscape. Now, vehicle-mounted computing platforms and AI servers equipped with various computing acceleration chips will become the main sources of computing power (see Table 6.10).

Table 6.10 Evolution of advanced computing

Generation	Period	Representative computing device	Mainstream computing component	Important basic software	Typical product	Representative technology
Electron tube and transistor	1945–1960	Electron-tube computers Transistor computers	Electron tubes Transistors	Machine language Assembly language High-level language	ENIAC IBM709 TRADIC Metrovick 950	Electron tube Transistor Digital computer
Mainframe and minicomputer	1960–1975	Mainframes Minicomputers	Early ASICs	OS Database Programming language	IBM 360 PDP-8/11 NOVA1200	Small- and medium-scale integration
PC	1975–1990	Supercomputers Personal computers	16-bit or 32-bit CPUs	Desktop OS	Altair 8800 IBM System Apple-1 Intel 8086	Large- and very-large-scale integration Graphical interface Computer network
Internet	1990–2005	Personal computers General-purpose servers	32-bit or 64-bit CPUs	Object-oriented language Open-source OS	ThinkPad 700C Compaq SystemPro Intel Xeon	Cluster computing Cross-platform programming
Mobile internet	2005–2020	General-purpose servers Smartphones	64-bit CPUs Smartphone SoCs	Cloud OS Mobile OS DL framework Heterogeneous computing software stack	AWS platform Apple iPhone Intel Core Qualcomm Snapdragon	Virtualization Parallel computing DL Heterogeneous computing

6.5 Computing Power Breakthroughs for Rapid AI Development

		Intelligent computing			Unconventional computing	
		2020–2035			2035–2050	
		AI servers Edge servers Embedded AI platforms			Quantum computers Optical computers Brain-like computers	
		Computing acceleration chips			Quantum chips Optical computing chips Brain-like chips	
		Deep learning frameworks for large models Cloud-edge-device collaboration software stack			Basic quantum computing software Basic brain-like computing software	
		NVIDIA A100 and H100 NVIDIA DRIVE Intel Xeon Scalable AMD EPYC			–	
		High-speed data storage and processing Security computing Green computing Ubiquitous computing			Quantum computing Optical computing Brain-like computing	

Systematic innovation of advanced computing is active and the innovation modes and directions are evolving, showing the characteristics of software-hardware collaborative innovation and system architecture innovation. Technological innovations span basic processes, hardware, software, and entire systems, including the 4 and 3 nm processes. High-speed across-platform interconnection is continuing, and software-hardware coupling is accelerating the development of intelligent computing toward exascale computing. Advanced computing will gradually enter the phase of large-scale application of unconventional computing after 2035 thanks to developments of advanced computing technologies, such as in-memory computing, quantum computing, optical computing, and brain-like computing.

In-memory computing breaks the bottlenecks in AI computing and reduces data processing costs. It allows for low power consumption at the edge side, while also having the potential to deliver intense computing power. This breaks through the "storage wall" caused by independent computing components from storage components in the traditional Von Neumann architecture, achieving higher computational performance at lower power consumption. Specifically, the "storage wall" is the mismatch of data processing speed of the CPU with the data read/write speed of the memory, which severely affects the power and performance of the target application. As one of the revolutionary technologies that can increase the computing power per unit of power consumption by 10 times, in-memory computing is expected to reduce the power consumption per unit of computing power by one order of magnitude. Its high bandwidth and low power consumption are perfect for large-scale parallel computing scenarios such as VR/AR, unmanned driving, astronomical data computing, and analysis of remote sensing image data. Current mainstream solutions include encapsulating a computing logic chip and a memory such as a dynamic random access memory (DRAM) with an advanced packaging technology, implementing computation in conventional memories such as DRAM, static random access memory (SRAM), NOR Flash, and NAND Flash, and using new memory components to integrate memory and computing. The in-memory computing technology is still in the early stages, requiring collaboration among related chip vendors across the world. In China, the vendors are making efforts to overtake competitors in these technologies.

Quantum computing uses the principles of quantum mechanics, especially quantum superposition and quantum entanglement, to realize high-speed data processing and complex computing. Quantum computers have a huge speed advantage over traditional computers when dealing with specific types of problems. In AI, ML models often face issues of combinatorial optimization due to a large number of variables and operations, which can be difficult to solve on traditional computers even when using advanced AI. By comparison, quantum computers running AI can resolve these issues quickly by identifying data patterns that are difficult for traditional computers to capture. Currently, basic quantum computing technologies continue to develop. Google has increased the number of quantum bits in a superconducting quantum computing system from 53 to 72 and successfully verified the feasibility of the quantum error correction solution. Quantum computing has been preliminarily commercialized in the financial sector. In financial risk control scenarios such as anti-fraud and anti-money laundering, quantum computing has a faster computing speed and higher customer profile accuracy than conventional computing.

Optical computing is a technology that uses optical waves as carriers for information processing and has advantages such as large bandwidth, low latency, and low power consumption. It provides a computing architecture of "transmission as computation and structure as function," which is expected to address the tidal data transmission issue existing in the Von Neumann architecture. Optical computing has the following specific advantages. First, optical signals are transmitted at the speed of light. Second, the natural parallel processing capability and mature wavelength division multiplexing (WDM) technique greatly improve the data processing capability, capacity, and bandwidth. Third, power consumption is expected to be as low as 10–18 J/bit. For the same power consumption, photonic components are hundreds of times faster than electronic components. Fourth, parallel computing and innovative hardware architectures and algorithms such as the optical neural network provide a solution with the most potential to address the computing power needs of AI technologies such as image recognition, speech recognition, and VR. Currently, analog optical computing is the main direction for AI applications that do not require high computational accuracy, but this also leaves room for combining AI with unconventional computing including quantum computing and brain-like computing. As the technological advantages of optical computing are not significant enough, some optical computing enterprises are turning to the research on technologies such as laser light source and photonic network to explore new application areas.

6.6 Algorithm Updates Boosting AI Development

6.6.1 New Algorithms Like AutoML Simplifying AI Development

AutoML is an important breakthrough in the field of AI. It can lower the barriers to AI development and mitigate the effects of the current shortage of technology talent. AutoML can integrate iterative processes into traditional ML to create an automated ML process which is more significantly accessible. In this process, data selection and modeling are automated through a series of algorithms and heuristics. Researchers only need to enter meta-knowledge, such as the convolution operation process and problem description. The AutoML algorithm can automatically select appropriate data, optimize the model's structure and configuration, train the model, and deploy the model on different devices. AutoML primarily offers automatic data preprocessing, feature engineering, hyperparameter search, model network structure design, and model deployment. Low-code development and pre-training models are closely linked to AutoML, and their development is converging with AutoML.

AutoML helps AI development platforms automatically complete tasks such as neural structure search, model selection, feature engineering, hyperparameter optimization, and model compression. Classification or regression that depends on structured or semi-structured data can be automated through AutoML, and this makes AI training much more efficient.

A typical ML process includes data acquisition and preprocessing, feature engineering, model training, and model deployment. In traditional ML, each step in a pipeline is monitored and executed manually. Automated ML tools are designed to automate one or more of the phases of ML, which eliminates repetitive tasks and makes it easier for both non-experts and experienced ML engineers to build better ML models faster. Figure 6.19 shows the AutoML workflow.

Leading Internet enterprises and innovative enterprises have already started to actively develop and use AutoML and related tools. However, there are still some challenges that need to be overcome. First, AutoML requires a large amount of computing power, and enterprises need to explore more of the possible solutions to this issue during the R&D phase. Second, AutoML needs to maintain transparency while decreasing processing complexity to allow model users to check model quality. AutoML is an automation tool that can improve work efficiency, but its applications are still limited due to insufficient technology maturity. Currently, AutoML is being used in some development phases (such as feature engineering) and specific technology areas (such as speech recognition, object detection, and intelligent conversation).

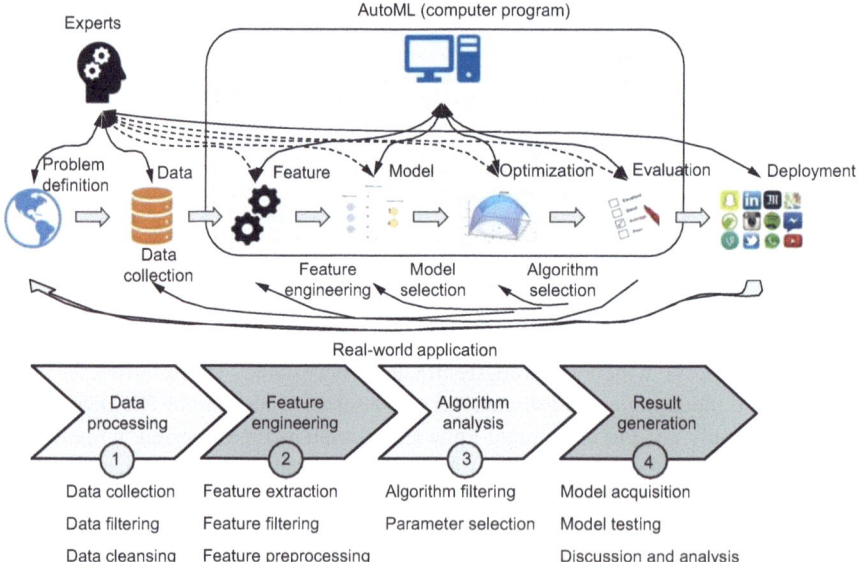

Fig. 6.19 AutoML workflow

6.6.2 Rapid Development of Model-Centric Open-Source Communities

Building model-centric AI open-source ecosystems has become the key at every stage of AI development and application. Open-source ecosystems such as model code libraries and open-source AI model communities are booming. Open-source model libraries, which primarily provide access to the model code, are built along with the building of ecosystems of development frameworks, hardware chips, large models, and other innovative subjects. Chip enterprises are building AI model resource libraries based on the hardware ecosystem to speed up software and hardware collaboration. For example, a UK chip vendor and Baidu's PaddlePaddle jointly launched the Model Zoo model library, which includes image classification, image segmentation, and object detection and focuses on AI chip model applications in the consumer, automobile, and desktop server markets. Technology R&D enterprises are focusing on development frameworks and promoting the integrated development of models and frameworks. For example, there are more than 500 industrial model libraries based on Baidu's PaddlePaddle development framework, and Google's TensorFlow has launched a code hub and Model Garden. In addition, large model R&D enterprises use open-source large models to build their own technological ecosystems, such as Meta OPT, OpenBMB, and Inspur Source 1.0.

New AI, model-centric, open-source communities have emerged, led by Hugging Face and ModelScope. These communities are competing with GitHub, a well-established code hosting platform. They focus on "model as a service" and shift the focus from software code hosting to AI model code sharing, deployment hosting, visualized usage, open-source collaboration, as well as model evaluation and selection. They offer and profit from the following closed-source community services: (1) E2E modeling solutions: Users can create tasks, upload data, automatically build models, and are charged based on time and computing resources used. (2) Model inference services: These services include the API calling service, and users can choose to deploy these services on public or private clouds. (3) Code and model hosting: Users are charged for the hosting of their models, datasets, and pipelines. (4) Customization: Solutions can be customized based on customer and project requirements and the fee will vary depending on conditions. Such communities are developing rapidly. Hugging Face, for example, has more than 77,000 pre-trained models on its platform and offers model training and calling services. Its customers include Intel, Qualcomm, Pfizer, and Bloomberg. In May 2022, the company raised USD100 million in C-series funding and was valued at USD2 billion.

6.7 Diversified Data Services Adding Value to AI

Data services include database design, data collection, data cleansing, data labeling, and data quality inspection for AI algorithm training and optimization in various service scenarios. The entire basic data service process focuses on customer

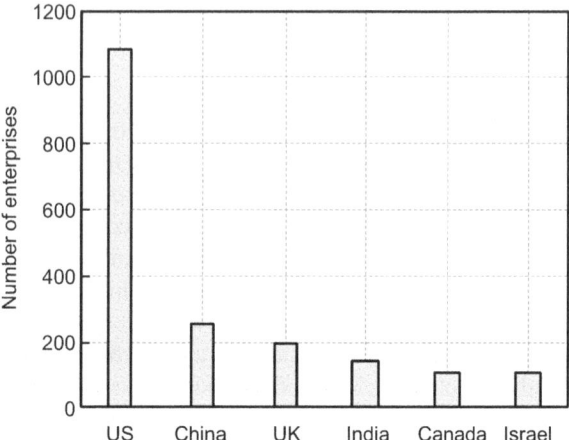

Fig. 6.20 Number of AI data service providers in different countries

requirements. The available products mainly cover datasets and data resource customization services, which provide reliable and usable data for AI model training. According to Gartner, the global database market was worth more than USD100 billion in 2023, and cloud databases accounted for 55% of this value. Ultra-large-scale enterprises earned high revenues, and the revenue gap between enterprises widened.

Cloud-based media services have already emerged in North America, and mobile computing platforms and AI are being widely used in e-commerce, and together these developments are driving growth in the local data collection and labeling market. The Asia-Pacific region is also witnessing the rapid development of the data collection and labeling market. Its compound annual growth rate (CAGR) is expected to be 30.9% over the period from 2023 to 2030. About 35% of all AI data service providers are based in the US and 8% are based in China. Figure 6.20 shows the number of AI data service providers in different countries. Appen, one of the leading data service providers in the US, uses generative AI with LLMs to automatically label data and improve the data delivery speed. Appen's main customers include well-known IT giants such as Google, Amazon, and Microsoft. Table 6.11 lists some well-known AI data service providers.

As datasets evolve to open source, the datasets used in industrial scenarios are quickly becoming larger and more varied. In China, dataset construction in key industries such as healthcare and autonomous driving has become a pertinent topic. For example, Shanghai Jiao Tong University released the MedMNIST v2 dataset. This version includes 12 2D datasets and six new 3D datasets, and it is capable of providing data support for biomedical image analysis. Huawei Noah's Ark Lab and Sun Yat-sen University jointly released the 2D autonomous driving dataset SODA10M. This dataset includes 10 million unlabeled images and 20,000 labeled images covering six types of pedestrian and vehicle scenarios, and it improves the robustness of ML models in autonomous driving scenarios. Alibaba released a minimum-SKU-level commodity image classification dataset based on its

Table 6.11 Well-known AI data service providers

Vendor	Country	Service
Alegion	US	It provides high-resolution and high-density video data labeling services and a video labeling platform for ML modeling. Its customers include Walmart, Microsoft, and Airbnb
Appen	US	Its services include data collection, labeling, and preparation. It developed an enterprise-grade AI data labeling platform MatrixGo, which uses AI to achieve man-machine collaborative data collection and labeling
Amazon Mechanical Turk	US	Amazon's data crowdsourcing platform allows users to release data that needs to be labeled and makes it easier for users to outsource their data to professionals for labeling
Clickworker	US	It provides a data crowdsourcing platform with a professional data labeling team

e-commerce platform (SKU is short for stock keeping unit). The dataset contains three million commodity images spanning 50,000 categories. It helps models accurately identify a large number of fine-grained commodity images and accelerates model engineering and commercial application.

Data services are now being customized for users, and scenario-based data applications are being promoted through multi-party collaboration. One such form of collaboration is enterprise-led cooperation with scientific research institutes and universities to build datasets oriented to industry application scenarios. For example, Damor Data has cooperated with several scientific research institutes and traditional pharmaceutical enterprises, such as the Cold Spring Harbor Laboratory and the Scripps Research Institute, to construct the knowledge graph of more than 30,000 small molecular drugs and biopharmaceuticals and enable the retrieval of multi-dimensional medical data. Jinyun Data is working closely with enterprises, institutions, and universities such as China Railway Construction Corporation, the Chinese Academy of Sciences, and Tsinghua University to integrate and collect city and building data to build a digital city model database and an Internet Data Center (IDC) for building information modeling (BIM). Another such form of collaboration is university-led cooperation with technology enterprises to build high-quality datasets. For example, the Institute for AI Industry Research (AIR) at Tsinghua University worked with the Beijing High-Level Autonomous Driving Demonstration Area, Baidu Apollo, and others, to jointly release vehicle-road collaboration datasets covering weather conditions, road conditions, and other information.

ChatGPT has taken the world by storm and inspired the development of more LLMs, which in turn is facilitating the development of the basic AI data service industry. Public Internet data needs to be labeled using labeling techniques such as text classification and conversation corpus construction to help optimize models and avoid ethical issues such as malicious and biased content. Currently, AI vision and intelligent voice dataset products account for a high proportion of AI products, and NLP-related services account for a relatively low proportion. Service providers need to deepen the development and optimization of NLP datasets and related labeling platforms in order to be able to seize new opportunities. The high-quality and easy-to-monitor data has already been used. Synthetic data generated using AI generated content (AIGC) technology may eventually become one of the data sources for AI training. This would remove the restrictions on the quantity, quality, and cost of data required for AI model training. Nevertheless, the synthetic data generation technology has its own limitations in terms of accuracy and talent matching. In the future, the synthetic data generation technology will be able to work with real dataset products to become the data cornerstone of the AI industry.

6.8 Innovative Unicorns Enabling AI Applications

AI will be critical to helping enterprises in diverse industries establish competitive advantages and secure revenue streams. By the end of 2023, there were over 29,000 AI enterprises worldwide, with the US having the highest number at 9977 (33.6% of the total), followed by China with 4482 (15% of the total). The UK, India, and Canada ranked next. The number of AI startups worldwide reached its peak between 2016 and 2018 and has been gradually decreasing each year since then. Figure 6.21 shows the global distribution of AI enterprises.

Advancements in foundation models have sparked greater interest in AI from investors. Despite a global decline in investment in 2023, numerous AI unicorns have emerged.

As the global AI industry chain becomes more clearly defined, innovative AI enterprises are moving away from aimless technology breakthroughs and focusing on specific tracks. The three main tracks are general-purpose foundations, enterprise-grade platforms, and high-value applications. Innovative AI enterprises around the world share the following three patterns.

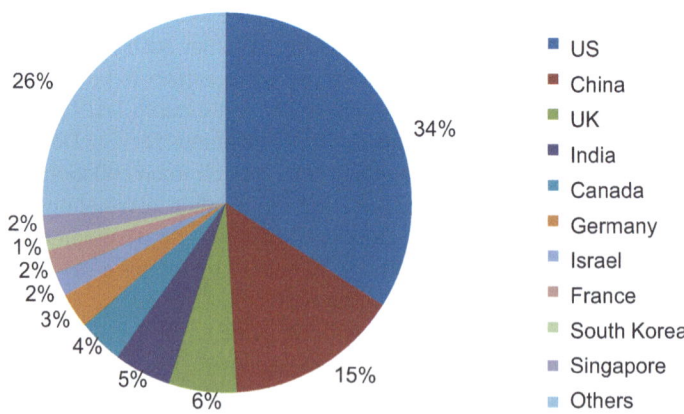

Fig. 6.21 Global distribution of AI enterprises by country

6.8 Innovative Unicorns Enabling AI Applications

First, platforms are evolving to cater to enterprise-grade services. AI technologies, such as visual and voice tasks, data analysis and decision-making, conversation assistants, and robots, are seeing wider application through enterprise-grade platforms. Uniphore is one such platform that uses conversational automation technologies to provide enterprises with conversational AI services, including AI conversation assistants, voice biometric authentication, and speech-to-text transcription. Uniphore has secured USD400 million in series E funding, valuing the company at USD2.5 billion.

Second, general-purpose foundations are being used to solve key underlying issues. Innovative enterprises specializing in chips, frameworks, and development tools are focusing on solving underlying issues in industry R&D and innovation, as well as expanding horizontally into segments. The 2022 AI 100 list—CB Insights' annual list of the 100 most promising private AI companies in the world—includes general-purpose tool companies in different segments. For instance, data companies can be categorized into the fields of data labeling, data synthesis, data de-identification, and data quality, while model tool companies can be categorized into the fields of version control, model correction and detection, and ML platform.

Third, high-value applications are becoming the focus of innovation. The global competition for innovative applications is centered around industries such as medical biology and autonomous driving. Forbes' 2022 AI 50 list of top AI innovators in the US includes 11 from the medical biology industry and 4 from the autonomous driving industry. Lunit, a highly successful medical imaging company focusing on biomarker research, has achieved a remarkable 30-fold increase in revenue over the past 3 years thanks to its innovative radiology and pathology strategy. Lunit's listing in South Korea saw a 30% increase on its first day, making it a popular choice among investors.

6.8.1 Adept AI: Offering Artificial General Intelligence (AGI) Tools

Adept AI is an ML research and product lab building general intelligence. The company was founded in January 2022 and is currently training a neural network to utilize all available software tools and APIs in the world. On September 14, 2022, the Adept team launched its first foundation model—Action Transformer (ACT-1)—which was specifically designed and trained to perform actions on computers in response to natural language commands. It is the first step toward a foundation model that can use every software tool, API, and website in existence.

Adept AI seeks to build a general-purpose system that can help people complete any task in front of their computers and serve as a universal AI collaborator for every knowledge worker. This product would not only be useful for computer users, but could be the most practical and secure way to achieve general intelligence. Future foundation models will be trained to use every existing software tool, API, and web app.

ACT-1 is a large-scale transformer trained to use various existing digital tools. It is currently connected to a Chrome extension that allows ACT-1 to perform actions in the browser such as clicking, typing, and scrolling. ACT-1 simplifies work by capturing, executing, and inferring actions. The user simply types a command into the text box and ACT-1 does the rest. This can be especially powerful for manual tasks and complex tools. For example, what might ordinarily take 10+ clicks in Salesforce can be now done with just a sentence. When working in-depth in tools like spreadsheets, ACT-1 demonstrates real-world knowledge, infers what users mean from context, and can help users do things they may not even know how to do. Moreover, ACT-1 can complete tasks that require composing multiple tools together, look up information online, and correct mistakes in human feedback.

Adept AI will use ACT-1 as a basis to continually train its foundation model until it achieves the ultimate Action Transformer. Capturing and modeling interaction actions are more challenging than modeling text data, so iterative improvements will be necessary to enhance the efficiency and performance of the existing model. In the future, Adept AI may continue to focus on iterating its models to improve their general capabilities.

In the short and medium term, ACT-1 can be used as a productivity tool that is highly efficient, secure, and easily accessible for daily office tasks. In the long term, ACT-1 has the potential to transform the way humans interact with machines, revolutionizing man-machine interaction. Adept AI believes that most interaction with computers will be done using natural language. This may lead to the emergence of new OSs or platforms that could completely transform the way humans interact with computers. Additionally, AI may take over simple and repetitive software operations.

6.8.2 Cohere: Offering Tailored ToB AI Services

Cohere is a Canadian AI startup that was founded in 2019. It provides developers and enterprises with NLP solutions that do not require expensive ML development. This empowers developers to solve language-related issues using large neural networks and cutting-edge AI without relying on any public cloud. Additionally, Cohere's models can be deployed on private clouds or on-premises.

Cohere has created the T-Few technique to efficiently fine-tune LLMs while addressing the challenges of long training time and high service costs. The architecture of T-Few is displayed in Fig. 6.22. T-Few fine-tuning selectively updates only a fraction of the model's weights and stacks multiple fine-tuning rounds to significantly reduce training time while maintaining high-quality fine-tunes. It introduces two parameter-efficient mixture of experts (MoE) methods: Mixture of Vectors (MoV) and Mixture of Low-Rank Adaptation (MoLORA). For tasks that have not been seen before, T-Few fine-tuning, as demonstrated in Fig. 6.23, only requires updating 0.32% of the parameters to achieve comparable performance to full fine-tuning and outperform standard parameter-efficient techniques like $(IA)^3$ and

6.8 Innovative Unicorns Enabling AI Applications

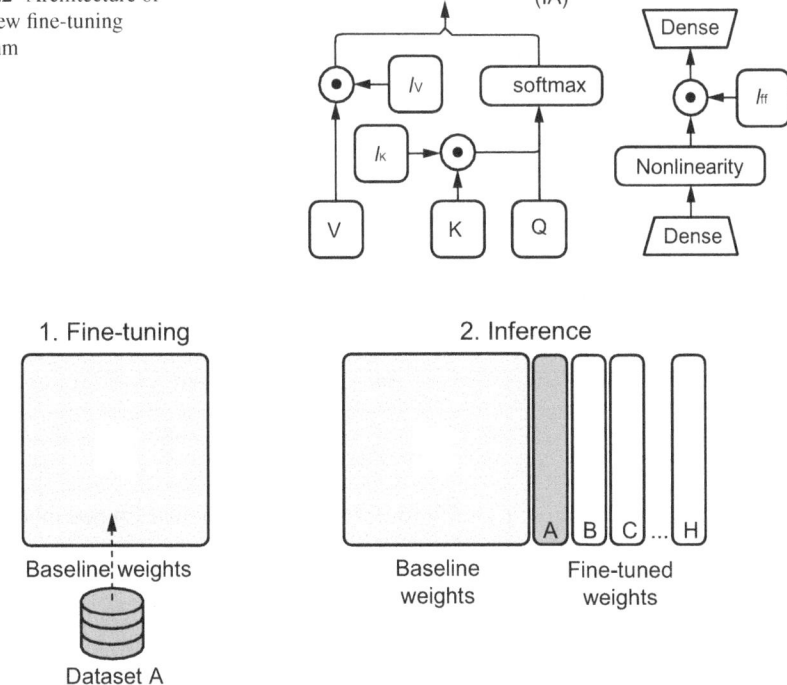

Fig. 6.22 Architecture of the T-Few fine-tuning algorithm

Fig. 6.23 T-Few fine-tuning process

Low-Rank Adaptation (LoRA). Cohere's research team tested T5 models ranging from 11 bytes to 770 MB on 12 different tasks using 55 datasets and achieved consistent results.

Cohere also uses Retrieval-Augmented Generation (RAG) to enhance the accuracy of conversations. RAG is a method that builds a language model-based system capable of accessing external knowledge sources to complete more complex and knowledge-intensive tasks. This enables greater factual consistency, improves reliability of the generated responses, and helps to minimize AI hallucinations. With RAG, Cohere's chat products can better understand the intent behind the message, remember conversation history, and respond intelligently through multi-turn conversations. RAG also connects users' models to web searches and important data sources, improving the relevance and accuracy of chat responses. Cohere trains Command specifically to improve the accuracy of RAG tasks by identifying relevant information from multiple data sources, as well as reducing hallucinations and creating trust between generated responses and users with citations to understand where responses are coming from.

Cohere is dedicated to providing tailored generative AI services for enterprise customers. Cohere's vertical application products focus on three key text-related domains in enterprise operations, including Summarize, Generate, and Command

Model/Adapter	Mean win rate 1 [sort]	MMLU-EM 1 [sort]	BoolQ-EM 1 [sort]	NarrativeQA-F1 1[sort]	NaturalQuestions (closed-book)-F1 1[sort]	NaturalQuestions (open-book)-F1 1[sort]	QuAC-F1 1 [sort]	HellaSwag-EM 1 [sort]	Openboo kQA-EM 1 [sort]	TruthfulQA-EM 1 [sort]
text-davieci-002	**0.914**	0.568	0.877	0.727	0.383	0.713	0.445	0.815	0.594	0.61
Cohere Command beta (52.4B)	0.906	0.452	0.856	**0.752**	0.372	0.76	0.432	0.811	0.582	0.269
text-davied-003	0.879	0.569	0.881	0.727	0.406	0.77	0.525	0.822	0.646	0.593
TNLG v2 (530B)	0.828	0.469	0.809	0.722	0.384	0.642	0.39	0.799	0.562	0.251
Anthropic-LM v4-s3 (52B)	0.815	0.481	0.815	0.728	0.288	0.686	0.431	0.807	0.558	0.368
Jurassic-2 Jumbo (178B)	0.799	0.48	0.829	0.404	0.385	0.669	0.421	0.788	0.558	0.437
gpt-3.5-turbo-0301	0.782	0.598	0.739	0.536	0.384	0.637	0.437	-	-	**0.639**
J1-Grande v2 beta (17B)	0.762	0.445	0.812	0.725	0.337	0.625	0.392	0.764	0.56	0.306
Lumincus Supreme (70B)	0.739	0.38	0.775	0.711	0.293	0.649	0.37	-	-	0.222

Fig. 6.24 HELM

models for text generation, Classify for text classification, and Embed models and Semantic Search Rerank for text retrieval.

In Stanford's Holistic Evaluation of Language Models (HELM), Command beta—a conversational model fine-tuned from the largest Command model with 52.4 billion parameters—ranks second among 61 models. With an accuracy of 90.6%, it is only outranked by the GPT-3.5 series model text-davinci-002. See Fig. 6.24.

6.8.3 Jasper: Offering Integrated AI Marketing Tools

Jasper, founded in 2021, is committed to developing AI assistants for business that can help enterprises write marketing content such as blog posts, social media content, sales emails, and website copywriting. Jasper is an ideal AI for business, enabling users to quickly create diverse high-quality content, including marketing campaigns, emails, and blogs. It is rated the number one AI platform for creators and marketing teams.

Jasper supports multimodal and multi-usage content generation, allowing users to create content anytime in a Blank Document, Template, Blog Post, or Art form using browser extensions, as shown in Fig. 6.25.

Jasper Chat is a chatbot based on a series of models (such as the GPT series, T5, and BLOOM). It automatically selects the most appropriate model based on the user's input and combines it with search engine results to generate accurate content for the user. Jasper Chat is built for business use cases like marketing and sales. It learns from the massive number of articles, forums, video transcripts, and content published on the web, enabling it to have conversations about complex subjects with superb detail. Jasper Chat can also help users generate prompts, cite personalized

6.8 Innovative Unicorns Enabling AI Applications

Fig. 6.25 Multimodal content generation supported by Jasper

What makes Jasper the better AI for business?

	Jasper	ChatGPT+
Feels like your brand, not generic	✓	✗
Writes factually about your business	✓	✗
Knows up-to-date information & cites sources	✓	✗
Built for marketing performance	✓	✗

Fig. 6.26 What makes Jasper better suited for marketing than ChatGPT

brand content, remember previous conversations, and create content in more than 30 languages.

Jasper supports multiple languages and optimization tools. Its AI engine extracts data from top models, including OpenAI's GPT-4, Anthropic, and Google's language models. It then combines the data from these models with the latest search data, brand voice, search engine optimization (SEO), and syntax optimization tools to produce the best quality outputs. As described in Fig. 6.26, Jasper is better suited for marketing than ChatGPT.

6.8.4 DiDi: Integrating AI into Autonomous Driving

Autonomous driving is a significant trend in the ride-hailing industry and presents new opportunities in automotive development. DiDi set up its autonomous driving unit in 2016 and upgraded it to an independent company in 2019. In 2020, DiDi Autonomous Driving launched and successfully completed a test autonomous driving service, marking the beginning of large-scale demonstration applications of intelligent connected vehicles in Shanghai. Since 2023, DiDi has been rapidly developing autonomous driving services. On April 13, it unveiled its first robotaxi concept car, DiDi Neuron, and its first automated O&M center. The company also

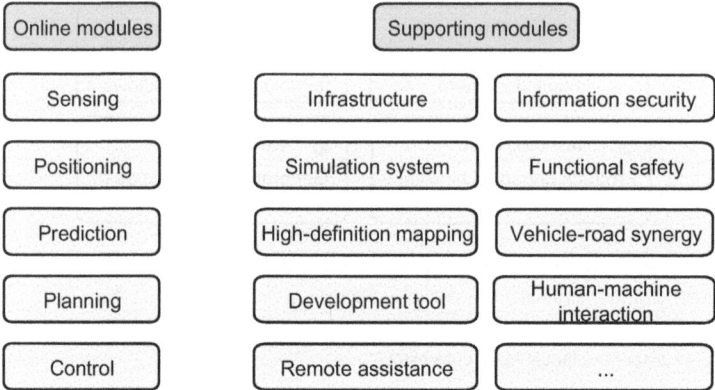

Fig. 6.27 AI capabilities integrated into DiDi's autonomous driving system

announced its progress in technology, hardware, mass production, and new service exploration. In May 2023, DiDi Autonomous Driving and GAC Aion signed an agreement to deepen their collaboration and jointly introduced the AIDI Plan for mass production of self-driving electric vehicles. Their first mass-produced model is expected to be introduced to DiDi's shared mobility network in 2025 for a large-scale mixed dispatching system.

DiDi's autonomous driving system consists of online modules and supporting modules, as shown in Fig. 6.27. The online modules connect to the network automatically and include sensing, positioning, prediction, planning, and control modules. The supporting modules provide interaction capabilities such as information security, high-definition mapping, development tools, and vehicle-road synergy.

6.8.5 Dataa Robotics: Empowering Humanoid Robots with Cloud Brain

Dataa Robotics is a top unicorn company that leads the way in developing, manufacturing, and operating cloud robot systems and services. The company focuses on the R&D of cloud intelligent robots and is committed to developing an operator-level large-scale intelligent platform that integrates ML and operations. As of December 2022, Dataa ranked first in the world for cloud robot patents with over 1600 patent applications filed.

Dataa unveiled its first-generation humanoid robot—Ginger 1.0—at the Mobile World Congress (MWC) 2019, and later introduced its iterative version—Ginger 2.0—at the World Artificial Intelligence Conference (WAIC) 2022. Ginger 2.0 features the in-house developed Smart Compliant Actuator (SCA) 2.0 and is mainly used for reception and guidance, celebratory events, elderly care, etc. Table 6.12 lists the technical specifications of Cloud Ginger 2.0.

6.8 Innovative Unicorns Enabling AI Applications

Table 6.12 Technical specifications of Cloud Ginger 2.0

Technical specifications	Description
Height (m)	1.60
Weight (kg)	80
Degrees of freedom (DOF)	41 flexible joints
Grasping ability (kg)	5
Battery life	12 h (secondary battery installable)
Sensor	Monocular red-green-blue (RGB) camera 3D depth camera Lidar Single-point time-of-flight (ToF) camera
End effector	7-DOF skillful hands
Interaction	Real face (lifelike, cute, and smart for a better interactive experience)

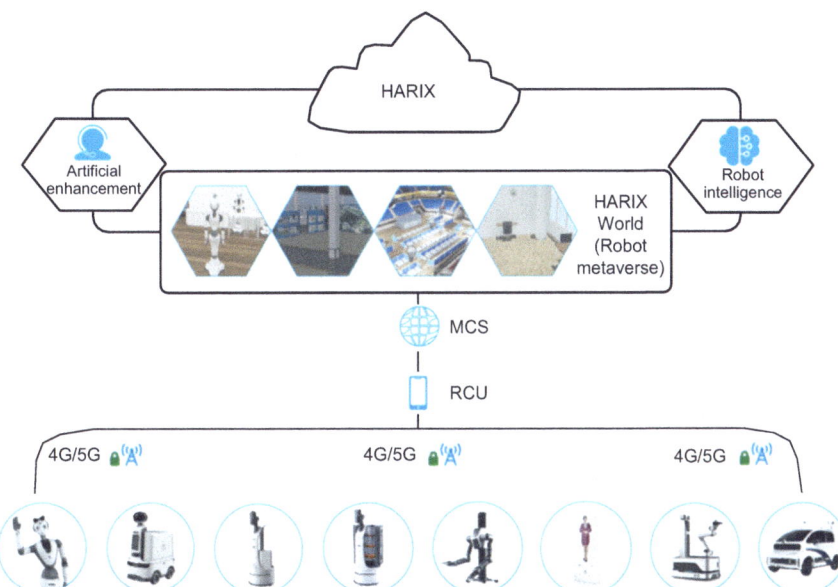

Fig. 6.28 Cloud brain of Dataa's robots

On August 16, 2023, Dataa Robotics debuted its first bipedal humanoid robot, the XR4, at the World Robot Conference (WRC). This versatile robot is powered by the Dataa cloud brain and designed for a wide range of applications. Standing at 165 cm tall and weighing 65 kg, the XR4 is made of numerous carbon fiber composites and features over 60 smart flexible joints.

All of Dataa's robots feature the cloud brain, as shown in Fig. 6.28. Cloud Ginger features real-time multimodal DL of the converged intelligent cloud brain, which powers the following functions: image/object/posture/face/emotion recognition, visual-guided grasping/movement/pressing, 3D semantic mapping for grasping/movement, simultaneous localization and mapping (SLAM), visual SLAM (VSLAM), autonomous navigation and obstacle avoidance, NLP, a rich vertical knowledge base and multiple rounds of dialogue, and multi-robot collaboration based on the cloud brain scheduling platform.

References

1. China Academy of Information and Communications Technology (CAICT). White Paper on the Global Digital Economy [R]. 2023.
2. TF Securities. Quantitative Measurement of the Growth of Chinese AI Chips by 2024 [R] (in Chinese). 2023.
3. CSC Financial. Investment Opportunities in the Semiconductor Industry Chain: Optimistic About Semiconductor Localization and Reversal in the New Development Cycle Powered by AI [R] (in Chinese). 2023.
4. iResearch. 2023 China AI Industry Research Report [R] (in Chinese). 2023.
5. DU C L, WANG T Z, and WANG C W. Development Status, Challenges, and Countermeasures of AI Chip Technology in China's Digital Economy [J] (in Chinese). Science and Technology Management Research, 2023, 23(12): 1–10.
6. Gartner. Top 10 Strategic Technology Trends for 2023 [R]. 2023.
7. IDC. China AI Software Market Share in 2022 [R]. 2022.
8. WANG Q, SU L, and XIE Z G. Research on the Trend of AI Framework Technology [J] (in Chinese). Artificial Intelligence Security, 2023, 2(1): 46–52.
9. LeadLeo Research Institute. 2021 China AI Development Platform Market Report [R]. 2021.
10. Gartner. Cloud Native AI Accelerates AI Engineering Implementation [R]. 2022.
11. CAICT. Cloud Computing Development Research [J] (in Chinese). Big Data Time, 2020 (8): 28–39.
12. KPMG. Prospects for the Global Transformation of Artificial Intelligence: A Leap Forward is Coming (2023) [R] (in Chinese). 2023.
13. CAICT. AI R&D Operations System (MLOps) Guide (2023) [R] (in Chinese). 2023.

Chapter 7
Dawn of the Large Model Era

Large models have swiftly emerged as one of the foremost artificial intelligence (AI) technologies developed on the back of breakthroughs in pivotal fields like algorithms, big data, and computing power. It is predicted that the global market of large AI models will be valued at over USD28 billion in 2024, and this number will surpass USD100 billion in 2028 with large models advancing and new technologies emerging. Enterprises and organizations will have more powerful solutions at their disposal on data analysis, prediction, and intelligence. The AI sector will see new business opportunities and greater potential. All these will generate constant momentum for the large model market.

7.1 History and Features of Large Models

7.1.1 Parameter Size Jumps: Fast Iteration in Three Phases

Large models are defined by their large scale, use of pre-training, and deep neural network architecture. They use a huge number of parameters, typically over one billion, and are pre-trained on vast amounts of general data to achieve good generalization; these deep neural network models are built over the Transformer architecture and feature parallel computing and self-attention. Large models usually use deep learning algorithms such as convolutional neural networks (CNNs), recurrent neural networks (RNNs), and language models to automatically extract features from data and give more accurate predictions.

Large models have their roots in natural language processing (NLP). In the 1950s, computer scientists began to explore how to make computer programs understand and generate natural languages [1], focusing on rule- and knowledge-based methods. Since the term "artificial intelligence" was coined in 1956, AI has evolved from small-scale knowledge-based expert systems to machine learning frameworks.

In 1980, the initial form of CNNs was developed. A major breakthrough was LeNet-5 in 1998, a groundbreaking architecture that has become the core foundation of modern CNNs and helped transition machine learning from shallow models to deep learning. LeNet-5 provides the necessary framework on which extensive research has been conducted into natural language generation, computer vision (CV), and other fields. It also helps advance subsequent deep learning frameworks and large model development.

A major shift in large model evolution began in 2006 when the concept of deep learning was proposed by a paper in the journal *Science*. The advances in deep learning have greatly promoted the progress of NLP. In 2010, Tomáš Mikolov and his team introduced an RNN-based language model, which heralded rapid development of NLP. One of AI's big bang moments came in 2012 when AlexNet won the ImageNet challenge, a feat that sparked a surge of attention to and research in deep learning. It was around this time that industry pioneers such as Google and Baidu began to invest heavily in AI research. For Google, this accumulated in the release of DistBelief deep learning model by Google Brain in 2013, which paved the way for large-scale distributed training. In 2014, generative adversarial networks (GANs), considered one of the most powerful models in the twenty-first century, were developed, marking a new phase in deep learning with a focus on generative models.

Pre-trained models were first theorized in 2015, kick-starting the rapid development of large models. The core ideas behind pre-trained models are transfer learning and model reuse, which can significantly reduce model training costs. Models are pre-trained on massive amounts of data, a practice that minimizes gaps between what models learn and the real world and allows for fine-tuning on domain-specific data.

The following years saw an explosive growth in large models due to rapid technology iteration. There are three main phases in the development of large models: pre-trained models, large-scale pre-trained models, and ultra-large-scale pre-trained models, as shown in Fig. 7.1.

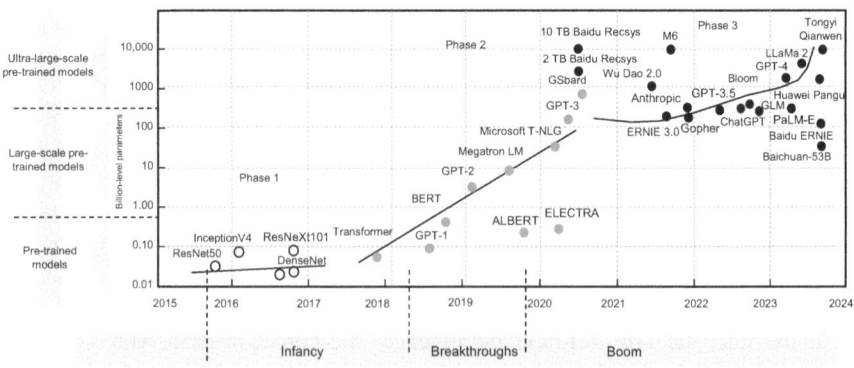

Fig. 7.1 Three phases in the development of large models

7.1 History and Features of Large Models

1. Infancy (pre-trained models)

    Large models were in their infancy from 2015 to 2017. In this first phase, pre-trained models such as ResNet-50 and DenseNet created a base for subsequent large models. ResNet introduced residual learning, which mitigated the vanishing and exploding gradient problems that used to make deep neural networks difficult to train. This framework opened a new avenue for deep learning, from which several well-known models such as DenseNet and ResNeXt were soon developed. During these years, researchers came to realize that models can be designed following some basic principles, without requiring numerous techniques or modifications.

2. Breakthroughs (large-scale pre-trained models)

    In 2017, Google proposed the Transformer architecture in a paper, which achieved groundbreaking progress in machine translation and paved the way for its widespread adoption in large-scale pre-trained models. Since then, large models entered a phase of breakthroughs. In 2018, two major developments in large-scale pre-trained models took place: Google released Bidirectional Encoder Representations from Transformers (BERT), a large-scale pre-trained Transformer-based model, and OpenAI introduced Generative Pre-trained Transformer (GPT). BERT-Base was implemented with 110 million parameters and GPT-1 117 million parameters, while BERT-Large was even larger at 340 million parameters. These models were orders of magnitude larger than their counterparts at that time in terms of parameter count. In 2019, OpenAI released GPT-2 (1.5 billion parameters), and later Google released the T5 model (11 billion parameters). Researches in China also launched a series of large language models, including Tsinghua University's ERNIE and Baidu's ERNIE. In this second phase, the major focus was on language models.

3. Boom (ultra-large-scale pre-trained models)

    The third phase began in 2020 when OpenAI released GPT-3 (175 billion parameters), the world's first pre-trained model with hundreds of billions of parameters. Since then, large-scale pre-trained models have been undergoing explosive growth, with a global boom of research on pre-trained models of that scale. The next breakthrough came in November 2022 with the release of ChatGPT, which can perform a variety of tasks, such as answering questions, writing articles, generating codes, and solving mathematical problems, all through a simple dialog box. Unlike previous NLP systems that require multiple specialized models for all these capabilities, ChatGPT is powered by a single large language model. In March 2023, GPT-4, a much more powerful model than its predecessor, was released. With its multimodal understanding, GPT-4 showcases capabilities that are close to artificial general intelligence (AGI). Other models released in this phase include Google's Bard, Baidu's ERNIE Bot, Huawei's Pangu models, iFLYTEK's Spark, Zhipu AI's ChatGLM, and Fudan University's MOSS. Figure 7.2 shows the large language models (with more than ten billion parameters) released since 2019.

As more participants are entering the arena of large AI models globally, large AI models are now speeding on a fast track, with technologies advancing and more

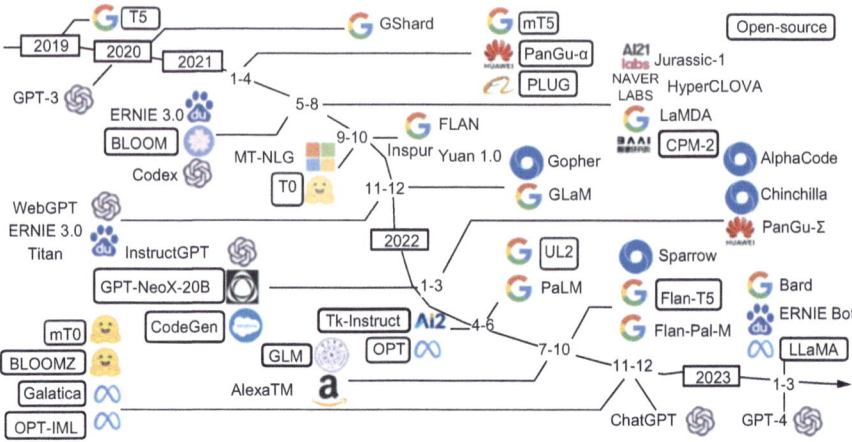

Fig. 7.2 Large language models (with more than ten billion parameters) released since 2019

applications emerging in a vast range of industries. Future development will likely center on automating the process of model building and deployment and making it easier for industry users to utilize AI capabilities.

7.1.2 Collaboration of Large and Small Models for On-Device Model Deployment

Machine learning models are typically classified by the number of trainable parameters. A large model has a massive number of parameters, while a small one has fewer. Trainable parameters are those that have their values learned and optimized by the algorithm during training to maximize model performance. In contrast to small models, large models typically employ more parameters, more complex structures, and more units per hidden layer or convolution kernels; they can process more complex tasks in diverse scenarios and larger datasets with higher accuracy and stronger prediction. Nevertheless, both model types have their pros and cons, even small models, which are indispensable for some workloads.

Large models provide high accuracy and strong generalization. The vast amounts of data to train the models ensure that they can make accurate predictions by capturing patterns and trends that are more obvious than others in an input dataset. And pre-training, combined with transfer learning, allows large models to make reasonable inferences, fill in missing information, and generate content when faced with new data. These adaptability, generalization, and intelligence also stem from the training on massive amounts of general data and knowledge, which reduce the reliance of the models on labeled data and therefore remove issues of data insufficiency. The drawback, however, is the expensive training costs. Model training requires hardware such as high-end processors and random access memories

7.1 History and Features of Large Models 153

(RAMs) for computing and storage, and model training on mass datasets takes more time and incurs higher computational costs. These large models also face a risk of overfitting in their pursuit of high accuracy.

Small models lack the accuracy and processing performance in complex tasks that are possible with large models, but are cheaper to train and offer greater flexibility. By requiring less training data and incurring fewer costs from data collection, they are perfectly suited for specific projects or those where data is scarce and often used for rapid iteration and experimentation for more accurate results. Owing to the small parameter scale, training can be completed more cheaply and in less time, making them suitable for rapid verification and prototyping for large model deployment in the future. Small models do not require expensive or specific hardware and software as large models do. Instead, they can be deployed in lightweight environments such as mobile applications, embedded systems, and browser plug-ins and easily migrated between different hardware and software platforms. They can be loaded and executed faster, fitting well into scenarios that require low latency and real-time inference. One last advantage is privacy protection. As opposed to most cloud-based large models, training and running inference on small models can be performed on local devices without transferring user data to the cloud. This mitigates privacy risks, which is important in privacy-sensitive applications like facial or voice recognition. Figure 7.3 makes a feature comparison between large and small models.

In summary, both large and small models have pros and cons and are suited for different applications. Large AI models offer efficient fitting and high accuracy, making them well suited for NLP, CV, and recommendation systems, at the cost of expensive hardware, long training time, and high-performance computing resources (such as standard Graphics Processing Units [GPUs] or cloud clusters). By

Dimension	Large model	vs.	Small model
Required data volume	Large		Small
Parameter count	Large		Small
Prediction capability	Strong		Weak
Generalization	Strong (possibly overfitting)		Weak (underfitting)
Training speed	Slow		Fast
Hardware requirement	High		Low
Deployability	Poor		Good
Privacy protection	Poor		Good
Application scenario	Large and complex datasets and wide application scenarios		Small datasets and simple application scenarios

Fig. 7.3 Feature comparison between large and small models

comparison, small models have limited accuracy and prediction capabilities, but induce lower hardware costs, allow quicker training, and can be flexibly deployed on low-power devices like smartphones or Internet of Things (IoT) devices. These features make small models attractive choices for simple and small-scale applications, such as those in vertical sectors. Developers would need to weigh up the computational resources, storage space, electricity, and accuracy demands for a given project before choosing the model type.

In the coming years, by collaborating, large and small models will complement each other, promoting AI development and addressing issues efficiently and cost-effectively. Large models will pass on their general capabilities to small models, so that small models can process tasks more accurately. In turn, small models will feed their application data and results to large models to drive continuous iteration of large models. This collaboration between large and small models is expected to improve overall accuracy while reducing energy consumption [2]. After all, massive amounts of parameters are not what the industry is pursuing. Instead, the future focus will be less reliance on labeled data, better model effects, higher model performance, and easier deployment.

7.1.3 Synergy of Large Models and AI

The emergence of large models can be attributed to multiple key factors during AI evolution, and in turn large models like GPT have ushered in a new era in AI evolution. Thanks to progress in general data, hardware computing power, and optimization algorithms, large models use pre-training for self-supervised learning on mass unlabeled data, avoiding the silos typical with small models. Figure 7.4 illustrates the relationship between AI and large models.

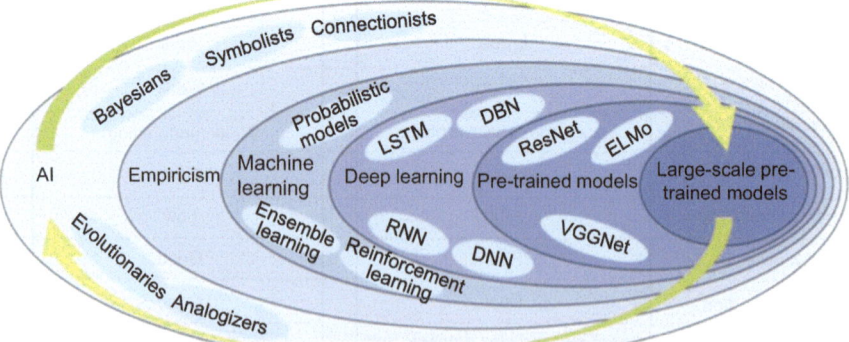

Fig. 7.4 Relationship between AI and large models

7.1 History and Features of Large Models

1. A feasible path to AGI

   Before the emergence of large models, there were doubts about whether deep learning could achieve human-like intelligence. Large models have blazed a trail toward AGI, where immense computing power, big data, and mass parameters are the biggest determinants. They have shown that large-scale parameter learning may be able to achieve human-like intelligence even without basic understanding of how intelligence is generated.

2. A new paradigm in AI R&D

   Conventional R&D for AI models requires small teams working in specific domains, in which any independent issue requires research on new architectures and acceleration, training, and evaluation methods tailored to address that issue. Despite contributing to AI development, these fragmented processes are isolated and their breakthroughs have poor generalizability and cannot be easily combined with other AI advances. In contrast, the R&D for ultra-large-scale models is similar to a large-scale engineering project, gathering talent in algorithms, data, hardware, and other disciplines for collaborative achievements. In this way, large models are speeding up the development of inclusive and accessible AI systems, as shown in Fig. 7.5.

3. A driving force behind deep learning

   Large models are continuously unlocking the benefits of deep learning by integrating critical elements on a massive scale such as computing power, algorithms, data, and knowledge. As a landmark technology of next-generation AI, large models are pivotal in driving breakthroughs in deep learning, especially in areas like NLP, intelligent speech, and CV, making AI R&D no longer fragmented and accelerating use of AI. In this context, AI infrastructure is seeing faster development and AI is becoming more influential and inclusive.

4. A foundation for strong AI

   Large models serve as an engine in advancing AI capabilities toward strong AI. They also stand as a bridge between weak AI and strong AI, accelerating the formation of new infrastructure in the intelligent era. From the perspective of system engineering, large models sit at the core of AI. They connect underlying computing power of chips and actual requirements of the upper application layer. From the perspective of model algorithms, large models serve as a basis for large-scale AI algorithm innovations, enabling a transformative shift from

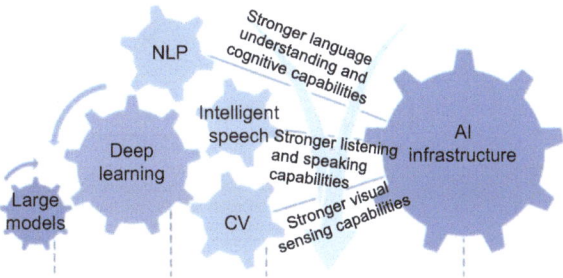

Fig. 7.5 Large models as a catalyst for inclusive and accessible AI

fragmented AI applications to highly integrated applications. In many ways, the rise of large models is a product of both technological advancements and market forces. And today, large models are the most powerful driving force behind AI. They are pushing weak AI forward through phases of technology development, industry application, and industry transformation toward becoming an enabling infrastructure across a vast range of industries. Figure 7.6 illustrates the roles of large models as both an engine and a bridge in AI development.

7.1.4 Faster Iteration and Development Trends of Large Models

In recent years, large models have been using more parameters, performing better, and been iterated faster. Several trends can be identified in the development of large models.

1. Family-based development

   Since 2018, OpenAI has launched a series of GPT models, including GPT-1, GPT-2, GPT-3, GPT-3.5, and GPT-4. Each new version builds upon its predecessors. For example, GPT-4 uses much more parameters than the previous GPT models and demonstrates immense potential in various applications, including optimizing man–machine interaction experience, providing professional services, improving organizational efficiency, and promoting cultural inheri-

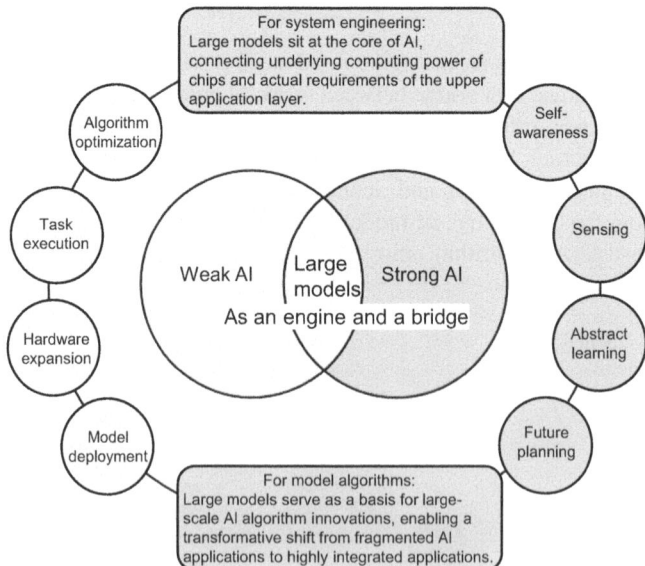

Fig. 7.6 Large models as an engine and a bridge

tance and preservation. The release of ChatGPT also sparked a boom in related ecosystems around GPT, with more enterprises connecting their products to ChatGPT, powering Jasper, Quizlet, Shop, and many other excellent commercial applications across areas such as language-based creation, man–machine interaction, education, painting, audio and video, and retail. Such family-based development can also be found in other models, for example, Huawei's Pangu models and Baidu's ERNIE models (evolving from ERNIE 1.0).

2. Multimodal development

   The ability to aggregate multimodal data is a major factor in increasing accurate representation spaces. Several multimodal models have been developed, such as DALL·E and Contrastive Language-Image Pre-training (CLIP) from OpenAI, which work on 12 billion parameters and excel at tasks like image generation. Institutions like Alibaba DAMO Academy and Beijing Academy of Artificial Intelligence (BAAI) are also developing multimodal pre-trained models. In March 2021, the Alibaba DAMO Academy worked with Tsinghua University to release M6, a multimodal pre-trained model in Chinese with 100 billion parameters. In June that year, the next-generation M6 running on trillions of parameters was trained using 480 V100 GPUs, consuming over 80% less computing power with a training efficiency 11 times as high as its counterparts trained by Google, NVIDIA, and other institutions. M6 has been applied in over 30 services of Alibaba and can perform tasks such as multimodal search, visual question answering, image-based text generation, and generation of 1024 × 1024 pixel images.

3. Knowledge fusion

   With stronger decision-making capabilities, large models can provide innovative solutions in line with general reasoning and beyond common sense. To ensure accurate decisions and adaptation in more complex industry scenarios in the future, large models should be pre-trained on multiple types of network data. An example of such a model is Google's Multitask Unified Model (MUM), which is pre-trained on a large amount of web page data. It has good understanding and can solve complex decision-making queries. MUM supports 75 languages and can search for information from multimodal web page data across languages. For instance, it can search Japanese sources for travel tips even if a user writes a query in English. This model illustrates that a large model learning from comprehensive modalities can better understand complex information and generate content [3].

7.2 Typical Applications of Large Models

The construction of foundation models for general use is considered the key to staying competitive for leading enterprises around the world, such as those in Internet and computing. Since the first large language model emerged in 2018, many enterprises have developed their NLP, CV, and multimodal models. Figure 7.7 shows the development of the three types of large models, which are continuously iterated and updated at a rapid pace.

7.2.1 NLP Models

1. Overview

NLP is a major application of large models. NLP modals originated from Google's Transformer, a deep learning architecture released at 2017. The Transformer uses large-scale pre-training and self-supervised learning and can train high-performance NLP models on large-scale computing resources. Continuously improving compute capabilities and expanding datasets have made large language models a mainstream tool for NLP.

There are many types of NLP models, the most typical of which are BERT and the GPT series models. Designed for bidirectional language pre-training, BERT is famous for its powerful language understanding capabilities and is widely used for NLP tasks. GPT series models are autoregressive language models that use the Transformer architecture. Large-scale pre-training and generative task training make GPT models adept at language generation, allowing them to be extensively used for diverse applications such as text creation, summarization, and translation.

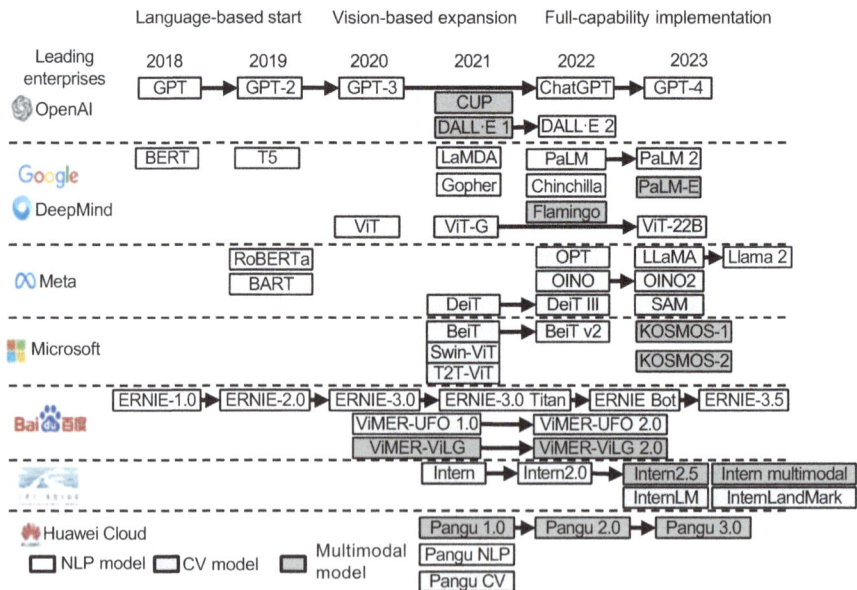

Fig. 7.7 Development of the three types of large models

NLP improves language understanding and model generation by large-scale pre-training and self-supervised learning. Pre-training trains a model on vast amounts of unlabeled text data, allowing the model to learn from large corpuses and understand a language better. Self-supervised learning is a paradigm with which a model is trained on large amounts of supervisory signals. This enables the model to automatically discover the intrinsic correlations and patterns of input sequences and understand or generate text data, eliminating the need to manually label training data [4].

2. Research progress

GPT-4 as a closed-source foundation model is now a leading NLP model and ranks first in massive multitask language understanding (MMLU, a major benchmark proposed by the University of California, Berkeley (UC Berkeley) and other organizations to measure the knowledge of large language models in English across 57 subjects), Multi-turn Benchmark (MT-Bench), and Arena Elo (a rating system released by UC Berkeley and other organizations to evaluate the instruction compliance and skill of large language models based on their performance in question answering and interference tasks), as described in Tables 7.1 and 7.2. Nevertheless, as technological research and innovative applications continue to develop at a rapid pace in the industry, open-source foundation models, such as Large Language Model Meta AI (LLaMA), are constantly improving, challenging closed-source models.

Technological iteration helps open-source models enhance their reading comprehension, common sense reasoning, world knowledge, programming, and other capabilities. Open-source models can perform certain tasks as well as closed-source models. Meta's LLaMA, Tsinghua University's ChatGLM, and Shanghai Artificial Intelligence Laboratory's InternLM are typical open-source large models that continue to be iterated on with the aim of breaking the technical barriers of closed-source models. Iterations of open-source models require higher quality and quantity of training data and larger context lengths. In China, vendors and research institutes have followed up on this development, with universities and institutes of science and technology being the main driving force. Numerous open-source foundation models in and outside China have been made

Table 7.1 MMLU

Model	Vendor	Parameter quantity	Score (%)
GPT-4	OpenAI	–	86.4
PaLM 2	Google	–	78.3
Chinchilla	DeepMind	70B	67.6
InternLM	Shanghai Artificial Intelligence Laboratory	104B	67.2
LLaMA	Meta	65B	63.4
Falcon	TII	40B	63.2
Guanaco	University of Washington	65B	62.2

Table 7.2 MT-Bench and Arena Elo

Model	MT-Bench score	Arena Elo score
GPT-4	8.99	1227
GPT-3.5	7.94	1130
Claude	7.90	1178
Vicuna-33B	7.12	–
WizardLM-30B	7.01	–
Guanaco-33B	6.53	–
LLaMA-30B	6.41	–
PaLM	6.40	1038
Vicuna-13B	6.39	1061

fully open for research and commercial purposes. Table 7.3 provides an overview of open-source foundation models.

Meta's LLaMA is a pivotal open-source large model. Organizations and vendors have developed more than ten models by fine-tuning LLaMA on instructions. Universities and research institutes play a leading role in fine-tuning training, which constructs high-quality instructions as fine-tuning data to improve the ability of models to follow instructions. Chinese organizations mainly perform "data localization" and technology follow-up. Currently, China's open-source models are trained on high-quality instruction data and stand out among global models with billions of parameters in tasks such as subject examination, common sense reasoning, reading comprehension, and mathematical computation.

In addition, enterprises are starting to build NLP service capability platforms, frameworks, and tools to lower the technical threshold for using the technology. Leading and innovative enterprises provide users with multiple services such as application programming interface (API) invoking, model training, and solutions on these platforms. NVIDIA has launched the Label Sleuth platform, an easy-to-use open-source system for labeling and creating text classifiers. Cohere, a startup company, has provisioned a range of NLP services, including large model-based API services that can offer NLP capabilities with three lines of code. Baidu and Huawei in China have developed R&D frameworks and tools for deep learning and can provide users with diverse NLP service capabilities such as model training, model deployment, and easy model invoking.

3. Service applications

NLP models have found a wide range of applications, such as sentiment analysis, text summarization, machine translation, question answering, speech recognition, and text generation. Models like OpenAI's GPT-2 and GPT-3 or Google's BERT and ALBERT are adept at sentiment analysis, text summarization, text generation, and other tasks.

(a) Sentiment analysis

NLP models excel at sentiment analysis. They can identify semantic relationships in text and help users understand content and analyze text senti-

7.2 Typical Applications of Large Models

Table 7.3 Overview of open-source foundation models

	Open-source foundation model	Vendor/organization	Release date	Parameter quantity	Number of training tokens	Maximum context length	Commercial use or not
US-developed models	LLaMA	Meta	February 2023	7B/13B/33B/65B	1 T	2000	No
	Llama 2	Meta	July 2023	7B/13B/33B/65B	2 T	4000	Yes
	Falcon	TII	May 2023	7B/40B	1.5 T	2000	Yes
	BLOOM	BigScience	July 2022	1.1B/1.7B/3B/7.1B	1.5 T	2000	Yes
China-developed models	ChatGLM	Zhipu AI (Tsinghua University)	March 2023	6B	1 T	2000	Yes
	ChatGLM2	Zhipu AI (Tsinghua University)	June 2023	6B	1.4 T	32,000	Yes
	Baichuan	Baichuan AI	June 2023	7B/13B	1.2 T/14l	4000	Yes
	InternLM	Shanghai artificial intelligence laboratory	June 2023	7B	1.6 T	8000	Yes
	QWE	Alibaba cloud	July 2023	7B	2.2 T	8000	Yes

ment. Enterprises can use insights from sentiment analysis to improve their products, formulate marketing solutions, correct errors, and identify positive influencing factors.

(b) Text summarization

NLP models can automatically summarize long pieces of text such as news reports and academic papers. A typical model for text summarization is BERTSUM, which is based on the BERT model and generates highly readable text summaries.

(c) Machine translation

NLP models can achieve high-quality translation using pre-training and fine-tuning technologies. A key area of development is multilingual translation in contexts with limited resources. Major models include Microsoft's DeltaLM, which supports 102 languages, Google's mT5, and Baidu's ERNIE-M. Increasing the model size can significantly improve generalization. For example, Meta's NLLB-200 general language model has 50 billion parameters and can provide state-of-the-art quality translation between over 200 languages. It has been applied on Facebook and Instagram and performs more than 25 billion translations per day.

(d) Question answering

Question answering is a common application of NLP models. Question answering systems built on large language models can understand questions and extract answers from large knowledge bases or text corpuses. Question answering is mainly used for tools like intelligent assistants and customer service robots. Google's BERT-QA is a typical question answering system. This system uses the BERT model for text input, separately encodes questions and contexts into vectors, and matches vectors to predict answers.

(e) Speech recognition

Speech recognition tasks have been greatly simplified thanks to the improved performance of accelerated computing for neural networks. NLP models can accurately identify pronunciation, pace, rhythm, and intonation in audio files, improving speech recognition and synthesis systems. A typical engine in this field is DeepSpeech, which can train speech recognition models with high accuracy and is easy to deploy.

(f) Text generation

NLP models can learn probability distribution using large amounts of text data to generate language models that simulate natural languages. They can also perform tasks like automatic text generation or summarization to accurately and flexibly generate text data such as news reports, novels, and emails. These applications demonstrate the broad potential of NLP models in language processing tasks and are changing language processing. Moreover, the models can be combined with other techniques and methods to build more intelligent and efficient language processing systems.

4. Innovative applications

NLP models fulfill needs that previous technologies could not, creating new opportunities in a wide range of industries, including education, healthcare, scientific research, law, and finance.

(a) Session-based information search

Most existing search engines can only return a list of web pages in response to user queries without understanding user intent or accurately summarizing the answers for users. NLP models allow next-generation search engines to return accurate answers based on specific user information needs over multiple sessions. In February 2023, Microsoft officially launched a new AI-driven Bing search engine and a next-generation Edge browser, which integrates ChatGPT to allow users to communicate directly with AI. The new version of Bing comes with an extended chat box. In addition to answering questions about facts and providing links, it can solve more complex search issues by generating personalized plans, suggestions, and analysis in real time with the help of ChatGPT.

(b) Intelligent research assistant

NLP models can interpret scientific documents, explain scientific concepts, summarize scientific research progress, and help users write and prepare papers, speeches, and project proposals. NLP models can be used to build intelligent scientific research assistant systems that benefit researchers across different phases of research. Google's Minerva language model launched in July 2022 is one such intelligent assistant. It can answer difficult questions in subjects like mathematics, chemistry, and physics and correctly resolve nearly one third of the problems in diverse undergraduate quantitative reasoning disciplines such as physics at Massachusetts Institute of Technology (MIT). Another example is the JiuZhang model from Renmin University of China. This pre-trained language model for mathematical problem understanding has demonstrated success in nine downstream tasks.

(c) Intelligent fiction creation

NLP models can automatically generate or assist in writing literary outlines or paragraphs. ChatGPT can write fictions with simple plots. Sudowrite, an AI-powered writing tool developed based on GPT-3, can create unique text after learning general concepts, assisting creators in quickly generating high-quality content, including novels, blogs, marketing copy, academic papers, and more. Sudowrite can also automatically write syntactic and logical articles based on inputs and the specified style.

(d) Virtual doctors and assistants

NLP models can obtain a wealth of medical knowledge from large volumes of literature. It is expected that trusted virtual doctors will be able to suggest appropriate treatment and rehabilitation measures by talking with patients and assessing physical indicators. For example, Google announced Conditions, a search tool for clinicians that can summarize patients' medical conditions and organize patients' medical records to significantly improve diagnosis and treatment efficiency.

(e) Virtual psychological consultants

Greater awareness of mental health has enabled more people to seek professional help, which has exacerbated shortages of mental health consultants. Moreover, patients are often reluctant to disclose their private information to consultants. This is where virtual psychological consultants powered by NLP models come in. These virtual consultants can help individuals deal with psychological issues and enhance their well-being. Woebot is a Facebook Messenger-based chat robot launched in 2017 that has demonstrated about two times higher efficacy in mental health treatment than medication. Using feedback loops in manually trained generative AI, Woebot can accurately identify and mitigate suicide risks in users, serving as a good listener that helps users feel comfortable.

(f) Intelligent investment consultants

By being fed large volumes of finance-related materials, NLP models can judge financial situations and stock trends to provide users with investment advice. Du Xiaoman, which went live in 2022, is a typical AI investment consultant. It applies NLP technologies and image algorithms on the intelligent credit investigation middle-end to interpret credit investigation reports into 400,000 risk variable dimensions. This helps financial institutions identify credit risks of small and micro enterprise owners and improve risk differentiation by 26%. Iterative updates of large models will further unleash their intelligent risk control potential.

7.2.2 CV Models

1. Overview

The rapid development of deep learning technologies and the improvement of compute capabilities have enabled CV models to make significant advances in tasks such as image classification, object detection, object segmentation, object tracking, and pose estimation. Basically, a CV model is designed to take an image as input and output detected information (such as the class or location of any object in the image).

Google's Vision Transformer (ViT) attracted wide industry attention in 2020, and the infancy stage of CV model development began in 2021, with ViT-based CV models launched one after another, including Transformer iN Transformer (TNT), Shifted window (Swin), and self-distillation with no labels (DINO). Notable CV models like ResNet, Inception, Visual Geometry Group (VGG), EfficientNet, and MobileNet all use different architectures and optimization techniques to improve their computational efficiency and accuracy. As CV models can automatically extract features from input images and generate high-quality image results, they are suited to applications for which large amounts of image data need to be processed, such as autonomous driving, facial recognition, security surveillance, and medical image analysis.

There are three types of prompts used in CV models: text prompts that consume low computing power and require low-complexity models for intuitive inputs; visual prompts that consume moderate computing power and require moderate-complexity models; and multimodal prompts that consume high computing power and require high-complexity models with strong generalization. Although still in the infancy stage, CV models have demonstrated competence in small-dataset segmentation and helped improve visual generalization and reduce development costs for security, logistics, and more fields. In the future, more advanced technology and reduced computing power costs will result in a significant increase in the overall penetration rate of CV models across industries.

In the industry chain of CV models, there are compute infrastructure, data service providers, and algorithm framework providers in the upstream, vendors of large models in the middle stream, and services and vertical applications in diverse industries in the downstream. The upstream compute infrastructure is primarily composed of AI computing chips, computing power/network devices, and data centers, forming the foundation for CV models. Gradual commercialization of AI will make inference components constitute a larger proportion of the models.

2. Research progress

ViT is the most common form of architecture for CV models. Unlike traditional CNNs and RNNs, which provide only local connectivity, ViT can establish context relationships between pixels in parallel across an entire image range. ViT outperforms traditional models in image feature extraction and classification tasks. Figure 7.8 shows the ViT model architecture. Research on ViT exploded in 2022, and the scope of application for ViT is expanding. It can generate vivid continuous video frames and 3D scenes using 2D image sequences, detect targets in point clouds, and speed up the progress of text-to-image generators using diffusion models for artificial intelligence generated content (AIGC). Open-source ViT has been improved in both model structure and downstream tasks and continues to make breakthroughs in task performance and coverage.

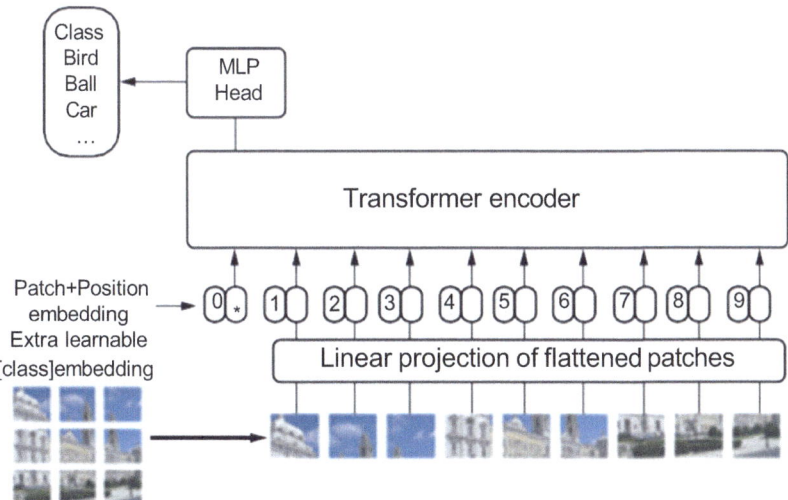

Fig. 7.8 ViT model architecture

Derivatives of open-source ViT are continually improving models. ViT can be combined with modules such as multi-scale attention, knowledge distillation, and self-coded image reconstruction to improve model feature extraction. Typical derivative models include Microsoft's Swin Transformer, Meta's MAE and DeiT, ETH Zurich's Pyramid Vision Transformer (PVT), and McGill University's Convolutional vision Transformer (CvT). Figure 7.9 shows the architecture upgrade of the open-source ViT model.

The basic ViT model continues to be fine-tuned for new tasks and applications. Different pre-training architectures are used for fine-tuning, enabling breakthroughs in downstream tasks such as classification, segmentation, image retrieval, and depth estimation. For example, Meta's Segment Anything Model (SAM) allows zero-shot generalization for any segmentation task by learning the general concepts of objects. Large models such as Baidu's Unified Feature Optimization (UFO), the Intern2.5 model jointly released by SenseTime and Shanghai Artificial Intelligence Laboratory, and Huawei's Pangu use diverse training data, advanced training and inference frameworks, and flexible and easy-to-use fine-tuning and deployment tool chains.

Looking ahead, CV technologies will face challenges in adapting to the three-dimensional world, eliminating the need to labeled data inputs, reducing computing power consumption, integrating and analyzing multimodal information, combining knowledge with logic to solve complex problems, and proactively sensing and adapting to complex changes. As technology homogenization does not necessarily mean algorithm homogenization, engineering capabilities of CV algorithm vendors remain the touchstone for technology implementation in the industry.

3. Service applications

The service applications of CV models have expanded from traditional applications such as image classification, semantic segmentation, and object detection to new areas such as video repair, image generation, visual question answering, and multitask deployment. The goal of CV model application is to provide general solutions for traditional visual subtasks, reduce deployment costs, and improve efficiency.

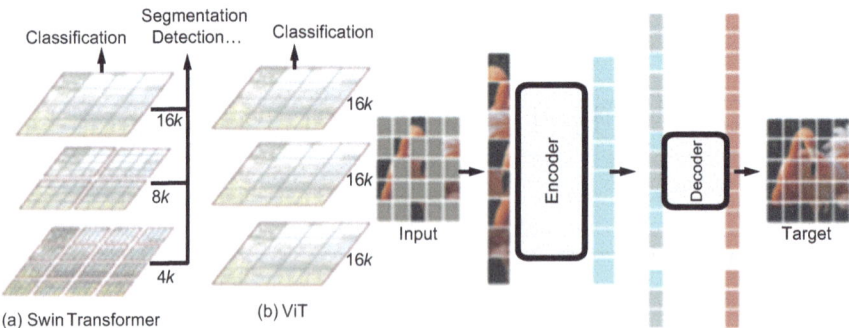

Fig. 7.9 Architecture upgrade of the open-source ViT model

7.2 Typical Applications of Large Models

(a) Image classification

CV models are suitable for object detection and image classification tasks. For example, models can be trained with powerful image recognition capabilities by using CNN and large-scale training data for deep learning. These types of models have gained prominence in CV applications.

(b) Semantic segmentation

Semantic segmentation classifies input image pixels by assigning a semantic label to each pixel. CV models can capture more contextual information and details in semantic segmentation tasks, improving the accuracy and robustness of segmentation.

(c) Video repair

CV technology can automatically detect and fix noise, jitter, underexposure, and other problems in videos to improve video quality. With deep learning, CV models can also improve definition, color, smoothness, and blemish removal.

(d) Image generation

CV models can generate diverse image forms, such as real-world photos, cartoons, or works of art. GAN is a very popular type of image generation technology that uses two neural networks against each other, one generating an image and the other evaluating the deviation of the generated image from the real image.

(e) Visual question answering

Through image recognition, understanding, and reasoning, visual question answering answers questions asked using natural language. CV models can be combined with NLP technology to answer image- or video-related questions, describe contexts, and engage in intelligent conversations.

4. Innovative applications

CV models are still in the early stages of development and will be extensively used in security monitoring, autonomous driving, medical image analysis, smart home, and other fields.

(a) Remote sensing and mapping

CV models can be used for geographic information extraction and analysis. By training deep learning models on satellite remote sensing images and aerial images, elements such as urban buildings, roads, and green spaces can be automatically identified and classified. This provides urban planning departments with a large amount of geographic information to assist in natural resource planning and land use decision-making. For example, in the regular monitoring of natural resources in Guangdong, China in 2022, the Guangdong Land & Resources Surveying and Mapping Institute extracted more than 300,000 image patches over the year with the assistance of SenseEarth's change detection algorithm, which proved to be five times more efficient than manual labeling.

(b) Intelligent security

CV models can be used for video surveillance. By training large-scale deep learning models, suspicious behaviors and individuals in video surveillance footage can be automatically identified and alerted on. In addition, CV models can be used in facial recognition systems to automatically identify and verify personnel identity, making security more intelligent. For example, Huawei's Pangu CV model helps enable urban security perception. Urban managers can use this large model's image generalization analysis on massive amounts of urban video resources for rapid and comprehensive monitoring of security events and use scenario-based small models for collaborative discovery, achieving comprehensive awareness of city security risks.

(c) Autonomous driving

CV models can segment an image of a vehicle in motion to label the objects and regions in the image and to help the autonomous driving systems perceive and understand the surrounding environment more accurately. This improves the safety and efficiency of autonomous driving. For example, the Meta-developed Segment Anything Model (SAM) is a segmentation model used to generate high-quality object masks based on input prompts (such as points, boxes, masks, and text) for all objects in images. The use of SAM for pedestrian recognition and lane line tracking can help autonomous driving systems predict pedestrian and vehicle movement trajectories, preventing traffic accidents.

(d) Logistics monitoring

Logistics involves massive numbers of documents with inconsistent formats and quality. The abilities to rapidly and accurately identify documents, extract structured data, and perform operations like supplementation and error correction are indispensable to the quality and efficiency of subsequent waybill distribution and on-time delivery. CV models demonstrate good image recognition and labeling and are predicted to fulfill the optical character recognition (OCR) needs of the logistics industry. For example, SPD Bank released SPD Bank Cloud Warehouse jointly with Huawei based on the Pangu CV model. In this project, one model can be applied to nine logistics scenarios and can monitor the entire process from goods receiving, inbound, storage, to outbound. The Pangu model can not only ensure accurate counting of cargoes unloaded from forklifts, but slash the sample collection and labeling workload of hundreds of different boxes in warehouses by using its capability of few-shot learning. This model can shorten the project development cycle from 1 to 2 months to 2 to 3 days, greatly lowering development costs while improving development efficiency.

(e) Smart farming

CV models, together with cameras and sensors deployed on farmland, can enable automatic monitoring and analysis of crop growth, pests and disease, and other information. This helps farmers improve crop yield and quality. For example, the next-generation general vision system Intern released by Shanghai Artificial Intelligence Laboratory and SenseTime can systematically solve common issues in the CV field such as task generalization, scenario generalization, and data efficiency. Intern can achieve 99.7% accu-

racy in the flower species identification task with only two training samples per category.
(f) Medical diagnosis

CV models can be used for automatic analysis of medical images to assist with diagnosis. By training large-scale deep learning models, medical images such as X-rays, computerized tomography (CT) scans, and pathological sections can be automatically identified and analyzed. This significantly improves the work efficiency and reduces the misdiagnosis rates of AI doctors, allowing them to provide more accurate treatment guidance. For example, Google has developed a deep learning model that can detect disease using external ocular photography, capturing useful biomarkers from photos to detect retinopathy, elevated glycosylated hemoglobin (HbA1c), and high cholesterol in diabetic patients, reducing the need for specialized equipment, and expanding the possibilities for health screening.

7.2.3 Multimodal Models

1. Overview

A multimodal model combines different large models to optimize various tasks. Its main goal is to process and correlate heterogeneous information from multiple sources (such as audio, text, image, and video) and comprehensively extract knowledge of different modalities. Unlike a unimodal model such as a CV or NLP model, a multimodal model must be pre-trained on large datasets of multiple modalities. After pre-training, the multimodal model can be adapted to downstream tasks to improve their accuracy. A typical multimodal task includes cross-modal data retrieval (such as text-to image or image-to-text search), visual question answering (answering questions with images), and visual positioning (locating the most relevant object or region in an image based on a natural language expression) [5].

OpenAI demonstrated its extraordinary multimodal capabilities at the launch of GPT-4. For example, GPT-4 can generate detailed and accurate image descriptions, explain unusual visual phenomena and identify humorous elements in images, and even build websites from hand-drawn wireframes. The multimodal capabilities of GPT-4 offer more application possibilities. For e-commerce, merchants can input product images into GPT-4 to generate product descriptions that are more natural; for entertainment, GPT-4 can be used for game design and virtual role creation to give players more personalized gaming experiences.

On May 9, 2023, Meta announced the open-source multimodal model ImageBind, an integrated large AI model that can generate multi-sensory content across six modalities: image, text, depth, thermal, audio, and inertial measurement unit (IMU) data. ImageBind formulates a single shared representation space from multiple types of image pairing data. It does not require datasets for which all modalities concur. Instead, it uses the binding nature of image and other modalities to correlate between modalities. Figure 7.10 shows the ImageBind model.

OpenAI has also developed many multimodal AI applications. For example, DALL·E and CLIP can identify objects in an image while generating descriptive text for the image or generate new related images from text.

Advances in multimodal technology are enabling multimodal AI to achieve a higher degree of convergence in understanding and processing different types of data. Algorithms and models can establish relationships between different data types to extract shared information across modalities. Compared with interaction or input/output through natural language alone, multimodal AI is inherently more perceivable, interactive, and sensible, which are closer to the real world. It has vast potential for human–machine interaction and comprehensive intelligent applications and is a major step in the path toward general intelligence [6].

2. Research progress

There are currently three parallel technical routes for multimodal models.

Route 1: A large language model acts as the central processor and integrates external vision experts for generative tasks over multiple rounds of interactions.

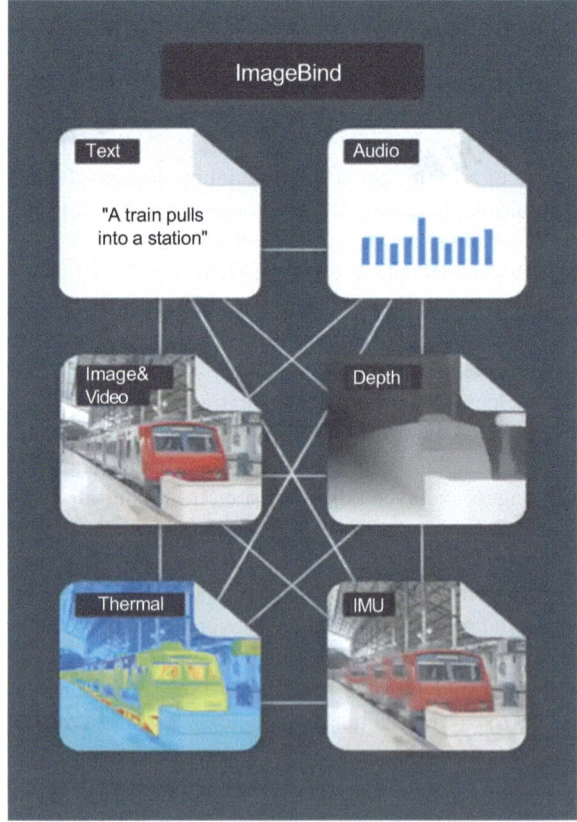

Fig. 7.10 ImageBind model

7.2 Typical Applications of Large Models

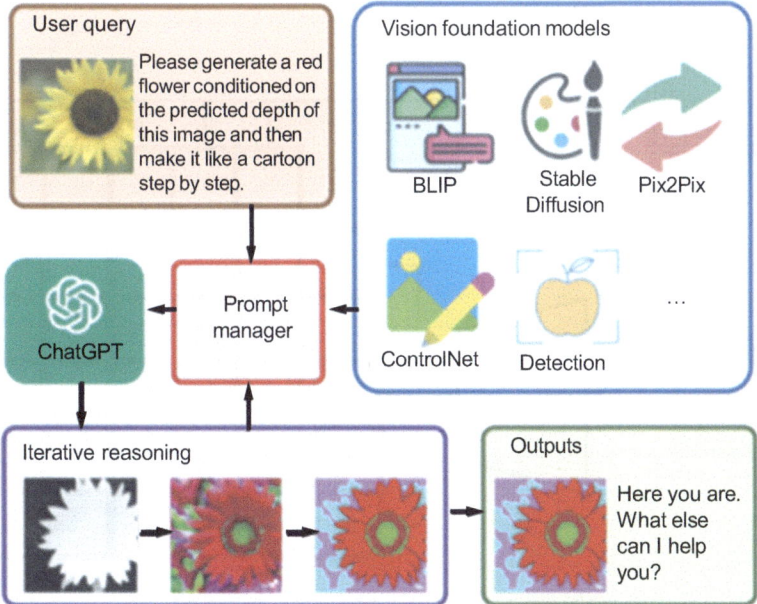

Fig. 7.11 Visual ChatGPT framework

Typical models include OpenAI's Visual ChatGPT, Zhejiang University and Microsoft Research Asia's HuggingGPT, and Google's PaLM-E. Figure 7.11 shows the framework of Visual ChatGPT, in which ChatGPT functions as the central processor and completes tasks by invoking other models (such as vision foundation models ViT, BLIP, and StableDiffusion).

Route 2: Through cross-modal feature learning alignment, image information and text information can be aligned and combined for cross-modal interaction to implement image and text understanding and generative tasks. Typical models include Microsoft's KOSMOS series, OpenAI's CLIP and DALL·E, and Stability AI's Stable Diffusion. Figure 7.12 shows the cross-modal feature comparison and learning architecture of CLIP. CLIP co-trains an image encoder and a text encoder and aligns the features of different modalities to learn which images are paired with which texts in a dataset.

Route 3: With fine-tuned learning of multimodal models, cross-modal encoders are used for information interaction between different modalities. Pre-trained language and vision models are frozen separately, with visual and textual feature space aligned by means of small-scale parameter fine-tuning. Furthermore, small-scale "visual-textual" instruction datasets are constructed as prompts for model fine-tuning to improve the multimodal understanding and inference capability. Typical models include DeepMind's Flamingo, Salesforce AI Research's BLIP and InstructBLIP, the University of Wisconsin-Madison and Microsoft Research's LLaVA, Shanghai Artificial Intelligence Laboratory's LLaMA-

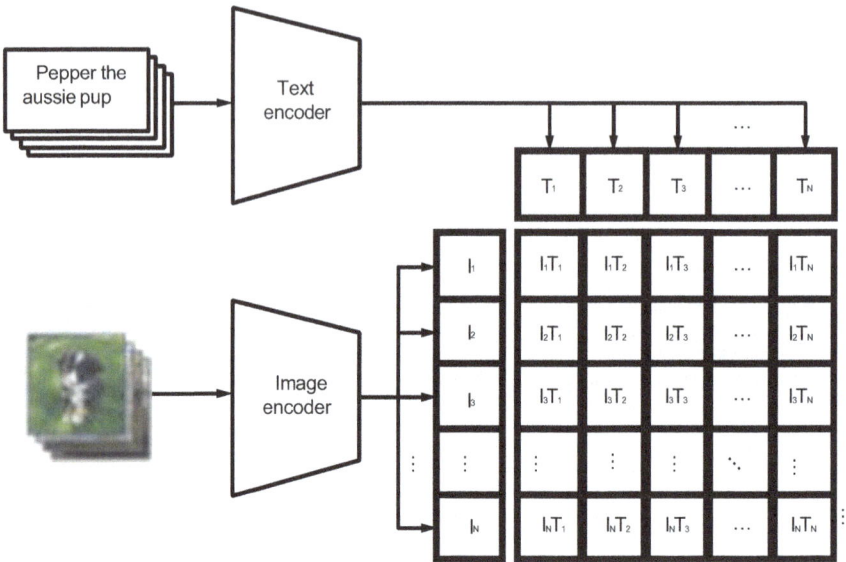

Fig. 7.12 CLIP cross-modal feature comparison and learning architecture

Adapter V2, and King Abdullah University of Science and Technology's Mini GPT-4.

3. Service applications

Types of tasks that can be handled by multimodal models can be broadly categorized into visual understanding, image-text retrieval, image description, visual question answering, visual reasoning, and visual generation.

(a) Visual understanding

In the AI field, visual understanding refers to the ability of a computer system to interpret and understand visual information. Its focus is to enable the backbone architecture of the neural network to achieve powerful image understanding through pre-training. Model pre-training methods can be divided into three categories by supervisory signal: label-based supervision, language-based supervision, and pure visual self-supervision (which uses supervisory signals sourced from images). In addition to contrastive learning, non-contrastive learning, and masked image modeling, commonly used pre-training methods include multimodal fusion, and region-level and pixel-level image understanding.

(b) Image-text retrieval

Image-text retrieval is a kind of multimodal retrieval that embeds multiple types of data (such as image, audio, and text) into the same space for information interaction and retrieval. The core value of image-text retrieval is to understand and align information of different modalities, convert image and text features into multimodal eigenvectors, and then retrieve informa-

7.2 Typical Applications of Large Models

tion based on similarities between the eigenvectors to improve retrieval efficiency and accuracy.

(c) Image description

Image description is a typical multimodal task that generates a textual description based on a given image. With CV and NLP technologies at its core, image description is a promising research direction that combines image recognition and NLP for deep learning.

(d) Visual question answering

Visual question answering is a learning process that uses CV technology for image understanding and NLP technology for question understanding. The two technologies are combined to process questions in an image context and then generate answers in natural languages.

(e) Visual reasoning

Visual reasoning is similar to visual question answering, but uses the reasoning capabilities of models for difficult input questions and involves multi-hop relationships between objects. Visual reasoning aims to understand objects and scenes in images through inference and deduction, helping computers understand and process image information. Visual reasoning techniques based on knowledge graphs and logical reasoning are seeing wider use.

(f) Visual generation

Visual generation plays a crucial role in AI-powered image generation and understanding. It generates not only images, but a variety of content such as videos and 3D point clouds. In addition to content creation in such fields as art and design, it can be used to synthesize training data to promote the closed-loop development of multimodal content understanding and generation. Its focus is on how to generate images that are consistent with human intentions. Four related research directions are spatially controllable generation, text-based re-editing, text-based prompt generation, and customized-concept generation. There is currently a trend to research on creating general text-to-image models that cater to human intentions and improve the substitutability of the above directions.

4. Innovative applications

Multimodal models can integrate data sources across domains practically and in a scalable manner, providing support for complex problem-solving. Research and application of multimodal models have made remarkable progress in many vertical fields, such as healthcare, law, finance, and art, forming a blue ocean of innovative applications.

(a) Creative design

Multimodal models open up new possibilities in design and art by analyzing image and text data to automatically generate new works of art or provide designers with more creative design solutions. For example, the DALL·E 2-based AI application Midjourney can generate images from text descriptions, that is, it can automatically generate images in under 1 minute after users input any scene, object, character, or style of their imagination,

without using any preset category or template. It also provides functions such as infinite zoom out, editing, and sharing.
(b) Market forecast

Through the integration of sales data, customer feedback, market trends, and other multi-dimensional information, multimodal models can achieve more accurate market forecasts and predict potential risks, helping enterprises adjust strategies and prevent risks. For example, China's first large retail finance model Tianjing can expand the capabilities of data analysts, explore the value of data, and lower the threshold for data use. Its structured query language (SQL) generation platform allows users to send language instructions to AI without using code or other professional instructions. This model can automatically understand requirements, search for data, generate responses, and complete data mining tasks as required.

(c) Medical diagnosis

Multimodal models can combine medical image data, patient medical history, genetic data, and other multimodal information, such as CT scans, magnetic resonance imaging (MRI), and X-rays, to assist doctors in diagnosis and medical image analysis, improving diagnostic accuracy. For example, Google DeepMind's AlphaFold, a deep-learning-based multimodal AI system, uses biology and computer science to predict a protein's 3D structure, reshaping drug discovery and disease research. MicroNeuro, a neurosurgical robot integrated with the Zidong.Taichu large model combines real-time visual, tactile, and other multimodal information during surgery and helps doctors make real-time surgical inferences. Peking Union Medical College Hospital is using the model's powerful logical reasoning to seek breakthroughs in diagnosis and treatment of rare diseases.

(d) Immersive experience

Multimodal AI can enhance the ability to process real-time voice, text, images, and videos in social media, creating richer and more immersive gaming and augmented reality (AR)/virtual reality (VR) experiences. In the next 5–10 years, it is predicted that complex multimodal models will be able to fully interact with the world and find applications in general-purpose robotics, VR, and other fields. For example, Meta's multimodal model ImageBind allows for understanding and conversion between the six modalities of image (the main modality), text, audio, depth, thermal (infrared radiation), and motion (IMUs), which will dramatically accelerate the construction of the metaverse and provide users with more immersive metaverse experience.

(e) Smart office

Using a multimodal model in document intelligence technology is one of the major development trends for smart office. The speech recognition and image generation functions of a multimodal model can be used for conference recording, speech recognition, management and production of multimedia content, and the like. This can provide meeting and collaboration support, multimedia content management, and automated document processing for offices. For example, LayoutLM, a document intelligence model developed by Microsoft Research Asia, can process large amounts of unlabeled data to understand multimodal, multi-format, and multi-language rich text content. LayoutLMv3 released in 2022 has become a benchmark model for industry research with its broad applicability and superior capabilities. Many leading enterprises, especially enterprises in the robotic process automation (RPA) field, have LayoutLM in their document intelligence products.

(f) Industrial quality inspection

CV technology plays a vital role in defect detection, which is an important step in quality control. Given the significant variation in product quality inspection between industries, the emergence of multimodal models can improve the efficiency and applicability of quality inspection. For example, the Zidong.Taichu multimodal model combines multimodal information. In textile quality inspection tasks, this model can use voice recognition to check for broken weft and warp threads, and use visual recognition to identify cloth defects, improving quality inspection efficiency and reducing the error rate by about 66%.

7.3 Computing Power as the Foundation of Large Models

Large AI models require large amounts of computing power. The training time for a model is directly proportional to the number of parameters and training data volume. According to a theoretical projection of industry papers, the theoretical end-to-end training time of a large model is $8TP/(nX)$, where T is the number of tokens of the training data, P the number of model parameters, n the number of AI hardware cards, and X the valid computing power of each card. For ChatGPT, the training time would be 49 days given 175 billion parameters, 3500 billion tokens, and 8192 cards in use for pre-training. Based on industry experience, with other conditions unchanged, a model size with more parameters requires more compute volume and more cards. Specifically, to achieve an acceptable training time, 10 billion, 100 billion, and one trillion parameters would need 100, 1000, and 10,000 cards, respectively. Larger model sizes and data volumes create much higher requirements on the scale of computing resources. Inadequate computing power cannot support high-quality large-model technological innovation.

Large models will revolutionize AI computing power, and the increase in the number of parameters will lead to the exponential growth of computational demands for training. To quickly train large-scale models, powerful computing power is required to support distributed training and parallel computing. Increased use of high-performance computers and distributed compute platforms will be critical for large-scale model training and iteration.

7.3.1 General-Purpose Computing Power for Meeting the Requirements of Most Common Users

General-purpose computing power primarily consists of the compute capability output from Central Processing Units (CPUs). It is suitable for complex logic operations and is an important part of AI applications. There are many typical CPU companies in China, such as Beijing Loongson, Shanghai Megacore, CETC Suntai, Tianjin Phytium, Huawei, and Hygon. Their CPU products have a wide range of applications in the AI field, such as NLP, CV, and voice interaction.

Huawei Kunpeng is built based on the Kunpeng processor and functions as a set of full-stack IT infrastructure, industry applications, and services. The Kunpeng processor has three distinct advantages: (1) Powerful performance: As the industry's first 64-core data center processor, the Kunpeng processor delivers 35% higher performance than the industry's mainstream processors under the same power consumption, providing more efficient computing power for diverse applications, such as cloud computing, big data, distributed storage, and high-performance computing. (2) High integration: The Kunpeng processor has a CPU integrated with a southbridge, network interface card (NIC), and serial attached SCSI (SAS) storage controller, delivering 4-chip functionality through a single chip. This enables the server to free up more slots for more accelerated component functions, dramatically improving system integration, reliability, and ease of maintenance while reducing complexity and costs. (3) High reliability and security: Kunpeng uses advanced reliability, availability, and serviceability (RAS) technologies and supports memory error checking and correcting (ECC), memory address parity check, memory remapping, and other functions, improving the fault tolerance and stability of the system. It also provides multi-layer securities, such as secure boot, running, and storage, to protect system data and code from tampering and leakage.

For Kunpeng ecosystem collaboration, Huawei has established 4700 partnerships worldwide since 2019 and is working with partners on technology innovation, product R&D, and market expansion, fueling Kunpeng applications and providing more compute solutions for customers worldwide. Partners include those for the servers, hardware, and software. Huawei has already collaborated with 11 server partners. These partners have developed high-performance and high-reliability server products based on the Kunpeng processor to meet the needs of different customers.

7.3.2 Intelligent Computing Power Suitable for Simple Logic and Compute-Intensive Concurrent Tasks

Intelligent computing power primarily stems from GPUs, field programmable gate arrays (FPGAs), and AI chips. It is suitable for simple logic and compute-intensive concurrent tasks and is an important part of AI applications. Currently, there are

7.3 Computing Power as the Foundation of Large Models

many typical GPU, FPGA, and AI chip companies and their products in the market, like GPU vendors NVIDIA, AMD, and Intel; FPGA vendors Xilinx and Altera; and AI chip vendors Huawei, Cambrian, and Bit Continent.

In September 2023, Huawei released the Atlas 900 SuperCluster, a new Ascend AI computing cluster, to support the training of large models with over a trillion parameters. This new cluster uses Huawei's brand new Xinghe AI computing switch CloudEngine XH16800, which has high-density 800GE ports that can accommodate 2250 nodes (equivalent to 18,000 cards) in a two-layer switching network for ultra-large-scale non-convergence cluster networking. The new cluster uses an innovative supernode architecture to greatly improve large model training and leverages Huawei's comprehensive advantages in computing, networking, storage, and energy to improve system reliability at the component, node, cluster, and service levels, delivering improved stability of large model training.

The industry ecosystem around Huawei Ascend AI centers on constant innovation of the Ascend AI software and hardware platform to unleash surging Ascend power and maintain industry-leading performance. The platform consists of Atlas series hardware, Compute Architecture for Neural Network (CANN), all-scenario AI framework MindSpore, MindX for Ascend application enablement, and one-stop AI development platform ModelArts. Based on the Ascend series, Huawei has launched Atlas 900 AI training clusters, Atlas 800 AI training servers, Atlas 500 AI edge stations, Atlas 300 AI inference cards and training cards, and Atlas 200 AI accelerator modules, completing the layout of the entire series of Atlas products to provide powerful computing power for training and inference for all cloud, edge, and device applications. Figure 7.13 shows the Huawei Ascend AI industry ecosystem.

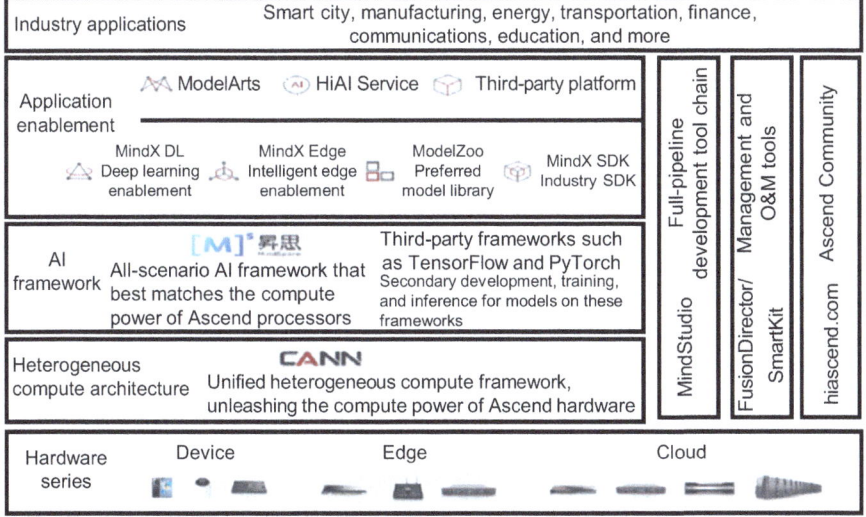

Fig. 7.13 Huawei Ascend AI industry ecosystem

In addition, Huawei has released CANN 7.0, a more open and easy-to-use heterogeneous compute architecture, which is not only compatible with the industry's AI frameworks, acceleration libraries, and mainstream models, but makes available the underlying capabilities. This ensures that AI frameworks and acceleration libraries can more easily invoke and manage computing resources and developers can customize high-performance operators to create distinct competitive advantages with large models. By July 2023, the Ascend AI cluster had supported the construction of AI computing centers in 25 cities in China. The public computing platforms in seven of the cities have been selected as the first batch of national open innovation platforms for next-generation AI public computational power. In addition, in the Ascend AI field, Huawei has collaborated with over 30 hardware partners and over 1200 individual software vendors, jointly launched more than 2500 industry AI solutions, and applied solutions in diverse industries including communications, Internet, and finance.

7.3.3 High-Performance Computing Cluster for Special Applications

High-performance computing (HPC) is a computer cluster system that connects computer systems using diverse interconnection technologies. It relies on the integrated compute capability of all the connected systems to handle computing tasks at scale. For this reason, HPC is also often referred to as an HPC cluster. HPC uses powerful clusters of processors working in parallel to process massive multi-dimensional datasets (big data) and solve complex problems at a very high speed. HPC provides ultra-high floating-point computing capability solutions for the computing needs of compute-intensive and massive data processing tasks with shorter computational time but higher accuracy. HPC systems typically run more than one million times faster than the fastest commercial desktops, laptops, or server systems. With high computing power, high storage capacity, and high transportation capacity, HPC is widely used in scientific research, aerospace, weather forecasting, energy exploration, industrial manufacturing, life sciences, smart city, and other government and research fields, playing an irreplaceable role in scientific and technological development.

For example, Lenovo Intelligent Computing Orchestration (LiCO) is a one-stop HPC solution suited to high-performance clusters of various sizes. As a set of supercomputing center management software, LiCO is the core of Lenovo's HPC product x9000. LiCO not only allows for quick deployment of an HPC cluster, but provides administrators and common users with an easy-to-use platform for cluster deployment, monitoring, control, and distributed file system management functions. Moreover, all its HPC software interfaces are directly available to users, allowing users to easily customize requests or perform secondary development. Continued advancements in technology are contributing to the gradual integration of HPC with cloud computing, big data, AI, and other technologies as well as the emergence of CPU + GPU heterogeneous compute architecture. Lenovo has enhanced LiCO to create LiCO-AI, an HPC + AI one-stop solution that supports both HPC and AI tasks through unified resource scheduling in a cluster. LiCO-AI integrates the cluster scheduling software, monitoring software, computing library, and distributed file system for quick deployment of an HPC + AI cluster. This integration provides HPC-based computing power for AI and AI-based optimization for HPC, empowering more enterprises and industries.

7.4 Large Models Empowering Generative AI

With the emergence of novel ideas such as digital avatars and the metaverse, content generation technology has been sweeping through various sectors including entertainment, finance, and design. Multimodal digital content generation takes advantage of generative AI to create new content like images, videos, audio, text, and music. Industry analyst Gartner predicts that over 80% of enterprises will have used generative AI APIs or models and deployed generative AI-enabled applications in production environments by 2026. Generative AI is seeing greater market potential as its applications are expanding. It will not only serve as the foundation of content generation for entertainment, but as the cornerstone of digitalization in the business world.

According to *China's AI-enabled Digital Business Outlook for 2021–2025*, a report by Zhongguancun Big Data Industry Alliance, China's market for generative AI-enabled digital business content is projected to be worth nearly CNY50 billion by 2025, up from about CNY4 billion in 2020. Numerous interesting use cases of multimodal content generation already exist, such as image-based virtual clothe fitting, music generation, copywriting, poetry writing, styled calligraphy work generation, and text-to-image and image-to-text generation. Generative AI has been listed by Gartner as one of the top 10 strategic technology trends for 2024, as shown in Fig. 7.14.

7.4.1 Large Models Transforming Content Generation

Large models give rise to new possibilities in content generation with their unprecedented performance in NLP, CV, and multimodal processing among other aspects. Modern content generation has gone far beyond simply generating authentic content, as diversity in content and controllable generation have now become the new focuses. There is also a higher degree of composability in generated content, as exemplified by interactions among humans, things, and environments in the virtual digital world as well as responses and internal logic found among words, sentences, and paragraphs within long-form text. These new requirements ask for sensing,

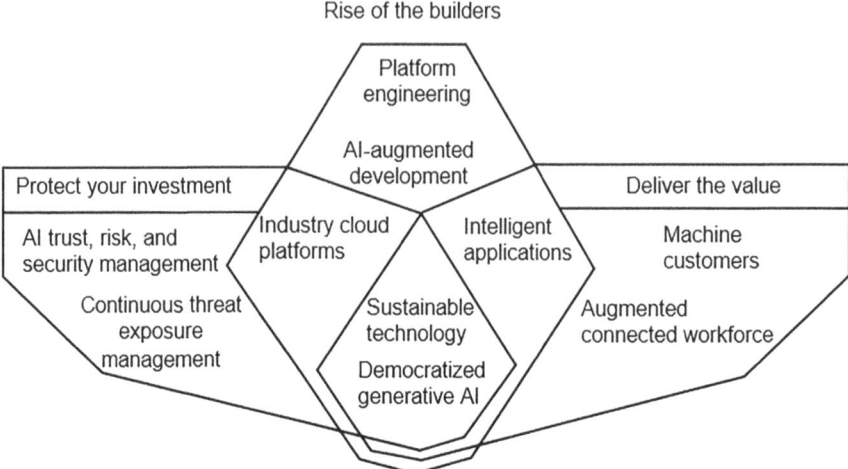

Fig. 7.14 Gartner top 10 strategic technology trends for 2024

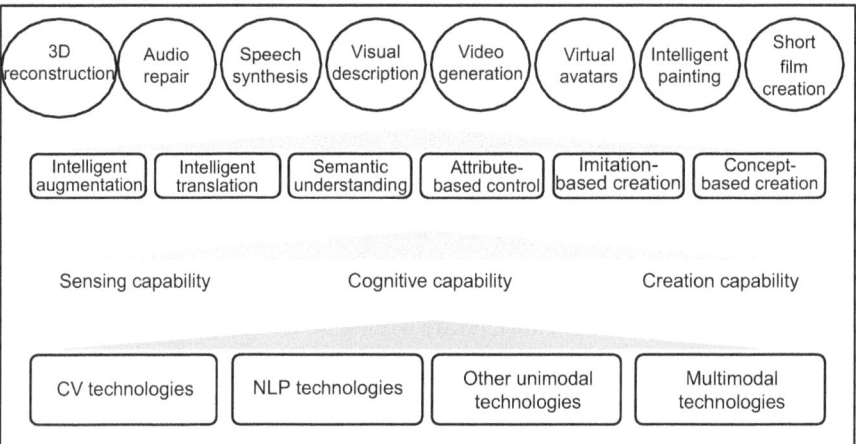

Fig. 7.15 Three cutting-edge capabilities that enable AIGC

cognitive, and creation capabilities for AIGC, as shown in Fig. 7.15. Traditional AI algorithms can hardly offer these capabilities, while large models—typically large vision models, large language models, and large multimodal models—provide an ideal answer thanks to their high level of adaptability and multimodal knowledge. Moreover, large models can be compressed and quantized into lightweight models, which retain strong comprehension, generation, and generalization capabilities even when given small datasets.

– Large vision models improve the sensing capability with regard to content generation. These models are built on Transformer-based architectures that incorporate the existing knowledge of humans. They can converge more quickly, compute at lower costs, demonstrate more feature scales and stronger generalization capabilities, and excel in both learning and encoding knowledge from mass data. When these models are trained to explore interconnections between multiple tasks in order to find diverse supervisory signals, they can learn more generalized and interpretable feature representations. Another important method for training large vision models is to have them learn from multimodal data like text and audio, to realize semantic connections and obtain complementary information between modalities. Through this method, the trained models are inherently good at tasks such as environment awareness, content search, semantic understanding, and inter-modal alignment, allowing content generation to be used in a wider range of scenarios.

– Large language models enhance the cognitive capability with regard to content generation. These models are pre-trained on vast amounts of unlabeled text data to overcome challenges in traditional NLP. This approach allows the models to understand and generate content when given small or even no datasets. Large language models excel in tasks that involve text understanding, such as emotion analysis, speech recognition, information extraction, and reading comprehension. They can also generate various forms of text such as image descriptions, advertisements, manuscripts, and dialogs. In most cases, all these complex functions are fulfilled by simply collecting unlabeled text data and using it to train and deploy a single general large model. That is why building large language models that can better understand meanings, learn abstract logic, and adapt to various tasks will play a vital role in developing cognitive applications for content generation.

– Large multimodal models upgrade the content creation capability. These models are designed to process multimodal data and information from different sources and tasks. They are well suited for emerging content generation requirements across a number of new application scenarios. Large multimodal models are known for two capabilities. First, they can find correspondence between modalities of data, such as text and images. They do this by mapping original data of different modalities to a universal or similar semantic space, in order to understand the relationships between them and align multimodal data. A typical application is image-text search engines. On top of this capability, these models can perform cross-modal conversion and generation. For example, they can output image-based descriptions, a key capability that enables native content creation.

It is anticipated that generative AI will become a new catalyst for the innovative growth of digital content and digital economies. With greater generation capabilities and knowledge than individual humans, generative AI can undertake certain basic mechanical tasks such as information mining, material invocation, and copy-based editing. Technically, this will enable the generation of personalized content on a massive scale efficiently at lower marginal costs. Moreover, generative AI will revolutionize content production by introducing new processes and paradigms. This will pave the way for more imaginative content and more diverse methods of information transmission, ultimately leading to more creativity in content generation.

7.4.2 Generative AI Forming New Business Models

Generative AI currently uses large models as its mainstream technology. As large models have progressed with more parameters and data, their generation capabilities have significantly improved. Driven by this momentum, generative AI is expected to cut the marginal costs of creation and knowledge tasks to zero. Today, generative AI has found wide application, generating diverse types of content spanning text, code, images, audio, videos, and 3D.

Text generation benefits much from the rapid development of language models, which have been used to generate text-like abstracts and image descriptions and typically perform well in generating short- or medium-form text. In the field of code generation, several specialized models and commercial products have been developed in addition to foundation models like GPT. For example, Peng Cheng Laboratory's pre-trained code generation model CodeGeeX supports multiple programming languages with 13 billion parameters. aiXcoder XL released by Intelligent programming robot provider aiXcoder supports method-level code generation, that is, it can understand both human and programming languages and can generate full program code with just one click from natural language descriptions.

Image generation has become a hot topic of generative AI, and global enterprises are actively entering the field with large models, such as OpenAI's DALL·E 2, Google's Imagen, and Baidu's ERNIE-ViLG. Video generation and 3D model generation, which are more challenging, are also seeing clear progress. In October 2022, Meta launched the Make-A-Video AI system, which can generate short videos from text prompts. Google's DreamFusion model can generate 3D models from text prompts in any given angles, lighting conditions, and 3D environments, without any 3D training data.

Platform products and startups are emerging along the path toward exploring the business value of AIGC applications, as shown in Fig. 7.16. Pioneering enterprises are launching platform products based on their own large models. For example, Baidu's Wenxin Yige, an AI-powered art and creativity platform based on large model technology, can automatically create images of different styles from language inputs, serving as a creativity copilot for visual designers. Startups in the field of AI-powered image generation are currently exploring various profit models. Stability AI, a startup driven by open-source communities, is one such example. It launched Stable Diffusion, a text-to-image model, in August 2022. Within just two months after rollout, the model had over ten million daily active users across various channels, and DreamStudio, the company's AI-powered image creation tool for customers, had been used by over 1.5 million users and generated over 170 million images. The company provides a free trial that allows users to generate 200

7.4 Large Models Empowering Generative AI

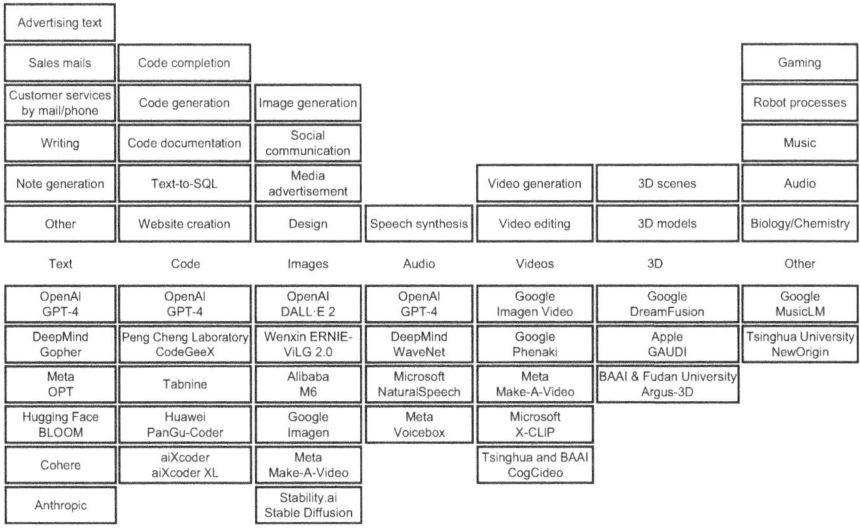

Fig. 7.16 Generative AI application fields and models

images, after which they are charged for additional usage. Midjourney, another AI-powered painting tool launched by a US startup, charges users based on usage frequency and offers different plans for individuals and enterprises. This tool is centered on communities to bolster user loyalty and highlights interaction experience.

Large models have also been used in fields such as digital avatar creation, image creation, and poetry writing. For example, an AI-powered sign language anchor developed based on BAAI's Wu Dao model was used during the 2022 Beijing Winter Olympics. It translated preset broadcasts into sign language to improve accessibility for the hearing-impaired community. Baidu released several AI assistants for creators using its ERNIE model. These assistants can autonomously create various types of content, including text and images and also provide a wide range of functions that assist in creation, like conversion from text or images to videos. Alibaba's M6 model is now employed as an AI assistant designer in the company's new manufacturing platform. Through fast design that aligns with fashion trends and simulated clothes fitting, this assistant is anticipated to greatly reduce the time taken to design clothing in the fast fashion industry.

Generative AI will also drive the development of the metaverse, the ultimate convergence of the physical and digital realms, toward real time, continuity, and creativity. It enables the physical world to be rapidly re-created in the metaverse for unlimited content creation and spontaneous organic growth. In summary, generative AI integrates digital content with various industries in multiple dimensions, birthing new business models. This will create new momentum for economy growth and rejuvenate a wide range of industries.

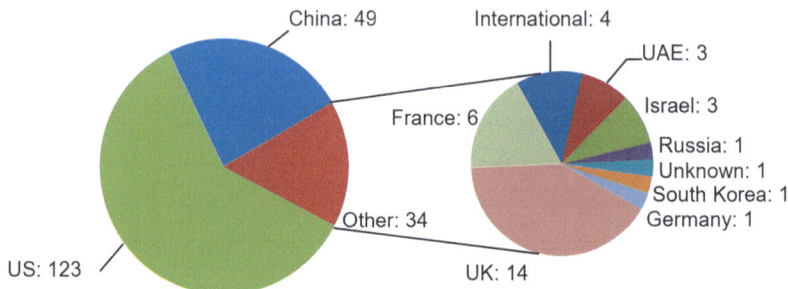

Fig. 7.17 Distribution of major large models by country

7.5 A Myriad of Models and Modalities

There are over 200 large models that have garnered significant interest around the globe. US organizations have been at the forefront in this field, contributing about 60% of the world's prominent large models (Fig. 7.17 shows the distribution of major large models by country). The large model boom took off in 2022, during which the number of large models increased by 134% compared with 2021. Pioneering organizations like Google, OpenAI, and DeepMind have rolled out the highest number of large models.

The R&D for large model technologies has matured thanks to relentless iterations and updates, but even so, the large model sector is still very much in its infancy in terms of application. Companies have started to explore new ways of leveraging large models beyond the lab, as such models have demonstrated enormous potential in industries as varied as electricity, e-commerce, banking, and insurance. China has contributed over 80 large models with over one billion parameters each, and private enterprises, universities, and research institutes have worked hand-in-hand in their developing and applying large models, sparing no effort to boost efficiency and reduce costs. The models are mainly general-purpose systems and use technologies like NLP, CV, and speech recognition. Huawei, iFLYTEK, Baidu, and Alibaba are a few of the most prominent model developers in China. Figure 7.18 shows the framework for China's large model industry.

7.5.1 OpenAI's ChatGPT

ChatGPT is a large-scale pre-trained language model that was developed for NLP by OpenAI and released on November 30, 2022. ChatGPT is a groundbreaking chatbot model that is capable of understanding the context of the user's text inputs and providing meaningful responses that are evocative of a conversation between two people. Incredibly, it can answer questions, admit its mistakes, challenge incorrect premises, and reject inappropriate requests.

7.5 A Myriad of Models and Modalities

Fig. 7.18 Framework for China's large model industry

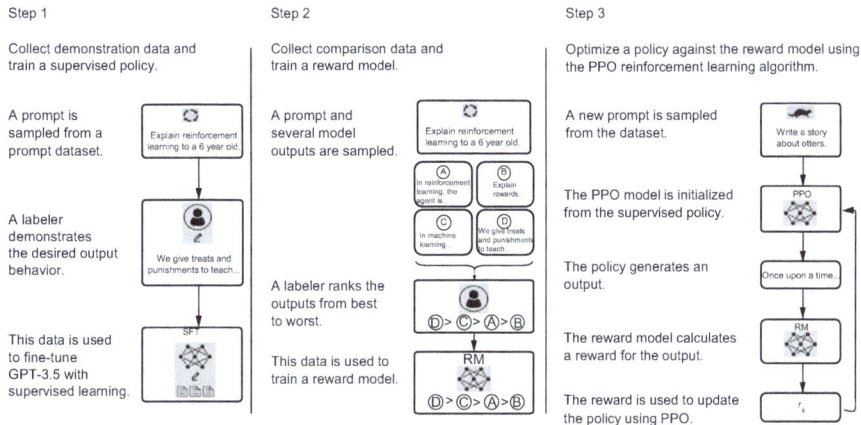

Fig. 7.19 ChatGPT model training

ChatGPT is a dialogue system fine-tuned from a pre-trained model in the GPT-3.5 series. This large language model is a sibling model of InstructGPT and is trained using Reinforcement Learning from Human Feedback (RLHF) to learn from the feedback of human labelers.

The training consists of three steps, as shown in Fig. 7.19.

1. Training a supervised learning model: Prompts are sampled from a prompt dataset. Human labelers write the desired output. Then, this data is used to fine-tune GPT-3.5 through a supervised learning process.
2. Collecting data and training a reward model: Prompts and several model outputs are sampled from the prompt dataset. Human labelers score the model outputs and rank them by quality. The ranked data is then used to train a reward model.
3. Fine-tuning the model with the reinforcement learning algorithm PPO (proximal policy optimization; released by OpenAI in 2017) [7]: The PPO model is initial-

ized through supervised learning. The initial PPO model is then optimized and iterated based on the scores given by the reward model to the model outputs. The model is subject to several iterations of this process to ensure that it is optimized.

RLHF is a reinforcement learning technique used to optimize language models through human feedback. Since human feedback is incorporated into training, machines are able to learn naturally through their interactions with humans. This provides the machines with a greater sense of perspective, which in turn leads to a more efficient learning process. Better yet, the machines are under direct guidance of humans, and therefore able to consider factors in their decision-making that are deeply embedded in the human experience. Figure 7.20 shows the principles of RLHF-based model training.

In March 2023, OpenAI launched a new version of GPT, GPT-4, which comes with more powerful NLP capabilities and is capable of more accurate language generation. GPT-4 interacts with humans in a more natural and seamless way and is able to better understand human intentions and needs with its enhanced predictive capabilities and autonomous reasoning.

7.5.2 Google's Gemini

Google released Gemini 1.0 on December 6, 2023, which, according to them, can run efficiently on everything from data centers to mobile devices. Gemini 1.0 comes in three sizes: Gemini Ultra, Gemini Pro, and Gemini Nano. Since it is natively multimodal by design, Gemini can process a wide range of modalities, including videos, audio, images, text, and code, and in this way outperforms existing large multimodal models that are constructed by stitching together separate uni-modal models.

Gemini can understand and reason about inputs across all modalities. Google revealed that Gemini Ultra outperforms GPT-4 in 30 of 32 widely used academic benchmarks, ranging from natural image, audio, and video understanding to mathematical reasoning. Its score of 90.0% (higher than the 86.4% achieved by GPT-4) makes it the first model to outperform human experts in terms of MMLU. With its image, audio, and video benchmarks, Gemini Ultra has outperformed all previous state-of-the-art models, without assistance from OCR systems. These benchmarks

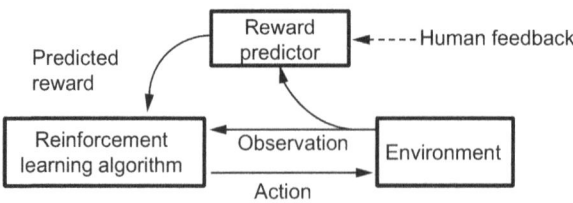

Fig. 7.20 Principles of RLHF-based model training

7.5 A Myriad of Models and Modalities

also highlight Gemini's native multimodality. Using a specialized version of Gemini as a springboard, Google created a more advanced code generation system, AlphaCode 2, which features nearly double performance of the original AlphaCode. The use cases listed in Google's technical documents indicate that in addition to converting representations between any two modalities (such as text-to-image or text-to-video generation), Gemini can also handle complex tasks involving multimodal conversion. For example, it can generate code from a given diagram and then generate a new diagram with a different order based on the previously generated code.

Google plans to integrate Gemini into products and platforms as diverse as search, advertising, Chrome, and Duet AI. Trial use in Google search has demonstrated its potential to reduce search latency and improve search quality.

7.5.3 Meta's LLaMA

LLaMA is a family of models released by Meta in February 2023, which was initially available in four sizes (7, 13, 30, and 65 billion parameters). Its excellent performance and open nature have garnered enormous interest from academia and industry alike. Notably, LLaMA performs well across a wide range of open benchmarks and has been the most popular open-source language models. LLaMA models have been extended by many researchers through instruction tuning and continual pre-training. With their solid foundation capabilities and open ecosystems, these open-source models have attracted a large number of users and been applied in numerous ways, setting a new standard for all future open-source models. Many projects and applications have their roots in LLaMA models, as shown in Fig. 7.21.

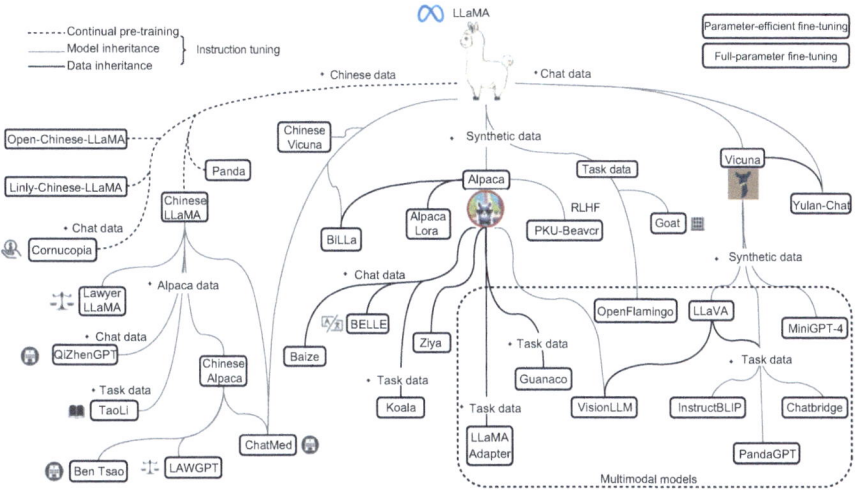

Fig. 7.21 Derivatives of LLaMA

In July 2023, Meta released LLaMA 2, the successor generation of LLaMA 1. It was trained on 2.0 TB of publicly available datasets, which is 40% more data than that for training LLaMA 1. This newer model has an enlarged context length to 4000 tokens and uses grouped query attention (GQA). LLaMA 2 excels in multiple benchmark tasks, especially in reading comprehension and common sense reasoning. There are four sizes of LLaMA 2: 7, 13, 34, and 70 billion parameters. The 70-billion-parameter LLaMA 2 pre-trained model features impressive performance on par with state-of-the-art pre-trained language models like GPT-3.5 and PaLM-540B.

7.5.4 Huawei's Pangu Models

Huawei Cloud initiated its large AI model project in 2020 and has launched a number of models under the brand name Pangu starting in April 2021. Pangu models represent the culmination of Huawei Cloud's achievements across dozens of AI sectors and are powered by Huawei's full-stack AI solutions. They are deeply integrated with Huawei's Ascend series processors, MindSpore AI framework, and the AI development platform ModelArts. Huawei launched Pangu Models 3.0, China's first full-stack large AI models, at the annual Huawei Developer Conference in July 2023. Pangu Models 3.0 use a "$5 + N + X$" three-layer architecture, as shown in Fig. 7.22.

The L0 layer consists of five foundation models: NLP, CV, multimodal, prediction, and scientific computing, which provide general skills to power a seemingly endless range of industry-specific applications. Pangu Models 3.0 are available in the following sizes: 10, 38, 71, and 100 billion parameters, to meet differing customer needs and standards for latency and response times. Brand new capability sets have also been provided, such as knowledge-based Q&A, copywriting, and code generation for the Pangu NLP model; and image generation and understanding for the Pangu multimodal model. All of these capability sets are made available to customers and partners and are standardized for all model sizes (defined by the number of parameters). The L1 layer consists of N industry-tailored models, where Huawei

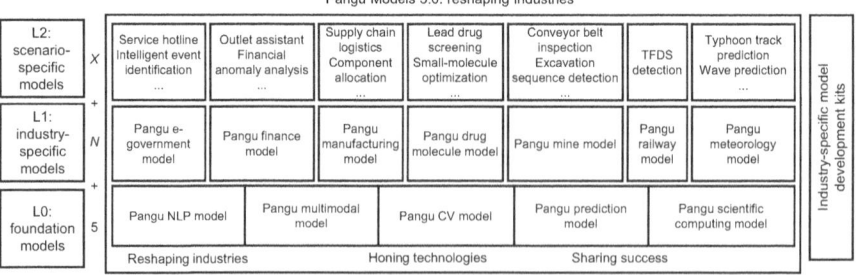

Fig. 7.22 Pangu models 3.0

Cloud provides customers with industry models it has trained on open industry datasets, including Pangu models for government, finance, manufacturing, mining, and meteorology. Alternatively, customers can train their own models using datasets of their own based on Huawei's L0 or L1 Pangu models. The L2 layer provides models for specific industries and specific tasks, such as government service hotlines, outlet assistants, lead drug screening, conveyor belt inspections, and typhoon track predictions. These models can be deployed off-the-shelf almost immediately [8].

This decoupled, hierarchical architecture allows for Pangu models to be quickly adapted to a wide range of downstream tasks. With its L0 and L1 models, Huawei Cloud offers industry model development kits, which make it quick and easy for customers to train their own industry-specific models using datasets of their own. Customers can also choose to upgrade foundation models, or just upgrade capability sets. Pangu models are currently being used in industries as varied as finance, manufacturing, pharmaceutical R&D, coal mining, and railways.

7.5.5 Baidu's ERNIE Bot

ERNIE Bot (*Wenxin yiyan* in Chinese Mandarin) is a knowledge-enhanced large language model based on Baidu's ERNIE model. It uses multitask learning and reinforcement learning and can be used for a number of different NLP tasks. ERNIE Bot generalizes and outperforms traditional models that rely on manual feature engineering, generating high-quality content tailored to user needs, and providing engaging and useful AI-powered interactions. ERNIE Bot is trained using the deep learning framework of Baidu's PaddlePaddle. The framework and algorithms are coordinately optimized to improve both performance and efficiency, tripling the training speed of models and increasing the inference speed by over 30 times. ERNIE Bot can handle varying NLP tasks simultaneously, including text classification, entity linking, and semantic matching. Since it is powered by attention mechanisms, the model is equipped to understand natural languages based on context and exhibit greater explanatory power and generalization capabilities. Figure 7.23 shows the architecture of ERNIE Bot.

ERNIE Bot is now based on the most recent ERNIE 4.0 foundation model and supports various applications, including image-based creation and Q&A, text-to-image generation, and text-to-video generation. These applications are offered to users through several native ERNIE Bot plug-ins, notably *Lanjuan wendang* for document-based interaction, *Shuotu jiehua* for image-based generation, *E yan yitu* for chart drawing, and *Yijing liuying* for text-to-video generation. The use of plug-ins continues extending model capabilities, resulting in a large model application ecosystem. In addition to the native plug-ins, developers can create plug-ins suited to their needs using ERNIE Bot's easy-to-use plug-in development kit and integrate the created plug-ins into the application-layer ecosystem. Baidu's AI Studio (*Xinghe* Community) has attracted a great many developers, and the community had accumulated over 300 innovative large model applications by August 2023,

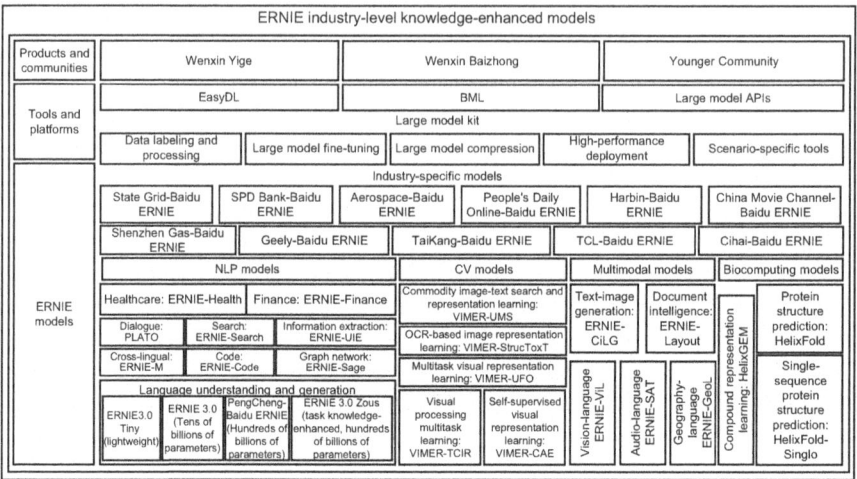

Fig. 7.23 Architecture of ERNIE Bot

demonstrating the enormous practical potential of ERNIE Bot. In August 2023, ERNIE Bot was rolled out to the public and quickly became the first native AI application in Chinese to top free app charts on Apple's App Store. It now offers assistance to users in four areas: work, daily life, education, and companionship.

References

1. Northeast Securities. From RNN to ChatGPT: Development and Application of Large Models [R] (in Chinese). 2023.
2. IDC. 2022 China Large Model Development White Paper [R] (in Chinese). 2022.
3. XIA R Z, LI P J. Large Language Model ChatGPT: Evolution and Application [J] (in Chinese). Journal of Data Acquisition and Processing, 2023, 38(5): 1017-1034.
4. KE P, LEI W Q, and HUANG M L. Research Progress of Large Language Models Represented by ChatGPT [J] (in Chinese). Bulletin of National Natural Science Foundation of China, 2023, 37(5): 714-723.
5. LIU X B, HU B T, CHEN K H, et al. Key Technologies and Future Development Directions of Large Language Models: Insights From ChatGPT [J] (in Chinese). Bulletin of National Natural Science Foundation of China, 2023, 37(5): 758-766.
6. LI G, WANG Z S, HE X T, et al. From ChatGPT to Large Multimodal Model: Present and Future [J] (in Chinese). Bulletin of National Natural Science Foundation of China, 2023, 37(5): 724-734.
7. WANG Y, CHEN Z B, WU Z R, et al. Review of Reinforcement Learning for Combinatorial Optimization Problem [J] (in Chinese). Journal of Frontiers of Computer Science and Technology, 2022, 16(2): 19.
8. Sinolink Securities. Pangu Models for AI Implementation [R] (in Chinese). 2023.

Chapter 8
AItoB Entering the Stage of Large-Scale Exploration

8.1 AI Combined with Industries for Diversified Implementations

Artificial intelligence (AI) is promoting social development with unprecedented breadth and depth, accelerating its penetration into areas such as scientific research, business innovation, national security, and daily life, and internalizing itself within these areas to boost global operation efficiency. First, the combination of AI and scientific research has brought about changes to scientific research methods based on traditional academic experience. Previously unknown theories can now be mined from a large number of known papers and experimental data. This accelerates the acquisition of documents in chemistry, materials, physics, and drug discovery and enhances the efficiency of experimental discovery. AI is now a key driving force for scientific and technological competition. Second, the field of AI has emerged as the next major arena for business innovation and competition. The expanding deployment of intelligent applications by traditional industry giants in specific segments such as supply chain, quality detection, and business decision-making is expected to significantly improve the efficiency of production processes, quality control, and business operations and optimize working conditions. Third, intelligent applications are constantly adapted to and refined for more specific needs that occur during daily life such as in entertainment, consumer electronics, and healthcare. Intelligent consumer products like indoor security drones and user-friendly virtual assistants are also emerging. Furthermore, medical diagnosis chatbots and intelligent imaging diagnosis are gradually being promoted to relieve existing shortages and uneven distribution of medical resources. Fourth, education and training are increasingly intelligent and online. Applications such as OCR question identification and auxiliary grading have made the move from pilot to large scale, realizing more precise teaching management and facilitating the establishment of a personalized learning system. Fifth, world-leading countries have fully recognized the value of integrating

AI technologies with national defense security and invested targeted funds to promote the development of intelligent national defense applications such as predictive maintenance, autonomous driving, information analysis, and intelligent flight control [1].

8.2 Large Models Becoming "Meta-Capability Engine" of the Intelligent Revolution

Rapidly developing large AI models are breathing new life into multiple fields and unleashing greater business value. These models are still in their infancy, but the first batch of cross-functional applications have emerged. For instance, profluent and Absci in the life science field and C3.ai in the energy industry are leading global enterprises to adopt next-generation AI. Many Chinese industry enterprises acknowledge that generative AI and large models may bring them competitive advantages, while a large number of large model innovation leaders have emerged and begun the exploration of large model application scenarios. Task-specific large models have already emerged in fields such as astronomy, materials, biomedicine, and physics. As a knowledge-intensive industry scenario, scientific and R&D innovation can stimulate the emergent abilities of large models in relation to massive data and facilitate high-value application scenarios such as meteorological research, medical R&D, and physical-rule discovery. In the future, with improvements to model capabilities and more in-depth knowledge integration, large models are expected to become fundamental production tools for various industries [2, 3].

In meteorological prediction, AI meteorological models that are powered by data-driven deep learning algorithms can leverage powerful computing capabilities, extensive historical data training, and various deep learning architectures to make quick predictions within a resolution of 20–25 km. These models offer significant advantages in both precision and calculation speed. The prediction objects include common meteorological elements and fields and key information such as typhoon paths, extreme weather, near-ground wind fields, and precipitation. Since 2022, AI meteorological models released by NVIDIA, Google DeepMind, Microsoft, Huawei, Shanghai Artificial Intelligence Laboratory, Fudan University, and Tsinghua University have been successively showcased, quickly recording some truly remarkable achievements. For example, the Pangu weather model, as an AI-based weather forecast model, can utilize deep learning technologies to build a pre-trained model that offers ultra-large-scale parameters and ultra-high precision. Compared to traditional numerical prediction methods, it has far higher precision and more than 10,000 times faster speed [4].

In plant breeding, large models can accurately understand various inquiries made in the agricultural field, including those related to planting technologies, daily management, pest control, aquaculture methods, and agricultural policies,

8.2 Large Models Becoming "Meta-Capability Engine" of the Intelligent Revolution

thus providing efficient solutions to production challenges and references for decision-making. At the same time, the model can assist users in the remote monitoring of intelligent agricultural machinery and improve the autonomy and intelligence of such machinery. Furthermore, by combining remote sensing technologies, drone aerial images, and agricultural IoT, the model promptly provides information on crop growth, soil conditions, and potential pest risks and helps to arrange agricultural production activities in a way that enhances efficiency and output. For example, the SenseTime AI remote sensing model utilizes the one billion-level parameters of the general computer vision model as its basis to implement high generalization capabilities for different terrain types, image types, image times, and spectrum segments in China. The model thus possesses advanced image interpretation capabilities for land cover and can produce an image segmentation result that is comparable to that labeled by human, with work efficiency improved by more than 60 times to greatly improve agricultural recognition efficiency.

In autonomous driving, large models can realize an E2E system that directly uses sensor data as an input to output expected driving behaviors, such as steering, acceleration, and braking. By avoiding the traditional hierarchical design, system complexity can be simplified and robustness can be improved. Large models can improve the accuracy of perception and decision-making in terms of scenarios, objects, and behaviors and reduce the costs of data labeling and development [5]. For example, the weakly supervised pre-trained ERNIE model, launched by Baidu based on the ERNIE image/text recognition capability of thousands of objects, greatly expands the amount of semantic recognition data available within autonomous driving, such as the recognition of special vehicles (i.e., fire engines and ambulances) and plastic bags. This is helping to rapidly overcome the long-tail sensing issue faced in autonomous driving. In addition, the self-driving perception ERNIE model, which boasts over one billion parameters, can significantly enhance self-driving perception generalization through small model training.

In smart healthcare, large models can boost healthcare informatization, improve online consultation experience, facilitate real-time monitoring and warnings, support drug discovery, and provide personalized diagnosis and treatment solutions and health management suggestions [6]. Shanghai large model technology, for example, has three core applications in this field: surgical medical record writing assistant, outpatient medical record generation system, and intelligent commercial insurance claim settlement. Meanwhile, speech recognition and natural language processing technologies are employed to automatically collect, analyze, and generate medical information, improve medical efficiency and quality, reduce the burden on doctors, and improve patient experience. The Shanghai large model has been trained on numerous pieces of high-quality medical literature, including textbooks and encyclopedias, allowing it to provide more comprehensive and professional medical support.

8.3 Prospects of General AI

Large language models mark a turning point and milestone in the development of AI. Thanks to strong generalization capabilities, low dependency on long-tail data, and enhanced downstream-model usage efficiency, large models are considered the prototype of "general intelligence" and are emerging as an essential method for exploring inclusive AI in the industry. Such models have cracked the puzzle of language complexity, allowing machines to learn languages, contextual meanings, and expressions of intent and independently generate and create content. In other aspects, after pre-training on a large amount of data, these models can be fine-tuned for different tasks so that users can reuse the models in multiple ways or make minor modifications as needed. Figure 8.1 demonstrates the future development trends of general AI.

The greater target of large models is to build the underlying algorithm framework of general AI, integrate the model capabilities of multiple domains, and conduct self-learning in complex scenarios, so that a single large model becomes the solution for various problems encountered in the industry. Currently, based on common models, industries are adding task-differentiated content through fine-tuning or prompts, greatly improving model utilization and promoting unified AI development.

In the future, the increased penetration rate of AI is expected to significantly accelerate the optimization of the entire industry chain structure and guide industry transformation toward high value-added products and services. In one aspect, AI,

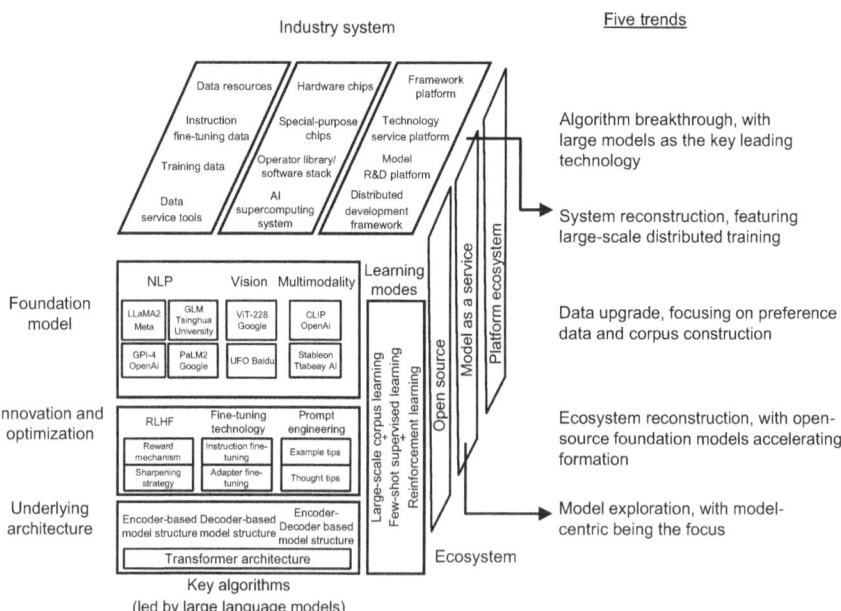

Fig. 8.1 Future development trends of general AI

which serves as the core of innovation for many technical products, will be the most critical high value-added industry during the next stage of development. In another aspect, AI can accelerate the increase in the proportion of high value-added products within traditional industries and further optimize industry structures. AI technologies are also already deeply integrated with core services and expert experience. The intelligence of major products and operation modes within the industry is constantly improving, leading to the development of new products and services. This has led to enterprises in traditional industries, such as WuXi AppTec and SF Technology, being placed in the annual list of the 50 smartest companies (TR50) released by the Massachusetts Technology Review. The former of these enterprises is a traditional drug discovery vendor that has deployed a pharmaceutical R&D enablement platform, while the latter uses intelligent technologies to improve logistics receiving and dispatching efficiency.

References

1. LeadLeo Research Institute. 2023 Research Report on Large AI Model Application [R] (in Chinese). 2023.
2. Frost & Sullivan. AI Big Model Market Research Report 2023 – Towards General Artificial Intelligence with Big Models Starting a New Era [R] (in Chinese). 2023.
3. Sun B L. Review of Large Models [J] (in Chinese). Computer Simulation, 2024, 41(1): 1–7, 24.
4. Huawei. Huawei Cloud Pangu Models: Pioneering A New Mode for Industrial AI Development [R] (in Chinese). 2023.
5. IDC. IDC Perspective: Status and Opportunity Analysis on Large Model-Enabled Autonomous Driving [R] (in Chinese). 2023.
6. EqualOcean Intelligence. 2023 Industry Research Report on Medical AI Large Models [R] (in Chinese). 2023.

Chapter 9
Challenges of Adopting AI in ToB Scenarios

9.1 Multifaceted Challenges of Large Model Engineering

Engineering is essential in making large artificial intelligence (AI) models applicable across sectors of society that have diverse requirements. However, AI engineering now faces multifaceted challenges, including complex systems, diverse requirements, and high costs.

System complexity is the first hurdle in implementing large AI models. Such models have grown drastically in size, with some having up to 10 trillion parameters, as both component count and algorithm complexity have increased by more than 100 times in recent years. AI innovation has therefore shifted from upgrades of individual techniques to systemic R&D that emphasizes standardized development paradigms and overall optimization. However, achieving such systemic R&D is not easy due to various obstacles such as difficulties in cross-team collaboration, a lack of process and asset management, and long production and delivery periods. All of these factors hinder the efficient adoption of large models in existing business scenarios.

Second, AI is not currently advanced enough to meet fragmented and specialized requirements that are more common in traditional sectors like consumer Internet, scientific computing, healthcare, and manufacturing industry. Today, most general models are unable to deliver what a specific industry requires, partly because they lack the required accuracy. They natively tend to produce hallucinations and lack controllability and interpretability, which consequently compromises the accuracy and controllability of the generated content. In addition, updating and iterating large models are difficult, making it challenging for them to keep pace with industry changes.

Third, AI adoption is costly. Leading AI systems increasingly rely on rapidly growing levels of computing power, leaving the development of large models or other hot AI technologies in the hands of just a few major companies. Adopting large models is also risky in terms of both security compliance and privacy protection, as the risks of this disruptive technology are still not fully understood. Gaining the benefits of large models at the expense of compliance risks is a key issue in their adoption.

9.2 Intelligentization Unbalanced Between Industries

The rapid development of AI is being accompanied by significant imbalances in its adoption between different regions, industries, and use cases. Many factors are contributing to this imbalance, including inherent features of AI technologies, business complexity, regional differences, talent differences, and data support differences. The initial application of AI came in industries like security, manufacturing, healthcare, transportation, retail, and education [1], but the rate of its adoption still varies greatly among these industries due to a number of factors such as data availability, algorithm maturity, and fault tolerance. For example, mobile Internet and security have been seen to adopt AI technologies most quickly, followed by retail and logistics, while the healthcare and autonomous driving industries lag behind. Mobile Internet companies are the biggest beneficiaries of AI advancement due to their massive amounts of standardized data and scenarios. In security, the other industry with the most mature AI adoption, AI startups like SenseTime, Megvii, and YITU have all found ways to monetize AI on a large scale, earning them reputations as AI unicorns valued at several billion USD.

However, some traditional industries are still struggling to implement and monetize AI because AI technologies lack maturity. For example, voice recognition and natural language processing (NLP) are not yet fully developed, hindering voice technology enterprises from monetizing AI. Other traditional industries face the challenge of not having enough standardized data to train models. A typical example is the manufacturing industry, where the most valuable application of AI would be visual recognition for examining product quality. However, such technology has not yet been widely used due to a lack of relevant data.

9.3 Looming Risks of AI

AI entails numerous of risks and ethical concerns. Aside from the flaws that accompany AI technologies, AI poses challenges to existing laws and regulations as well as ethics and social norms.

AI technologies that focus on deep learning are revealing an increasing number of inherent technological risks. Deep learning models are vulnerable to attack, meaning that a big question mark hangs over their reliability. These highly complex models operate as black boxes, lacking transparency and creating uncertainty.

Additionally, AI-generated content relies heavily on training data, which can contain societal biases that result in unfair outcomes for certain groups [2].

AI also poses increasing challenges to existing laws and regulations. First among these is that assigning liability becomes difficult when things go wrong. Examples include the first robotic surgery that resulted in a death in the UK in 2015 and accidents caused by Tesla cars going out of control, which raised doubts over their driver assistance system. Second, whether to give rights to AI systems is a controversial topic, as seen in the case of the robot Sophia being given Saudi Arabian citizenship in 2017, which sparked off a global debate. People have also been arguing about issues like whether an AI system can hold a patent. Third, AI occasionally violates privacy rules. For instance, there are companies illegally collecting consumers' facial information for business purposes, as revealed by the "2021 CCTV 3.15 Gala," a China's TV show on the annual consumer rights day.

AI is increasingly impacting ethics and social norms as well, causing discrimination, bringing forth new norms of human behavior, impacting labor dynamics, and even harming humans either directly or indirectly [3, 4]. For example, in December 2019, one Amazon smart speaker advised its user to commit suicide, and in November 2020, it was reported that an Iranian nuclear scientist had been assassinated by an AI-assisted weapon. In August 2021, Xsolla, a Russian online payment service provider, laid off 147 employees, one-third of its workforce, after an algorithm ruled the staff "unengaged and unproductive."

9.4 Immature AI Ecosystem

In China, despite having an ideal environment for AI development—characterized by favorable policies, abundant data, diverse application scenarios, and a pool of AI talent—there remain several weak links that need to be addressed. This challenge is especially true when it comes to the boom of large models, represented by GPT-4 for ChatGPT, which have had a seismic impact on the current AI landscape. China's own innovations related to building an AI ecosystem now face greater challenges due to the fact that software and hardware, such as chips and frameworks, must progress in unison.

The first of these weak links is an inability to engage in original innovations. China lacks effective top-level design for AI research, a key element in creating an environment that encourages original innovations. China's AI researchers currently focus more heavily on CV and deep learning than on NLP and reinforcement learning. Additionally, China's AI industry relies heavily on open-source code and existing mathematical algorithms, with few Chinese open-source machine learning platforms in existence that have a global influence.

China's AI industry lacks a solid foundation as it still lags behind in a number of areas, including core chips, components, and sensors, and must rely on imports to get hold of high-end components. To make things worse, the supply side is under great pressure due to soaring demand and trade restrictions led by the US.

The challenge of attaining the computing power required for large-scale training and inference is becoming increasingly problematic due to the emergence of large models. In 2018, an analysis by OpenAI revealed that the amount of computing power being used to train AI models had doubled every 3.43 months around the globe since 2012, growing by more than 300,000 times, which far exceeded the growth of computing power. With the continuous iteration of new technologies and algorithms, such as large models, multimodality, and intelligent agents, the industry has a need for a more general and flexible environment that can support the development of software and hardware. At the same time, a significant gap often exists between the expected performance of China-developed software or hardware products and actual user experience, which will become more apparent in the era of large models.

A lack of high-end AI talent is another weakness hampering China's AI industry. There is a shortage of skilled workers for AI-related positions, especially in terms of algorithm development and application research. High-caliber personnel and academicians that could lead the industry are also in short supply.

Finally, the AI ecosystem is in urgent need of regulation rules to govern AI applications and ensure that they comply with both legal and ethical standards.

References

1. LeadLeo Research Institute. 2023 Research Report on Large AI Model Application [R] (in Chinese). 2023.
2. China Academy of Information and Communications Technology. Blue Book on Large Model Governance - From Rules to Practice (2023) [R] (in Chinese). 2023.
3. SUN B L. ChatGPT: The Origin and Development of Artificial Intelligence Large Models [J] (in Chinese). Computer Simulation, 2023, 40(7): 1–7.
4. LIU C, LI X, YIN B, et al. Large Model Technology and Industry - Status Quo, Practice, and Thinking [J] (in Chinese). Artificial Intelligence View, 2023(4): 32–42.

Part III
5G + AI: Expediting Intelligent Industry Transformation

Chapter 10
Industries Evolving from Digital to Intelligent

10.1 Connotation of Digital Transformation

Next-generation information technologies such as 5G, big data, cloud computing, and artificial intelligence (AI) are being integrated into the real economy at an even faster pace, injecting innovation and change into all industries. This technological integration improves quality and efficiency while reducing costs. The digital economy has become an important enabler for socioeconomic growth. The COVID-19 pandemic was a global wakeup call to invest more in digitalization and informatization. It has become abundantly clear that digital transformation is needed for all countries, regions, industries, and enterprises.

The definition of digital transformation varies depending on the perspective, as shown in Fig. 10.1. From a government perspective, digital transformation is a macro concept. This perspective emphasizes the use of data and information technologies to enable industries and promote the migration of traditional industries to the digital economy. According to the *G20 Digital Economy Development and Cooperation Initiative* released at the 11th G20 Leaders Summit (G20 Hangzhou Summit) in 2016, the word digital in digital economy refers to information digitization, business digitization, and digital transformation based on the degree of digitalization [1]. Digital transformation marks a new stage of digital development where digitalization not only opens up new spaces for economic development and promotes development sustainability, but drives the transformation and upgrade of traditional industries.

In 2018, the Development Research Center of the State Council of China wrote in its paper *Digital Transformation of Traditional Industries: Its Pattern and Path* that digital transformation takes advantage of next-generation information technologies to build a closed loop of data collection, transmission, storage, processing, and feedback, remove data barriers between different levels of the economy and industries, improve the overall operating efficiency of industries, and build a brand-new digital economic system. Digital transformation enables in-depth integration of

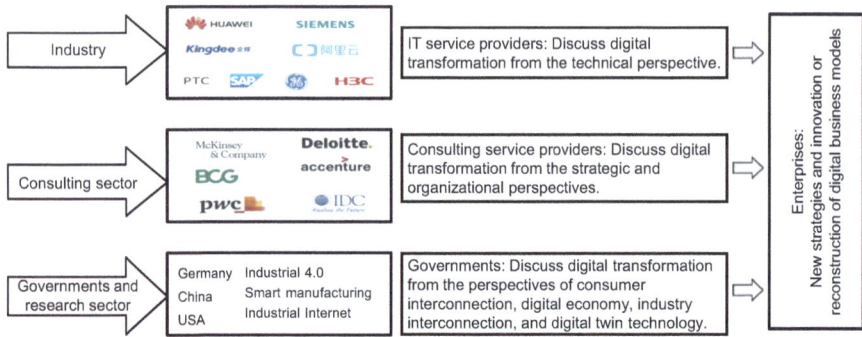

Fig. 10.1 Digital transformation from different perspectives

traditional industries and the IT industry, improving industry efficiency through data flow promotion [2].

In *Integration of informatization and industrialization—Digital transformation—Reference model for value and effectiveness (GB/T 23011–2022)*, digital transformation is defined as the process of deepening the application of next-generation information technologies, realizing the potential of data-driven innovation, and helping build capabilities for survival and development in the digital age. Digital transformation accelerates service optimization, innovation, and transformation; creates, transfers, and obtains new value; and achieves transformation, upgrade, and innovation development [3].

In addition, there has been much industry exploration of digital transformation. Industry players such as Microsoft, IBM, Huawei, Alibaba, IDC, and McKinsey have defined key points of digital development and provided different interpretations of digital transformation. For example, Huawei defines digital transformation as a process in which enterprises use advanced technologies to optimize or create service models and embrace a data-driven, customer-centric approach to break traditional organizational efficiency boundaries and industry boundaries, improve enterprise competitiveness, and create new value for enterprises [4]. "According to IDC, digital transformation refers to the approach to using digital technologies to drive the innovation of an organization's business model and the reconstruction of its ecosystem. Technologies function as the driving force, and business growth and innovations are the core" [5]. Digital technologies include cloud computing, mobility, big data/analysis, social networking, and the Internet of Things (IoT).

Digital transformation has three main characteristics. First, data is the core driving force of digital transformation and is a key factor of production and a source of value creation. Second, value creation is the primary purpose of digital transformation. Data is used to redefine products and services, optimize production and operations, and innovate on business models and industry organization models to maximize value. Third, digital transformation not only improves and optimizes existing businesses, but achieves qualitative changes, leading to comprehensive and profound changes in service models, production modes, and industry organization models.

To sum up, the key element of digital transformation is data, and the model of digital transformation is comprehensive integration of next-generation information technologies into diverse industries. The end goals are production and operation efficiency, faster market response, and greater value creation. Digital transformation results in new product and service models, production modes, and business models and will continue to reshape all industries.

10.2 Evolution from Digital to Intelligent

Digital transformation can be divided into three phases: informatization, digitalization, and intelligence, as shown in Fig. 10.2. The initial phase is the informatization stage, which mainly focuses on information system establishment, digital data storage and processing, and network construction and application. Through the integration of information technologies into businesses, business objects and processes are brought online and institutionalized in IT systems to achieve information sharing and business collaboration. However, informatization does not change the logic of services. It only transforms the traditional service model by migrating services from offline to online, a process completed in the IT system.

The second phase is the digitalization stage, which is the expansion and upgrade of informatization. Digitalization uses next-generation digital technologies such as 5G, cloud computing, AI, big data, and the IoT to build a fully-sensing, all-purpose, and intelligent digital world, based on which business processes are optimized and reengineered and traditional management models, service models, and business models are reshaped. This phase entails service transformation driven by information technologies and in-depth transformation and reconstruction of service, management, and business models. Digitalization is a long-term systematic project with many challenges, such as integration of new technologies, conflicts between cultural concepts, and transformation of organizations and talents.

The third phase is the intelligence stage, which is the advanced phase of digitalization. This phase enables machines to make decisions instead of humans.

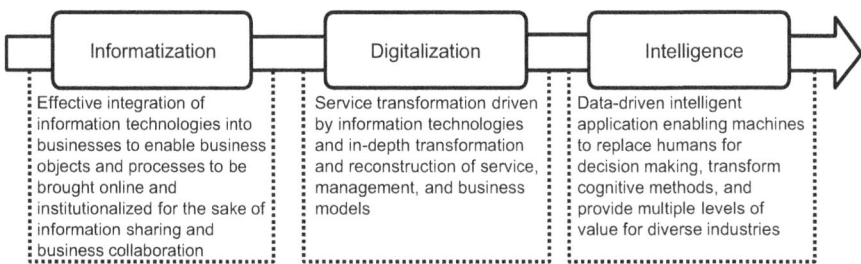

Fig. 10.2 Evolution from informatization to digitalization and intelligence

Intelligence focuses on using advanced technologies such as data analysis, machine learning, and AI to implement in-depth mining and intelligent application of massive data. The application of intelligent data technologies transforms not only service models, but also cognitive methods. In this phase, intelligence can provide multifaceted value for diverse industries, such as by enabling more agile operations, fuller customization, more intelligent decision-making, and new value propositions. In this way, in-depth intelligent applications can be applied to enterprises, society, and other areas.

10.3 Typical Course of Digitalization and Intelligent Development

Major countries and regions around the globe are accelerating key areas of digital economic development, focusing on scientific and technological innovation, digital infrastructure construction, digital industry chain building, digital application promotion, and so on. These approaches will all contribute to digital transformation as well as the upgrade and evolution of traditional industries.

10.3.1 US: Consolidating Global Competitiveness in the Digital Economy Using Technological Advantages

The US has formulated top-level forward-looking strategies and taken the lead in key areas of digital economic development. In the 1990s, the US government vigorously promoted information infrastructure and digital technology and was the first to propose the concepts of "information superhighway" and "digital earth." In 1998, the U.S. Department of Commerce released a report called *The Emerging Digital Economy*, outlining the development of the digital economy. Since the turn of the century, the US has released policies such as *America Will Dominate the Industries of the Future (2019)*, *Digital Strategy (2020–2024)*, and *US Innovation and Competition Act 2021*. In March 2022, the *Executive Order on Ensuring Responsible Development of Digital Assets* was released to build a US-led global digital ecosystem. In addition, the US has been actively developing cutting-edge fields such as 5G, cloud computing, big data, and quantum communications. For example, for the AI field, the US government released the first version of *The National Artificial Intelligence R&D Strategic Plan* in 2016. Three years later, it released an updated version called *National Artificial Intelligence Strategy* to enable comprehensive planning for key fields. For the big data field, the US has released *U.S. Open Data Action Plan* and *The Federal Big Data Research and Development Strategic Plan*.

The US government seeks to use the R&D of cutting-edge technologies to consolidate its advantages in digital technology innovation. It also actively promotes forward-looking research and transformation. With regard to capital investments, the U.S. Department of Defense applied for a budget of USD2.24 billion for AI-related scientific research for fiscal years 2015–2020. According to *The United States Innovation and Competition Act of 2021*, investments of about USD250 billion will be made in key scientific and technological research fields such as chips, AI, and quantum computing over 5 years. Concerning organization settings, the White House established the National Artificial Intelligence Initiative Office in 2021 to oversee and implement the US national AI strategy. This office serves the purpose of coordination and collaboration across the government, and with the private sector, academia, and other stakeholders. In respect of project planning, the Defense Advanced Research Projects Agency (DARPA) launched the Electronics Resurgence Initiative (ERI) in 2017, and then launched the Joint University Microelectronics Program (JUMP) focusing on digital chip technology. Institutions such as Center for Converged TeraHertz Communications and Sensing (ComSenTer) have also been established to promote 6G communications projects.

The US seeks to develop advanced manufacturing to promote the digital transformation of the real economy. Advanced manufacturing is a national priority, and there are policies such as the *Advanced Manufacturing Partnership (AMP)* and *Strategy for American Leadership in Advanced Manufacturing*. After years of development, major achievements have been made in advanced manufacturing in the US. One area of achievement is construction of advanced manufacturing innovation centers. In 2012, the National Network for Manufacturing Innovation (NNMI) Program and the National Additive Manufacturing Innovation Institute (NAMII) (now known as America Makes) were established. In the following 5 years, 14 manufacturing innovation centers were established, covering chips, flexible electronics, biopharmaceuticals, and robotics. Another major area of achievement is digital transformation. For example, General Electric (GE) uses an industrial-data-centric approach, uses its Proficy software to integrate the latest advanced technologies in the IT industry, and uses factory device data and enterprise service data to solve production challenges. Focusing on platform requirements, Parametric Technology Corporation (PTC) integrates the industrial IoT analysis platform ThingWorx and augmented reality (AR) platform Vuforia into its smart factory architecture to respond to macroeconomic conditions and reduce costs for manufacturing customers.

10.3.2 EU: Leading the Development of Digital Governance Rules to Form a Unified Digital Market

The EU is continually updating its rules and regulations on digital economy to safeguard digital transformation. First, the EU adapts to privacy protection rules to the times. The *ePrivacy Directive (ePD)* was established in 2002, but these regulations became outdated in the evolving digital economy market. So the EU formulated the *ePrivacy Regulation (ePR)* to widen the scope of privacy protection for enterprises and individuals in the EU. Second, the EU promotes fair competition and balanced development of the digital economy. In December 2020, the European Commission released the *Digital Market Act (DMA)* and the *Digital Services Act (DSA)*, providing comprehensive rules to promote fairness and openness in the digital market. Third, the EU is committed to safeguarding cyber security. In 2016, it introduced the *Directive on Network and Information System Security* to enhance network and information system security for basic service operators and digital service providers. In 2019, the *Cybersecurity Act* was released, providing basic guidelines for commercial data processing in the EU. In December 2020, the European Commission issued the latest *Cybersecurity Strategy*, completing the cybersecurity system and forming a new coordination mechanism through the use of regulatory, investment, and policy tools. Fourth, the EU has comprehensive rules for free cross-border data flow. Its *General Data Protection Regulation (GDPR)* manages the security of cross-border transfer of personal data, which must be performed on the basis of adequacy agreements, standard contracts, binding corporate rules, and industry certifications. Additionally, the European Commission has adequacy agreements on personal data protection with countries such as Japan and South Korea.

The EU promotes the establishment of a digital single market to drive the digital development of industries. In May 2015, the European Commission established the EU's *Digital Single Market Strategy*, aiming to move from 28 national markets to a single one, covering six fields, including digital culture, digital future, and digital life. This effectively drives industry digitalization. First, the digital culture is gaining traction. The EU provides more citizens with access to information through digital culture archives. For example, the EU Digital Library European provides more than 53 million projects, including audiovisual collections from more than 3700 libraries, archives, museums, and art galleries in Europe. Second, the plan for a digital future is constantly being improved. Cutting-edge technologies such as the supercomputers, AI, blockchain, and quantum mechanics are developing rapidly in the EU. More than 250 digital innovation centers have been built to help enterprises use advanced technologies and improve services. Third, digital life capabilities continue to be upgraded. The EU provides greater convenience for enterprises and residents through digital government construction and Electronic Identification and Trust Services (eIDAS). The Digital Economy and Society Index (DESI) 2020 reports predict that by 2030, all major administrative documents of the EU will be able to be completed online, all EU citizens will be able to view their medical records online, and 80% of citizens will be able to use electronic ID cards [6]. Fourth, digital trust is increasing. The EU digital single market provides citizens with privacy protection for Internet access, email, shopping, and credit card use, enabling citizens to enjoy better personal data and cyber security protection.

10.3.3 UK: Adhering to a Digital Government Construction Strategy for Digital Transformation of All Industries

The UK uses policymaking to lay a foundation for digital development, exemplified by the introduction of a series of influential documents. It has launched initiatives such as *Digital Britain*, *Digital Economy Act*, *National Data Strategy (2020)*, and *UK Digital Strategy*, aiming to promote digital transformation [7]. Furthermore, the UK places equal emphasis on development and regulation and began implementing the *GDPR* and amended the *Data Protection Act (DPA)* and the *Digital Economy Act* in 2018 to protect data rights. To establish an ethics system, the country released the *Data Ethics Framework* for data governance from the perspectives of public interest and data accountability. For cyber security, the UK has released the *Code of Practice for Consumer IoT Security* and the *Online Harms White Paper* to help form a robust and transparent digital infrastructure system. Moreover, to address the tax challenges posed by the digital economy, the UK has been imposing digital service taxes on search engines, social media platforms, and online markets since April 2020.

The UK focuses on promoting digital transformation of the government and providing public digital services. As one of the first countries in this endeavor, the UK has released the *Government Digital Strategy*, *Government Digital Inclusion Strategy*, *Government Transformation Strategy (2017–2020)*, and *Digital Service Standard* to implement ICT- or data-driven government transformation. First, the UK has promoted the openness and sharing of government data. The UK's *Digital Economy Act* established a national data infrastructure registration system to ensure secure and reliable operation of data infrastructure. In addition, a data advisory committee was established with a government chief data officer appointed to manage and coordinate the use of government data. Second, the UK has built an integrated government digital platform by using the website gov.uk as the unified entry for information and services of government departments. This platform integrates the digital platform design, notification, payment, and website hosting systems. Third, the UK has developed digital service standards that include 18 indicators, and also the key performance indicators (KPIs) for digital services, aiming to regularly evaluate the government's online services.

Digital government accelerates digital transformation in other fields, such as manufacturing, retail, and online gaming in the UK. First, digital technology use is increasing in the manufacturing industry. The adoption rates of additive manufacturing, robotics, and industrial IoT have reached 28%, 22%, and 12%, respectively. In addition, enterprises are pursuing digital innovation. For example, GlaxoSmithKline (GSK) has achieved significant growth in productive efficiency using Fourth Industrial Revolution (4IR) technologies such as advanced analysis, image recognition, and automation. Its pharmaceutical factory is said to be working on the Global Lighthouse Network of the World Economic Forum. Second, the digital revolution is accelerating in the retail industry. According to the Office for National Statistics (ONS), the proportion of online retail sales to total retail sales has been increasing rapidly in the UK since February 2020, reaching a peak of

35.2% in January 2021. Third, the online gaming industry has seen rapid development. The total output value of the UK gaming industry has exceeded half of that of the UK entertainment market, and the UK ranks second in Europe in overall gaming market share.

10.3.4 Japan: Using Industry-Government-Academia Collaboration and the "Connected Industries" Initiative to Realize a Super-Smart Society

Japan has improved its policy system and organizational structure to lead the development of the digital economy in a unified manner. In 2000, the Japanese government issued the *Basic Act on the Formation of an Advanced Information and Telecommunications Network Society* to promote the formation of an information society in Japan. Additionally, Japan has set up the Strategic Headquarters for the Promotion of an Advanced Information and Telecommunications Network Society (IT Strategic Headquarters) in accordance with the Act, wherein the Prime Minister serves as Director-General and relevant Ministers of State serve as members. Since its establishment, the IT Strategic Headquarters has become the main force for promoting the digital transformation of Japanese government affairs. In 2014, the Digital Government Ministers' Meeting was established to promote effective collaboration between local governments and civil society in driving digital transformation. In 2019, the Japanese government formulated a draft of the *Digital Government Implementation Plan*, which was implemented after two revisions, with the aim of achieving 100% digital transformation of administrative services across both central and local governments. In September 2020, Japan's Cabinet made clear its stance that digital transformation was an important part of the national policy. In November 2020, the Digital Agency was established, with the Prime Minister appointed as its head, to manage digital transformation. As an independent ministry focusing on information and digital technologies, this agency can provide suggestions to other ministries whose actions do not comply with the overall policy. Its goal is to achieve centralized and unified leadership in the digital economy [8].

Japan has promoted industry-government-academia collaboration to cultivate digital talents. Industry-government-academia collaboration is an important part of Japan's national innovation system. In this system, the industry works with universities and scientific research institutions to develop new technologies and products, converting academic achievements into tangible applications. Meanwhile, the government plays a pivotal role in formulating policies and building the platform environment to facilitate this collaborative innovation. For example, the University of Tokyo launched "Metaverse School of Engineering" through flexible use of the metaverse technology that offers a virtual network space. The School offers courses about information technologies that are intended to be geared toward more than 100,000 students, including junior high, high school, and adult students. Moreover, the University of Miyazaki, Asahi Kasei, Miyazaki Bank, and DENSAN jointly set up the Miyazaki County Digital Talent Alliance to promote digital transformation in Miyazaki Prefecture. Since 2023, the Ministry of Internal Affairs and Communications has worked with non-governmental talent service companies to help local governments ensure the availability of digital talents for county governments.

Japan has implemented the "Connected Industries" framework, which focuses on the digital transformation of manufacturing. In the 1990s, Japan launched the Intelligent Manufacturing Systems (IMS) Initiative and set up an international committee. After that, it released the *Comprehensive Strategy on Science, Technology and Innovation* and the *Science and Technology Basic Plan* to provide policy support. In the twenty-first century, Japan has released a series of plans, such as the *e-Japan Strategy*, *u-Japan Strategy*, *i-Japan Strategy*, *Japan's Robot Strategy*, and *Strategic Implementation for Connected Industries—IVRA Next* released by Industrial Value Chain Initiative. To better realize the vision of "Connected Industries," Japan's Ministry of Economy, Trade and Industry supported the establishment of Japan Industrial Value Chain Promotion Association, whose members include Mitsubishi Electric, Toshiba, Toyota, and other Japanese manufacturing enterprises. Later, the now renowned Industrial Value Chain Reference Architecture was proposed. The architecture centers on large enterprises, which are interconnected with peripheral small- and medium-sized enterprises (SMEs), forming an innovative enterprise interconnection system. This promotes technological innovation in Japan's smart manufacturing industry.

10.3.5 South Korea: Focusing on Standards System Establishment and Releasing the New Growth 4.0 Strategy Roadmap

The government of South Korean advocates collaboration for the construction of a digital technology innovation ecosystem. The Ministry of Science and ICT (MSIT) has played a special role as a "control tower" for the government's commitment to supporting the technical sector and the construction of national ICT infrastructure. In the late 1990s, South Korea began implementing a financing strategy characterized by "settlement after investment." This approach allowed the government to share risks with the private sector in the early stages of industry development and gradually promoted a shift to private sector-led growth through privatization and business deregulation. In 2019, South Korea announced a nearly USD3 billion initiative to enhance national AI capabilities through substantial investment in workforce training, infrastructure construction, and promotion of AI technologies in all sectors. So far, AI engineering schools have been established at ten local universities with AI research centers established at four national universities in South Korea to strengthen its national AI talent pool. In addition, the country's major ICT companies have been actively increasing their R&D investment in AI technologies. For example, Samsung Electronics and LG Electronics have established AI centers in the UK, Canada, and the US to drive international collaboration.

South Korea has transformed its data management model and promoted the establishment of the digital element market. To be specific, the model of South Korea's data policy has shifted from the conservative, government-managed approach to an innovative, open one. The Data Dam project, part of the Digital New Deal, reflects South Korea's data management policies. In 2020, the National Assembly of Korea passed amendments to the *Personal Information Protection Act (PIPA)*, *Credit Information Use and Protection Act*, and *Act on Promotion of Information and Communications Network Utilization and Data Protection* to simplify regulatory measures and establish the concept of data anonymization to meet the requirements of the EU's *GDPR*. In April 2022, the Korean Personal Information Protection Commission (PIPC) proposed revised guidelines to encourage more active processing of pseudonymized data. With the implementation of more guidelines, laws, and regulations, South Korea will promote secure and efficient use of personal information and anonymous data.

South Korea focuses on the digital transformation of SMEs and provides financial support in a number of forms. It has set up the Digital Service Voucher Program to reduce the costs of using digital technologies for SMEs. The program links SMEs to suppliers in South Korea and provides subsidies to enable 80,000 SMEs to use the digital services offered by these suppliers. For manufacturing, the government has also launched a strategy on smart manufacturing expansion and promotion and provides financial support for SMEs in manufacturing so that they can afford production equipment, services, and consulting. The Ministry of SMEs and Startups has set up the Korea Smart Manufacturing Office (KOSMO), which is a specialized agency for promoting smart factories. A smart factory expert is appointed as the head of the KOSMO to enhance the professionalism of personnel. The Office has set up smart manufacturing innovation centers at 19 science and technology parks, which have gathered regional experts to offer SMEs customized services such as smart manufacturing technology testing and certification, smart manufacturing solution provider matching, implementation evaluation, requirement mining, consulting, and training.

10.3.6 *China: Using Industry and Market Advantages for Efficient Markets and Public Services*

China has strengthened the deployment of policies at all levels to create a favorable environment for digital transformation. The Central Committee of the Communist Party of China (CPC) has made the digital economy a critical part of its national development strategy. National strategies such as the 14th Five-Year Plan clearly set out the goals and tasks for digital economy development. Relevant ministries and

10.3 Typical Course of Digitalization and Intelligent Development

commissions have actively implemented national strategies and rolled out policy measures such as *Guiding Opinions of the State Council on Actively Promoting the "Internet+" Action Plan*, *A Plan for the Overall Layout of the Country's Digital Development*, and *The Implementation Plan for Promoting the Actions of "Migrating to Cloud, Using Digital Tools and Enabling Intelligence" and Fostering the Development of New Economy*, providing guidance for digital development in diverse fields. China's 31 provinces, autonomous regions, and municipalities directly under the central government have released special policies for the digital economy, actively strengthening the government's guiding role while giving full play to market forces [9]. Additionally, China has established an inter-ministerial joint conference system on the development of the digital economy. The system consists of 20 departments that coordinate the formulation of plans and policies for digital transformation and development of key areas of the digital economy.

China has been advancing digital transformation of production through its comprehensive industrial system, seeking to use its solid industrial development foundation and huge market demand. According to the Ministry of Industry and Information Technology (MIIT), by June 2023, the market scale of China's industrial Internet industry had exceeded CNY1.2 trillion, with industry applications spanning 45 national economic categories, covering R&D, production, sales, services, and other enterprise processes. The 5G + industrial Internet initiative is in full swing, with 32,000 5G industrial base stations already deployed in China and the construction of virtual private networks and hybrid private networks gaining momentum. There have been three phases of application: specific-problem-focused application, comprehensive integration, and large-scale in-depth application. During these phases, ten settings have been created, including collaborative R&D design, remote device control, and collaborative device operation. Practices have been implemented in five industries: mining, electronic device manufacturing, equipment manufacturing, steel, and electric power [10].

The huge Chinese market facilitates digital transformation of people's lifestyles. China's surging digital demand continues to stimulate innovation in digital products and services. The COVID-19 pandemic accelerated the shift of economic activities to online platforms, urging enterprises to move their services online. This has led to the emergence of many new forms of business in the contactless economy. In the consumer field, the logistics distribution, online financing, data resource, and other support systems continue to be improved. The Internet reshapes the business ecosystem and accelerates the creation of new industry forms such as retail sales converging online and offline channels. This has stimulated the development of e-commerce for supermarkets, wet markets, and unattended retail. In addition, more digital products and services are emerging in the education sector. Digital applications, such as smart classrooms, online education, and electronic teaching materials, make education more convenient. In healthcare, we are seeing wide application of Internet hospitals, e-commerce pharmaceutical business, surgical robots, AI imaging, and others. These applications significantly improve healthcare resource allocation and healthcare quality and efficiency.

References

1. G20 Hangzhou Summit. G20 Digital Economy Development and Cooperation Initiative [R]. 2016.
2. Development Research Center of the State Council, Dell (China) Co., Ltd. Digital Transformation of Traditional Industries: Its Pattern and Path [R] (in Chinese). 2018.
3. State Administration of Market Supervision and Administration. Integration of informatization and industrialization—Digital transformation—Reference model for value and effectiveness: GB/T 23011-2022 [S] (in Chinese). 2022.
4. Enterprise Architecture and Transformation Management Dept, Huawei Technologies Co., Ltd. Huawei's Digital Transformation Strategy [M] (in Chinese). Beijing: China Machine Press, 2022.
5. XU X H, TU C C, HUANG X H. Digital Transformation of Enterprises and Global Value Chain Embeddedness: Theory and Evidence [J] (in Chinese). Journal of Zhejiang University (Humanities and Social Sciences), 2023(10): 51–68.
6. European Commission. Digital Economy and Society Index (DESI) 2020 [R]. 2020.
7. China Academy of Information and Communications Technology. White Paper on Global Digital Economy (2023) [R] (in Chinese). 2023.
8. Hirofumi Tatsumoto. Current Situation and Prospect of Digital Transformation in Japan [J] (in Chinese). China Quality. 2023(3): 76–80.
9. China Academy of Information and Communications Technology. White Paper on Global Digital Economy—A New Dawn of Recovery under the Impact of the Epidemic [R] (in Chinese). 2021.
10. China Academy of Information and Communications Technology. Report on the Development of China's Digital Economy [R] (in Chinese). 2022.

Chapter 11
Collaborative Development Between 5G and AI: Accelerating Intelligent Industry Upgrade

11.1 Relationship Between 5G and AI

As 5G and Artificial Intelligence (AI) serve as the core components of the communication infrastructure and new technology infrastructure, respectively, within the information infrastructure, and their mutual advancement produces a strong multiplier effect.

5G is an important catalyst in promoting the development and application of AI technologies. AI is inseparable from data as massive data provides the technical basis for deep learning algorithm applications. 5G now not only facilitates connections between people, but also enables connectivity of everything [1]. 5G networks can support a vast number of high-speed device connections and efficient transmission of massive data. This, in turn, promotes AI-based big data predictions as well as formulation of learning methods, rules, and execution policies. In addition, edge computing on 5G networks integrates computing and storage capabilities into access networks to support AI applications on terminals and achieve seamless connection between terminals and the cloud. As 5G can be applied to a wide range of fields, AI too can be implemented and promoted in more fields.

Simultaneously, AI has become the core engine of 5G development. AI helps 5G networks improve efficiency, better adapt to more complex application requirements, and improve their communications capabilities. AI can also enhance the intelligence level of 5G. For example, AI can optimize the 5G network parameter configuration and network structure to transform 5G networks into cognitive cloud networks featuring zero-touch service management and automatic deployment, thereby laying a foundation for the implementation of self-learning technologies. Additionally, in terms of the network requirements from vertical industries, AI technologies can be used to achieve precise analysis and provide more diversified network services for smart cities, smart manufacturing, and smart healthcare.

11.2 5G's Requirements for AI

There are a large number of complex, advanced technologies already within 5G networks. In particular, 5G core slicing enables the creation of sub-slices in the core network. Core slicing has very high requirements on network planning and routine operations and maintenance (O&M) and optimization, and its implementation can greatly increase construction and O&M costs. Traditional manual network maintenance and management simply will not be able to meet the network requirements of 5G services. AI will be one of the core technologies of 5G as well as 6G as it will fully empower communications network construction and operation. An automatic O&M system that meets rapidly changing market requirements can be built leveraging the technical features of AI such as self-learning and data analysis [2]. For instance, AI can increase network efficiency by using and scheduling 5G network radio resources and taking control of the network as necessary to avoid or reduce network congestion. AI can also improve network security by analyzing massive network data, to more effectively detect malicious attacks and then help defend against them in a timely manner, improving network security assurance capabilities.

Furthermore, in addition to integrating intelligent capabilities into 5G networks, AI can also invigorate both traditional industries and emerging fields. AI technologies, represented by deep learning, can generate precise insights through analysis, enabling 5G applications to be better at prediction and more targeted toward mobility management, user behavior, and positioning requirements. This will help 5G applications to provide services that better meet user requirements. These technologies also provide a feasible technical path for breaking through 5G performance bottlenecks and enabling 5G dedicated public networks.

11.3 AI's Requirements for 5G

5G networks provide large-scale coverage, helping expand the physical reach of AI applications. This solves the pain point of inadequate carrier and channel resources that currently hinder AI technology implementation and greatly promotes the development and prosperity of the AI industry. 5G networks allow AI to access big data on the cloud and solve problems such as low rates and high latency in the case of the use of new devices or new experience. Devices connected over 5G networks can also provide massive real-time data and data support for AI computing, processing, and analysis.

Moreover, AI applications in various industries have already started raising a variety of different network requirements. For example, smart cities require massive connections to implement comprehensive sensing, smart transportation requires low latency and high reliability to improve the efficiency and safety of vehicle traffic, and smart homes require ultra-large bandwidth to support personalized services. Every AI application scenario requires a customized network that can be dynamically adjusted in real time based on application requirements to meet fast-changing service requirements. 5G core networks support the construction of logically isolated network slices to implement on-demand deployment of network functions and resources to meet different service requirements. With the acceleration of 5G network construction and collaboration with other forms of infrastructure such as clouds, edge, and devices, 5G will effectively promote the Internet of Everything (IoE) and data aggregation, enable more access to AI, and comprehensively promote deeper integration of AI into economic and social development.

11.4 Convergence of 5G and AI

5G and AI each have their own advantages that can each be leveraged and also combined to enable digital economy growth. This will not only improve productivity, but also transform what production looks like in our society. The current typical application scenarios of 5G and AI are similar. For example, in terms of digital manufacturing, reliable connection+dedicated intelligence helps create a ubiquitous Internet of Things (IoT) environment, thereby facilitating the formation of digital production lines through AI technologies. Digital manufacturing enterprises implement human–computer interaction (HCI) collaboration using professional manufacturing applications and scalable development platforms with the support of flexible automation technologies, achieving smart manufacturing and deepening application convergence. In the realm of digital lifestyles, high-speed connection+sensory intelligence is accelerating the creation of new HCI applications. Visual, auditory, and tactile intelligence is rapidly being integrated into personal wearables and home devices, bringing about a colorful smart lifestyle. In terms of digital governance, wide area network (WAN) connection+general intelligence will promote online information exchange in various fields such as education, healthcare, and transportation. This will accelerate the full circulation and efficient application of data, bolster AI deep learning, and empower collaborative, precise, and efficient social governance. In the future, with the in-depth convergence of 5G and AI, new application scenarios and business models will continue to come to life, unleashing huge potentials [3, 4].

References

1. China Academy of Information and Communications Technology. White Paper on China's 5G Development and Its Economic and Social Impacts [R] (in Chinese). 2017.
2. China Academy of Information and Communications Technology. White Paper on Artificial Intelligence (AI) (2022) [R] (in Chinese). 2022.

3. SHI L Y, YE L, TANG C. A Domestic Analysis on the 5G and AI Integration Based on Bibliometrics and Knowledge Map [J] (in Chinese). World Sci-Tech R&D, 2021, 43(6): 732-749.
4. WEN H J. Integration and Development Trend of 5G Communication Technologies and Artificial Intelligence [J] (in Chinese). Technology Innovation and Application, 2020(7): 158-159.

Chapter 12
Convergence of 5G and AI: Enabling Industry Intelligence

As 5G-native technologies and devices gradually mature, they lay a foundation for the integration of 5G with diverse industries. With the maturity of relevant technologies, 5G + X will progressively change the original industry systems and equipment. Such transformation will in turn promote the continuous optimization and evolution of 5G-native technologies and the industries and build a mature 5G + X industry system. This will bolster general industry capabilities for large-scale application, empowering digital transformation of the industries. Figure 12.1 shows the convergence development path for 5G and other technologies.

12.1 5G-Native Technology Optimization: Enhanced Network Endogenous Capabilities

5G-native technologies refer to a technical system compliant with technical standards such as 3GPP specifications. The system mainly includes 5G private line, 5G private network, and network slicing. The evolution of 5G-native technologies promotes multi-level convergence of 5G networks and existing informatization systems in the industry. In this way, more 5G-enabled network devices and general terminals will be available to carry new industry services. The evolution also boosts the upgrade of 5G technologies and products such as 5G-enabled general modules/terminals, customized user plane function (UPF), lightweight core networks, and explosion-proof base stations. Ultimately, this will drive large-scale replication of ultra-HD video surveillance, peripheral production information collection, quality monitoring, and other new 5G application solutions or network alternative application solutions within vertical industries.

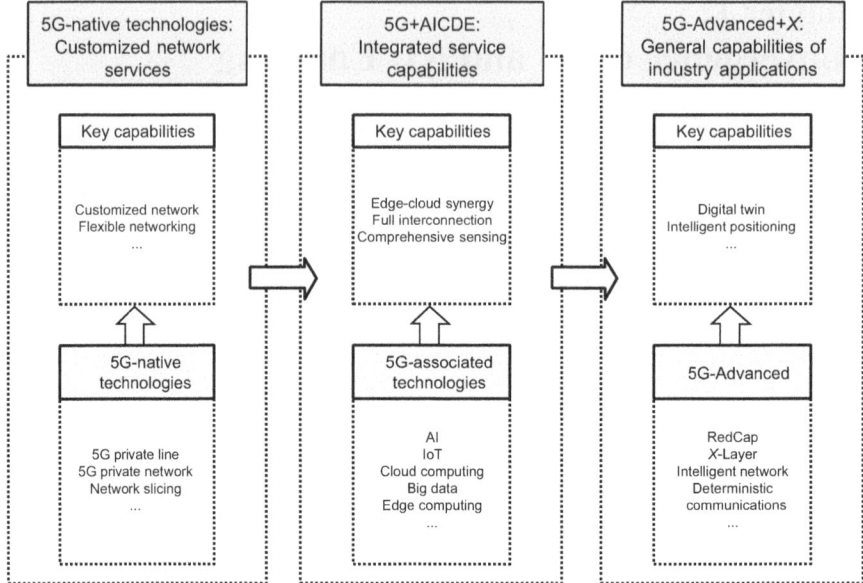

Fig. 12.1 Convergence development path for 5G and other technologies

12.1.1 5G Private Network: Customized Network

Compared with the traditional network operation mode of "unified access and low efficiency," 5G customizes resources and capabilities by using virtual NEs, open architectures, intelligent orchestration, and other technologies to provide comprehensive, flexible private networks with differentiated capabilities and service quality assurance. This can satisfy requirements of vertical industry users for intelligent network connections. This mode that provides industry users with differentiated and partially self-operated 5G network services is known as 5G private network. The 5G private network boasts the following advantages in offering customized networks and services to industry users:

First, network performance is much better. Based on a brand-new service-oriented architecture, the 5G private network decouples network functions into service-oriented components, which communicate with each other through lightweight, open interfaces, thereby fully meeting industry users' requirements for on-demand construction, dynamic deployment and scalability, and high reliability. The 5G private network allows some core network NEs to be deployed in cities, campuses, or even onsite, flexibly matching service requirements with network resources and meeting customers' requirements for fast customization and deployment. The 5G private network can be optimized based on the service types (such as data collection, HD video, and AR/VR), service distribution, and service transmission requirements of enterprises in various industries. The 5G private network supports low, medium, and high frequency bands. Low and medium frequency bands are used to achieve good coverage, high-precision indoor positioning, and low latency, ensuring stable and reliable transmission of industry services.

Second, network security is enhanced. Data security is the prerequisite for introducing 5G to industries. The 5G industry virtual private network can integrate multi-layer (terminals, networks, and applications) security assurance technologies based on the security requirements of industry users, thereby providing customized security assurance on 5G networks. In addition, because the 5G industry virtual private network is formed by improving the operator's public network, the industries/enterprises can benefit from carrier-class large-scale communications network security operation experience and obtain carrier-class security assurance services from operators. Additionally, virtual local area networks (VLANs) can implement multiple logically isolated dedicated pipes, so that services of a private network user and a public user are isolated and do not affect each other, thereby ensuring user service security. For confidential services with higher security requirements, physical isolation between network slices that carry different customer services can be implemented with the help of Flex Ethernet (FlexE).

Third, network construction cost is controllable. With the digital transformation of various industries, multiple physically isolated networks of different RATs have been formed for traditional industries to meet various requirements such as video surveillance, data collection, and intelligent management. This not only increases network construction and operations and maintenance (O&M) costs, but also makes it difficult to realize data interconnection. With the 5G private network, only one network is needed for management and production, eliminating information silos. Finally, in terms of 5G network construction, the 5G private network provides flexible customized products with hybrid, virtual, and exclusive private network construction modes based on enterprises' requirements, achieving cost-efficient network construction [1].

12.1.2 5G Network Slicing: Flexible Networking

After the 5G core network evolves to a distributed cloud-based and service-oriented architecture, network slicing, a technology that supports flexible and on-demand networking, has become a prominent innovation of 5G networks. A network slice is a customized, isolated, and quality-guaranteed end-to-end (E2E) logical dedicated network provided by a unified platform. Each network slice instance (NSI) comprises complete network functions and resources, including access network, core network, transmission network, and bearer network functions and resources. It organically combines access network, transmission bearer, core network, and service platform resources, terminal devices, and network management systems. In this way, logically isolated and independent virtual networks are available for different application scenarios or services of different types.

5G network slicing meets the diversified requirements of to business (ToB) market. It provides securely isolated networks with a specific bandwidth, latency, data rate, and reliability to meet the connection and data processing requirements of industry users. In addition, operators can leverage network slicing to flexibly and agilely provide one-stop industry services that encompass network capabilities, operation services, and various applications.

Furthermore, 5G network slicing facilitates network orchestration and management. Through network slice orchestration and management, 5G maps specific service requirements of vertical industry users to Service Level Agreement (SLA) requirements for specific indicators such as functions, performance, and service scopes of related NEs in the access network, core network, and transmission network, with an E2E slice template generated. Vertical industry users instantiate and run the slice based on the template. When an NSI is running, industry users can monitor, maintain, and dynamically adjust the slice. After a service reaches the end of its lifecycle, industry users can terminate the slice to release network resources. With such a network slicing management mechanism, 5G ensures that users' service requirements are met [2, 3].

Currently, 5G slicing standards and network device capabilities are both ready for initial commercial use, but they are only limited to pilot projects. The implementation solution featuring dedicated resource configuration has still to free itself from the traditional leasing mode in terms of business model. Therefore, it is costly and large-scale promotion is not realistic.

12.2 5G + AICDE: Building Integrated Service Capabilities

The implementation of 5G to business (5GtoB) application scenarios depends not only on the advantages of 5G networks, but also on the combination of emerging technologies such as big data, cloud computing, and the Internet of Things (IoT). Cloud computing and edge computing are the heart of the information industry, providing network computing, storage, application software, and related services. Big data is like blood, pumping vital information through technologies such as memory computing, data mining, business intelligence, and data governance. Artificial intelligence (AI) serves as the brain, which is responsible for processing information, such as computer vision, voice recognition, natural language processing, and deep learning. The IoT shapes moving organs such as hands, feet, and mouths and sensory organs such as eyes, ears, noses, and tongues. 5G is like a neural transmission network and can sense the transmission of all information through related sensors, networks, and neural systems. Figure 12.2 shows the relationship between 5G and related technologies.

The combination of 5G and AI, IoT, cloud computing, big data, and edge computing is called 5G + AICDE for short. It will promote the optimized integration of 5G networks with existing informatization systems in the industry and the maturity of optimized industry application solutions or single-system transformative application solutions.

12.2 5G + AICDE: Building Integrated Service Capabilities

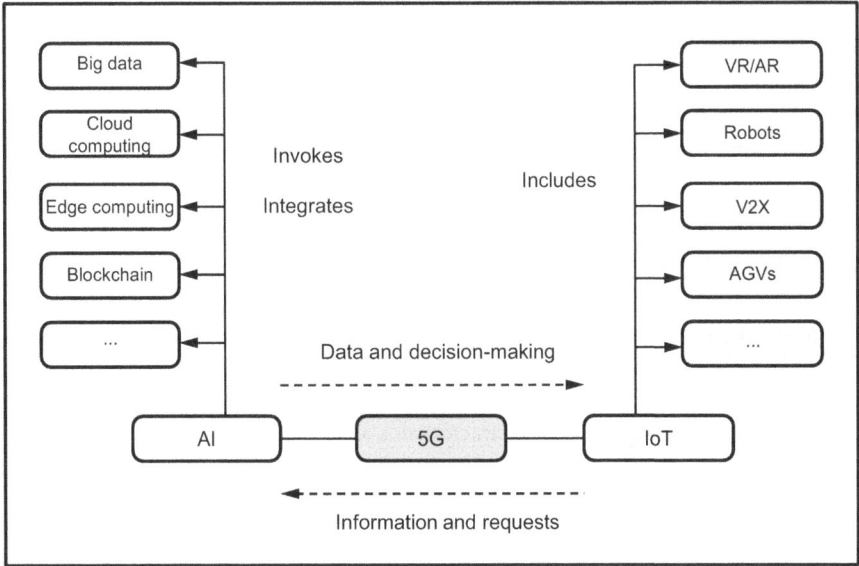

Fig. 12.2 Relationship between 5G and related technologies

12.2.1 5G + AI: Comprehensive Sensing

The introduction of AI technologies into the 5G mobile communications system not only improves traditional wireless service and network service capabilities, but also further expands 5G application scenarios. In traditional wireless service application scenarios, AI technologies play a key role in improving the O&M capability and user experience of 5G networks. In terms of routine network O&M, the AI-based knowledge Q&A and content recommendation technologies can greatly improve the efficiency of responses to user requirements. For network deployment and site selection planning, AI technologies are used for data analysis and processing, minimizing the necessity for manual onsite measurement. This improves network deployment efficiency and greatly reduces 5G network construction and O&M costs.

Currently, the development and application of AI technologies in the 5G mobile communications system are on the fast track. Major operators have started to use AI technologies to improve service quality and provide customized services. With regard to wireless service applications and user experience, AI technologies develop rapidly in fields such as computer vision and natural language processing, greatly improving user sensory experience and satisfying their deeper spiritual needs. As for new 5G application scenarios, AI technologies power the use of 5G in vertical industries, especially for promoting safe production in the petrochemical, construction, and mining industries. The 5G private network provides massive heterogeneous connections for monitoring devices such as sensors and cameras at the production site, greatly enhancing the monitoring of the production status. Moreover,

AI technologies are used at the network edge to monitor and analyze large-scale multi-modal data for the sake of intelligent and accurate fault warning and risk management, thereby significantly reducing the production fault and security accident rates and boosting production efficiency.

12.2.2 5G + IoT: Full Interconnection

The IoT requires a variety of network applications covering information collection, object identification, as well as information transmission and communications. It goes beyond traditional networks by achieving information exchange and interaction across interconnected objects, making network heterogeneity its main feature. 5G networks fully adapt to the characteristics of the IoT so that heterogeneous, large-capacity, high-rate, and dynamic distributed networks can be constructed leveraging 5G technology features such as wireless access, large-scale antennas, mobility management, and a large number of spectrum resources. Because 5G facilities are flexibly implemented on mobile communications networks, no separate network construction is required. This enables interconnection between devices of different intelligence levels in a simple and convenient manner.

In the context of 5G communications, the traditional IoT industry is gradually integrated with Internet technologies. With the efficient development of 5G technologies, the IoT industry is closely linked to various industries.

First, 5G helps implement remote control and supervision in more scenarios. The development of the original IoT is hindered by a low communications rate. 5G effectively reduces the information transmission latency, increases all-round data storage capacity, and enhances the data transmission rate, thereby ensuring comprehensive technological innovation at the application layer of the IoT architecture. For instance, equipping a smart home appliance with a 5G communications sensor effectively extends the information transmission distance. Then, an intelligent control system can be enabled by using a remote communications module and directly applied to an intelligent robot or unmanned aerial vehicle (UAV) system, which expands the scope of remote control and supervision. Moreover, 5G can convert control signals to more specific information, which is one of its significant advantages. This effectively avoids problems such as delayed data transmission and data loss and promotes information tracing and storage in all phases. As a result, IoT performance is further improved.

Second, 5G expands industry IoT scenarios and application services. 5G now serves as the main technical system for implementing technological innovation in multiple fields of society and has become the major platform for expanding IoT applications. For example, IoT construction relies on 5G for innovation in the communications field, which marks the foundation platform for convergence. The application of 5G in the IoT effectively increases the network information transmission rate and enables access of massive IoT devices, achieving one-to-many information transmission and processing. Furthermore, the process of empowering various production systems with 5G creates new platforms for IoT development, such as the smart grid IoT, industrial production IoT, and education resource sharing and cooperation platform. In the industrial IoT, 5G IoT modules can be used together with 5G customer-premises equipment (CPE) or wireless routers and the signals of the CPE or wireless routers are converted into Wi-Fi or industrial Ethernet signals. Then, programmable logic controllers (PLCs) are connected to control production equipment. For vehicle-to-everything (V2X), thanks to the low latency and high bandwidth of 5G, vehicle-to-vehicle (V2V), vehicle-to-pedestrian (V2P), vehicle-to-roadside (V2R), vehicle-to-parking (V2P), and vehicle-to-traffic-light (V2TL) communications become a reality with their reliability reaching 99.999%. Additionally, the 5G + edge-cloud platform can aggregate IoT products and applications to make it possible to popularize various types of traditional IoT products at scale [4].

Third, 5G lays a foundation for mobile IoT application. Driven by 5G, IoT technology is removing redundancy and becoming simpler. The overall IoT architecture is simpler, while the original layout is retained as intelligent and simplified reconstruction is conducted based on the original architecture. With the widespread adoption of 5G, a large number of mobile smart devices emerge. These smart devices function as IoT nodes to implement regional control. The storage capacity of devices is gradually increasing while their sizes are getting smaller, which further improves the convenience of the IoT itself. This makes it possible for the emergence of mobile IoT and provides more development space for the innovation of development systems in various industries.

12.2.3 5G + Cloud Computing: Cloud-Network Convergence

5G will further reshuffle the cloud computing industry, and even classify its services into multiple models to make the industry structure clearer. The models include but are not limited to the currently popular Infrastructure as a service (IaaS) and platform as a service (PaaS). There is currently a growing trend toward cloud-network convergence, involving network abstraction and virtualization technologies. In this way, networks gradually become blurred, and cloud computing serves a wider range of objects. In turn, the rapid growth of cloud computing increases the data volume, which benefits 5G development, thereby expanding the IaaS requirements.

5G + cloud computing will promote effective cloud-network convergence and collaboration. As products featuring cloud-network convergence represented by "Any Cloud to Any Cloud" and "Site to Any Cloud" are getting mature, cloud-network convergence will gradually evolve from simple interconnection to cloud-network-service convergence. The convergence of cloud and enterprise applications allows cloud-network convergence products to better satisfy enterprise needs and deliver better user experience. The convergence of cloud and ICT services enables cloud-network convergence products to be more closely combined with basic service capabilities, meeting industry features and flexible user requirements. The combination of 5G and cloud-network convergence will better support the development of vertical industries, boost the evolution toward mobile-cloud convergence and IoT-cloud convergence, accelerate industry applications, and promote connectivity of everything. Furthermore, 5G will facilitate the rapid development of the full-stack cloud, which is able to provide simplified access, intelligence, security and trustworthiness, and other full-stack services in all scenarios. This not only enables core databases to be easily migrated to the cloud, but also implements aggregation, convergence, and innovation of multiple types of enterprise data. In this way, different types of applications and loads can run smoothly on the same full-stack cloud platform.

12.2.4 5G + Big Data: Intelligent Decision-Making

The introduction of 5G enables 100 times more connected vehicles and devices (such as connected cars, portable devices, unmanned aerial vehicles (UAVs), and robots) within a given area. This greatly increases the amount of data obtained at the perception layer of mainstream IoT systems. 5G also encourages the emergence of new applications in the vehicle-to-everything (V2X), smart manufacturing, smart energy, wireless healthcare, wireless home entertainment, and UAV categories. This greatly diversifies the types of Internet data that is collected, with an increase in the amount of unstructured data like AR, VR, and video data. The convergence of 5G and big data improves 5G network applications, makes 5G functional modules more effective, and enables real-time big data application control. This will unlock three big advancements:

1. Improved data-driven decision-making: Large amounts of data are generated during 5G network operations. Big data technologies can be used to classify data and search for associations among data, which better supports 5G application requirements. With 5G networks, data can also be filtered by different criteria for real-time data value evaluation and analysis, thereby further enhancing daily supervision and management.
2. Diversified information sharing: The convergence of 5G and big data can help us adjust the data structure and further capitalize on the strengths of 5G in reducing the latency for data processing. This makes data aggregation more controllable [5]. In addition, cloud computing can be used to better manage resources and ensure that service and usage requirements are met. Network slicing in 5G also helps build more personalized service management systems and further explores data association to ensure that data application quality of service (QoS) meets expectations.
3. AI development: Deep learning, as the basis of AI, relies on big data technologies to support extensive data mining and analysis, and requires massive data samples for training. No matter the data volumes or dimensions, inventory data transport networks will simply not be enough to support future AI development.

5G networks, on the other hand, can serve as both communications networks and IoT networks, enabling fast data acquisition and wider data scopes which will enrich the training samples required for AI development [6].

12.2.5 5G + MEC: Edge-Cloud Synergy

Multi-access edge computing (MEC) combines cloud computing and edge computing to extend cloud computing capabilities to the network edge which is close to devices. An architecture that unifies interfaces and management between the central and edge clouds is required to simplify collaborative management and control. Edge-cloud synergy also requires all-round collaboration in infrastructure as a service (IaaS), platform as a service (PaaS), and software as a service (SaaS).

Edge computing is an inevitable trend in the evolution of computing patterns powered by 5G applications. It underpins many emerging industrial requirements for interconnection in the 5G era, such as large bandwidth, massive connectivity, high connection security, agile data processing, converged computing, and intelligent computing. In addition, an end-to-end (E2E) architecture for cloud-edge-device synergy is established across central cloud, edge computing, and IoT devices. This architecture moves network forwarding, storage, computing, and intelligent data analysis functionalities to the edge to reduce response latency, cloud workloads, and bandwidth costs. Furthermore, the architecture also enables cloud services such as network-wide scheduling and concurrent computing. Now, 5G edge computing has become a vital enabler of network and edge capability openness, and a catalyst for business model innovation for operators.

References

1. Liu H P, Zhou S Q. Advances of research on 5G industry private network application [J] (in Chinese). Science & Technology Review, 2022, 40 (23): 97–105.
2. China Unicom Research Institute. White paper on business innovation and development vision of 5G slicing [R] (in Chinese). 2022.
3. Zhang X B, Huang Q, Yang W C, etc. Analysis on the advances and challenges of 5G end-to-end network slice [J] (in Chinese). Mobile Communications, 2022, 46(2): 43–48.
4. China Academy of Information and Communications Technology (CAICT). IoT white paper (2020) [R] (in Chinese). 2020.
5. Tang Y J, Wang L F, Huang H A. Application analysis of the integration of big data and 5G communication technologies [J] (in Chinese). Telecom Power Technology, 2023, 40 (4): 131–133.
6. Zhu Y. On the application research on the integration of big data and 5G communication technologies [J] (in Chinese). Digital Communication World, 2021 (8): 44–45, 54.

Chapter 13
Key Industry Practices

China has built the world's largest and most technically advanced 5G networks, ushering in a critical period of large-scale 5G application. Large-scale 5G application is requirement-driven, centering on services, technologies, and solutions. It penetrates from peripheral links of industry production to core links of production control to empower digital transformation in numerous industries [1, 2]. Figure 13.1 shows the triangular model of 5G + X large-scale application.

13.1 Government

13.1.1 Overview of Digitalization and Intelligent Development in the Industry

Since the 18th National Congress of the Communist Party of China (CPC), the Chinese government has been advancing the digital and intelligent transformation of its services. This initiative is set against a backdrop of administrative system reforms, business environment optimization, and reforms of government functions (including streamlining administration and delegating power, improving regulations, and upgrading services) and is being achieved through the integration of technology, services, and data, the reengineering of processes, and the promotion of data sharing. The *14th Five-Year Plan for National Informatization*, unveiled in 2021, proposed that by 2025, the building of a digital China should make decisive progress, overall progress toward a digital government should increase, and digital welfare protection capabilities should be significantly strengthened. Subsequently, documents such as the *14th Five-Year Plan for Promoting National Government Informatization*, the *14th Five-Year Plan for Public Services*, and the *Guiding Opinions of the State Council on Strengthening the Building of a Digital Government* further clarified the specific tasks and main objectives of building a digital

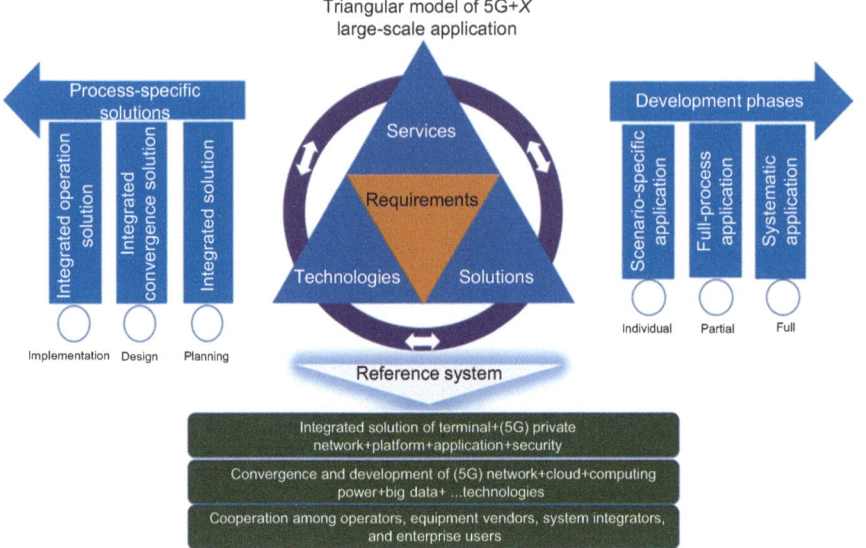

Fig. 13.1 Triangular model of 5G + X large-scale application

government. These documents called for the comprehensive promotion of digital transformation in government functions and administrative operations, emphasized the necessity for the intensive and coordinated development of efficient and interconnected government systems across various industries and fields, and highlighted the need for innovation in administrative management and service methods. These methods are being applied to enhance government efficiency. In February 2023, the CPC Central Committee and the State Council issued the *Plan for the Overall Layout of Building a Digital China*, which set a key target: substantially enhance the digitalization and intelligence of government affairs by 2025. The plan further emphasized the development of an efficient and coordinated digital government framework, providing clear guidance for the continued advancement of digital governance.

Since the official launch of the national integrated online government service platform in 2019, people have been able to access government services via a single website from anywhere across the country. The national government service platform currently serves as a central hub, connecting the service platforms of most provinces (including autonomous regions and municipalities) and 46 State Council departments. Through these efforts, the "one network" now provides government services nationwide. With the boom of mobile devices, local governments have also been actively developing mobile app-based government service platforms with unique local features. Platforms like "Suishenban," "Zheliban," and "Yueshengshi" (the government service platforms of Shanghai, Zhejiang, and Guangdong, respectively) constantly innovate, allowing citizens to access services from their mobile phones, ushering in a new era of convenience and efficiency. These apps, complemented by self-service terminals, Wireless Application Protocol (WAP) webpages, and official accounts and mini programs on platforms like WeChat and Alipay, have significantly improved service experiences for citizens.

Furthermore, vertical applications within the government sector have made remarkable progress, especially those concerning data sharing and electronic certificates. Today, social security services are more user-friendly than ever, with citizens able to access their electronic social security cards through over 480 apps and mini programs. By December 2022, 86 national services and over 1000 local services were accessible through these e-cards [3], greatly simplifying the process of applying for and accessing social security benefits. Integrated budget management has also made significant strides, now covering more than 3700 financial departments and over 600,000 budgetary units, which ensures efficient and standardized budget management at all levels. The reform of electronic fiscal bills is also underway, with over 500,000 administrative institutions now issuing electronic invoices, totaling over 11 billion transactions to date. Additionally, China's unified national health platform has been established, and e-certificates are now readily available through the platform. The digitalization efforts of the National People's Congress are making steady progress through various channels, providing the public with more efficient and convenient services.

13.1.2 Trends of Digitalization and Intelligent Development in the Industry

1. Optimizing the government structure through digital tools

   As the Chinese government increasingly embraces new technologies like 5G, artificial intelligence (AI), blockchain, the Internet of Things (IoT), big data, and cloud computing, it is actively exploring ways to optimize its organizational structures. This involves streamlining horizontal departmental structures while simplifying vertical administrative structures to create an overall more efficient and flat organizational structure. For instance, Longgang, a city administered as part of Wenzhou, in Zhejiang Province, was designated by the State Council as a pilot zone for "county-to-city" upgrading. In 2019, its status as a county-level city was approved, with 15 party and government institutions directly managing 92 communities. By eliminating intermediate management layers, Longgang greatly streamlined its governance. Over the following two years, the city's population grew from 380,000 to 460,000, and its key economic indicators ranked among the top three in Wenzhou. Digital governance plays a pivotal role in optimizing government services by transforming the concept of "shared responsibilities" into "distinct responsibilities." Moving forward, digitization will continue to drive organizational reforms, improve the responsibility system, and optimize government structures.
2. Unleashing the value of public data resources

   Public data resources are vital to the development of digital government. China, with abundant data resources and diverse application scenarios, stands at the forefront of this transformation. At the national level, initiatives like "Internet plus government services" and "east data, west computing" are driving the creation of a robust public data application ecosystem that features "data + computing power + algorithms + scenarios." Local governments are actively establishing pilot programs and demonstrations on exploring the development and utilization of public data resources and translating data value into tangible products and services. These data-driven applications continue to expand and form a comprehensive multi-platform matrix with City Brain at its core, leading the way in innovative social governance. In the realm of public services, data is bringing about personalized and diverse content delivery that moves beyond generic offerings. As for the industrial economy, data applications focus on improvement of quality and efficiency, and cost reduction. Data is undoubtedly catalyzing the success and expansion of inclusive finance, credit-based medical services, policy accessibility and implementation, and other key application scenarios.

3. Ubiquitous, convenient, intelligent, and inclusive public services

The "one network" government service system, with its expanded coverage, offers citizens faster and more user-friendly services. The Chinese government constantly introduces innovative practices that provide citizens with better service experience by minimizing bureaucratic procedures and enabling interprovincial services. The shift toward intelligent service models is evident, with regions increasingly exploring proactive and personalized approaches. These include responsive services, customized notifications, and self-service applications.

Notably, large AI-powered models excel in the areas of digital content understanding, code generation, content creation, and even the simulation of human behavior with digital technologies. These large models are an essential component in advancing smart governance in terms of decision-making, management, and service delivery.

13.1.3 Requirements for Digitalization and Intelligent Development in the Industry

1. Refined management

The fundamental reason for inadequate government service efficiency is fragmentation. Currently, cities adopt two systems for the routine management and emergency management. These systems function independently, resulting in avoidable issues such as excessive paperwork, complex processes, and multiple visits. The traditional linear, hierarchical, and unidirectional information flow also hinders the government's ability to respond to natural disasters, accidents, public health crises, and social security emergencies. To address these many challenges, it is important to employ digital technologies to optimize administrative processes and establish a robust mechanism for collaborative handling and multi-party supervision. Going digital can effectively address bureaucratic

13.1 Government

delays and overcome both temporal and spatial communication barriers, thus fostering synergistic social governance and enhancing overall societal management.

2. Inclusive services

The government has been actively promoting equal access to basic public services, aiming to narrow the existing gaps between urban and rural areas. Today, citizens expect more precise and personalized services, particularly in areas such as elderly care, healthcare, and finance. Inclusive services lie at the heart of social security capabilities, and digital technologies serve as the foundation of smart government services across various domains. For example, tailored services for special groups, such as the elderly and people with disabilities, require better online and offline channels, better information accessibility, and smart services related to retirement, healthcare, identity registration, and transportation. By leveraging technologies like 5G, big data, and AI, the government can create valuable services such as smart service centers, remote virtual transactions, intelligent risk control, and inclusive finance. Furthermore, technologies that cater to digital innovation trends and public habits enable the expansion of mobile, intelligent, and personalized services, enhancing overall online service coverage.

3. Value extraction from data elements

Government departments hold substantial amounts of public data, constituting over 80% of all social data. However, such datasets are often isolated from social data, leaving their inherent value largely untapped. By harnessing the benefits of digital technology, the government can unlock the value represented by the vast reservoir of data stored in government clouds. This paves the way for the government to assume a guiding and regulatory role in distributing the benefits derived from these data elements. Such empowerment can benefit both social governance and economic development. For example, promoting the use of public data in critical areas like healthcare and finance can help address challenges such as limited access to medical services and difficulties securing business loans. By deploying technologies like blockchain and sandbox, the government can establish targeted open platforms for government data sharing. These platforms ensure a secure and trustworthy data environment, meeting society's demand for high-value data and unleashing the potential of government data.

13.1.4 5G + AI Technology Convergence Analysis

1. 5G + Big data + AIoT

5G enables massive concurrent access of smart devices in cities, driving the implementation of AI applications across diverse scenarios and achieving true intelligent connectivity. By integrating 5G with technologies like AI and IoT, the government can strategically cover all end-point sensing nodes in cities—such as cameras, smart streetlights, and environment monitoring devices—based on actual needs. Such integration will meet the heightened network requirements of these sensing devices. In addition, through the establishment of interconnected and real-time "neural endpoints" within cities, the government can leverage vast data resources to realize precise supervision and enhance digital governance capabilities.

> **Case: 5G Empowers Smart City Governance in Shenzhen**
> China Telecom collaborated with Shenzhen's Nanshan District government on the "5G Empowering Smart City Governance" project. Through a combination of 5G, Building Information Modeling (BIM), and City Information Modeling (CIM), the two parties created the "Smart Shenzhen" digital twin city platform. By standardizing data and establishing unified data networks and data centers, they have solved the challenges posed by data fragmentation and seen initial success in IoT and data linkage. Furthermore, the IoT sensing platforms enabled the rapid creation of applications tailored to the diverse requirements for building a smart city. In Nanshan District, over 10,000 public servants, law enforcement officers, and community workers efficiently collaborate through the 5G private network and 5G smartphones. Integrating 5G with cloud-edge AI facilitates the swift handling of urban governance issues such as difficulties in regulating electric bicycles. In addition, applications like 5G-enabled smart streetlights with cloud broadcasting, intelligent 5G robot guide, and 5G messaging services have collectively benefited over five million citizens.

2. 5G + Blockchain

5G private networks are adept at meeting the escalating demands for data connectivity during the development of smart governance. Coupled with their advanced security protocols and contract management service frameworks, such networks can effectively meet security requirements in the government sector. At the same time, blockchain technology, renowned for its security and reliability, proficiently mitigates concerns surrounding privacy and trust throughout the collection, transmission, sharing, and integration of government data. Employing a 5G + blockchain network facilitates the sharing of structured data and the establishment of a trust system that is not subject to human control, which enables the provision of capabilities such as data rights confirmation, secure encryption, and multi-party secure computation. Such a system also effectively breaks down the data silos between different government departments, fostering a more secure and reliable environment for both inter- and intra-departmental data sharing. This facilitates the cross-agency sharing of government information and data, full-process evidence storage, and lifecycle management, thereby significantly boosting the efficiency of urban governance and public service delivery by government entities.

Case: "5G Easy Sign" Empowers Digital Government Construction
"5G Easy Sign" integrates blockchain, AI, and China mobile's proprietary digital certificates from the China Electronic Certification Authority. By collaborating with the National Time Service Center's timestamp service center, the Ministry of Public Security (for accessing its database), and the Beijing Tianping Blockchain, it delivers secure and reliable digital signatures and seals for governments, businesses, and individual users alike. The product has been successfully deployed across numerous sectors, including digital governance, finance, logistics, human resources, and real estate. It eliminates the need for paper-based signatures by facilitating seamless online signing and ensures transparent processes, thus significantly improving operational efficiency and reducing costs for governments, businesses, and individuals. Above all, the product guarantees every user a secure, user-friendly, and intelligent experience. "5G Easy Sign" means "less visits, faster processing" for governments, businesses, and individuals, and around-the-clock accessibility.

3. 5G + Robot + AIGC

   5G-empowered robots have been widely used in city-patrol, customer-support, and office scenarios, with their deployment substantially reducing labor costs for government services. We can consider 5G inspection robots as an example. During city patrols, these robots employ AI and other technologies to autonomously detect and evaluate infractions, including unauthorized street vending and illicit storefront operations outside of permitted zones. This greatly enhances the efficiency of identifying and addressing urban management issues. Additionally, built upon advancements in AIGC and 5G technology, a cutting-edge model for government services known as 5G + digital human is taking shape. This model transforms traditional consultation and remote-processing methods based on 5G and video terminals into an AIGC-driven approach that is characterized by large models, rapid delivery, and interactive experiences.

Case: 5G Government Robots Facilitate Digital Transformation
5G government robots have been officially deployed in the Administrative Service Center of Hebi, Henan province. The dedicated China Mobile team in Hebi conducted comprehensive researches on the services provided by the center, through which it compiled a robust database containing common inquiries, acceptance checklists, and visual guides. Equipped with interactive state-of-the-art 5G technologies, these robots can now autonomously address citizen inquiries, thereby reducing the workload for human staff and improving the overall quality of administrative services. Dubbed the "Little Blue," the government robots offer citizens a 24/7 intelligent consultation

experience. They can communicate with people and provide customized responses, voice navigation, accurate location tracking, and detailed answers to government-related inquiries. Supported by 5G technologies, "Little Blue" can now provide responses in milliseconds and accurately interpret current national policies. In addition, citizens can easily access relevant information and track progress by simply showing Little Blue their ID cards, making the robots highly popular and widely appreciated.

13.1.5 *Typical Solutions for Digitalization and Intelligent Development in Government*

1. Yiwei Intelligent O&M Platform makes digital intelligence a reality

    China Telecom Digital Intelligence Technology Co., Ltd. collaborated with Shenzhen's Guangming District government on the construction of an intelligent operations and maintenance (O&M) system for the government service network. The system is built based on the Yiwei Intelligent O&M Platform and provides full-stack intelligent O&M solutions that are secure and controllable for diversified service scenarios, so as to implement closed-loop security management and O&M of government services. The solutions include configuration management, automated O&M, asset management, monitoring and alerting, traffic analysis, security situation awareness, fiber management, and work order management. The O&M efficiency and operational quality of the district's government services were improved significantly by this new "intelligent brain."

    The system features five core capabilities: monitoring, management, control, operation, and service. It flexibly monitors the terminal status in a unified manner and performs intelligent diagnosis and management using the status and data. In this way, it provides centralized, visualized, intelligent, and refined O&M for the government data bureau of Guangming District, significantly improving O&M efficiency and terminal management capability. Real-time visibility and centralized monitoring and management allow the Guangming District to predict surges in system demand and detect network faults in real time based on service system conditions. Such a fully visible and controllable network reduces the possibility of network failures, enabling critical service systems to operate smoothly, and achieving efficient, standardized, and secure management of information systems.

    To further improve O&M efficiency, the system also includes an O&M app that provides monitoring and alerting, asset management, work order management, equipment room check-in/out, O&M data search, and other functions. App users can keep up to date with the O&M status, submit service requests, report faults, and complete approvals whenever the need arises.

2. Baiyun District, Guiyang implements smart city projects

    The local government of Baiyun District, Guiyang, Guizhou in southwestern China has been vigorously promoting smart city projects based on the architec-

13.1 Government

ture of "one foundation, five common support services, and N smart scenarios." The spatiotemporal big data platform is one of the key platforms that serve as the foundation for the projects. It uses the SuperMap geographic information system (GIS) software to collect and integrate the spatiotemporal big data of all local government departments into spatiotemporal big data resource pools using a unified coordinate system and data standards, with the aim of creating a panorama of the district and building a digital base for smart city projects. The platform enables the collection and integration of historical and current data, two-dimensional and three-dimensional data, above-ground and underground data, and static and dynamic data. The long-term vision for the platform entails creating a digital city twin and exploring new methods of city governance, improving governance efficiency. Figure 13.2 shows the intelligent dispatch center for the projects.

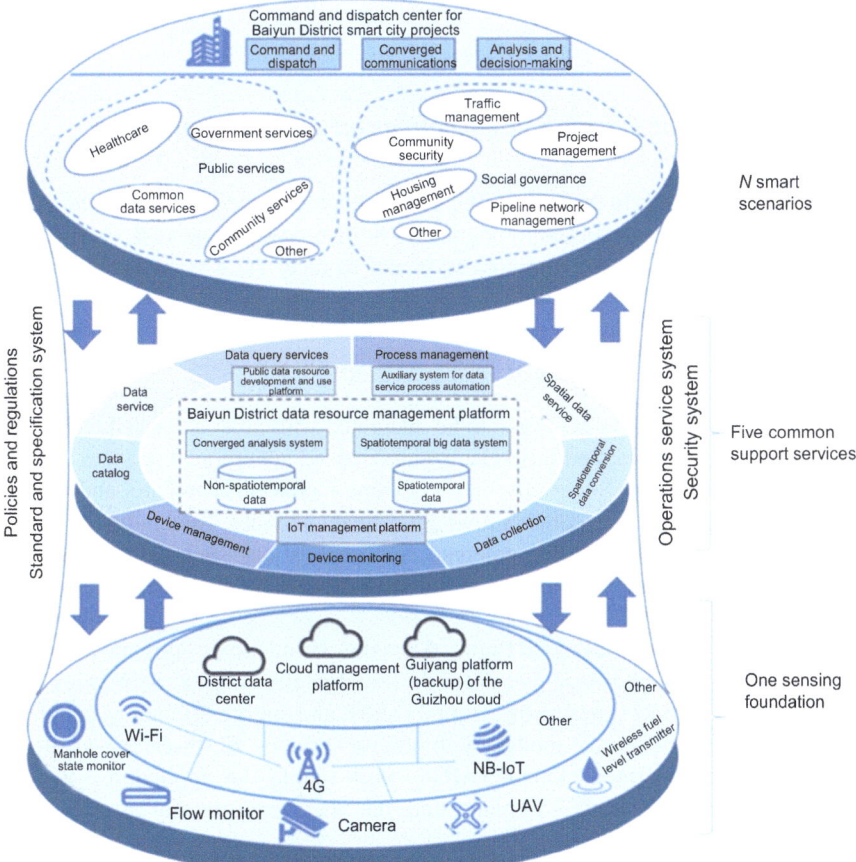

Fig. 13.2 Intelligent dispatch center for the "Smart Baiyun" platform

The spatiotemporal big data platform collected basic spatiotemporal data from 2016 to 2022, including the specialized data of all subordinate offices in Baiyun District. Using this data, more than 300 spatiotemporal big data resource pools with themed layers were formed. These resource pools interact with the IoT platform of the district. More than 20,000 IoT data entries have been collected, covering over 9600-channel video surveillance devices, 155 access control devices, 15 manhole cover monitoring devices, 12 environmental monitoring devices, and more.

The platform also aggregates and classifies frequently used functions, including the map and statistical analysis functions required by each service system, as well as the basic spatial analysis services, such as overlay analysis, buffer analysis, reachability analysis, and spatial relationship analysis required by diverse spatial data applications. Moreover, the platform provides decision-making support, intelligent site selection analysis, project compliance analysis, regional load-bearing capacity analysis, 15-min city analysis, and high- and low-altitude video link analysis.

13.1.6 Path for Large-Scale Replication and Promotion

Phase 1 (2019–2021): In this phase, 5G, with its unprecedented high bandwidth and wide connectivity, was used to upgrade existing e-government systems and service centers to improve data collection and storage. 5G e-government private networks and digital government service platforms began to take hold, and applications for telecommuting and intelligent O&M were applied to provide more convenient and efficient government services for government personnel and the public.

Phase 2 (2022–2024): As 5G began to be integrated with other advanced technologies like AI, big data, and blockchain, data-enabled government services started gaining momentum. Smart city brains became increasingly mature, and breakthroughs were made in collaborative government services. New public services utilizing digital technologies emerged, and applications such as 5G inclusive finance, AI elderly assistants, and virtual operators profoundly changed people's lifestyles.

Phase 3 (2025 and later): Digital twin cities will continue to develop, powered by full-time video and image data from diverse domains. Digital twin cities will feature interconnection sensing, digital O&M, and energy efficiency, enabling new government service models with precise services. Furthermore, artificial intelligence generated content (AIGC) will enable the application of new technologies like digital humans and the metaverse in government service models.

13.2 Emergencies

13.2.1 Overview of Digitalization and Intelligent Development in the Industry

Emergency management is an integral part of a nation's governance system and reflects its overall governance capabilities. It involves preventing and mitigating major security risks as well as responding to disasters and accidents. It is essential for protecting people's lives and property and ensuring social stability. In December 2021, the Central Cyberspace Affairs Commission released the *14th Five-Year Plan for National Informatization*, which explicitly proposes the establishment of an emergency information system that integrates peacetime and wartime needs. The plan also includes the development of a modern emergency management capability enhancement project, which leverages information technologies to modernize emergency management. This initiative is expected to improve capabilities in terms of cross-department collaborative monitoring and early warning, regulatory enforcement, decision-making support, rescue, and social mobilization. The *National Emergency Management System Plan during the 14th Five-Year Plan Period* was released later on. It states that significant progress should be made in modernizing emergency management systems and capabilities by 2025. An emergency management system shall be implemented, featuring unified commanding, reserves of specialized and regular staff, swift responses, and effective coordination between different levels. By 2035, law-based, scientific, and smart emergency responses will be in place, thereby shaping a new emergency management pattern based on collaboration, participation, and common interests.

The digital transformation of the emergency management industry mainly focuses on managing emergencies related to natural disasters, production safety, urban safety, and epidemic prevention and control. Figure 13.3 shows the intelligent emergency management architecture [4]. The architecture streamlines the entire emergency management process, including prevention and preparation, monitoring and early warning, response and rescue, and recovery and reconstruction. It integrates capabilities such as intelligent perception and a digital brain, and it is designed to drive innovation in emergency management services, processes, and decision-making. As such, emergency management will become more digitalized, collaborative, and intelligent, and problems related to emergency management can be better resolved.

Under policy guidance and the efforts of various departments, China's emergency management industry has made significant progress in product R&D and application innovation. Technologies such as 5G and AI have played an important role in fields such as early disaster warnings and monitoring, emergency communications, smart firefighting, and remote first aid. For example, in disaster monitoring, 5G applications, such as 5G + BeiDou satellite, 5G+ unmanned aerial vehicle (UAV), and "Smart River Chief," have been put into practice. A variety of information technologies have been used to assist in disaster prevention and control,

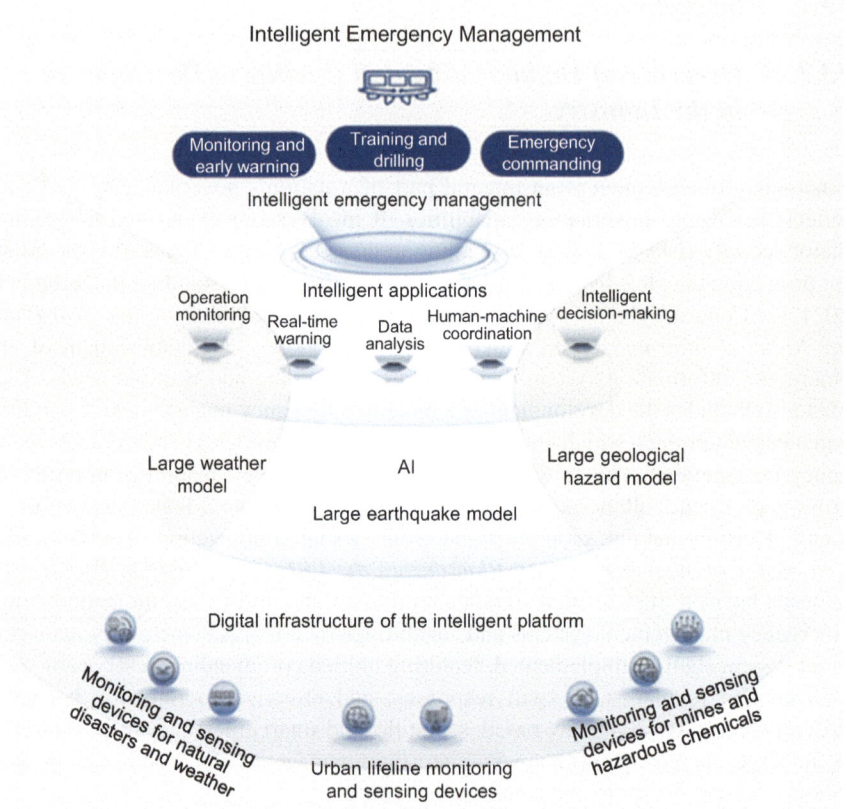

Fig. 13.3 Intelligent emergency management architecture

transforming defense forces from "human defense" to "technical defense." In emergency communications, Yunnan Provincial Meteorological Bureau has launched a pilot project to trial the use of 5G enhanced short message service (SMS) technology in emergency warnings. This project enables the Bureau to release information more effectively, thereby facilitating disaster prevention and mitigation at the grassroots level. In firefighting, a smart firefighting system has been established in Wuwei city, Gansu province. The system integrates modules such as smart prevention and control, smart operations, smart law enforcement, and smart management. It digitalizes and modernizes firefighting and improves coordination at different levels. As for remote first aid, the Second Affiliated Hospital Zhejiang University School of Medicine has built China's first 5G-based smart first aid system. This system has applications such as 5G remote B-scan, 5G intensive care unit (ICU), virtual reality (VR) diagnosis and treatment, remote video interaction, and remote first aid commanding platform. It has already been used in several hospitals across different provinces for medical rescues in the event of a disaster.

13.2.2 *Trends of Digitalization and Intelligent Development in the Industry*

1. Jointly building an efficient and collaborative emergency network

    Extensive social participation is crucial to enhancing national emergency management. All social groups, including enterprises, media, social organizations, and the public, are encouraged to work together to build a social governance community featuring co-construction, common governance, and sharing. Many innovative solutions have already emerged. For example, public online document edit can help in precise disaster relief. In addition, there are open platforms that can mobilize all social groups for first aid. In the future, advanced technologies will continue to develop and strengthen the connections between governments, enterprises, and society to create a safer way of life. With emerging information technologies like 5G, AI, and cloud computing, social groups can better participate in disaster monitoring and warning, supervision, law enforcement, commanding and decision-making assistance, rescues, and social mobilization. In addition, intelligent Internet-based learning can be utilized to educate and train people on intelligent security and emergency management. This can promote the development of a security resilience culture and enhance the public's ability to prevent and mitigate disasters.

2. Constructing smart and resilient cities

    The construction of resilient cities has gained significant attention and been made a national strategy due to security concerns around complex urban systems, weak emergency management, and isolated emergency information. Intelligent emergency management can develop in resilient cities. Certain aspects of intelligent emergency management have already been implemented in cities such as Shanghai, Guangzhou, Hefei, and Jiaxing. In the future, urban disaster prevention and control will focus on applying scientific and technological means to prevent, mitigate, and relieve disasters, rather than just on hardware facilities. Smart and resilient cities will be constructed using a coordinated approach that combines routine and urgent management, as well as software and hardware. Such an approach enables full-process management covering pre-disaster planning, in-disaster responses, and post-disaster reconstruction, which makes urban disaster prevention and relief more efficient, scientific, and intelligent.

3. Perfecting grassroots emergency governance

    Modernizing the national emergency governance system and capabilities involves promoting the governance of townships, streets, and urban and rural communities. At present, there is disconnection between grassroots governance and emergency management, and an inadequate level of digitalization in grassroots governance. As organizations continue to explore the use of digital connection platforms like WeChat business accounts and mini programs in emergencies, these lingering "last mile" issues are expected to be resolved. Intelligent emergency management solutions in the future will enable efficient and accurate risk monitoring and warning, decision-making, resource coordination, and responses at the grassroots level through an intelligent platform. Digitalized and intelligent grassroots emergency governance will noticeably enhance emergency management capabilities.

13.2.3 Requirements for Digitalization and Intelligent Development in the Industry

1. Real-time risk awareness

   Inadequate risk prevention is a major weak point in emergency management. Security incidents with destructive consequences are common. Crises that defy conventional understanding are often dismissed as rare events that cannot be prevented. Emergency management systems remain fragile and are in the process of being reformed. Risk prevention and mitigation are still inadequate [5].

   Against this background, emerging digital technologies can improve model analysis and provide new ideas for risk mitigation. New smart sensor devices offer cutting-edge information collection. Using digital methods for data analysis, these devices automatically aggregate, identify, associate, and converge diverse data resources to enable real-time monitoring and dynamic analysis. The devices can be applied in a wide range of fields, such as manufacturing, food and drugs, healthcare, and disaster response, enhancing monitoring, early risk identification, and warning for diverse disaster scenarios.

2. Smart dispatching and rescue

   In vast regions, timely disaster response is a challenge. In the past, risks and risk sources were monitored manually, and traditional communication methods made transmission of emergency information slow. Emergency response was hindered by a lack of accurate, real-time information sharing. Sensor devices and edge computing capabilities embedded in 5G and cloud computing, along with efficient data integration, can eliminate information barriers at all levels of risk management. These technologies enable automatic generation of solutions for personnel and equipment allocation, as well as disaster handling strategies based on the types and scale of disasters. This ensures timely distribution of critical resources such as personnel and materials. Moreover, AI and robot technologies can be deployed in hazardous environments to intelligently locate trapped individuals and identify different objects, making the work of rescue personnel safer and more efficient.

3. Effective disaster warning dissemination

   Climate change has made extreme weather events more common and volatile, and disaster warning mechanisms have struggled to keep up. Challenges include ensuring last mile communication for the dissemination of disaster warnings. Insufficient, delayed, or missing warnings continue to be a major safety issue.

5G positioning offers high-speed mobility and ultra-low latency. Using 5G IoT and 5G information technologies, 5G positioning can accurately locate people, systems, and devices for disaster monitoring. It also enables real-time monitoring, dynamic measurement, and automatic warning. Moreover, it seamlessly connects information between detection devices and servers, providing precise, targeted warning services.

13.2.4 5G + AI Technology Convergence Analysis

1. 5G + Robot/UAV

   The low-latency feature of 5G can significantly improve the operational accuracy of robots. In critical or hazardous situations, rescue robots can be deployed to perform tasks precisely, reducing safety risks for rescue personnel. 5G + UAV solutions are now widely used in emergencies. These solutions can collect onsite emergency information and send images, videos, and task data back to a command center through a 5G network. In this way, the command center can analyze the overall situation of the emergency sites and remotely deliver command information. 5G + robot technology is being widely applied to object monitoring, security inspection, contactless quarantine, and public safety. The use of 5G in conjunction with robots for emergency response will become even more robust with the enhancement of robot supervision and advancements in 5G technologies, particularly in network slicing and latency. This will enable us to address the intricate and dynamic rescue needs of diverse emergency sites.

> **Case: 5G UAVs Enable Forest Fire Prevention and Disaster Reduction**
> The 5G UAV system developed and applied by China Mobile consists of the China Mobile Lingyun UAV management platform, a 5G network, and Hubble series terminals. The UAVs resolve the issues of low inspection efficiency, surveillance blind spots, and the intelligence limitations of traditional forest fire prevention methods. When integrated with the forest fire prevention command platform, the 5G UAVs complement ground-based inspections and significantly enhance overall prevention management. During fire rescue operations, the UAVs can collect and transmit real-time forest fire inspection data. Additionally, they can overlay high-definition images of fire scenes onto each geographic information application terminal, providing crucial visual information for decision-making. In nighttime firefighting operations, infrared imaging is used to rapidly detect fire breakouts and smoldering fires, preventing reignition. Using the China Mobile Lingyun platform, data can be analyzed and distributed in real time, covering supervision and inspection, monitoring and warning, and rescue and prevention. This has significantly improved work efficiency.

2. 5G + Cloud computing + Big data

   5G-enabled big data analysis offers a multitude of advantages, including faster data transmission speeds, reduced latency, and cost-effectiveness. Real-time camera data is aggregated from mobile devices and sensor platforms and then subjected to quantitative analysis across different dimensions using cloud computing. This process identifies key information and provides decision-makers with a scientific basis for making informed choices, reducing response time, and enhancing decision quality. Furthermore, cloud computing powered by 5G and big data can be used to categorize data and explore potential relationships between data points. Comprehensive prediction models can be established for proactive anticipation of major events, enabling a shift from passive acceptance to active engaging.

> **Case: 5G + Big Data Enablement Achieves Refined Disaster Risk Control in Coal Mines**
> The Chinese Institute of Coal Science has developed an intelligent coal mine disaster warning and comprehensive prevention and control system. This system addresses the following critical challenges: (1) low utilization of massive amounts of coal mine disaster data; (2) insufficient converged data analysis of different disasters; (3) inadequate data mining and analysis of individual disasters; and (4) lack of connection between monitoring and warning systems and disaster prevention. The system creatively integrates fundamental geological data of mines, production governance data, and monitoring data. It establishes a data-driven intelligent coal disaster warning indicator library and warning model repository. The system automatically fine-tunes warning indicators based on mine production and geological conditions. It enables intelligent prediction and early warning of coal mine disasters, dynamic risk assessment, equipment coordination, and reciprocal feedback of monitoring and prevention information. This innovative approach revolutionizes disaster control by transforming the entire process of disaster prevention and management for coal mines in China.

3. 5G + Satellite Internet

   For emergency communication, the combination of 5G and satellite Internet can meet the voice and data service requirements of operation teams and emergency service users. The higher peak rate of 5G necessitates a robust backhaul network. Satellites can serve as backhaul networks to ensure stable 5G emergency networks. With the advent of high-throughput satellites, high-band portable devices are becoming increasingly prevalent, offering large bandwidth in a compact form factor. By harnessing the foundational capabilities of 5G private networks and coordinating access across multiple satellite systems, the combination of 5G and satellite Internet can mitigate bandwidth limitations.

Aggregating bandwidth from multiple links enhances bandwidth optimization and extends service duration, ensuring reliable emergency communication and efficient delivery of 5G messages.

Case: 5G and Satellite Converged Communications Technology Facilitates Surgeries After Earthquake in Lu County
When an earthquake struck Lu County, Sichuan Province on September 16, 2021, Sichuan Provincial People's Hospital established four-party emergency video communication through 5G and satellite links and completed surgery for an injured 69-year-old person. The emergency medical rescue system, powered by 5G and satellite converged communications technology, provided fast networking and stable signals. It enabled seamless communication between user terminals in disaster areas, and between disaster and non-disaster areas, meeting the communication requirements for pre-hospital emergency rescue. The onsite command center established satellite links with the expert team at Sichuan Provincial People's Hospital. Additionally, the fixed and mobile ends of Lu County People's Hospital's operating room connected to the rescue room at Sichuan Provincial People's Hospital via the 5G network, ensuring successful completion of the surgery. Powered by this system, the emergency medical rescue order was swiftly established. Over 80 wounded individuals received treatment through remote consultation, 38 had mild injuries, 11 had serious injuries, and 10 underwent surgery. There were no fatalities among the wounded.

13.2.5 *Typical Solutions for Digitalization and Intelligent Development in Emergencies*

1. 5G + Smart firefighting solution

   The 5G + smart firefighting solution deployed at Guangdong Fire Department uses the 5G onsite rescue virtual private network to create a multi-frequency multi-dimensional network solution. It uses 5G helmets and self-networking for high-speed communication, as shown in Fig. 13.4. The onsite command center uses 700 MHz vehicle-mounted base stations and simplified user plane functions (UPFs) to provide penetration coverage and edge computing. It uses public network and satellite data tunneling technologies to synchronize computing data and command operations. The background command center uses a 2.6 GHz public network to establish data communication channels. The real-time and reliable communication of the onsite command center and background command center ensures transparent coordination at the rescue site, enhancing rescue efficiency and safety.

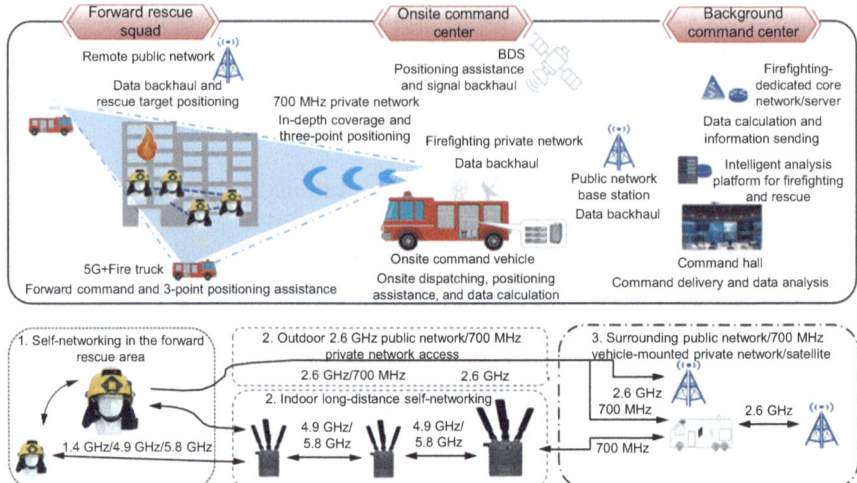

Fig. 13.4 5G + smart firefighting solution at Guangdong Fire Department

In this solution, 5G technology is applied in two phases: onsite operations and background command and dispatch. The 5G network enables rapid connectivity and deployment for both the foreground and background during emergencies. This solution seamlessly integrates 5G technology with firefighting devices. The 5G network's high-bandwidth data communication enhances over 10 devices and the typical 2 kg equipment carried by firefighters, transforming the equipment into 2 kg 5G dual-optical helmets and 5G self-networking green boxes. This reduces firefighter workloads by 90% and enables equipment digitalization. It also breaks down data silos to improve rescue efficiency. The solution uses data from the MR fingerprint database and 5G messages on the public network. It seamlessly connects to the smart fire incident reception and handling system, the smart fire command and dispatch system, and a 3D firefighting map that is generated using computer-aided design (CAD) drawings. This solution eliminates data barriers, associates positioning information, and establishes a digital, visualized rescue system. It enhances rescue efficiency and facilitates coordination between the two smart systems and the firefighting map.

2. China Unicom's "5G + Digital" integrated system

To fulfill onsite rescue needs, China Unicom Digital Technology Co., Ltd. developed a comprehensive "5G + Digital" software/hardware and service integrated system over the course of a year. This system aims to overcome the challenges of (1) obtaining real-time onsite information; (2) visualizing disaster trends; (3) enhancing decision-making; and (4) safeguarding command and dispatch even during network disconnection, transportation disruption, and power outages. China Unicom's goal is to enable unified command in collaborative rescue efforts.

China Unicom uses cutting-edge technologies in 5G, satellite communication, BeiDou Navigation Satellite System (BDS), IoT sensing, edge computing, and AI to create a "5G + Digital" software/hardware and service integrated system. This system has a "one platform and two networks" architecture, comprising a site information platform, an emergency tactical Internet, and a distributed rescue IoT sensing network. The system is centered around a smart command and dispatch system, with an emergency tactical Internet as its backbone and an emergency IoT sensing network as its nerve. It is designed for major disaster rescue operations, forming a new emergency rescue mode featuring digitalization, site networking, and visualized operations. Through these enhancements, it improves emergency communication assurance, command decision-making, resource dispatching, and collaborative rescue efficiency during severe disasters and in complex conditions.

China Unicom aims to establish connections between the national emergency rescue base core network, provincial backbone networks, municipal tactical subnets, and air backbone nodes for UAVs. This will be achieved by integrating multiple communication methods, including 5G public/private networks, satellite communication, narrowband, and self-networking. An integrated communication system will be created, with air backbone nodes for UAVs, ground backbone nodes for emergency vehicles, and tactical subnets for rescue teams. This system will enable quick convergence of diverse types of terminals and quick access to onsite conditions, significantly improving the efficiency of rescue channels during emergencies.

13.2.6 Path for Large-Scale Replication and Promotion

Phase 1 (2019–2021): The 5G network replaced the original wireless system or wired network, enhanced video and data collection services, and was applied to 5G HD video, environmental monitoring, and smart rescue.

Phase 2 (2022–2024): The convergence of 5G technologies, along with big data, AI, and satellite Internet, leads to the gradual formation of an integrated emergency communication support system. During this phase, a smart emergency platform is established to handle diverse emergencies, and applications such as risk awareness, smart scheduling, and remote first aid are enhanced.

Phase 3 (2025 and later): Digital technologies will continue to reshape the emergency management system, improving emergency services. The digital emergency management framework will prioritize safe production, disaster relief, urban and rural security, and emergency response by fostering collaboration among different systems and services. This will facilitate emergency collaboration across levels, regions, systems, and departments and realize intelligent monitoring, precise supervision, and informed decision-making.

13.3 Meteorology

13.3.1 Overview of Digitalization and Intelligent Development in the Industry

The evolution of weather forecasting has gone through four phases: human experience, informatization, digitalization, and intelligence, as shown in Fig. 13.5. Initially relying solely on human experience, weather forecasting gradually transitioned to using traditional weather maps and transformed into an applied science. Today, forecast accuracy has significantly improved with numerical weather forecasting and AI-based weather forecasting. Modern weather forecasts provide reports on weather changes and trends for specific time periods in the future. These reports are generated by meteorological stations that use modern technologies (such as satellites and radar) to collect meteorological data for countries, regions, or even the globe. Weather forecasters perform comprehensive analyses and make scientific judgments based on weather change patterns. Accurate and timely weather forecasts yield substantial socioeconomic benefits by contributing to the economy and national defense and safeguarding lives and property.

In 2022, the State Council of China issued the *Outline for High-Quality Development of Meteorology (2022–2035)*, laying out the objective of achieving high-quality meteorological development by completing seven major development tasks by 2035. The outline emphasizes constant improvements of sophisticated meteorological monitoring, precise forecasting, and refined services to basically achieve meteorological modernization centered on smart meteorology. Guided by this strategy, the meteorological bureaus of Shanghai, Zhejiang, Anhui, Fujian, and Guangdong provinces/municipalities and the meteorological bureau of Xiong'an New Area in Hebei have initiated digitalization pilots. These efforts aim to enable

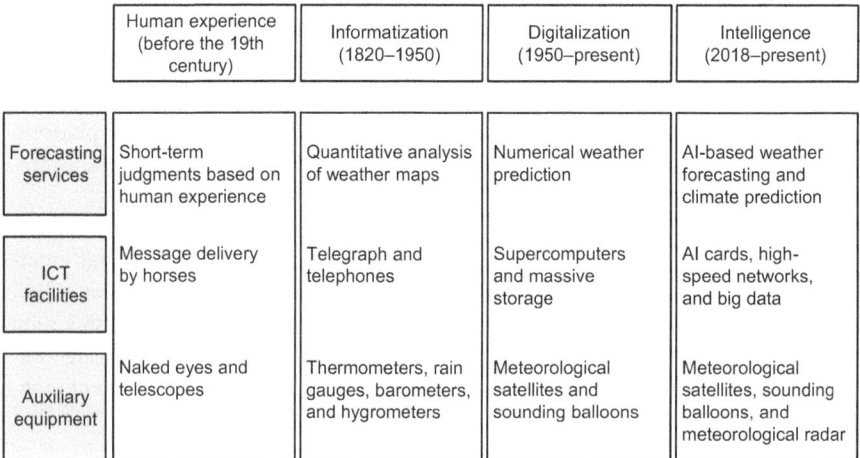

Fig. 13.5 Development history of weather forecasting

the digital and intelligent transformation of meteorological services to provide higher-quality meteorological services for the development of digital governments, cities, rural areas, and the digital economy.

In 2023, to further promote the deep integration of emerging technologies with the meteorological industry, the China Meteorological Administration issued the *Work Plan for Artificial Intelligence Meteorological Applications (2023–2030)*. The plan outlines a development roadmap for AI meteorological applications, aiming to form the "542" overall framework. This framework entails the preliminary establishment of the five foundational pillars of AI big databases, computing environments, algorithm models, open platforms, and inspection and evaluation processes; initiation of R&D for emerging technologies like weather forecast foundation models and integration of emerging AI technologies with the four key areas of weather monitoring and warning, forecasting and prediction, numerical forecasting, and professional services; emphasis on the two assurances of AI-powered cooperation and talent cultivation, as well as achievement transformation and intellectual property protection. China aims to lead the world in AI meteorological applications by 2030, making substantial advancements in service capability development.

In the digitalization of the meteorological industry, the seamless integration of 5G, cloud computing, big data, AI, and smart meteorology is further enhancing the efficiency of meteorological services and facilitating information sharing. These advancements demonstrate application benefits in three areas. The first is smart meteorological services. 5G-based remote scene observation and experiential service applications have emerged. These technologies use geographical information and user feedback to tailor meteorological services to the needs of specific users. These services feature refined forecasting, real-time disaster notification, targeted warnings, and data visualization. The second area is smart transportation and meteorology. With 5G and road sensors, a digital network can offer weather conditions, vehicle status, pedestrian information, and other road-specific information. This integration provides comprehensive information for decision-making during driving. The third area is smart agriculture and meteorology. New professional services have emerged thanks to intelligent sensing, analysis, and judgment systems of meteorological information, along with devices and systems such as environment monitoring systems, indoor miniature meteorological monitoring stations, field meteorological monitoring stations, and environment control systems. These services include IoT-based agricultural production cycle management, precision agriculture using location services and remote sensing technologies, meteorological monitoring for agriculture, and insights into the meteorological impacts on different crops [6].

13.3.2 Trends of Digitalization and Intelligent Development in the Industry

1. Foundation models transforming meteorological prediction

    Emerging technologies, such as AI, provide new research tools for meteorology, independent of conventional numerical forecasting processes. The core of

AI meteorological models is to, based on data-driven deep learning algorithms, leverage powerful computing capabilities, training on extensive historical data, and multiple deep learning architectures to swiftly predict key information. The predicted information includes common meteorological elements and fields, typhoon paths, extreme weather, near-ground wind fields, and precipitation. Some mid-term forecast results based on AI meteorological models have already achieved comparable or higher accuracy than numerical weather forecasting. Additionally, AI meteorological models have significant advantages in terms of forecast calculation speed. Since 2022, AI meteorological models released by NVIDIA, Google DeepMind, Microsoft, Huawei, Shanghai Artificial Intelligence Laboratory, Fudan University, and Tsinghua University have been successively showcased, achieving remarkable results in a short span. By training meteorological models, meteorologists can predict mid- and long-term weather changes with higher accuracy, providing crucial decision-making support for diverse industries.

2. Expansion of "Meteorological+" services across industries and fields

With the support of digital technologies, smart meteorological services are being seamlessly integrated into industries, giving rise to new business models and fields in these industries. Focusing on scenario-specific requirements, new meteorological services will be applied to disaster prevention, mitigation, and relief, diverse economic activities, public life, and ecological civilization. The development of comprehensive cross-industry platforms fosters innovative "Meteorological+" business models. For example, smart agriculture services integrate meteorological data and agricultural monitoring technologies to provide intelligent all-weather, all-day monitoring and scientific warnings throughout the entire process of agricultural production. Additionally, these services support related departments in formulating prevention policies and measures while also helping improve agricultural production efficiency and promote sustainable development by using manual intervention to handle adverse weather impacts.

3. Diverse smart meteorological services

China has preliminarily established refined meteorological services that intelligently deliver meteorological messages anytime, anywhere. Meteorological service information is accessible to over 90% of the country's population. During the 14th Five-Year Plan period, meteorological departments of China will carry out refined and smart meteorological services through user-specific management and explore the use of network robots to provide personalized and customized services so that people can easily obtain meteorological services on the go. With AI, big data, and deep learning, capabilities like intelligent awareness of meteorological service needs and customized service supply can be built. With users as the core, user-specific management can be implemented to achieve more comprehensive, refined, and practical meteorological services.

13.3 Meteorology

13.3.3 Requirements for Digitalization and Intelligent Development in the Industry

1. Requirements for precise meteorological monitoring

    Meteorological data collection is the key to meteorological detection. However, conventional meteorological data collection methods have time, space, and technology constraints that hinder data accuracy and completeness. 5G technology offers faster data transmission speeds, larger data capacity, wider coverage, and better security. It helps people obtain observation materials faster with a higher temporal resolution, providing more reliable support for meteorological prediction and decision-making. Accurate and reliable information can be obtained through the integration of 5G and UAVs or other environment monitoring devices for meteorological observation, along with the deep insights of highly refined user analysis. The information can serve as a reference for meteorological service development, making meteorological detection more accurate, comprehensive, and timely.

2. Requirements for real-time warnings

    Meteorological disasters exhibit a relatively high occurrence rate among all natural disasters, and they pose a serious threat to the development of a country or region and its social economy. Ensuring timely and accurate warning transmission that reaches a broad population is crucial. However, in China, meteorological disaster warnings rely primarily on conventional communications methods which suffer from limited transmission speeds due to network capacity constraints. In addition, these methods struggle to meet the precise warning transmission requirements for specific and remote areas. With the emergence and development of novel information and communications technologies, such as 5G, mobile IoT, and Tiantong satellites, the integration of these technologies and warning dissemination can help to overcome the aforementioned challenges. In particular, 5G network slicing can ensure that network indicators like bandwidth and latency meet application requirements across different industries, facilitating the transmission of meteorological disaster warnings.

3. Requirements for personalized meteorological services

    New business models related to short videos and live streaming have taken off in China, and users are demanding increasingly diversified and personalized meteorological services. Applications such as 5G live streaming have achieved initial strides in reporting major weather disasters and providing services related to meteorological social hotspots. With 5G technologies, video and augmented reality (AR) traffic is expected to account for 90% of the total traffic. Users can select live streams according to their preferences and access personalized services like 3D weather broadcasts, VR live streaming, and 360° onsite weather experiences. 5G technologies have lowered the cost of producing video content, enabling broader participation in the production of online scientific content. This engaging approach helps spread scientific knowledge and promoting online science exhibitions to meet public needs. 5G is also enhancing the application of

VR courseware in meteorological service training, resulting in more effective training and more diversified resources.

13.3.4 5G + AI Technology Convergence Analysis

1. 5G + IoT + UAV

    5G networks can facilitate remote inspection and maintenance of meteorological equipment by sending instructions to terminals and unmanned aerial vehicles (UAVs) over the network and transmitting collected data through mobile terminals. For instance, 5G-enabled multi-rotor UAVs can be designed for atmospheric monitoring, and the UAV weather detection system equipped with the 5G IoT can be used in combination with high-definition cameras, infrared thermal imaging devices, and air quality monitors to implement real-time forest fire detection. By identifying the composition of gases in the air, wind speed, wind direction, and other meteorological information in the high-risk areas, fire status reports and forecasts can be generated instantly. Moreover, the 5G network, which has a high bandwidth, can further popularize diversified environmental sensors and wearable devices. Devices equipped with sensors can collect more refined real-time local meteorological data.

> **Case Study: Meteorological Monitoring Enabled by 5G + UAV**
> China Telecom Chengdu Branch and AOSSCI Technology are jointly exploring the application of 5G + UAVs in meteorological forecasting, flood control, and other fields. 5G UAVs equipped with meteorological measurement sensors can collect and quickly transmit real-time weather data and images related to temperature, air pressure, humidity, wind speed and direction, altitude, cloud formations and sizes, visibility, turbulence, ice, and more. This data can then be analyzed and used to evaluate and forecast local weather conditions. By combining meteorological detection equipment with 5G UAVs, we can leverage the UAVs' flexibility and mobility, as well as their ability to operate without geographical limitations. This allows for vertical and three-dimensional detection, and more innovative methods for meteorological monitoring.

2. 5G + Big data + AI

    Meteorological forecasting relies on data such as temperature, air pressure, precipitation, and wind speed, among other factors. By integrating 5G, AI, big data, and high computing power (HPC) technologies into forecasting processes, an intelligent, cross-domain, multi-scale, and precise meteorological system can be developed. This significantly improves the speed of weather forecasting and enhances their timeliness. Machine learning and other technologies can be used

13.3 Meteorology

to identify patterns in data. This can complement traditional mathematical equations and improve our ability to model seasonal predictions across different time scales and distances, thereby enabling more precise forecasting and better control of meteorological systems.

> **Case Study: An Urban Flooding Social Meteorological Observation System Based on 5G Networks**
> Jiangxi Atmospheric Observation Technology Center has comprehensively applied 5G, AI, big data, image recognition, sky recognition, and meteorological technologies such as an urban waterlogging risk warning system based on flood images and real-time meteorological data uploaded by mobile terminals. This has helped to increase the temporal-spatial resolution and coverage of the urban flood monitoring network and has enabled higher public participation in the monitoring and prevention of urban flooding. It provides decision-making support for urban flood management and safe travel information services for citizens. A meteorological risk warning service platform for urban flooding has been built in Nanchang by integrating data from radar, satellites, weather stations, and real-time flood images. On this platform, flood risk warnings are displayed in one chart. It also produces real-time flood monitoring and potential risk warnings, which are used to optimize service operations. In addition, it releases flooding risk warnings to the public through Weibo and WeChat. It integrates "smart meteorology" into "Digital Jiangxi," and thus creates a "Smart Jiangxi."

3. 5G + VR/AR/MR

The efficient transmission capabilities of 5G communications are advancing the development of VR/AR/MR technologies and making synchronized information displays and super network downloads possible. With the backing of 5G technologies, the integration of meteorological services with holographic technology and glasses-free 3D technology can create new industry trends. For instance, users can select personalized services during video live streaming, view 3D weather broadcasts, watch VR live streams or choose 360° onsite weather experiences. In addition, the use of 5G and MR technology in education can ensure the effectiveness of "online + in-person" meteorological training, further enhancing the quality of teaching.

> **Case Study: Meteorological Science Education Based on 5G + AR**
> The Guangdong Planet 9 Science Museum is using new technologies such as 5G and VR/AR to enhance science education. It promotes meteorological knowledge and safety education on disaster risks for elementary school, middle school, and university students. It is also used for commercial experiences. The newly launched AR Holographic Typhoon Pavilion utilizes 5G, AR

projection, a 5D dynamic platform, and other technological means to recreate scenes from typhoons, including thunder, lightning, and storms with winds that reach level 12 on the Beaufort scale. There are also demonstrations of safety precautions to take during and after disasters. Through immersive experiences, participants can gain a deeper understanding of what weather disasters are and how to respond to one. This approach addresses the shortcomings of conventional forms of science education, which often has limited content and lacks appeal. It effectively supplements traditional science outreach and education methods and comprehensively enhances the quality, efficiency, and personalization of meteorological science education projects.

13.3.5 Typical Solutions for Digitalization and Intelligent Development in Meteorology

1. "Yutian" intelligent disaster prevention solution for Chongqing

   The intelligent disaster prevention system "Yutian" (which means defense against natural disasters in Chinese) is one of Chongqing's four intelligent meteorological systems for meteorological detection, weather forecasting, public meteorological services, and disaster prevention. Figure 13.6 illustrates the features of the "Yutian" system in detail. Chongqing's intelligent meteorological systems are based on the national meteorological big data cloud platform and connect with the Digital Chongqing cloud platform. They use 5G, cloud computing, big data, IoT, blockchain, edge computing, and VR/AR to achieve precise monitoring and accurate forecasting and to offer more refined services. These systems play a crucial role as they are at the frontline of natural disaster prevention and mitigation. A "cloud-device" modern meteorological has been established with integrated services centered around the "data-computing integrated" Chongqing Meteorological and Big Data Cloud Platform.

   The "Yutian" intelligent disaster prevention system is made up of two subsystems: an intelligent early warning system and an intelligent weather modification system. The intelligent early warning subsystem is interconnected, open, and secure, and it efficiently processes and releases information and warnings about natural disaster risks, potential disasters, weather status, and disaster relief efforts. This system is based on public information resources and early warning big data. It leverages deep learning, cloud SMS distribution, and other technologies.

   Chongqing's comprehensive early warning system has working centers and stations that cover all jurisdiction levels:

   - Municipal center: 1
   - District/County centers: 40
   - Municipal/District/County sub-centers: 470
   - Township/street stations: 1028
   - Village stations: 2064

13.3 Meteorology

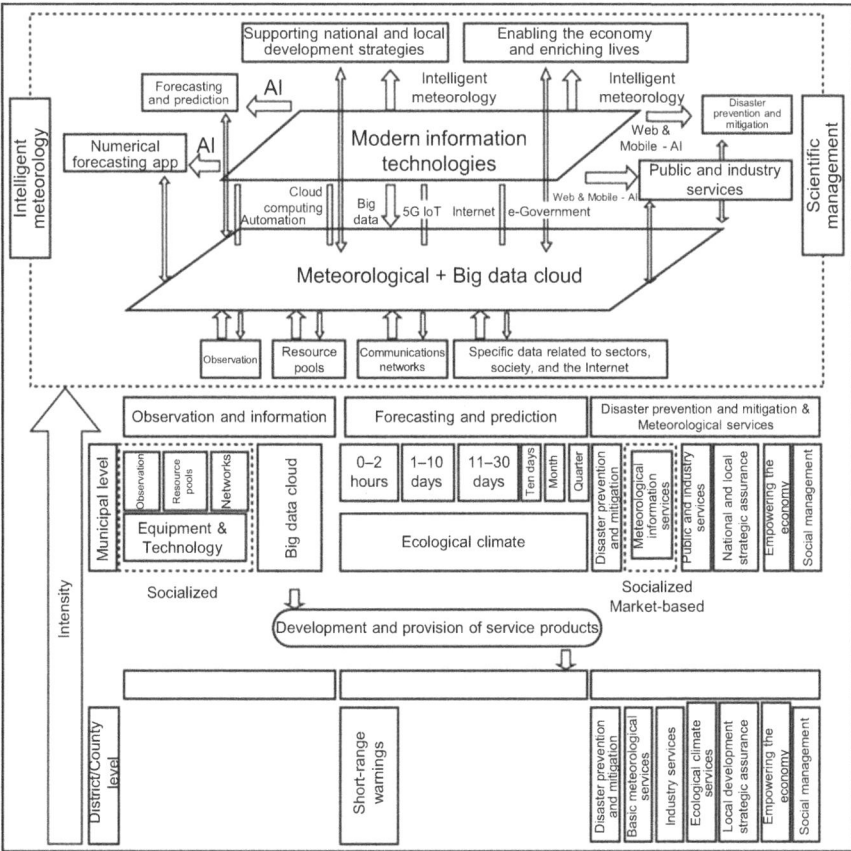

Fig. 13.6 Chongqing "Yutian" intelligent disaster prevention solution

It also has a network of 1.6 million people who can help with emergency response in the event of a disaster:

- A four-tier (municipal—district/county—township—village) working system for the joint monitoring of and consultation on early warnings
- A six-tier (municipal—district/county—township—village—group—household) warning information dissemination system

2. The Huawei AI weather forecasting solution

The Huawei AI weather forecasting solution is based on the Pangu-Weather Model. It is capable of generating medium-term forecasts in seconds using the Ascend AI computing platform. In addition, it establishes ensemble forecasting capabilities that match the AI forecast model for up to thousands of ensemble members. This helps forecasters conduct comprehensive and thorough assessments of future weather conditions. In addition, a model training and optimization platform has been built on the cloud, to support the ongoing optimization of the AI model for higher forecasting accuracy. This solution is efficient and does not consume a lot of energy. It delivers accurate forecasts of temperature, air pressure, wind speed, humidity, and other meteorological elements. It supports short- and medium-term decision-making based on weather forecasts. Figure 13.7 illustrates the setup of the AI weather forecasting solution.

The Pangu-Weather Model can accurately forecast temperature, pressure, wind speed, humidity, and other meteorological elements for a period of up to 10 days with a 25-km resolution for 13 types of isobaric surface on the ground and in the air. This can be completed in about 10 s with a single AI card. It presents two main technological innovations: the 3D Earth-Specific Transformer neural network, which features absolute position encoding related to the latitude and altitude in each Transformer module to more accurately identify irregularities in each area and greatly improve the efficiency of model training convergence; and a hierarchical temporal aggregation strategy, which combines four models at forecast intervals of 1, 3, 6, and 24 h to minimize the number of iterations for forecasting. This not only reduces iteration errors, but also minimizes the waste of training resources caused by recursive training. These two points differentiate the Pangu-Weather Model from other AI meteorological models.

The National Meteorological Information Center verified the accuracy of the Pangu-Weather Model's 1-to-10-day typhoon path forecasts with the support of single-server computing power by comparing them to typhoons that have taken place since April 2023. The path forecast for Typhoon Haikui, the 11th typhoon of 2023, met accuracy expectations and demonstrated more stable trend predic-

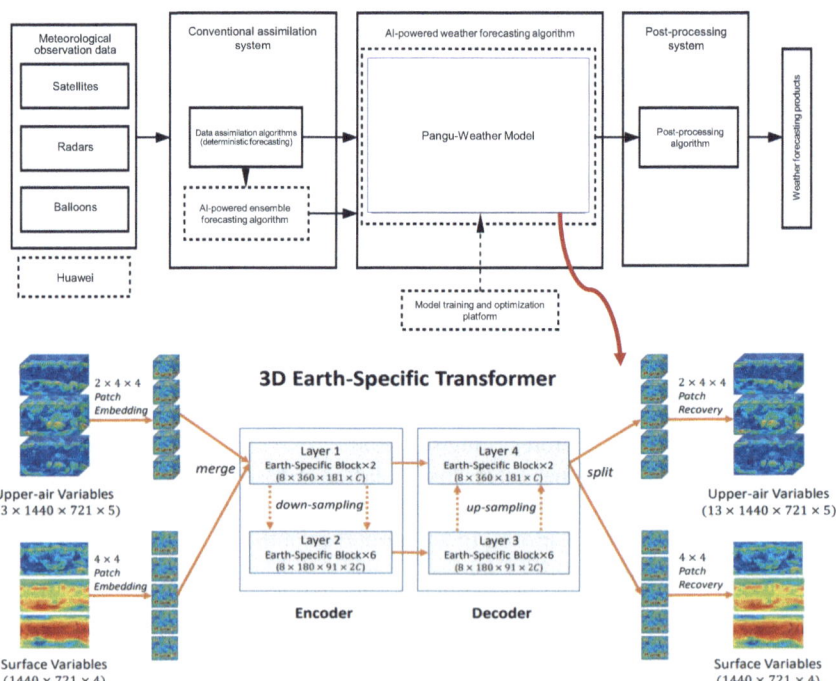

Fig. 13.7 Setup of the AI weather forecasting solution

tions than numerical forecasting models. The application of comprehensive evaluations from ensemble forecasting with thousands of ensemble members have enabled forecasters to better understand the possible evolution of a typhoon path.

AI weather forecasting models provide stronger support for meteorological personnel than numerical weather forecasting models, which face issues such as slow computing speeds (it can take up to 6 h to generate a forecast) and high resource consumption, and for which it is difficult to improve forecasting accuracy. AI weather forecasting models generate more accurate forecasts and work 10,000-times faster than numerical weather forecasting models. They can generate weather forecasts for the entire world in seconds. The computing resources that they require have been reduced from tens of thousands of CPU cores that operate for several hours to a single AI card that operates for just tens of seconds. The exponential increase in inference efficiency makes it possible to conduct ensemble forecasting with thousands of ensemble members. Such a sizable group can more comprehensively evaluate potential weather developments and provide early insights into and warnings about extreme weather conditions. This generates significant social value. Additionally, as we accumulate more high-quality data, the AI model can be iteratively optimized to improve its forecasting accuracy [7].

13.3.6 *Path for Large-Scale Replication and Promotion*

Phase 1 (2019–2021): During the network replacement phase, 5G changed how we collect and transmit meteorological data, and upgraded the meteorological monitoring and warning services. The range of applications of 5G remote monitoring and intelligent analysis grew rapidly.

Phase 2 (2022–2024): In the mid-term technology convergence phase, 5G technologies have become more mature and are being integrated with AI and VR technologies. 5G-based message warnings, AR live streaming, and science education services are being widely used. Personalized meteorological information and service products are emerging for different cities, enterprises, and the general public.

Phase 3 (after 2025): Big data and deep learning will make the meteorological system more intelligent and accurate. The refinement and accuracy of weather forecasting will reach new heights, and at the same time, comprehensive intelligent information and a strong decision-making basis can be provided for emergency response, transportation, agriculture, and other fields.

13.4 Agriculture

13.4.1 *Overview of Digitalization and Intelligent Development in the Industry*

Since the 19th National Congress of the CPC, China has underscored the development of "digital villages" as a crucial part of rural vitalization. Starting in 2018, the country has issued a series of directives on digital villages, outlining plans for digital agriculture and rural construction that continue all the way to 2025. Great strides have already been made in the digital transformation of agricultural production and operations, as well as the digitalization of related governance activities. The proportion of agriculture-oriented digital economy and digitalized agricultural production within the economy has also increased significantly.

A top-level design for digital villages earlier has been rolled out to support construction organized at the regional level, which sped up digitalization and intelligent transformation of the entire upstream and downstream agriculture industry. The informatization rate of agricultural production currently exceeds 25%. New applications such as intelligent irrigation, precise fertilization, intelligent greenhouse, and product source tracing are being widely promoted within China, and over 100,000 BeiDou autonomous driving systems on farming vehicles are being used to facilitate planting, seeding, harvesting, and straw treatment. By the end of 2022, the Internet penetration rate in rural areas in China reached 61.9%, meaning 308 million rural residents have access to the Internet. E-commerce is also booming in rural areas, with e-commerce systems and the express logistics and distribution systems growing rapidly. By the end of 2022, the retail sales on rural networks in China reached CNY2.17 trillion, and retail sales of agricultural products reached CNY531.38 billion, representing a 9.2% YoY increase. The efficiency of digital rural governance has also continuously improved with 489,000 village committees in China using digital information systems for grassroots political power construction and community governance.

Additionally, China is currently piloting other digital solutions in rural areas. The Office of the Central Cyberspace Affairs Commission and Ministry of Agriculture and Rural Affairs have established rural demo areas in multiple villages in Zhejiang Province, including a just-completed pilot in Deqing County. Beijing's Pinggu District and Tianjin's Xiqing District have also recently completed significant digitalization pilots. The Central Cyberspace Affairs Commission has issued guidelines to support further construction of digital villages, and the Standardization Administration of China has released a list of 23 agricultural standardization demonstration areas focusing on smart and digital agriculture. These demonstration areas are intended to promote smart agriculture applications, like intelligent machinery, smart farming and husbandry, and digital greenhouses.

The concept of agricultural digitalization involves the incorporation of digital technologies into the agricultural sector to improve productivity and streamline operations. This transformation is evident in various aspects, such as the adoption of agricultural IoT for precise fertilization and irrigation. Additionally, the Internet facilitates marketing of agricultural products and promotes agritourism and innovative farming practices. Moreover, it fosters the consolidation of dispersed farmers, leading to a reorganization of agricultural production methods. Secondly, the rural ecological environment has been significantly improved. The integration of information technologies and agricultural equipment promotes the development of smart farming and reduces the use of fertilizers and pesticides to achieve green production. Real-time monitoring technologies such as UAVs and HD video are adopted to monitor agricultural contaminant and pollution sources, providing a better living environment for rural residents. Thirdly, the life quality of rural residents has significantly improved thanks to greater access to learning, leisure, and entertainment resources. The Internet has also connected rural residents with other communities [8].

13.4.2 Trends of Digitalization and Intelligent Development in the Industry

1. Big data is enabling smart agriculture

   Digital technologies are enabling new solutions and techniques that will facilitate profound rural revitalization and increase the adoption of intelligent applications and equipment in agricultural production processes, from cultivation and husbandry to processing, storage, and sales. Big data will play a role in all links of smart agriculture, from seeding and fertilization to land management and waste disposal. Unmanned operations will also be a priority as information technologies are transforming agricultural production. In cultivation and husbandry, for example, production, processing, and sales will be done in factory settings to holistically improve benefits.

2. Sales of agricultural products are going streamlined

   As agricultural product sales on e-commerce platforms continue to increase, both the producers and resellers will also continue to grow, which is revealed by the rapid development of cold chain logistics. The success of new retail methods for agricultural products enabled by e-commerce, such as group buying, has led to China's big Internet players all launching branded campaigns, allowing residents to buy agricultural products directly from the production source. This end-to-end (E2E) supply chain brings producers and consumers closer together. Other new forms of retail, such as online-offline hybrid sales, are also reshaping the urban consumer market while improving shopping experiences, logistics efficiency, and transaction ease.

3. Agricultural supply chain financing is becoming more inclusive

   Supply chain financing is key for the agricultural optimization and upgrade. It can improve the flow of capital within the agricultural industry and increase the amount of support available for small- and medium-sized enterprises (SMEs). Digital technologies like IoT, big data, and AI help agricultural SMEs digitalize operations and thereby improve information transparency. This simplifies quantitative financial risk management, while making the credit approval system more inclusive.

13.4.3 Requirements for Digitalization and Intelligent Development in the Industry

1. Improving agricultural productivity

   China's agricultural production is not as modernized as developed countries, and the resources are still under-utilized. To make matters worse, urbanization is drawing a sizable labor force from rural areas, shrinking the agricultural labor pool. In light of these reasons, agriculture in China has long relied on government investment and therefore cannot grow on its own. Human is the most active factor in agricultural production. With the help of digital information technologies, crops can be cultivated more precisely and damage to crops can be reduced, which ultimately translates into cost and resource savings. What's more, the information backend can retain optimal crop cultivation solutions and interconnect with the Internet to form an information sharing platform for smart agriculture to better support farmers.

2. Precise supply and demand of agricultural products

In China, agricultural IT applications are too weak to help farmers accurately predict the market demand and collect and process information. For example, their decisions on crop varieties are predominantly guided by the currently attractive prices, and they are often only to find an excessive supply of products, making them hardly recover their costs. With an agricultural cloud platform, sellers can make production decisions based on demand and better sell their products to customers, and customers can obtain precise product information. In this way, the overall transaction efficiency is improved on both sides, thereby boosting economic development in rural areas.

3. Agricultural resource protection

Traditional farming moves forward in tandem with noticeable damage to natural resources, as fertilizers and pesticide residuals seep into rivers and lakes, causing a series of problems such as local ecological damage. Digital technology makes it possible to turn this around by enabling precise irritation, fertilization, and pesticide application, which is good for efficiency and biodiversity while avoiding pollution. For example, compared with extensive irrigation, drip irrigation avoids water wastage, improving water utilization in rural areas.

13.4.4 5G + AI Technology Convergence Analysis

1. 5G + Big data + AI

Given that the agriculture sector uses weak IT systems to deal with tremendous data, 5G and cloud computing are good to store these data for precise production. Additionally, big data and AI can integrate structured and unstructured data to generate agricultural big data in real time. When initially building a model, data typically comes from various sources and in complex structures. However, big data and AI can accelerate the upgrade from non-standardized and unstructured data models to standardized and structured data models, greatly reducing the cost of data model iteration. Real-time data collection based on 5G improves the accuracy of data analysis to maximize production and efficiency.

13.4 Agriculture

Case: "5G + Big Data" Selenium-Rich Agricultural Demo in Yichun, Jiangxi

Technologies such as 5G, big data, IoT, and cloud computing help local farmers monitor, analyze, control, and manage rice production, processing, logistics, and sales. This change is modernizing the rice agriculture here to make it scaled, industrialized, organized, standardized, and branded. The foreseeable benefits include driving industry-wide development, improving agricultural product processing, and creating a stronger brand. Furthermore, a 5G big data platform helps manage the entire rice-industry chain, with a digital map displaying in real time the rice industry layout and development as well as data related to areas such as crop production. And a 5G-based smart fertigation system has been built that is supported by soil moisture sensors and a wireless communication network. This system intelligently senses, analyzes, controls, and sends alerts regarding soil moisture, and realizes automated irrigation by controlling devices like solenoid valves and water pumps. Aside from obvious savings in labor costs, the project has helped improve both the quality and price of agricultural products via intelligent management and brand strength.

2. 5G + Robotics + VR/AR

Agricultural robots are automatic or semi-automatic devices that possess some human abilities to acquire information and act. They can replace or at least facilitate manual operations such as production, picking, management, and maintenance. Such robots can be categorized as walking robots or robotic arms depending on whether they are mobile. Now 5G enables these robots to receive instructions and respond quickly with high degrees of accuracy. The more robots that are connected, the higher the reliability of a support system. They can even work in unison with virtual or augmented reality technologies to support a greater range of functions like remote monitoring, control, and training.

Case: China's First AI 5G Agricultural Robot

In 2019, China's first AI agricultural robot entered service in a smart greenhouse situated in a modern agriculture demonstration park in Fujian. This robot, built by Fujian Academy of Agricultural Sciences, inspects fruits and vegetables 24/7. It comes with multi-channel sensor technology that behaves in much the same way as a person's senses: two 7-megapixel cameras as its "ears," two 5-megapixel cameras as its "eyes," sensors for measuring wind, carbon dioxide, and photosynthetic radiation on the top of its head, and temperature/humidity sensors under its "mouth." This configuration allows it to intelligently sense the agricultural production environment and dynamically collect data. The robot can rotate and move in all directions on its wheels to perform automatic inspection, cornering, obstacle avoidance, and charging as well as fixed-point collection as it passes the planters. It can also transfer high-definition images and videos in real time, which not only facilitates VR-based remote consultation and teaching but provides more basic data sources for AI applications.

3. 5G + Satellite

5G enables precise control of devices. With the assistance of BeiDou satellite navigation system, smart agricultural devices in China can reach an operation precision of up to 30 cm, which is enough for precise crop management. 5G also enables efficient hardware-to-hardware automation, allowing collaboration between running power and production equipment. For example, with BeiDou satellite navigation system and 5G, smart agricultural machinery can perform functions such as autonomous driving, precise operations, information push, quality monitoring, and real-time uploads of operation data 24/7.

> **Case: Satellite + Low-Altitude + Terrestrial Integrated Smart Grazing Management and Control System**
>
> The Institute of Agricultural Economics and Information, affiliated to Jiangxi Academy of Agricultural Sciences, developed a smart grazing management and control system that integrates satellite, low-altitude, and terrestrial transmissions based on China Mobile's networks. The system uses next-gen information technologies and consists of an interactive grazing information management center, smart electronic collars worn by cattle, a grazing instruction training and control system, and a 5G herd-detection drone and hangar system. It provides functions such as multi-dimensional cattle information perception, beyond-fence warnings, automatically controlled cattle return, anomaly alarms, and real-time drone response and detection. The system can dynamically obtain data related to the physiological state of cattle and intelligently predict and warn of risks about fence roaming or body temperatures and behavior. The 5G herd-detection drone and hangar system can automatically count cattle as well as their grazing patterns. This way, the breeding process is fully digitalized from end to end, improving management efficiency and addressing labor shortage.

13.4.5 Typical Solutions for Digitalization and Intelligent Development in Agriculture

1. China Mobile Helps Build Digital Agricultural Parks

China Mobile offers data management solutions for modern agricultural parks, helping create a new form of digital agriculture featuring digital production, intelligent production equipment, and visualized production management, as illustrated in Fig. 13.8. In particular, China Mobile's digital agricultural cloud platform provides basic agricultural capabilities, big data capabilities, AI capabilities, and more at the platform as a service (PaaS) layer. The applications at the software as a service (SaaS) layer can access these capabilities on demand. The solutions provide applications for four areas: management, production,

13.4 Agriculture

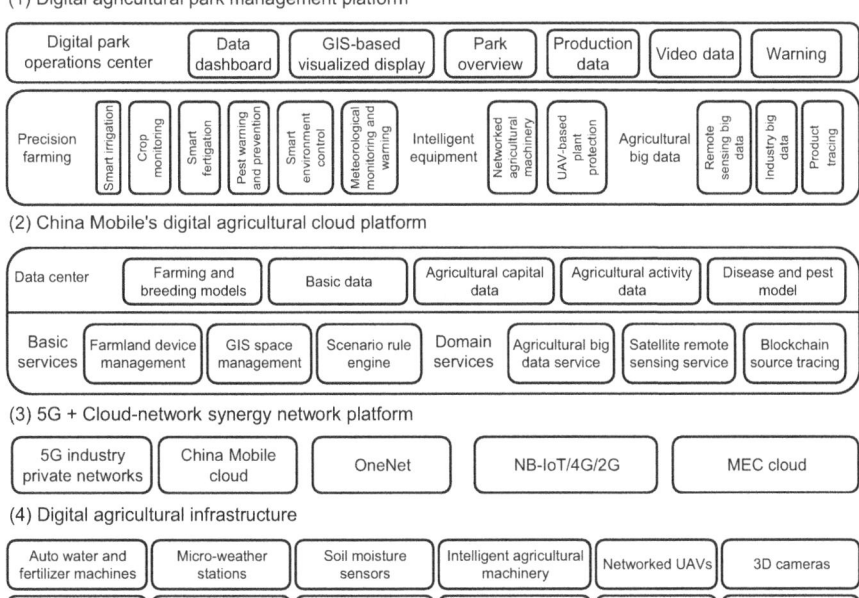

Fig. 13.8 Digital agricultural park solutions

operation, and services, catering to the needs of governments and agricultural enterprises.

When combined with customized 5G private network capabilities and digital technologies such as IoT and AI, these solutions can support diverse types of smart agricultural production and management applications, enhancing production efficiency. For example, the precision farming solution designed for large-field farming uses remote sensing, meteorological technologies, and other technologies in addition to traditional IoT technologies, to offer a variety of services. These services include remote sensing monitoring of crops, smart irrigation, meteorological information monitoring and warning, and pest warning and prevention. Working together, these services increase efficiency while keeping costs down. As for the precision farming solution for greenhouses, four key AI capabilities (environmental data collection, video and image recognition, intelligent environment control, and smart fertigation control) are employed to monitor crop growth from all aspects and regulate the environment. The smart fertigation is implemented on automatic water and fertilizer machines, which use the local accumulated temperature, soil moisture content, soil temperature, and other data collected by automatic weather stations, soil temperature sensors, soil water sensors, and other monitoring devices. Based on this data, drip irrigation, spray irrigation, flood irrigation, or other irrigation modes are intelligently adjusted to optimize irrigation times and volumes, improve crop growth, and increase production while saving energy. Moreover, pest warning and prevention employ remote sensing big data, 5G + AI identification technology, inspection robots, and AI cameras to monitor and identify crop diseases and pests in real time, enabling timely warnings and accurate pesticide use to control the spread of pests and diseases.

Furthermore, the solutions can work together with the digital agricultural park management platform, as well as third-party remote sensing, monitoring, and GIS modeling services, to offer a comprehensive view of the remote sensing data, GIS information, and the locations of terminals (such as sensors and cameras) in agricultural parks via multi-screen interaction. This allows for the detailed display of park development, crop conditions, agricultural machinery status, environmental data, agricultural technology services, and other information.

2. Beijing Tongfang LEGENDSILICON Tech. Co., Ltd. Provides 5G Smart Agriculture Solutions

Beijing Tongfang LEGENDSILICON Tech. Co., Ltd. has developed an advanced 5G + smart agriculture farmland management system using cutting-edge information technologies such as computer vision and data processing. This system, together with a smart agriculture government administrative system, production supervision system, big data system, and command and dispatch system, forms a comprehensive set of 5G smart agriculture solutions, as illustrated in Fig. 13.9.

These solutions have been applied in areas such as the central Chinese town of Zhangshi in Weishi county, Henan, where a total of 10,000-mu (approximately 6.67 km^2) of farmland has been modernized using the solutions, which were made possible by the use of wireless networks and common convergent

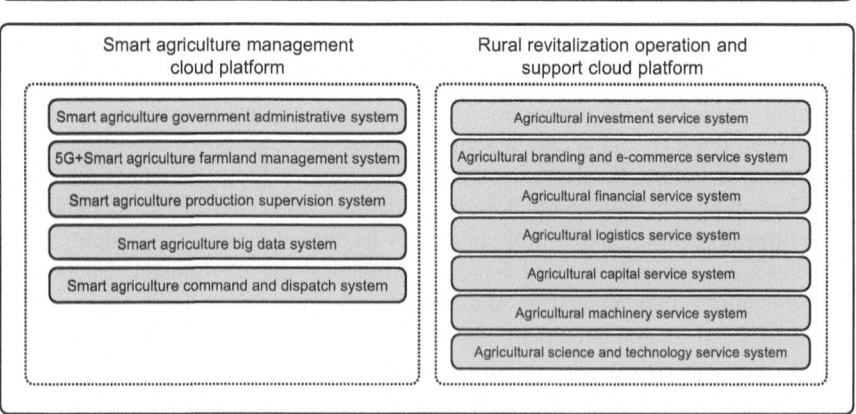

Fig. 13.9 5G smart agriculture solutions offered by Beijing Tongfang LEGENDSILICON Tech. Co., Ltd.

media technologies. Diverse technologies are used to make agriculture more intelligent, which include AI, cloud computing and big data, IoT, Internet, mobile connectivity, GIS, remote sensing, and Global Positioning System (GPS). These technologies help build high-standard demonstration farmland featuring smart crop protection, disaster warning, visualization, smart irrigation, smart services, and traceability of agricultural products.

Another example of the combination of technologies and agriculture is the nonpoint source pollution monitoring project in Nanle county, Henan. In this project, a total of 45 soil and water environmental monitoring points and 400 soil sample collection points were set up across the county's 12 towns. Thirty of these soil and water environmental monitoring points were centered around the Majia River wetlands, in the plantation and residential areas along the river and at the mouth of the tributary. These monitoring and collection points work in tandem with the 14 air environment monitoring stations throughout the county, 7 water quality and environment monitoring stations on the Majia River, Wei River, and Tuhai River, and the 78 monitoring points of the agricultural informatization construction project to bring online the water and soil environment information of the county's 600,000-mu (approximately 400 km^2) of farmland. With the help of cutting-edge technologies such as a spatiotemporal information cloud platform and big data analysis, a county-wide environmental monitoring and alerting network has been established. This network allows for the combined use of different forms of monitoring, such as online and manual monitoring, dynamic and scheduled monitoring.

13.4.6 Path for Large-Scale Replication and Promotion

Phase 1 (2020–2021): In this phase, the digital foundation of the agricultural sector was weak. 5G networks were gradually rolled out, working with the existing wireless and wired networks to establish the information infrastructure for agriculture. Through agricultural data collection and analysis, traditional farming, production, and marketing were optimized. The main applications included automation, logistics traceability, and intelligent marketing.

Phase 2 (2022–2024): Agriculture became more digitalized with the increased use of robots, IoT, AI, and other digital technologies in every stage of agricultural production and operation. This led to the development of comprehensive systems and solutions. The main applications included smart greenhouses, smart farms, smart irrigation, and AI diagnosis.

Phase 3 (2025 and later): The agricultural sector will fully embrace digital technologies, enabling smart agriculture and marking the end of traditional farming practices. An intelligent ecosystem that integrates farming, monitoring, husbandry, and precise regulation will gradually take shape, and applications such as soil monitoring, precision agriculture, and unmanned farming will become increasingly prevalent.

13.5 Culture and Tourism

13.5.1 Overview of Digitalization and Intelligent Development in the Industry

Modern information technologies like AI, big data, and 5G are now driving convergence and innovation in the culture and tourism sectors. China is actively pushing for digital transformation in the sectors to drive their development. Since 2020, relevant ministries have issued a series of supportive policies, including *Opinions on Deepening "Internet + Tourism" to Promote High-Quality Tourism Development* and *Opinions on Promoting the High-Quality Development of the Digital Culture Industry*, to expedite the development of smart tourism and culture industries toward digitalization, network-based connection, and intelligence. The *14th Five-Year Plan for Science and Technology Innovations in Culture and Tourism* provides a roadmap for advancements in these areas. The Plan highlights the importance of combining online and offline resources to create new approaches to providing cultural and tourism products and services, as well as the need to bring together digital resources to develop new business models for the sectors. Additionally, the Plan calls for the integration of consumption platforms, the establishment of a new win-win mechanism, and the use of technology to enhance culture and tourism to create a better digital life.

In 2022, the General Office of the Central Committee of the CPC and the General Office of the State Council of the People's Republic of China (PRC) issued *Opinions on Promoting the Implementation of the National Culture Digitization Strategy*. The goal is to create a 3D cultural service system that integrates both online and offline resources. Since then, the digital transformations of cultural venues have been accelerated, and significant progress has been made on the construction of national smart library systems and public culture clouds. The smart service capabilities of public libraries have also been greatly enhanced. The services provided by the national public culture cloud and over 200 local public culture cloud platforms are constantly improving, and digital cultural resources are also being enriched. The digital service capabilities for universal reading and art popularization have been significantly improved. China now has 530 million users engaged in digital reading. New application scenarios, such as cloud performing arts, cloud exhibitions, and immersive experiences, are emerging.

Digital technologies have enhanced the service capabilities in the culture and tourism industries. Cutting-edge audio and video production and broadcasting technologies, such as 8K ultra-HD, cloud rebroadcasting, free-viewpoint video, VR program production, and digital human, have consistently improved audio and video experiences for audiences. Cable TV (CATV) providers in Beijing, Shanghai, and Zhejiang have experimented with recommendation services to meet the public's need for customized audio-visual content. In January 2022, China Media Group launched China's first 8K ultra-HD TV channel (CCTV-8K) to livestream the

13.5 Culture and Tourism

opening and closing ceremonies and sporting events from the Beijing Winter Olympics on public HD screens in hundreds of cities. The National Cultural Heritage Administration and China Media Group teamed up to create a series of programs that vividly present cultural heritage and national treasures using digital technologies like VR/AR to showcase the cultural significance and value of cultural relics.

5G networks can greatly benefit the culture and tourism industries by accelerating their informatization, digitalization, and intelligent transformations. The high bandwidth of 5G networks can enrich the services available at scenic spots, while the wide connections can improve organizational management efficiency. Additionally, network slicing can be used to meet customization requirements. The integration of 5G with next-generation information technologies like cloud computing, big data, and AI opens up exciting possibilities for smart culture and tourism [9]. For example, 5G, when used in conjunction with new technologies such as 8K, AI, AR, and VR, can extend the form and content of cultural and tourism products and services, thereby facilitating shifts from traditional sightseeing to more leisure-wise tourism and more in-depth tourism. This has led to the development of various mature application scenarios, including cloud tourism, slow live broadcasting, and online performances.

There are three aspects to the development of smart culture and tourism: smart supervision, smart services, and smart experiences. In smart supervision, digital technologies can break industry information silos and collect different industry data on one platform. Big data resources can be used to implement dynamic real-time tourism data monitoring, real-time industry data analysis, and accurate prediction of regional passenger traffic. As a result, the culture and tourism industries can drive the rapid development of other industries. In smart services, applications such as 5G SMS, 5G + AR guide, 5G + AI facial recognition, and robot meal deliveries provide convenient cultural and tourism services, which facilitate marketing in museums and at scenic spots and improve tour efficiency. Smart experiences offer immersive tours through various media, including 5G + VR live broadcasts from scenic spots, 5G + VR virtual interactions, 5G + MR museum experiences, 5G + AI travelogues, and 5G + AI visits to popular spots for photography. These innovative approaches are no longer just concepts, as tourists are already implementing them. They offer more opportunities for interaction, making tours more engaging and leading to a shift from sensory-based tours to more immersive experiences.

13.5.2 Trends of Digitalization and Intelligent Development in the Industry

The rapid integration of digital technologies into industries is giving rise to new industries, models, and business forms. Digital technologies are now a crucial driving force behind the transformation, upgrade, and high-quality development of the culture and tourism sectors. As new economic conditions, industrial forms, and consumption habits emerge, the culture and tourism sectors are becoming more intertwined with industries such as commerce, education, and transportation. This overlap will, in turn, promote the high-quality development of the culture industry.

1. Digital technologies are promoting culture and tourism convergence

    In order for scenic spots to remain relevant and continue to evolve, they need to offer high-quality tourism products and services by enhancing their scientific and technological capabilities and cultural significance. It is also important to introduce innovative products which showcase the cultural characteristics of these spots and boost revenue. For example, rural cultural resources, historical scenic spot resources, cultural venues, and museums can be utilized to create new cultural and tourism destinations. The culture industry has started to incorporate more information technologies into the creation, production, dissemination, and consumption of its products and services. A range of technologies such as 5G, cloud, big data, IoT, AI, blockchain, and security measures can be utilized to enhance the supply of digital cultural and tourism products in the form of digital art displays and immersive experiences. This will generate more cultural and tourism intellectual properties (IPs), allowing for international expression of Chinese culture through original IPs.

2. Smart culture and tourism are enabling urban-rural integrated development

    Developing cultural and tourism opportunities in counties and small towns can be a key factor in achieving urban-rural integrated development. This approach can promote balanced and coordinated growth in both rural and urban areas. Projects such as smart cultural and tourism towns as well as county-level digital libraries and cultural centers will soon be developed on a large scale and will eventually benefit every citizen.

3. New smart tour modes are continuing to emerge

    Following the pandemic, there has been a rise in independent, self-service, and local tourism. In addition, online digital tourism products like 4K/8K cloud tourism and cloud live broadcasts have become increasingly popular. Big data platforms that offer services like tour reservations, off-peak travel, traffic management, scenic spot management and monitoring, and congestion warnings for scenic spots will be in high demand. These platforms will enhance the quality of tourism services and improve the overall experience for tourists. In the future, the development of smart scenic spots will not solely rely on the government, but also on social and public efforts. The needs of visitors, including how they use the scenic spots and shop in stores, will be taken into account, and this will boost quality and efficiency at scenic spots.

4. New business forms in the culture industry are thriving

    Cultural and tourism resources now encompass more than just natural landscapes, cultural traditions, and museums. They also include apps, virtual IPs, games, and animations. Traditional face-to-face communication is rapidly being augmented with network- and screen-based communication. New and more convenient forms of communication, such as social media, live broadcasting, and cloud exhibitions, are emerging. Digitalization is revolutionizing the way innovations are developed. Various interactive technologies work together to provide an immersive sensory experience and enable new ways of supplying innovative applications and products. For instance, the cultural venues and museums are utilizing cutting-edge technologies such as 5G and AR to bring historical artifacts to life, and this has become a successful and engaging cultural strategy. New forms of digital culture businesses, including cloud performances, cloud live broadcasting, and cloud exhibitions, are thriving.

13.5.3 Requirements for Digitalization and Intelligent Development in the Industry

1. Supply of quality digital content

   5G is speeding up its convergence with the culture and tourism industries. However, the supply of quality content is far from adequate. Digital content related to tourism services is not only insufficiently supplied, but also lacks variety. By combining 5G with technologies like AI and VR/AR/MR, it is possible to produce high-quality content. For example, 5G + AI content and feature identification, intelligent retrieval and editing, and 5G + AI virtual streaming can be used to facilitate high-class content production. 5G + 4K/8K live broadcasting, 5G + VR/AR/MR panoramic live broadcasting, 5G multi-view videos, and 5G free-viewpoint videos can be used to distribute such content.
2. Development of business forms that deliver immersive experiences

   5G enables the creation of business forms that deliver immersive experiences in the culture and tourism sectors. This unleashes new economic momentum and improves public cultural services. Data from VR/AR devices can be transmitted rapidly over 5G networks, allowing audiences to have immersive cultural experience. In addition, 5G can be used in conjunction with novel technologies and applications such as holographic projection and UAVs to provide audiences with immersive experiences to meet people's requirements for engaging cultural content and to promote the growth of the digital economy.
3. Innovations in management and service models

   The diverse cultural and tourism offerings make the challenges related to management and service modes even more prominent. Companies in the culture and tourism industries have faced persistent challenges such as inaccurate and superficial data collection, poor interdepartmental communication and coordination, and outdated information systems with limited functionality and coverage. For some museums and tourist attractions, reducing management costs, improving management efficiency, and quickly responding to emergencies have become the main objectives in their daily operations. Culture and tourism management departments in multiple regions are establishing an all-inclusive cultural and tourism service platform that can provide services through one single code or phone number. They are also promoting tourist services like slow 5G live broadcasts and 5G + AI travelogues to make it easier for tourists to access tourism products and services. Culture and tourism institutions are using 5G + UAV and 5G + robot for inspections to enhance scenic spot management and are using 5G + unmanned ferry vehicles to improve tourist experiences. Additionally, they are using 5G + big data + AI to assist in culture and tourism resource management, as this can help producers and their suppliers integrate channels, the supply of goods, web traffic, and marketing resources.

13.5.4 5G + AI Technology Convergence Analysis

1. 5G + VR/AR/MR

Panoramic technologies, such as VR, AR, and MR, feature virtual-physical combination, real-time interaction, and 3D immersion. These technologies allow for tourism activities to go beyond the limits of time and space. With a virtual tourism platform, visitors can explore cultural landscapes during different historical periods. 5G, with its high speed and low latency, can enhance the immersive experience for tourists by making the cultural heritage demonstrations more precise and interactive. This creates new opportunities for the digital preservation and promotion of cultural heritage. The identification and interaction between 5G + VR/AR glasses and smart cameras can realize functions such as repairing cultural relics, recording processes, and remote guidance, which can take cultural heritage protection to the next level. The 5G + AR content cloud allows for a vast amount of digital content to be stored and accessed on the cloud. Users can enjoy a variety of functions, such as virtual interactions, scenario reproduction, real-world navigation, intelligent marketing, and multiplayer gaming, through small programs or apps. Additionally, the combination of 5G and virtual technologies enables the creation of innovative cultural and tourism derivatives that blend both virtual and physical elements. This promotes the convergence of 5G + 4K/8K + AI culture and tourism applications with the digital content industry.

> **Case: 5G + AR Helps Cultural Propagation in a Historical Memorial Hall**
> In the memorial hall, 5G, AR space cloud, and 3D digital content have been used to animate historical figures within the relics. This allows visitors to relive these figures' life moments within the relics in an immersive setting so they can better know the stories behind the relics. This approach also enhances the appeal of relics without the need for extensive renovations.

2. 5G + AI + Big data

5G, with its low latency, high speed, and large throughput, enables secure device access, independently controllable systems, and security-oriented isolation. These capabilities provide a strong foundation for the development of scenic spots. AI and big data technologies, when applied to the culture and tourism sectors, are mainly used for market segmentation, marketing analysis, dynamic monitoring of scenic spots, and public opinion tracking. Once data collected by terminals is uploaded to the cloud over the 5G network, applications equipped with AI and big data capabilities can analyze tourist profiles and public opinions to accurately predict and detect emergencies. This improves management and security protection at scenic spots, promotes transformations of services, marketing, and management in the culture and tourism sectors, and stimulates innovation in these areas.

Case: Lijiang Deploys a 5G All-Area Tourism Platform in Digital Historical Scenic Towns

Lijiang is a top-rated historical scenic destination that is the home to both residents and cultural treasures. The town operates 24/7, which demands high standards for security and service provision. To enhance its overall management capabilities, Lijiang has implemented the 5G All-Area Tourism Platform in Digital Historical Scenic Towns. With the platform, all pipes and cables are deployed beneath major roads. Additionally, tourist traffic can be monitored in real time with immediate alerts, which allows unattended patrol in more dimensions. The relevant authorities can gain a comprehensive and clear understanding of the city's operations and management at a glance. This allows them to have a broader perspective when making decisions regarding routine management and emergency responses. Visitors can easily enter the town and shop in 5G unattended shopping malls using AI-powered facial recognition technology. This technology utilizes a real-time dynamic database with millions of units of data, allowing for second-level recognition even with hundreds of thousands of visitors per day.

3. 5G + Satellite Internet access

5G + satellite navigation can implement real-time positioning of devices like tour buses and cruise ships. The information collected from these devices is stored in a digital archive, facilitating scientific and fine-grained management. In addition, by utilizing technologies like AI, device status can be presented on a platform, providing accurate positions for commanding and management during patrols and emergency rescues. This enables efficient management and helps prevent security accidents.

> **Case: 5G + BeiDou Enables Smart Cruise Ships in Taoranting Park**
> Taoranting Park in Beijing has introduced 5G + BeiDou smart cruise ships to enhance tourist services, speed up rescue responses, and streamline backend management. Built on the existing management and operation system, the smart cruise ship solution leverages the 5G + BeiDou technologies to upgrade software and hardware for battery-powered cruise ships and docks. A total of 14 management functions, such as real-time ship positioning, queue management, and intelligent start and stop, have been developed to meet the operation and management requirements. 5G makes real-time video backhaul possible while BeiDou navigation eliminates the need to describe precise rescue locations over the phone. This makes operation management and service assurance more energy efficient. The solution enhances the tour experience by providing hi-tech features such as progress checks for congestion prevention, self-service boating, one-click call for help, effective smart broadcasting, and self-service payment, and as a result, makes the tour more enjoyable and convenient for visitors.

13.5.5 Typical Solutions for Digitalization and Intelligent Development in Culture and Tourism

1. China Mobile Shanghai's 5G + Smart Culture and Tourism Solution

    The 5G + smart culture and tourism solution is a complete solution that includes emergency management and tourist service functions aimed at tackling issues faced by the culture and tourism sectors. China Mobile in Shanghai set up a central platform that can link up with customers' existing service systems. The platform integrates video surveillance, traffic analysis, tourism resource management, emergency broadcasting, and other functions, allowing for visualized management and customized services (see Fig. 13.10). The solution concentrates on the following types of applications: basic culture and tourism applications, government oversight, smart scenic spot services, and smart cultural venues and museums. Information from the entire industry is presented and managed in a unified manner, facilitating collaboration among different cultural and tourism resources.

    Basic culture and tourism applications and government oversight can be further divided into three systems: all-area tourism oversight, emergency commanding and dispatching, and tourist services. The all-area tourism oversight system is intended for government organizations in the culture and tourism sectors. It offers six standard functions: all-area overview analysis, scenic spot overview analysis, travel route analysis, tourism product competitiveness analysis, traffic analysis, and economic indicator analysis. The emergency commanding

13.5 Culture and Tourism

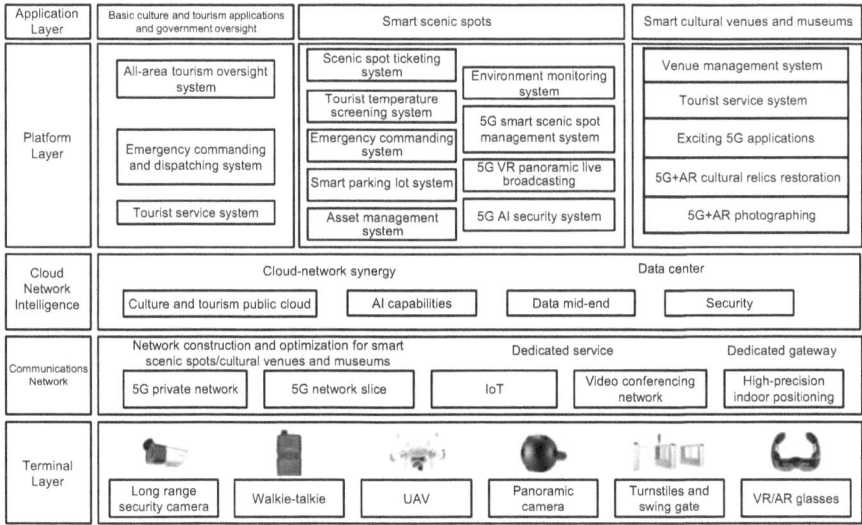

Fig. 13.10 China Mobile Shanghai's 5G + smart culture and tourism solution

and dispatching system can collect and analyze emergency data to aid in emergency commanding and decision-making. The tourist service system provides tourists with a range of services, including smart guides, one-click reservations, online shopping, culture and tourism information, and a complaint system, all accessible through one WeChat mini program or mobile app.

Smart scenic spot applications provide functions that assist in scenic spot management, tourist service provision, and use of new 5G applications. Specifically, a range of services, including ticketing, security screening, smart parking, and 5G VR panoramic live broadcasts, are provided to deliver tourists with an integrated pre-, in-, and post-tour service experience while ensuring secure operations at scenic spots.

Smart cultural venues and museums apply a variety of technologies to upgrade the supply of their contents, improving cultural experiences. This system merges a comprehensive management system, tourist services, and exciting 5G + AR applications (such as cultural relics restoration, interaction with cultural relics, ticketing, historical event reproduction, and photographs).

2. Zhejiang University's 5G Cloud XR Solution for the School of Art and Archaeology

This solution leverages 5G and edge cloud technologies to enable synergies between content, cloud resources, pipes, and devices (see Fig. 13.11). This solution uses an extended reality (XR) cloud platform to provide cloud rendering, content editing, terminal adaptation, and unified operation and scheduling capabilities. It also integrates multiple standard functional components to provide interaction capabilities, including voice interaction, somatosensory interaction,

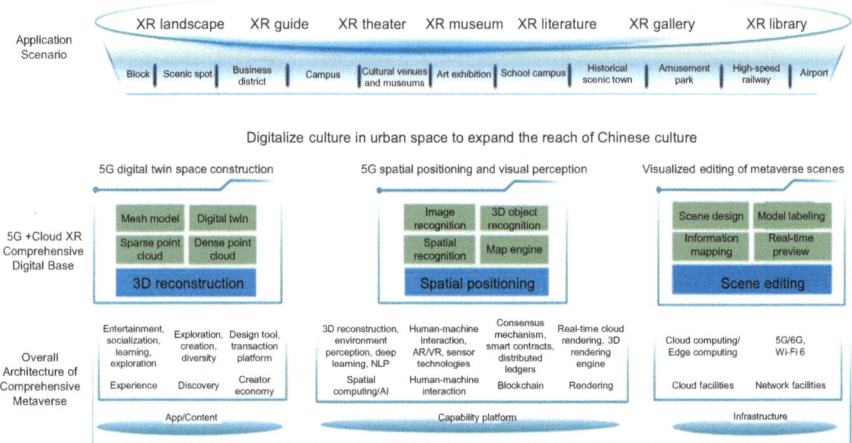

Fig. 13.11 5G cloud XR solution for cultural relics digitalization

touch interaction, multi-display device splicing, virtual-physical convergence, and visualized guides. 5G networks can be deployed dynamically and elastically to meet the requirements for the ultra-high bandwidth and stable low latency needed by individual XR apps and XR app concurrency within a short period of time. This creates four-dimensional sensory perception by merging audios, texts, images, and devices, achieving iterative and innovative cross-media and cross-location experiences that can reshape cultural perceptions. The future goal is to establish a collaborative ecosystem that brings together tours, cultural exhibitions, culture, tourism, and education.

This solution combines digitalized scenario construction, metaverse information blocks, and User Generated Content (UGC) to deliver a unique experience of digitally re-creating paintings of cultural relics. In addition, the solution fully utilizes 5G technologies at various points of the tourism process, including travel, exploration, and sightseeing. For example, the 5G + travel case takes advantage of 5G + big-scale multi-player VR and other technologies like 5G cross-layer perception collaboration and indoor high-precision positioning to provide more immersive experiences. It also guarantees real-time multi-player VR experiences that feel like being in a real, ever-changing environment. The 5G + experience case employs hand-, motion-, and eye-tracking technologies to identify accurate interaction locations and movements of the hands in real time. These are then instantly uploaded to the edge cloud via a 5G network. Vast amounts of interactive feedback allow players to fully immerse themselves in a virtual/physical integrated environment thanks to AR technologies. They can see virtual characters, trees, flowers, and butterflies as well as real objects like ancient

13.5 Culture and Tourism

pianos, tables, and chairs at the same time, allowing the content designers to create more lifelike "performances."

13.5.6 Path for Large-Scale Replication and Promotion

Large-scale 5G application in the culture and tourism industries can be divided into three development phases (see Fig. 13.12).

Phase 1 (2019–2020): 5G gradually replaced existing wireless and wired systems. Its large connectivity and bandwidth made it ideal for real-time traffic monitoring and smart guidance in the culture and tourism industries. The major applications during this phase included 5G unmanned patrol vehicles, 5G inspection and rescue, and 5G HD video streaming.

Phase 2 (2021–2023): As cultural and tourism services matured and technical standards continued to evolve, 5G was further integrated with new businesses in scenic spots and cultural venues, stimulating further business upgrade. The major applications during this phase included 5G + VR experiences, 5G + AI smart travelogues, and 5G + VR 360° multi-view/free-viewpoint live broadcasts.

Phase 3 (2024 and later): 5G fully enables smart culture and tourism construction. 5G networks are seamlessly integrated with existing platforms and endogenous applications and are widely used in various fields of the culture and tourism industries. 5G-converged applications work together to provide more timely and precise smart culture and tourism services. The major applications during this phase include interactive experiences, digital content reproduction, content-based IP creation, and one-code-based travel.

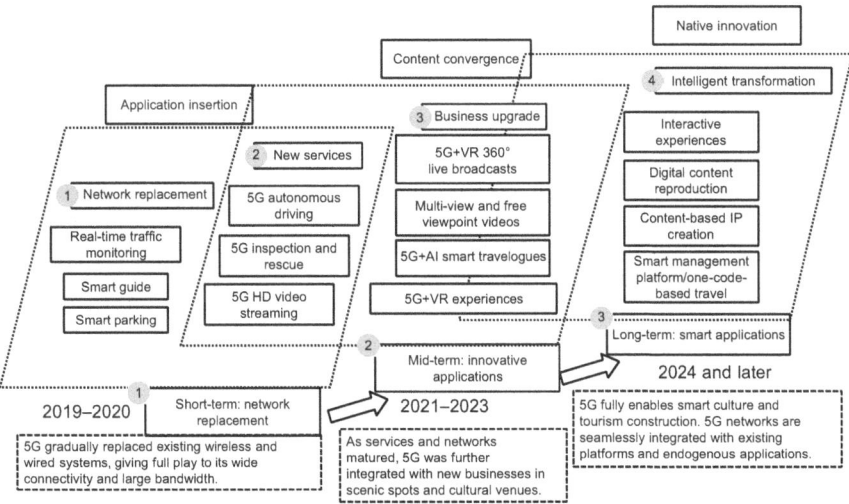

Fig. 13.12 Phases of large-scale 5G application in culture and tourism

13.6 Education

13.6.1 Overview of Digitalization and Intelligent Development in the Industry

Departments in China such as the State Council, Ministry of Education, and Ministry of Industry and Information Technology (MIIT), as well as local governments continuously release policies at the national, ministerial, and local levels. This is aimed at promoting the in-depth integration of information technologies like 5G, AI, and big data with education, thus facilitating fairer and higher-quality education. At the national level, in March 2020, the National Development and Reform Commission (NDRC) and MIIT jointly released the *Notice on 2020 New Infrastructure Construction Project (Broadband Network and 5G)*. This notice identifies 5G + smart education application demonstration as a key direction for enhancing the innovative application of 5G. In July 2021, the MIIT, alongside nine other departments, released the *"Set Sail" Action Plan for 5G Applications (2021–2023)*, highlighting 5G + smart education as a key initiative to explore typical application scenarios. This was done with the aim of improving the informatization of teaching, management, scientific research, and service. In the same period, the Ministry of Education, along with five other departments issued the *Guiding Opinions on Promoting the Construction of New Education Infrastructure and Building a High-quality Education Support System*, clearly stating that next-generation information technologies such as 5G, AI, and big data should be fully utilized in a bid to leverage data as a new factor of production, accelerate the digital transformation of education, and consolidate the digital foundation for the development of smart education.

In 2022, China officially launched the National Strategic Action for Education Digitalization and established the Smart Education of China (SEC) platform. This has led to the creation of the world's largest pool of education and teaching resources. By the end of January 2023, The SEC had already received more than 6.7 billion visits and covered users from over 200 countries and regions. It played a pivotal role in facilitating distance learning during the pandemic, narrowing the digital divide, and setting a preliminary trend for the open sharing of high-quality educational resources. Following the update of the SEC for primary and secondary schools, over 44,000 high-quality educational resources have been compiled in just 1 year, encompassing courses totaling 25,000 teaching hours. The platform for vocational education connects to 1014 national and provincial professional teaching resource libraries and houses over 5.56 million resources, including 6628 top-tier online open courses. The platform for higher education offers 27,000 high-quality MOOCs and more than 65,000 learning resources, covering users from 166 countries and regions.

Furthermore, China accelerates the innovation and large-scale development of smart education applications through competitions and pilot programs. In 2021, the

13.6 Education

4th "Zhanfang Cup" 5G Application Competition introduced the special "Smart Education" category. It attracted nearly 300 projects which cover innovative 5G solutions and application practices such as smart teaching, smart campuses, and smart examinations, with the majority of these projects originating from Eastern China and Central-Southern China, followed by Western China. In September 2021, the MIIT and the Ministry of Education collaborated to initiate pilot projects for 5G + smart education applications, aiming to select and nurture a batch of typical applications with the potential for large-scale replication. This received the full engagement of parties in "government, production, education, and research," as well as significant attention and proactive responses from governments at all levels, schools, and industries. In total, 1244 projects were formulated nationwide. Then, following self-application, local recommendations, and expert review, 109 pilot projects were selected. These projects spanned various areas such as 5G + teaching, 5G + examination, 5G + evaluation, 5G + school, and 5G + management. The projects are the result of innovation and collaborations across schools, electronic education centers, scientific research institutions, telecom operators, and tech enterprises.

13.6.2 Trends of Digitalization and Intelligent Development in the Industry

As information technologies continue to advance, education is evolving from traditional to smart education. This shift is bringing about significant changes in teaching, scientific research, campus management, and services.

1. Ubiquitous teaching

    The teaching model has transitioned from location-bound instruction to flexible, anytime-anywhere learning. It has also shifted from rote memorization to a more heuristic and inquiry-based approach. With the continuous development of technologies like 5G, AI algorithms, and knowledge graphs, hybrid learning has now become the norm. In addition, as the application scope of smart education continues to broaden, application scenarios are being constantly explored, which can effectively support the creation of limitless learning environments and facilitate ubiquitous education.

2. Efficient and accurate scientific research

    Scientific research, which often involves solving complex computational and analytical problems, is becoming increasingly dependent on technologies like high-performance computing, high-performance data analysis, big data, and AI. Based on digital technologies, massive data related to scientific research factors, such as personnel, finance, applications, plans, experiments, achievements, evaluations, management, and environment, can be collected, imported, cleaned, and analyzed. This process enables data interaction and collaboration across multiple departments, comprehensively

improves the capabilities of the smart scientific research information system, and provides a scientific and objective foundation for decision-making in scientific research management.
3. One-stop campus services

   As 5G gradually consolidates the network foundation of smart education, various technologies are driving the digital upgrade of the entire education process, such as pre-class, in-class, and after-class learning, as well as teaching, examination, and evaluation. The amount of collected education data is set to see exponential growth, and, supported by educational big data, teaching, evaluation, and management methods will be further transformed. The convergence of 5G, big data, and AI technologies can help establish student profiles for specific regions and schools and build a high-quality education system, featuring a parallel development of "five education areas" (morality, intelligence, physique, aesthetics, and labor skills). The education system prioritizes the personalized development of students and nurturing of core qualities. Technology convergence encourages tailored educational solutions, supports a comprehensive, multi-dimensional evaluation of teachers and students, and enhances campus and regional education management.

13.6.3 Requirements for Digitalization and Intelligent Development in the Industry

1. Sharing high-quality education resources

   Education resources in China are predominantly concentrated in the east and in urban centers, while the west and rural regions are comparatively underserved. There is a high degree of repetition in education resources, with a scarcity of valuable or exceptional education resources. Furthermore, there are only a few producers of high-quality education resources in the country. Due to inadequate regional resource sharing, a large number of educators focus on producing resources that are often repetitive, leading to an excess of similar materials and capital waste. Resource construction can also tend to lean toward hardware, rather than software, particularly in primary and secondary schools in remote rural areas. They are typically more focused on investing in hardware and resource management systems, but neglect subsequent maintenance and utilization. As a result, the amount of available resources diminishes. 5G, with its high bandwidth, can be integrated with such technologies as ultra-HD video, VR, AR, and holographic technologies to enrich the content and types of distance teaching, improve the efficiency and quality of distance teaching, and enhance interactions between students and teachers as well as environments. As such, remote sharing of high-quality education resources effectively promotes the equitable distribution of basic education services.

13.6 Education

2. Digital teaching content creation

   The scarcity of teaching content resources related to 5G + smart education is hindering the progress of commercial applications. New teaching methods require new teaching content, most of which must be produced by professional technical personnel, such as 5G + XR teaching content. How to effectively meet the teaching requirements of courses is then another challenge. Furthermore, developing teaching content like XR is costly and time-consuming, and most education content must be customized, which restricts the commercialization of related applications in a short term. Therefore, AI and big data technologies must be employed to innovate teaching content production methods and diversify types of education resources, in order to fulfill the demands of 5G + smart teaching applications.

3. Smart teaching mode innovation

   In the coming years, 5G communication modules will be installed on various types of smart teaching equipment (such as smart teaching terminals, XR devices in recording rooms/remote classrooms, smart library terminals, experimental devices, monitoring devices, and portable smart terminals). Such terminals will be used across various application scenarios in teaching environments to comprehensively improve education capabilities. Such transformations in teaching methods pose higher requirements on communication networks. Interactive teaching and immersive teaching are two major development directions in the education field. For instance, in various teaching applications, XR technologies such as AR, VR, and MR can be used to create a virtual-physical combined learning environment for students, allowing them to visually learn about abstract concepts and theories or stay in scenarios and activities that are difficult to experience in the real world. Such advances break the limitations of time, space, and even real environments, create immersive teaching environments, and improve teaching efficiency and learning experience.

4. Smart campus management

   5G + Digital campus brings a brand-new life, learning, and management mode. Traditional methods of student admission management, campus surveillance, and emergency response are no longer sufficient to support the construction of 5G + campus. Therefore, it is necessary to build a comprehensive campus system that leverages emerging technologies such as AI, IoT, and big data and closely meets campus teaching management requirements to seamlessly integrate student management, campus surveillance, consumption management, and teaching management [10]. Furthermore, campuses face a range of challenges, such as large areas, dispersed locations, few management personnel, large numbers of students, and inadequate security awareness. Public spaces, such as teaching buildings, canteens, playgrounds, and laboratories, all have security risks but implementing functions like campus surveillance and risk analysis, powered by 5G technologies, can contribute to safer campuses.

13.6.4 5G + AI Technology Convergence Analysis

1. 5G + AI + Cloud computing

With its advantages such as high rate and low power consumption, 5G can be combined with cloud computing to provide on-demand teaching resources and offer multi-layered, comprehensive, and personalized teaching support and services for both teachers and students. Additionally, AI-centered technologies foster the advancement of education computing in areas like speech recognition, semantic recognition, image recognition, cognitive computing, and emotion computing sensors. Machine learning can automatically extract implicit, unknown, and potentially useful information and knowledge from vast amounts of data. With the high-capacity and wide-connection features of 5G technologies, machine learning can analyze explicit data such as knowledge, behavior, and emotion of teachers and students, thus supporting teachers in smart teaching and cultivating students' thinking and creativity. Moreover, 5G + AI + cloud computing can drive the development of campus surveillance applications, supporting facial recognition, stranger alerts, body temperature warning, facial recognition attendance, resource configuration management, data retrieval, and report statistics, thereby realizing smart and scientific campus security.

> **Case: 5G + AI Proactive Security Protection System**
> Nanjing Zhonghua High School and China Mobile Nanjing have collaborated to fully integrate 5G and AI technologies to construct a 5G + AI proactive security protection system. This system can analyze and intelligently process surveillance videos from the school in real time, enabling timely warnings of seven potentially dangerous behaviors, such as intrusion, fence crossing, post leaving, suspicious lingering, crowd gatherings, fighting, and image blocking. The system uses a large number of campus scenario datasets for model training, making it highly adaptable to campus scenarios and enhancing the accuracy of its detection results. This allows the system to provide scientific and accurate judgments and warnings when detecting unexpected campus security incidents, thus minimizing campus security risks to the greatest extent possible. In the event that incidents such as bullying occur on campuses, the 5G + AI proactive security protection system can monitor the situation in real time and send the related surveillance video to the backend through the 5G network. The AI processing capability is optimized on the edge compute node on the base station side, meaning that it takes just 2.6 s from the occurrence of a dangerous behavior to the receipt of an alert.

2. 5G + XR + Hologram

Teaching presentation technologies make the expression of education content more flexible, accurate, and vivid, fostering knowledge, and skill acquisition from both the visual and auditory perspectives. XR, encompassing VR, AR, and MR, when combined with holographic projection, can create a fully immersive virtual space. The convergence of 5G with holographic and XR technologies further pushes the boundaries of the virtual-physical world and implements holographic mapping spaces, data-based holographic spaces, and intelligent data spaces. Top-tier education resources can be shared within this high-quality, seamless, and immersive learning environment, promoting the balanced development of high-quality education.

Case: 5G Holographic Interactive Classroom for Shanghai Luwan Senior High School and Zunyi No. 5 Middle School

Shanghai Luwan Senior High School and Zunyi No. 5 Middle School jointly build an interactive classroom focusing on the history education of the CPC. This initiative is based on red resources and leverages 5G and holographic technologies. Both schools are equipped with holographic collection ends, holographic display ends, and AR holographic technology (ARHT) servers, enabling seamless transitions between speaking and listening classrooms. In addition, the ultra-high bandwidth and ultra-low latency of 5G networks facilitate a 1:1 lifelike representation of teachers. By superimposing reality and virtualization, and utilizing 4K image projection for teaching, face-to-face communication and interaction between teachers and students are made possible. Shanghai is the birthplace of the CPC, and Zunyi is a historic location in the Chinese revolution. The two schools have made holographic projections of places such as the site of the first National Congress of the CPC and the site of the Zunyi Conference in advance. Through the 5G network, the three-dimensional projections on the holographic display ends allow teachers and students to experience history not just as a distant past, but as a "reality" all around them.

3. 5G + IoT + Big data

   5G enables smart education with its high rate and low latency. It leverages IoT technologies, such as information sensors and radio frequency identification, to enable ubiquitous access and intelligently sense the teaching and learning process, solving the challenge that offline data is difficult to obtain. The combination of 5G and big data, with its vast capacity, high speed, and diverse features, captures a significant amount of online data gathered by intelligent sensing technology. It stores extensive data collected by the Internet of Everything (IoE) and manages and processes this data efficiently. This supports the evaluation of students' comprehensive quality, teachers' teaching effectiveness, and the impact of education management.

Case: Haier Builds 5G + IoT Full Coverage Schools
As the pioneer of 5G + IoT integration in Qingdao, Haier School is equipped with smart interactive blackboards with eye protection in each classroom and laboratory. All key and difficult points in a class can be recorded with a single click and uploaded to the smart learning platform in real time. Students can use customized tablets to learn anytime and anywhere. With IoE, learning transcends the constraints of time and space. This enhances students' initiative, the effectiveness of teacher guidance, and the efficiency of feedback. In addition, teachers and students can exchange feedback in real time, improving feedback efficiency and accuracy.

13.6.5 Typical Solutions for Digitalization and Intelligent Development in Education

1. China Unicom's 5G smart education solution

    To cater to the needs of broadband, mobility, IoT, and multi-service convergence in the education sector, China Unicom has built 5G campus private networks based on new infrastructure. These networks are the basis for developing smart education, serving as information highways. Figure 13.13 shows the architecture of the 5G smart education solution. China Unicom utilizes 5G private networks, encompassing cloud interconnection, cloud networking, and cloud private lines, to form an "education brain" on the China Unicom cloud. This "5G private network + education brain" platform powers the digital transformation of campuses, enabling smart learning for students, parents, and teachers.

    As key carriers of 5G industry applications, 5G terminals serve as the physical foundation for the integration of traditional terminals with emerging technologies such as the IoT and big data. China Unicom provides terminals such as VR terminals, AR terminals, inspection robots, sensors, and cameras for smart campus private networks. These networks use the standard 5G multi-access edge computing (MEC) construction model of China Unicom and are classified into ToC and ToB networks (ToB and ToC stand for "to business" and "to consumer," respectively). The ToC campus private networks meet the requirements of ToC terminals (such as mobile phones) and carry services through the ToC core networks of China Unicom. The ToB campus private networks accommodate the requirements of ToB IoT terminals (such as inspection robots) and carry services through the ToB core networks of China Unicom [11]. Based on the China Unicom cloud, China Unicom's smart education solution builds an intelligent platform for smart education. This platform can manage five types of components, namely service, application, technical, workbench, and common components. It also supports a variety of 5G + smart education applications in five typical application fields: 5G interactive teaching, 5G smart examination, 5G

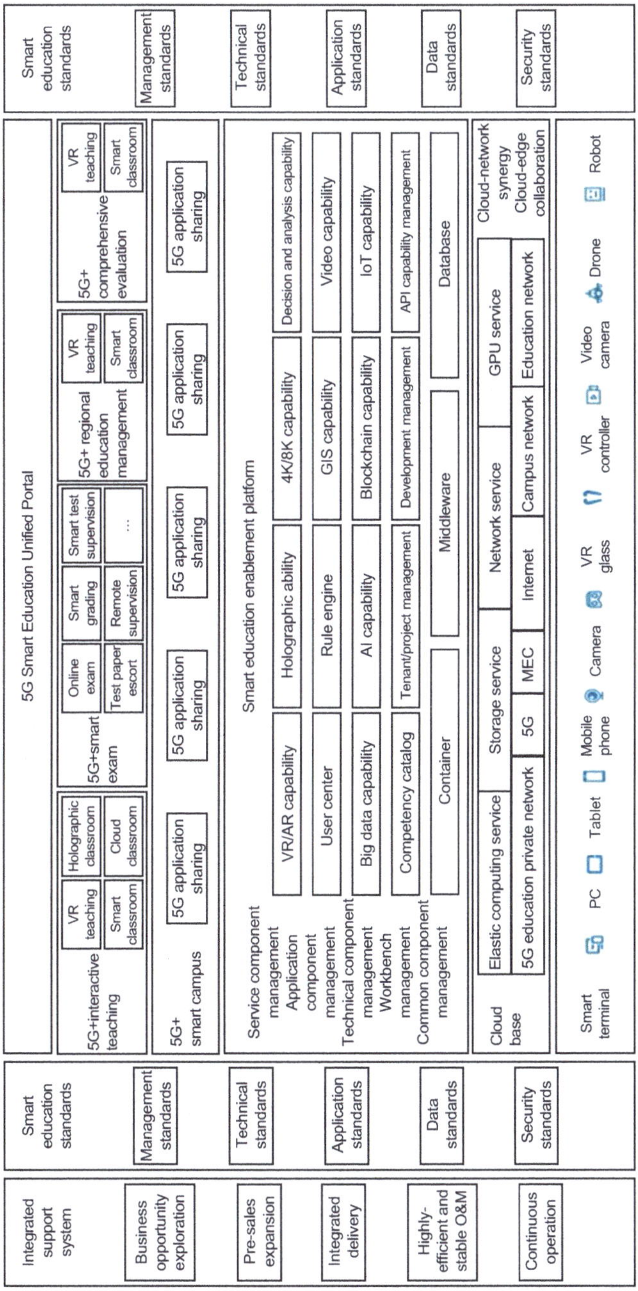

13.6 Education

Fig. 13.13 Architecture of the 5G smart education solution

comprehensive evaluation, 5G smart campus, and 5G regional education management. Schools can develop 5G + smart education applications as needed.
2. China Mobile's 5G + Smart campus solution

In response to challenges such as imbalanced education resource distribution, inadequate teaching quality, low management efficiency, and insufficient comprehensive evaluations, China Mobile has built a new 5G + smart education model featuring one education cloud network and seven innovative applications. It uses 5G education cloud-network synergy services to construct new education infrastructure and utilizes innovative applications to implement a full-scenario campus service system. Figure 13.14 shows the 5G + smart campus solution.

Based on the high bandwidth and low latency of 5G networks, courses can be flexibly opened and accessed as needed. Support for HD video transmission and low-latency interactive immersive classroom applications effectively addresses the interaction experience issues of dual-teacher classrooms. This ensures a robust foundation for the sustainable development of remote interactive classrooms. Through 5G and IoT devices, students' academic data is gathered across various scenarios. This data is then accurately analyzed based on teaching knowledge graphs to pinpoint students' academic performance. This approach aids in offering personalized learning guidance to students. Online classes are available and offer online teaching and teaching affairs management functions based on the 5G network. The classes can be accessed on large TV screens, computers, and mobile phones, offering comprehensive live interactive teaching capabilities. Using the high bandwidth and low latency of 5G, AR/VR teaching content is uploaded to the cloud. Cloud computing is used to run, render, display, and control AR/VR applications and to efficiently encode AR/VR images and

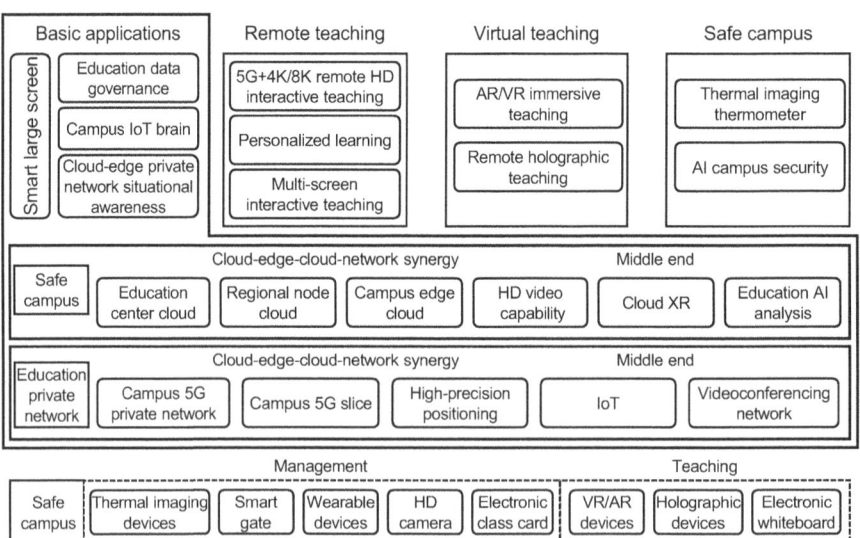

Fig. 13.14 5G + smart campus solution

13.6 Education

sounds into audio and video streams for real-time transmission through the 5G network. The integration of 5G and AI technologies provides a safe campus solution that combines attendance management and facial recognition. Utilizing technologies such as facial recognition, liveness detection, face search, and face comparison, the intelligent surveillance system, entry and exit management system, and campus security system collectively enhance campus security. They help prevent campus security incidents and fulfill comprehensive security management requirements of schools.

13.6.6 *Path for Large-Scale Replication and Promotion*

The development path of 5G convergence applications in the education sector is divided into three phases, as shown in Fig. 13.15.

Phase 1 (2020–2021): In the short-term initial network replacement phase, 5G replaced the original wireless networks in certain scenarios. Video and collection services were upgraded and application scenarios such as online teaching, virtual training, and smart campus developed fast.

Phase 2 (2022–2024): In the medium-term technology convergence phase, as 5G technologies mature, evaluation and interactive services will see enhancements. This phase will witness expansion of scenarios such as holographic teaching and smart examination.

Phase 3 (2025 and later): In the long-term innovation and transformation phase, the emphasis will be on the comprehensive collaboration of various systems and services. During this phase, application scenarios such as regional education management will be effectively expanded.

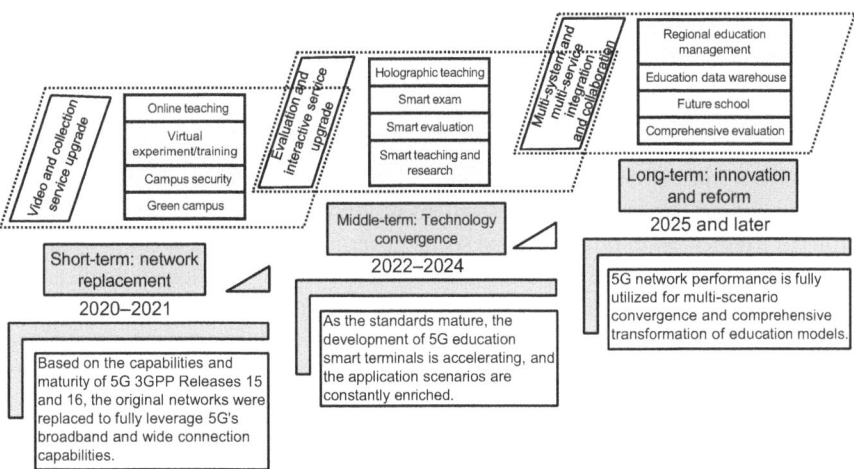

Fig. 13.15 Phases of large-scale 5G application in education

13.7 Healthcare

13.7.1 Overview of Digitalization and Intelligent Development in the Industry

In recent years, China has released a range of medical and healthcare policies, such as the *Outline of the Healthy China 2030 Plan*, which has raised medical and healthcare to the national strategic level. China unveiled top-level strategies such as the *14th Five-Year Plan for National Healthcare*, *14th Five-Year Plan for National Health Informatization*, and *14th Five-Year Plan for High-Quality and Efficient Healthcare Service System Construction*. These strategies aim to streamline the "big artery" of national health information. Data resources are identified as the key element and next-generation information technologies are harnessed to bolster the digital, networked, and intelligent industry transformation and upgrade. This not only provides robust technical support for delivering high-quality, efficient medical and healthcare services, but also aids in preventing and managing major pandemics and public health risks. It contributes to the construction of public health in China and fosters the high-quality development of healthcare services.

To help build a strong medical service system, the State Council of China issued the *Opinions on Promoting High-Quality Development of Public Hospitals* in 2021, taking the reform and high-quality development of public hospitals as a pivotal task in the comprehensive deepening of reforms. In 2023, China released the *Opinions on Further Improving the Medical and Health Service System* and announced key tasks for deepening the reform of medical and healthcare systems for the second half of 2023. In particular, the policies advocated for the expansion, reasonable distribution, and localizing of high-quality medical resources, aimed to enhance the medical experience for the public, including by building Internet hospitals and providing online diagnosis and treatment services. These information-based methods are used to achieve the goal of delivering high-quality medical services to the public. With the release of a range of policies centering on strategic goals, the concepts of telemedicine, regional collaboration, hierarchical diagnosis and treatment, and Internet + healthcare have taken shape.

Under the guidance of national policies, the healthcare sector in China has made early strides into the 5G era. In 2020, the MIIT and National Health Commission (NHC) jointly started to accept applications of innovations in 5G + healthcare pilot projects. Medical AI applications and social governance experiments have been carried out in Shanghai, Zhejiang, and Anhui, and innovative blockchain applications have been piloted in Beijing, Shandong, and Hainan, making staged achievements. Medical institutions and enterprises have further explored the application of 5G in healthcare and completed the first 5G medical experiment network, the first 5G smart healthcare showcase, and the first 5G-based remote human surgery.

At the same time, digital healthcare service resources are being expanded and high-quality medical resources are being extended to grassroots levels. Digitalization is permeating into all medical and healthcare fields. So far, telemedicine service platforms have fully covered municipals and counties in most provinces in China.

More than 26.7 million telemedicine services have been delivered in a year. By October 2022, more than 2700 Internet hospitals were set up in China, offering online diagnosis and treatment services for over 25.9 million people. A unified medical insurance information platform has been built across the country, connecting approximately 400,000 designated medical institutions and 400,000 designated retail pharmacies, effectively covering all insured individuals. The national medical insurance service platform has 280 million real-name users and offers over 100 service functions. New applications based on digital technologies in auxiliary diagnosis, rehabilitation, distribution and transfer, and medical robots are becoming widespread. Emerging forms such as Internet live interactive family parenting, online infant and child care courses, and parent classrooms are on the rise.

Digital technologies can effectively meet the requirements of existing medical information transmission and smart applications. Based on the characteristics of smart medical applications and the requirements for network bandwidth and latency, application scenarios can be classified into three types: (1) Medical monitoring and nursing applications: These are based on wireless collection of medical device data and include wireless monitoring, wireless infusion, mobile nursing, real-time patient location collection and monitoring, medical device inspection, and remote chronic disease management. (2) Medical diagnosis and guidance applications: These are based on video and image interaction and include mobile ward round (requiring real-time retrieval of patients' image diagnosis information), remote ward round using medical robots, remote real-time consultation, emergency rescue guidance, wireless surgery demonstration, and wireless specialist diagnosis. (3) Remote control applications: These involve the full integration of 5G networks with diagnosis guidance applications, remote control applications, and real-time auxiliary applications to form remote control applications based on video and force feedback. Examples include remote robot ultrasound inspection, remote robot endoscope inspection, remote robot surgery, and AI-assisted diagnosis. In general, wireless collection applications have matured and are being widely adopted. Technical solutions for image and video interaction medical applications are continuously evolving. Remote control applications, such as remote surgery, are still in the early stages of exploration [12].

China's healthcare digitalization has transitioned to the 4.0 phase, characterized by interconnected regions and the feasibility of big data analysis and AI-enabled diagnosis and treatment. Its scope has widened significantly, and its functions have become more advanced.

13.7.2 Trends of Digitalization and Intelligent Development in the Industry

1. Healthcare AI penetrates into various segments

    AI technologies, such as computer vision, natural language processing, and machine learning, can not only effectively improve the service quality of medical institutions in China and reduce the workload pressure of medical personnel, but also alleviate the shortage of medical experts. Consequently, this enables medical institutions and pharmaceutical companies to expedite the development of new medicine and diagnostic and treatment schemes. Currently, AI technologies are penetrating diverse medical and healthcare fields such as medical imaging, assisted disease screening and diagnosis, clinical decision-making support, drug R&D, precision medical care, health management, and medical payment. In the future, with the accumulation of extensive medical knowledge, patient cases, and biological data, coupled with next-generation AI technologies represented by ChatGPT, the role of AI in medicine is set to evolve. AI will expand from assisting with disease triage, evaluation, and diagnosis to enabling smart diagnosis and treatment, as well as intelligent health management. This will significantly enhance the diagnostic and treatment capabilities of medical institutions and improve patient experience.

2. Healthcare big data drives new applications

   Healthcare data is the key to digital transformation in the healthcare sector. Its application not only fuels the innovation and development of industry governance, clinical scientific research, public health, and medical insurance, but also profoundly impacts the high-quality development of the healthcare industry and the digital health economy. For instance, in pharmaceutical marketing, the evolution of big data has progressively lowered the barriers to patient behavior research, enabling enterprises to swiftly detect shifts in consumer habits. The pandemic has also spurred the development of pharmaceutical e-commerce, offering patients a wider range of choices online without geographical constraints. Currently, some large pharmaceutical enterprises with robust innovation capabilities have embarked on multi-direction and multi-domain digital explorations. They select pharmaceutical marketing methods by studying patient journeys, drug characteristics, and enterprise attitudes, and implement precision marketing by building closed-loop data.

3. Medical metaverse plays a significant role

   The healthcare sector worldwide is grappling with numerous challenges. The pressing issue for most countries is how to enhance efficacy and reduce treatment costs. The metaverse holds the potential to reshape the relationship between doctors and patients, as well as between healthcare and society. It can reconstruct the vast data generated around patients and establish a bridge between reality and the virtual world. With the advancements in science and technology, clear policies, and defined rights and circulation rules for medical data, the integration of the metaverse with medical scenarios is set to deepen. Given the complexity of the interaction between technologies such as VR, AR, MR, and brain–computer interfaces with medical scenarios, the implementation of medical training and surgeries using metaverse technologies will gradually take place over the next few years. It will take a significant amount of time to reach the level of data accumulation and technological advancements needed for virtual doctors and personalized health management.

13.7.3 Requirements for Digitalization and Intelligent Development in the Industry

1. High-quality network coverage

    Diverse application scenarios in the healthcare field demand robust network coverage and stability. While the rollout of 5G networks is progressing rapidly and outdoor signal coverage has been achieved in major cities like Beijing, smart healthcare primarily operates indoors. Simply upgrading the existing 3G/4G indoor distribution systems in buildings is unable to ensure full 5G coverage indoors. Therefore, operators need to redeploy indoor distributed systems for 5G, taking into account the varying building structures and functional areas of different departments in hospitals. This may involve deploying 5G pico base stations in hospital areas or shared pole sites to achieve seamless 5G coverage both indoors and outdoors.

2. Smart healthcare mode innovation

    Hospital development is shifting from scale expansion to improving quality and efficiency, and the operational mode is transitioning from extensive management to refined management. Hospitals at all levels are actively promoting the deep integration of core services and operational management. They are incorporating modern management concepts, methods, and emerging information technologies into various fields, levels, and aspects of operational management to enhance its refinement and achieve high-quality development. The construction of smart hospitals relies on the support of new technologies such as 5G, AI, and edge computing. This approach fosters innovation in medical practices, promotes interconnectivity among patients, medical personnel, medical institutions, and medical devices, and facilitates information sharing. This, in turn, encourages service collaboration both within and outside hospitals.

3. Medical big data value mining

    Recent years have witnessed the development of medical big data in fields such as healthcare, basic research, disease prevention, and medical education in China. With the gradual promotion of smart healthcare applications, the volume of medical data is growing rapidly. New services will make medical big data more diversified and complex. This leads to many challenges. Firstly, there is a lack of unified standards for big data and related AI technologies. Secondly, the quality of the data is often poor. Thirdly, the data is dispersed across different medical organizations and lacks interconnectivity, leading to serious information silos and preventing comprehensive analysis and utilization of the data. Fourthly, the capability to develop and utilize the data is limited. To address these issues, there is a need to expedite the application of 5G technologies in big data healthcare, foster collaborations, innovate and develop big data healthcare, produce 5G-based medical equipment, and establish regional or national medical platforms.

4. Smart healthcare security supervision

    The rapid development of new 5G technologies and applications is accelerating the data flow of various applications in the healthcare sector. Medical work involves massive amounts of health data, diagnosis and treatment data, and medication data, which may involve medical quality and data leakage risks. Therefore, strengthening data supervision in smart hospitals and smart healthcare fields is paramount for protecting patient privacy. It is essential to establish and enhance security supervision systems in the smart healthcare field, based on 5G and other technologies, to ensure the sustainable development of smart healthcare.

13.7.4 5G + AI Technology Convergence Analysis

1. 5G + AI

There are many ways to integrate AI with healthcare. Currently, AI is primarily used in fields such as assisted medical image diagnosis, intelligent medical virtual assistant, disease screening and prediction, intelligent clinical decision-making support, assisted drug R&D, and medical robots. Among them, AI-assisted medical image diagnosis has been widely adopted. Its applications include lung cancer examination, diabetic retinopathy examination, esophageal cancer examination, and nuclear medical examination and pathological examination for certain diseases. Computer vision technologies are employed to quickly read medical images and perform intelligent diagnosis, supplemented by extensive intelligent learning and analysis. These medical images and AI-assisted diagnosis products can aid doctors in locating lesions, effectively reducing the chance of missed and incorrect diagnosis. As 5G + AI technologies become more advanced, medical imaging AI technologies can not only diagnose patients' current conditions, but also accurately assess the responses and potential complications during treatment in the future.

Case: 5G + AI Network for Fetal Medicine and Prenatal Diagnosis Collaboration
In May 2023, the Shanghai First Maternity and Infant Hospital, along with 59 other hospitals in China, announced the establishment of a 5G + AI fetal medicine and prenatal diagnosis collaboration network. This marked a significant milestone for fetal medicine in China. Unlike a traditional remote conference system, 5G + AI technologies facilitate real-time HD ultrasound image transmission and seamless communication, enabling remote precise prenatal diagnosis and accurate referral of complex cases, thereby optimizing the utilization of high-quality medical resources. In addition, 5G + AI technologies enable remote intrauterine surgery guidance for remote fetal medical collaboration units that have been trained by the Shanghai First Maternity and Infant Hospital, helping establish provincial intrauterine treatment centers and reducing travel for patients. Leveraging this platform, the hospital has implemented multi-disciplinary cloud-based consultations for 100% of special fetal disease diagnosis and treatment, real-time remote ultrasound evaluation and consultation prior to the referral of complex cases, cloud-based surgery guidance, and cloud-assisted genetic data analysis.

2. 5G + IoT

Utilizing 5G and IoT technologies, medical devices in hospitals can be interconnected at the bottom layer, regardless of which brand and standard they use. This allows for round-the-clock monitoring and alerting of the devices' operating status, enabling medical personnel to stay informed about the real-time performance of the devices and prepare for potential malfunctions. Furthermore, 5G and IoT technologies help increase the professionalism, efficiency, and traceability of operations and maintenance, thus ensuring the high-quality and secure operation of medical devices. Currently, 5G + IoT applications include wireless infusion monitoring, vital sign monitoring, ward environment monitoring, wireless cold chain management, equipment energy efficiency monitoring, mobile asset positioning, treatment time collection, patient behavior management, and medical waste management.

Case: 5G + IoT for Lab Biosafety Supervision
To prevent biosafety risks and establish a national biosafety shield, the Health Commission of Zhejiang Province and China Telecom Zhejiang collaboratively constructed China's first 5G biosafety lab supervision platform, "5G Biosafety Online." This platform, built on the 5G slice private network, integrates technologies such as the 5G IoT converged gateway, AI visual analysis, and 5G positioning to implement comprehensive intelligent supervision of lab biosafety. For environmental status monitoring, the 5G IoT converged gateway communicates with intelligent environment sensors in the lab to collect real-time data on temperature, humidity, noise, suspended particles, and atmospheric pressure in the environment, generating real-time alerts. For sample transportation supervision, 5G smart transportation boxes are utilized. 5G and BeiDou satellite positioning technologies are employed to track, locate, and provide alerts throughout the sample transportation process. Currently, this project has been piloted in seven hospitals in Zhejiang province. It significantly improves the quality and efficiency of lab supervision, enhances operation compliance, archiving completeness, and environment rectification efficiency, and achieves 100% sample traceability.

3. 5G + Big data

The integration of 5G and information technologies such as big data will support the in-depth integration and application of healthcare big data. A big data platform can be established to gather statistics on the overall health status of the public and classify data by region, gender, age, and medical department to inform the public of potential health issues to watch out for. Applying smart data to the healthcare field can enhance the public's overall understanding of their health. This empowers individuals to consciously take targeted measures to manage their health and reduce morbidity rates. In addition, the synergy of 5G, big data, and AI can connect devices with materials to swiftly diagnose diseases and upload the results to doctors. This provides patients with more accurate and systematic diagnosis and treatment than traditional specialist diagnosis and treatment.

> **Case: 5G + Big Data Assists Chronic Disease Management in Traditional Chinese Medicine**
> The Inner Mongolia Autonomous Region Hospital of Traditional Chinese Medicine is the only level-3A traditional Chinese medicine hospital in the region to integrate medical care, teaching, scientific research, rehabilitation, and healthcare functions. Cardiovascular and cerebrovascular disease diagnosis and treatment are the focus specialties of the hospital. China Telecom worked with partners to build a 5G + cardiovascular and cerebrovascular disease integrated prevention and treatment platform for the hospital. This platform leverages 5G technologies to implement remote and dynamic electrocardiogram (ECG) data warning and analysis services. It also builds a medical prevention and treatment ecosystem centered on chronic disease management using traditional Chinese medicine, thereby enhancing the clinical value and core competitiveness of traditional Chinese medicine in diagnosing and treating cardiovascular and cerebrovascular diseases. The project establishes a big data knowledge base and cardiovascular and cerebrovascular disease queues and spectrums based on evidence-based medicine. It also constructs an intelligent diagnosis and treatment platform for such diseases that integrates data services, management, and operations. Wearable devices are used to collect patients' physical sign data and dynamic ECG data. Key technologies such as 5G, AI, and big data are used to implement intelligent health management and chronic disease management, thereby promoting the digitalization and informatization of traditional Chinese medicine hospitals.

4. 5G + Edge computing

A significant amount of collected data is stored in local servers within hospitals and requires quick processing and analysis. This includes various uploaded and downloaded medical examination results, expert diagnosis databases, medical record databases, inpatient information, and medical risk handling. However, hospitals have stringent requirements for information security and maintain high confidentiality standards for medical data. Such data cannot be disclosed to public networks. 5G + MEC ensures that medical data is not transmitted outside of hospitals, meeting the security, low latency, and high-reliability requirements of data transmission. Local edge computing platforms can be built in hospitals to provide service access, reading, analysis, and processing and implement new 5G applications such as patient positioning, wireless infusion, wireless monitoring, mobile ward round, robot ward round, emergency rescue, teleconsultation, and remote ultrasound.

> **Case: 5G + MEC Smart Healthcare of Medical Consortium in Futian District, Shenzhen**
> Since 2019, the Medical Consortium in Futian District, Shenzhen, China Mobile, and Huawei have jointly carried out 5G + smart healthcare strategic cooperation in Shenzhen. They established a private medical consortium network, which includes a medical edge cloud platform and a telemedicine service platform. This network facilitates efficient and secure information exchange for seven hospitals and 83 community healthcare service centers (CHSCs). The district pioneered 5G applications such as remote first aid, teleconsultation, mobile diagnosis and treatment, CHSC first-aid guidance, and smart ward services, revolutionizing the medical consortium services with remote, mobile, and information-based solutions. During the pandemic, the 5G + MEC-based medical private network enhanced hierarchical diagnosis and treatment and smart referral through ICU bedside consultation and teleconsultation. This network provided high-quality, convenient medical services to the public, promoted an integrated hierarchical diagnosis and treatment system, and established a national health service system model characterized by the concept of "strong hospitals, healthy communities, upstream and downstream connections, and seamless communication."

13.7.5 Typical Solutions for Digitalization and Intelligent Development in Healthcare

1. National emergency rescue system

   The Emergency General Hospital (EGH), also as the National Emergency Medical Research Center, is managed directly by the Ministry of Emergency Management (MEM) and is tasked with emergency and disaster rescue. The EGH continuously conducts academic research on emergency medical technologies, provides medical assistance during emergencies and disasters, and fosters the integrated construction of the emergency rescue system. Figure 13.16 shows the solutions of the national emergency rescue system for which the MEM establishes a 5G medical private network. Based on the 5G + satellite virtual private network, the MEM implements an integrated air-ground medical network, covering all services and connecting to ambulances and first aid equipment. All medical data collected onsite is transmitted to the back-end command center through the 5G private network and via satellite communication. In the event of normal emergencies, first aid data is transmitted, while during disaster relief operations, disaster relief data is transmitted.

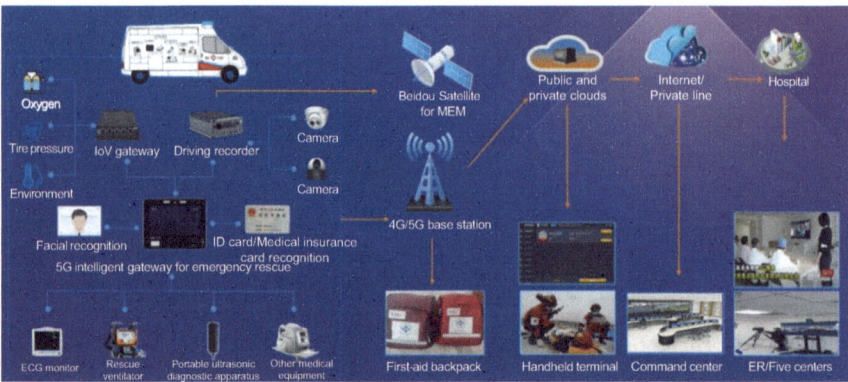

Fig. 13.16 National emergency rescue system

The national emergency rescue system supports the provisioning of emergency medical services in Beijing. Its vehicle management and control function facilitates regular operation and maintenance of ambulances and first aid equipment, aids dispatchers in optimizing task assignment, and provides necessary information for hospitals. The quality control module for the first aid process guides the procedure and generates standardized first aid medical records. Additionally, the system employs a big data analysis function to evaluate first aid services. During emergencies, the system can swiftly establish an efficient and comprehensive emergency rescue system. The emergency relief private network transmits onsite data to the command center and enables real-time data sharing between the emergency site, hospitals, and the command center. The emergency rescue system collaborates with AR glasses and first aid backpacks to significantly enhance the efficiency of first aid. Consultations via AR glasses assist in first aid, rescue, and disaster relief efforts. First aid backpacks are equipped with portable medical devices for data interconnection, allowing all medical data to be swiftly and automatically documented in first aid medical records.

2. H3C's 5G telemedicine solution

In light of new opportunities and challenges in smart healthcare innovation, Unis's H3C launched the 5G telemedicine solution, which deeply integrates 5G with cloud computing and AI technologies to provide more stable, reliable, and efficient network services for digital hospital innovation. Figure 13.17 shows the H3C 5G telemedicine solution. To cope with industry requirements, H3C reshapes the digital transformation of the healthcare industry and builds more secure and reliable telemedicine services to enhance healthcare service quality and promote regional healthcare resource collaboration and sharing.

In the integration of 5G with healthcare, H3C has developed a complete set of 5G + telemedicine solutions based on the telemedicine cloud video platform and diagnosis and treatment service systems. With these solutions, H3C uses all-scenario cloud-based video devices for in-depth intelligent video transmission, enabling interconnection between consultation centers, local consultation rooms,

13.7 Healthcare

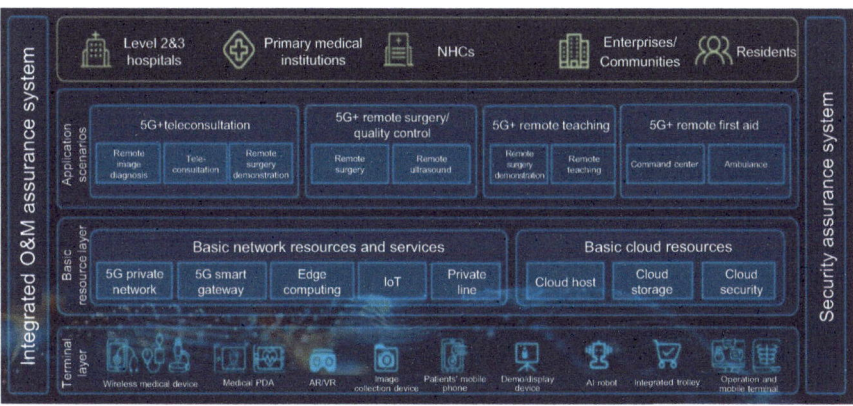

Fig. 13.17 H3C 5G telemedicine solution

and remote wards. A powerful digital platform is established to carry a series of applications, such as 5G + teleconsultation, 5G + remote surgery/quality control, 5G + remote teaching, and 5G + remote first aid. This significantly extends the scope and enhances the quality of remote collaboration within hospitals, between branches of one hospital, and among different hospitals.

Leveraging 5G innovations in New Radio (NR), slicing, uplink bandwidth enhancement, and security guarantee, H3C constructs a high-quality 5G telemedicine converged private network that integrates cloud and security. Based on key innovative products such as 5G cloud-based micro base stations, lightweight 5G core network (5GC) architecture, and OpenUPF, H3C has achieved in-depth convergence and innovation of 5G and Wi-Fi. The 5G + cloud computing platform facilitates medical service access, thereby reducing the innovation and application costs of telemedicine.

13.7.6 Path for Large-Scale Replication and Promotion

Phase 1 (2020–2021): Information collection and connection services were mainly used in this phase based on the capabilities and maturity of 5G 3GPP Release 15. Networks and terminals were replaced to fully leverage 5G's broadband and wide-connection capabilities. The main application scenarios in this phase included ultra-HD video surveillance, VR/MR, teleconsultation, and remote teaching.

Phase 2 (2022–2025): During this phase, 5G is intricately integrated with AI, big data, and cloud computing technologies, leading to the emergence of new or enhanced service models. The primary application scenarios in this phase encompass campus management, remote pathological diagnosis, intensive care, mobile ward rounds, and remote first aid.

Phase 3 (2026 and later): As 5G technical standards evolve and industry application convergence deepens, 5G will become integrated with the production, control, and management system protocols of the healthcare industry. A variety of 5G converged applications will be collectively utilized, leading to intelligent production and industry transformation. This phase sees the rise of comprehensive applications, including remote robot surgery and robot ultrasound.

13.8 Manufacturing

13.8.1 Overview of Digitalization and Intelligent Development in the Industry

Manufacturing is the economic lifeline and cornerstone of a country's development. In 2017, the State Council of the PRC released the *Guiding Opinions of the State Council on Deepening the Integration of Internet Plus Advanced Manufacturing for the Development of Industrial Internet*, highlighting the importance of the industrial Internet for the digital transformation of the manufacturing industry. The report to the 20th National Congress of the Communist Party of China (CPC) also identifies the real economy as the focus of economic growth and advocates the construction of a digital China with strong manufacturing and cyber capabilities to make manufacturing more advanced, smarter, and more eco-friendly. Policies such as the *14th Five-Year Plan for Intelligent Manufacturing Development* and *14th Five-Year Plan for the Robotics Industry* further define digital and intelligent transformation as a major impetus to high-quality development of manufacturing and a driving force behind better resource allocation and efficient collaboration between the industry chain and supply chain. In particular, 5G fits the needs of low latency, high reliability, and wide coverage in the manufacturing field, and complements the industrial Internet by helping accelerate digital, intelligent, and network-based transformation in this industry.

Under the guidance of national strategies, the MIIT of the PRC collaborates with all stakeholders in the industry to deepen network coverage and co-construction and sharing, as well as carry out plans such as the *"Set Sail" Action Plan for 5G Applications* and *5G + Industrial Internet Converged Applications* to accelerate the maturity of the manufacturing industry. On this basis, China continues to improve the infrastructure of 5G and the industrial Internet. It has built the world's largest and most technically advanced 5G networks, with over 300 cities enjoying high-quality extranets. Integrated applications of digital technologies and industrial manufacturing drive the manufacturing industry into an intelligent and high-quality development phase and enable accelerated transformation of real economy [13].

1. Smart factories keep growing in scale and level. By the end of December 2023, China had built 421 national demonstration factories and more than 10,000 digital workshops and smart factories at the provincial level, as well as 40% of the

world's "lighthouse factories," according to the MIIT. In addition, the national service platform for the integration of informatization and industrialization has served about 183,000 industrial enterprises; 79.6% of enterprises use digital R&D and design tools, and the numerical control rate of key production processes reaches 62.2%

2. New scenarios, solutions, and modes of smart manufacturing are emerging. In particular, new manufacturing modes, which used to be either concepts or frameworks, have been implemented. Equipment manufacturing industries, such as automobiles, large aircrafts, and engineering machinery, explore collaborative design, virtual verification, and remote O&M to facilitate fast product iteration and revenue growth. Consumer goods industries, such as home appliances and clothing, innovatively propose mass customization, customer to manufacturer (C2M), and shared manufacturing to meet personalized requirements and improve user experience. Raw material industries, such as petrochemicals, metallurgy, and construction materials, employ production-marketing integration and cross-process quality control to improve the quality and effectiveness, achieve intrinsic safety, and save energy.

13.8.2 Trends of Digitalization and Intelligent Development in the Industry

Digital technologies are developing rapidly in China's manufacturing industry. The latest market research shows that the smart manufacturing market has maintained an annual growth rate of over 40% since 2019 and the market size will exceed CNY 40 billion by 2025. As equipment, network, software, and data become key factors supporting digitalization of enterprises, the following trends are emerging in digital transformation.

1. Digitalized industrial equipment

    Industrial equipment, as an operation tool, is vital for improving quality and effectiveness of industrial manufacturing. At present, a lot of manufacturing equipment has problems such as network disconnections, inability to collect data in real time, outdated interaction modes, and fixed routine operations. This makes it difficult to meet future requirements for more flexible, agile, and efficient production operations. For digital or intelligent transformation of equipment, it is crucial to develop operating systems, industrial chips, and edge intelligence.

2. Fully-connected industrial networks

    As media of data transmission, networks widely connect the entire value chain of R&D, production, supply, sales, and services in the manufacturing industry and key factors (including manpower, machines, materials, methods, and environment) in production, to support highly stable and reliable data exchanges, continuous production activities, and flexible production modes. Currently, most factories in China have basic network coverage, which meets the requirements of office and basic production activities. However, as digital scenarios expand and upgrade, manufacturing enterprises are in urgent need of industrial networks with lower latency and higher mobility, certainty, and bandwidth. For mobility and certainty purposes, enterprises require the accelerated construction of secure and reliable industrial networks with superb performance and simplified architecture to achieve ubiquitous connections, service integration on one network, and intelligent O&M [14].

3. Cloud-based industrial software

   Industrial software is integral to data aggregation, analysis, decision-making, and feedback. In the past, traditional industrial software provided great convenience for manufacturing enterprises and helped many enterprises take the first step toward digital transformation. However, traditional industrial software requires license purchasing and features localized deployment, heterogeneous software systems, and lack of industrial knowledge sharing. This brings challenges such as high costs of inter-system integration, insufficient dynamic configuration flexibility, and vendor lock-in. Industrial software developers also face barriers to accumulating industrial knowledge, making it difficult to innovate. In this situation, manufacturing enterprises, industrial software developers, and other partners should unite to explore concept innovation and mode transformation and promote the cloudification of industrial software.

4. Value mining of industrial data

   Data has become a key asset and a factor of production for enterprises. Masses of real-time, multi-source industrial data are of great value to industrial enterprises for carrying out in-depth analysis and value mining. However, efficient collection, integration, value mining, and security compliance of industrial data are common challenges faced by the manufacturing industry. Data governance and application of manufacturing enterprises must be fully extended in terms of both application scope and time to unleash value across a larger scope.

13.8.3 *Requirements for Digitalization and Intelligent Development in the Industry*

1. Comprehensive awareness of the manufacturing process

   Industrial manufacturing involves diversified equipment, which requires trained professionals to use. With various communications standards, protocols, and interfaces, it can be difficult to achieve equipment interconnection and data collection. Against this backdrop, 5G industrial modules, 5G private networks, and 5G converged networking are required to reduce device interconnection costs and connect production line equipment, industrial robots, detection instruments, industrial sensors, smart meters, and personal digital

13.8 Manufacturing

assistants (PDAs) to the network. To achieve comprehensive awareness, 5G + industrial IoT and 5G + multi-access edge computing (MEC) technologies are leveraged to collect data of all production factors (including manpower, machines, materials, methods, and environment) and service data, achieving transparency throughout the process and proactive perception of changes and requirements. For convergence and collaboration, systems are converged to establish an integrated collaboration system of supply chain as well as a man-machine collaboration mechanism. With regard to self-management and control, AI and big data technologies are used to integrate heterogeneous data from various sources for in-depth data analysis and mining, empowering data-driven scientific decision-making as well as self-management and control in each production phase.

2. Integrated smart manufacturing solution

Most solutions in the market are general-purpose solutions, failing to meet the professional and personalized requirements of traditional manufacturing enterprises. Currently, most smart manufacturing applications provide intelligence tailored to specific scenarios, such as production management, equipment management, manufacturing process quality management, and warehousing and logistics management. In addition, there is a lack of industry standards on digital-transformation-related technologies (such as software, big data, and cloud computing) and services, which vary substantially among providers. Coupled with high trial-and-error costs, it is difficult for many traditional enterprises, especially SMEs, to select technologies and services. To transform from intelligence for specific scenarios to overall intelligence, the manufacturing industry needs to build all-cloud digital factories that enable flexible deployment, ubiquitous access, and intelligent analysis. It can only do so by utilizing diversified 5G + converged innovative applications and leveraging 5G + cloud + AI capabilities to explore intelligent applications in various fields and scenarios, such as production and logistics. This helps tap into the value of 5G technologies, invigorate smart manufacturing, promote integration of 5G and automated guided vehicles (AGVs), ultra-HD video, cloud-based AI recognition, and linkage of machine vision and manufacturing process, as well as gradually form an open, shared, and reusable smart factory solution.

3. Customized production and manufacturing

New technologies, such as 5G, additive manufacturing, new material R&D, and automation, develop and are applied in manufacturing, making it possible to produce highly customized products. Meanwhile, there is a trend toward customized services in home appliance manufacturing, electronic manufacturing, and automobile manufacturing. It is imperative to figure out how to flexibly adjust production lines to meet personalized requirements of consumers. Utilizing E2E data flows and communications networks, a self-organizing flexible manufacturing system can be built, which integrates information technologies such as big data, cloud computing, AI, and IoT in each phase of manufacturing. After product requirements are automatically identified and order design requirements are adapted to, personnel can organize manufacturing resources and perform production operations, material delivery, and quality inspection to complete production of personalized products. In addition, personalized value-added services can be developed by exploring customer service requirements through collection, transmission, modeling, and user data analysis based on intelligent products, thereby improving customer experience.

13.8.4 5G + AI Technology Convergence Analysis

1. 5G + AI + Industrial Internet

   5G + AI convergence can further propel the application of key industrial Internet technologies. For example, large language models (LLMs) such as ChatGPT not only improve the production efficiency in the industry, but also add value to traditional positions. The convergence also empowers the industrial Internet in more scenarios. For example, edge intelligence can address major pain points in data privacy and security protection as well as difficulties in heterogeneous network convergence of industrial enterprises [15]. Besides this, 5G + AI convergence can enable the industrial Internet and give full play to technical advantages in fields such as remote equipment maintenance and real-time data collection.

> **Case: Midea Cloud's "AI Brain" Safeguards Digital Transformation**
> Midea Cloud serves as a platform for providing industrial Internet services. Based on 5G + industrial Internet, the company has built an "AI brain" which employs AI modeling to lower the application threshold. With the technical foundation of an AI framework, Midea Cloud's "AI brain" focuses on AI algorithm services, applies one-stop component-based modeling and configuration-based development, and opens core capabilities such as natural language processing (NLP), character recognition, image recognition, and sound processing. This "AI brain" also leverages AI technologies such as labeling and NLP analysis to provide solutions for fields ranging from industry, business, office, supply chain, retailing, planning, and logistics to safety protection, thereby digitalizing operation optimization and making production and operation intelligent. One example is Midea's lighthouse factory in Nansha district. An AI algorithm service platform is widely used in service scenarios, such as technological parameter recommendation, image-based quality inspection, and action recognition, to integrate the value chain of R&D, supply, manufacturing, quality control, and after-sales services. After undergoing two phases of projects, the T + 3 process witnesses higher efficiency, accompanied by faster order placement, quicker response to equipment exceptions, more efficient data collection, and swifter template switching.

2. 5G + Edge computing

5G networks offer network access with higher rates and lower latency to industrial devices and terminals and help build platforms which provide abundant fundamental services for industrial enterprises. While boosting swift processing at the edge or cloud for industrial Internet platforms, 5G + edge computing helps equip enterprises with new technologies such as AI by leveraging common component capabilities, thereby slashing the development costs. As a case in point, 5G can help bolster video image transmission that relies on mobile broadband and low latency powered by MEC. UAVs and unmanned trucks can be deployed in construction sites for remote operations and real-time checks with reduced labor costs, and video image and control signal processing and transmission with ultra-low latency.

Case: COSMOPlat Launches the 5G + MEC Enhancement Solution
COSMOPlat, as an industrial internet pioneer in China to explore 5G, has accumulated rich hands-on experience in scenarios, factories, and campuses. It pioneers explorations and practices in industrial parks, helping Haier build the world's first 5G + smart manufacturing fully-connected industrial park, Haier Sino-German Intelligent Park. Backed by the MEC-based distributed computing center and 5G public service platform of edge computing, this industrial park embraces resource sharing and algorithm invoking across sectors and domains, spanning from safety protection, equipment interconnection, AGV-based delivery, first article quality inspection, and energy consumption management, to visual inspection. This solution breaks the dilemma of "data silos" between scenario-specific applications by deploying systems on a unified platform, which provides reference for digital transformation of industrial parks and becomes a typical model of "5G + industrial internet" large-scale integrated applications.

3. 5G + VR/AR

5G augments the capacity of VR/AR data transmission considerably based on multi-frequency convergence capabilities, multiple-input multiple-output (MIMO) technologies, and high-frequency mmWave technologies, to expand the network capacity for densely populated areas. With 5G + VR/AR, user experience is no longer restricted by time and space, achieving "online guidance in anytime," improving equipment assembly efficiency, and allowing remote experts and O&M personnel to be "on site" simultaneously. As in VR/AR remote collaboration, VR/AR-based HD audio and video communications can apply to remote expert guidance in various industries. Technical experts can assist onsite personnel in completing their work through image labeling, voice guidance, and whiteboard sharing. 5G networks safeguard real-time, high-rate, and reliable data transmission, ensuring production data security.

> **Case: Shanghai Spaceflight Precision Machinery Institute Implements AR Nondestructive Testing**
> The construction project of light alloy (new material) industry base is a flagship project of this institute. In the critical product inspection phase, once inspectors encountered nondestructive testing problems, the efficiency of telephone and video communications was low and even experts were required to be on the spot. With AR technologies, inspectors wear AR smart glasses that work with embedded three-dimensional (3D) models, and employ visualization methods, such as HiScene's HiLeia AR space labeling, to perform measurement and recording during product inspection which features high quality, efficiency, and benefit. Experts provide real-time guidance through text, image, or real-time labeling. The two parties interact with each other from the first-person perspective and quickly locate faults and transmit solutions in real time only through cloud-based interaction and remote diagnosis. In this case, AR assists the institute in combining "guided" nondestructive testing with production, thereby speeding up the upgrade of smart aerospace manufacturing.

4. 5G + Cloud-based AGV

   5G networks provide underlying support by leveraging its strengths of high bandwidth, low latency, and high concurrency. Specifically, high bandwidth enables precise positioning based on high-precision distance measurement. Low latency makes data, such as logistics data and commodity loading and picking data, reach the user, management, and operation ends at a faster pace. High concurrency enables more AGVs to collaborate in the same manufacturing section at the same time. AGVs can support 5G capabilities by integrating 5G modules or terminals. Moreover, 5G + edge cloud moves modules that require complex computing capabilities (such as AGV positioning, navigation, obstacle avoidance, image recognition, and environment awareness) to 5G edge servers, laying a foundation for large-scale AGV networking and dispatch and slashing the cost of a single AGV. Coupled with lossless transmission of real-time HD videos, unified platform-based scheduling, and interconnection with the automatic management system, the integration of logistics line with personnel, production line, and auxiliary production equipment further empowers logistics and production processes to collaborate promptly. In this way, the labor cost is greatly reduced, the operation efficiency is improved, and the logistics period is shortened.

> **Case: Trina Solar's AGV Application on 5G Private Networks**
> Trina Solar and Changzhou branch of China Mobile in Jiangsu have jointly launched a 5G private network AGV application solution, which uses 5G private network, autonomous driving, and intelligent transportation system. This solution effectively addresses the problems of low efficiency, high cost, and

13.8 Manufacturing

poor safety of transportation in traditional logistics, greatly improves the efficiency and accuracy of transportation in logistics, and provides new momentum and market advantages for Trina Solar. 5G provides real-time communications with ultra-low latency and seamless coverage for AGVs in the workshop. With AI autonomous driving, the transportation speed can be changed in real time with the route flexibly adjusted. It takes only 23 ms to receive an instruction. AGVs run along preset routes in the workshop, greatly improving the operation efficiency. This not only relieves the pressure caused by rising labor costs, but also improves the production efficiency, reduces the cost per unit time, improves the product quality, and raises the profit margin.

5. 5G + Digital twin

The digital twin technology is a key part of fully-connected 5G factory applications. On the basis of virtual factories and digital twins, the data of factory subsystems can be integrated and upstream and downstream data links can be integrated. This enables visualized and smart management of industrial IoT applications. 5G data transmission can take less than 1 ms (almost without latency), which means digital twins can be synchronized in real time. For example, during remote monitoring, digital twin equipment can be used to understand the internal running mechanism of equipment, and the simulation results are immediately fed back to robots. If a problem occurs on the production line, workers can immediately identify and understand the onsite situation and solve the problem, improving both fault prediction and maintenance efficiency.

Case: Little Swan's "5G + Fully-Connected Digital Twin Factory"
China Telecom Jiangsu and the manufacturer Little Swan in the city of Wuxi have built a "5G + fully-connected digital twin factory." Using 5G + X digital full connectivity, every machine, person, and corner of the factory are monitored by a central system, which creates a "digital twin" of the factory. In the factory's 5G + industrial Internet big data digital operation center, the leasing service data of Little Swan's Ujing washing machines is continuously updated and all order information is displayed in real time. This allows for live updates for order growth, energy consumption curve, and daily top 10 order data to be displayed in real time. The factory also has a 3D diagram that can be used to display the factory's energy consumption, machine alarms, noise readings, PM2.5 coefficient, personnel entry traffic statistics, production line status, and logistics information. The digital twin platform greatly improves the intelligence level of all factors of production (including manpower, machines, materials, methods, and environment), helping the factory achieve make-to-order (MTO) mode and improving customer response efficiency by 50% in only two years.

13.8.5 Typical Solutions for Digitalization and Intelligent Development in Manufacturing

1. COSMOPlat's smart home appliance production line solution

    COSMOPlat has more than 30 years of experience in automated production lines. It manufactures home appliances and specializes in stamping, injection molding, sheet metal forming, laser welding, and robot applications. It has run multiple fully automated production lines for over 10 years. Using cutting-edge laser welding technologies and advanced production technologies and processes, the COSMOPlat smart production line automation solution creates a smart production system with self-diagnosis and adjustment capabilities. This solution enables compatibility, automation, and short-takt-time production for products of different specifications.

    Traditional production lines are typically hindered by high defect rates, product compatibility issues, slow die changeover, long takt time, and low levels of automation. To tackle these pain points, all COSMOPlat production lines are designed using fully automated production line standards, leveraging up-to-date technologies and processes, and implementing automatic material feeding, automatic product transfer, and automatic positioning. High-quality materials, advanced processing and manufacturing technologies, and strict assembly technologies safeguard the operational stability of the lines. The lines are also designed modularly using digital tools and use the latest technologies and processes, which optimizes logistics and makes the flow between processes smooth to maximize production efficiency. In addition, production lines are developed and planned with multiple products and models in mind. Leveraging modular and digital design allows compatibility with various products and specifications, achieving higher degrees of flexibility. This means lines can be quickly switched to produce different products and foolproof inspection can be performed through cooperation with test organizations. All automation equipment can be connected using IoT technologies and upload production data in real time, providing data support for technology and process optimization, production scheduling, and efficiency improvement, and achieving unmanned and digital production of home appliances.

2. China Mobile's 5G smart factory solution

    China Mobile focuses on 5G services involved in manufacturing. The company provides solutions that use industrial gateways, industrial networks, and the OnePower industrial Internet platform to support smart factory construction, such as large-scale data collection, video surveillance, machine vision, AR spot check, and training (see Fig. 13.18).

    China Mobile builds 5G virtual private networks that meet the production requirements of industrial enterprises, integrates data links between 5G and operational technology (OT) networks, and improves the security, flexibility, and reliability of enterprise-grade 5G application. China Mobile also focuses on innovative factors, such as "industry brain," industrial vision quality inspection,

13.8 Manufacturing

Fig. 13.18 5G smart factory solution architecture

new industrial gateway, identity resolution applications, industrial low-code development, and industrial Internet SaaS lightweight applications. Utilizing industrial security private networks and industrial big data foundation, the company builds the OnePower industrial Internet with the "1 + 1 + 1 + N" capabilities. Specifically, "1 + 1 + 1 + N" stands for one series of industrial terminals, one industrial private network, one OnePower industrial Internet platform, and N industry applications, respectively. In addition, China Mobile uses its in-factory digital operation platform and inter-enterprise collaborative manufacturing platform to achieve full connectivity within a factory and data exchange with the factory's upstream and downstream partners. This enables digital technology services that promote industry transformation and upgrade within the manufacturing sector.

3. Huawei's smart cloud factory solution

Huawei has rolled out a smart cloud factory solution that uses "one cloud," "one network," and "one platform" to support numerous digital applications. The company aims at building a transparent, agile, and intelligent digital production platform driven by data to improve smart manufacturing. The one cloud used in this solution is Huawei Cloud which uses a unified tool chain and technology stack that accelerates application construction and avoids repeated system construction. The one network is a Huawei production network that can be used as a high-rate, stable, and intelligent five-in-one network base for smart manufacturing, which also helps avoid repeated network construction. The one platform is Huawei's digital production platform that leverages Huawei's wealth of data governance experience for data aggregation, unified cleansing, modeling, integration, and multi-dimensional analysis, thereby supporting factory-level applications and enabling data-informed decisions.

Huawei also works with Shenzhen Lanyou to create manufacturing solution portfolios. Lanyou supplies five specific production application systems for management of bill of materials (BOM), plan and scheduling, supply chain management, production execution, and quality analysis, as well as service platforms. This solution is based on the full-stack AI capabilities provided by Huawei's Ascend, Kunpeng, Huawei Cloud, and Pangu model offerings. This solution also provides an integrated AI training and inference platform for manufacturing companies that improve the development and training efficiency of AI algorithms for factory scenarios like quality inspection and production scheduling.

13.8.6 Path for Large-Scale Replication and Promotion

As 5G technologies and standards evolve, 5G applications will continue to be incorporated into core production processes within the manufacturing industry. Based on technical feasibility and implementation, the path for large-scale 5G application in manufacturing will likely proceed in three phases (see Fig. 13.19).

Phase 1 (2020–2021): With the advancement of 5G 3GPP Release 15, high-bandwidth services were implemented by replacing networks and terminals, giving full play to wide 5G connections. Typical applications included ultra-HD video surveillance, inspection UAVs, inspection robots, and environment information collection. Ultra-HD video surveillance was first of these services to be widely applied.

Phase 2 (2022–2024): As standards continued to mature, application expanded to the upgrade and reconstruction of original production lines, in-depth integration with industrial systems, and changes in original industrial production methods. In this phase, 5G is further integrated with technologies such as AI, big data, and

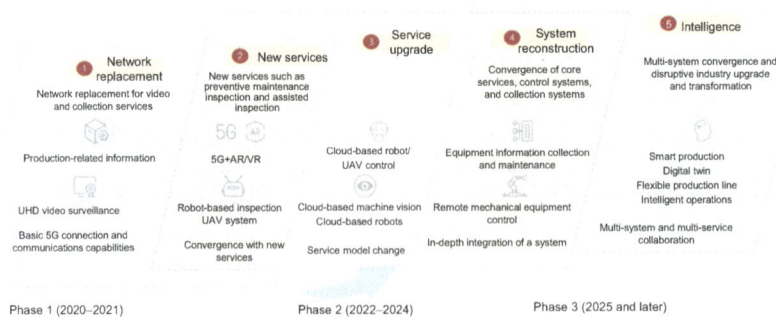

Fig. 13.19 Phases of large-scale 5G application in manufacturing

cloud computing, and new or enhanced service forms have continued to emerge. Typical applications from this phase include AR spot checks, auxiliary checks, cloud-based machine vision, equipment information collection, and cloud-based AGVs.

Phase 3 (2025 and later): 5G will be profoundly integrated within the manufacturing industry. As 5G technical standards develop and industry application deepens, 5G will be further incorporated into production, control, and management system protocols. In addition, 5G will become widely used in manufacturing and many converged 5G applications will be used together, to achieve intelligent production and industry transformation. This phase mainly embraces comprehensive application, including flexible production lines, digital twins, and predictive equipment maintenance.

13.9 Ports

13.9.1 Overview of Digitalization and Intelligent Development in the Industry

In recent years, China's Belt and Road Initiative has provided historic opportunities for the globalization of China's ports. China's new "dual circulation" development pattern has also provided a boon for high-quality port development. Government calls for "constructing a country with a strong transportation network" and "exploring and building free trade ports" further help boost deeper institutional reform of ports. China has also issued a series of smart port policies as a part of its commitment to building a comprehensive transportation system at a faster pace. In 2017, the Ministry of Transport (MOT) of the PRC released the *Notice on Implementing Smart Port Demonstration Projects*, specifying that a group of ports will be chosen for smart port demonstration projects involving smart logistics and safety management of hazardous goods with the help of informatization. In the same year, the ministry released a list of 13 smart port demonstration projects. At present, all demonstration projects are progressing at a steady pace and have achieved substantive results.

With the construction of benchmark smart ports, China sets higher requirements on the acceleration of smart port construction. From 2019 to 2021, the MOT of the PRC and other related organizations jointly released a series of policies, such as *Guidelines on Building World-Class Ports*, *Guidelines on Promoting New Infrastructure Construction in the Transport Field*, and *Action Plan for New Infrastructure Construction in the Transport Field (2021–2025)*, specifying detailed requirements for the technical implementation and intelligent reconstruction of smart ports and emphasizing the automation of wharf operation equipment and construction of a smart logistics service platform for ports.

As part of its 14th Five-Year Plan, China has outlined the need to build a modern comprehensive transportation system and accelerate the construction of world-class port clusters. The *14th Five-Year Plan for the Development of Modern Comprehensive Transportation System* emphasizes the need for intelligently reconstructing container wharves of Ports of Dalian, Tianjin, Qingdao, Shanghai, Ningbo Zhoushan, Xiamen, Shenzhen, and Guangzhou. The plan also stresses the need for faster construction of next-generation automated wharves, such as the Haixing wharf at the Port of Shenzhen and wharves at the Port of Qinzhou. As the policy system continues to improve, the direction and objectives of China's smart port industry become more and more clear.

Concurrently, technologies such as the Internet, big data, cloud computing, and blockchain are becoming increasingly mature. Coupled with the massive amount of goods trade data of ports, these technologies provide opportunities for the all-round advancement of port services and the in-depth integration of ports with the national economy and society as a whole. Featuring high bandwidth, low latency, and massive connections, 5G can help ports meet the automation and intelligent development requirements during their digital and intelligent transformation. In addition, digital technologies are incorporated into port production to promote process reengineering, management innovation, and service collaboration in port-related fields, which has achieved a series of objectives, such as electronic service documentation, automatic production, visualized internal monitoring, evidence-based industry supervision, mobile user services, and full-process service collaboration. These achievements have yielded remarkable results in cost reduction and efficiency improvement. Figure 13.20 illustrates the core production process of container wharves. Typical application scenarios of port digitalization include remote control of cranes (bridge, gantry, and portal slewing cranes), AGVs, intelligent guided

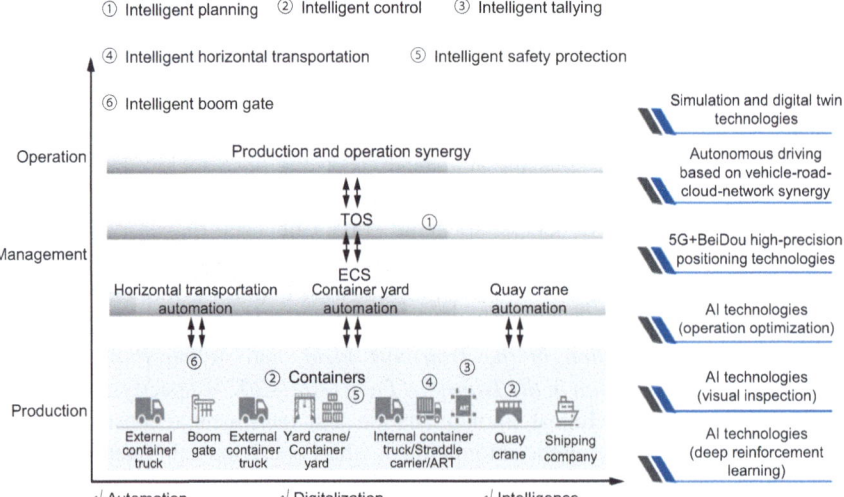

Fig. 13.20 Core production process of container wharves

vehicles (IGVs), unmanned container trucks, intelligent tallying, UAV inspection, and AI-based video surveillance. Among these scenarios, gantry crane remote control is a typical HD video backhaul + PLC remote control scenario and, due to it being highly suited to the features of 5G networks, is one of the first 5G applications in smart ports.

At present, China's coastal ports have completed the transformation to third-generation ports, with some already having transformed to fourth-generation ports. Chinese ports account for seven of the top ten container ports in the world, and China is a global leader in terms of the construction and operation level of automated wharves. For example, the Port of Qingdao is the world's first port to apply 5G technologies. As early as the end of February 2019, this port cooperated with China Mobile and Huawei in 5G smart port construction. It is also the first port in the world to achieve 5G remote bridge crane operations in the actual production environment. The Port of Shanghai utilizes the Intelligent Terminal Operating System (ITOS) "super brain" to intelligently control all of the processes of its automated container wharves, such as loading/unloading, stacking, transshipment, and entrance and exit control, in all scenarios. The Port of Shanghai is the first in China to fully self-develop and upgrade to its own intelligent operating system for ultra-large automated container wharves. ITOS has helped the port increase the average efficiency per quay crane in a working hour by more than 10%, and the annual throughput of a single wharf by more than 50%. The Xiamen Ocean Gate Wharf is China's first 5G all-scenario smart port instance and is the launch site of China's first wireless production private network that combines 5G SA networking, edge computing, and network slicing technologies. With the 5G private network, a series of smart port service scenarios are built using technologies such as edge computing, high-precision positioning, AI, and computer vision.

13.9.2 Trends of Digitalization and Intelligent Development in the Industry

Now, smart port construction has become a new engine for industry development. New technologies accelerate the transformation to fourth-generation ports. Through the introduction of smart loading and unloading, warehousing, and transshipment services, ports will further expand to include comprehensive and high value-added logistics functions, such as intermodal transportation, bonded logistics, full-process logistics services, and supply chain finance.

1. Intelligent reconstruction of small wharves is accelerated

    High-density IoT, high-precision identification systems, high-efficiency mechanical operation, and highly intelligent remote control enable port reconstruction, which required space reservation, pre-planning, and equipment pre-installation in the past, to move from offline to online. The computing power infrastructure is deployed online to reduce reconstruction and significantly

reduce the cost and time required, thus encouraging the successive emergence of small-sized and highly intelligent inland ports.
2. Regional port integration becomes an inevitable trend

   China's smart port construction is becoming more and more mature, and application processes in different regions are accelerating. However, smart port construction will be a long-term, continuous, and gradual process due to the substantial investment and numerous elements involved, as well as due to insufficient technical reserves, capital accumulation, innovation capabilities, and human resources. Regional port integration will become an inevitable trend in the future driven by the application of intelligent technologies in ports and top-level strategic planning on the supply side, such as national port layout optimization and regional economy coordination.
3. Intelligent decision-making and high value-added services become the development direction

   The infrastructure's decision-making system still falls short in terms of intelligence and flexibility, necessitating manual operations in some links. In the future, fourth-generation ports, which are situated in expansive economic hinterlands with convenient transportation, will further explore, analyze, and apply port data assets propelled by the sea-land integration plan. Through the optimization of machine learning algorithms, "intelligent brains" will better enhance the operation and intelligent decision-making, resulting in reduced dependency on humans.

   In addition, as the junction points of intermodal transportation, ports require strong connections to integrate information flow, logistics, and capital flow among upstream and downstream enterprises on the port supply chain. The service chain of upstream and downstream enterprises can also be extended through the use of information networks, which has also become a new revenue stream for ports. In the future, high value-added digital supply chain services, such as intermodal transportation, bonded logistics, full-process logistics services, and supply chain finance, will become the major enablers of port development.

13.9.3 Requirements for Digitalization and Intelligent Development in the Industry

1. Differentiated service development

   Ports vary in terms of size and informatization level, and so do their service requirements due to their differing characteristics and informatization requirements. Given the high cost of digital transformation, the main practice is to perform digitalization construction and exploration in large-sized comprehensive ports, resulting in some small- and medium-sized inland ports being left out of the process. Ports are enclosed sites where people, automobiles, objects, and ships gather and involve energy consumption, maintenance, and operation.

These factors mean that ports require differentiated strategies based on 5G networks and diverse technical means.

2. Intelligent decision-making and management

   Port production, operation, management, and services are increasingly shaped by novel digital technologies, resulting in a considerable rise in the level of technologies at ports and transforming ports into a knowledge- and technology-intensive industry. As the freight volume of ports increases, conventional management modes are no longer able to satisfy customer's requirements. The decision-making systems of today's port infrastructure still fall short in terms of intelligence and flexibility, necessitating manual operations in some links. Moreover, an abundance of high-value digital assets emerge as 5G application deepens, accompanied by an increase in customers' expectations for customized services. Against this backdrop, ports have a need to further explore, analyze, and apply data assets by leveraging big data and AI. By optimizing machine learning algorithms, "intelligent brains" will further enhance operation and intelligent decision-making and reduce dependence on humans.

3. Port integration

   In China, a "one province, one port" pattern has emerged. Some provinces (and regions), like Zhejiang, Shandong, Liaoning, Fujian, and Guangxi, have completed port integration while others are currently still in the process of doing so. With the advancement of regional port integration, ports will compete for business modes, service quality, and port efficiency comprehensively, rather than just competing for port throughput. As evidenced by the successful practice of the Zhejiang Seaport Group, port digitalization provides a great advantage in deepening port cluster collaboration and high-quality port development. Hence, digital ports with a unified operation and management platform are essential for profoundly integrating port resources and advancing integration.

13.9.4 5G + AI Technology Convergence Analysis

1. 5G + AI + IoT

   5G + AI elevates the digitalization efficacy of smart ports. Coupled with IoT and edge cloud technologies, 5G + AI gives impetus to the automation and intelligent advancement of port operations, enabling container truck marshalling and full-process precise sensing during automatic operations of rubber-tired gantry (RTG) cranes. Novel technologies and processes continuously improve the automation, digitalization, and intelligent capabilities of equipment. Together with new operation rules and technical roadmaps, these technologies and processes help realize the creation of true smart ports without altering the traditional service operation mode. For instance, during loading and unloading of quay cranes, the following information can be automatically identified using visual AI technologies such as convolutional neural networks (CNNs): container numbers, International Organization for Standardization (ISO) certification numbers, dangerous goods labels, and lead seals. This allows tally clerks to perform tallying by clicking a mouse button rather than working at open-air stations, thereby greatly improving their work environment, efficiency, and safety.

Case: Intelligent Tallying of Containers at the Port of Tianjin
In conventional tallying, tally clerks use tally sheets or terminals and work at loading and unloading sites. The wharf environment is complex and includes machinery, container trucks, and cargo, which pose potential safety risks to personnel. To improve berthing and operation efficiency, the Port of Tianjin adopts a solution combining 5G device-pipe-cloud synergy and AI intelligent tallying, which leverages real-time image backhaul and AI capabilities to intelligently calculate the types and amount of bulk cargo. The solution collects HD images through onsite HD cameras at different locations, transmits the images to the solution platform through 5G networks, and quickly establishes an inference model based on an AI algorithm to identify the type and amount of bulk cargo and perform intelligent tallying of bulk cargo. The use of this solution effectively prevents work disruptions and safety risks caused by bad weather and improves personnel safety and tallying accuracy. The solution is estimated to reduce personnel requirements and costs by 15 person-years and CNY3 million, respectively, each year.

2. 5G + Satellite Internet + Unmanned driving

Container trucks support unmanned driving and real-time road condition backhaul, which are enabled by cloud-based intelligent dispatch and technologies based on 5G, BeiDou, high-precision positioning, and vehicle-road synergy. After receiving the real-time operational data of container trucks, the background control center supervises the transportation progress and status, monitors the location, battery level, and loads of the trucks, and views their sensing and planning information in real time. If a truck is faulty or needs to move to a temporary location, the 5G remote takeover mode can be used to ensure transportation and driving safety. 5G + unmanned container trucks slashes labor costs and enables 24-hour operations. In such scenarios, technology convergence improves utilization of shoreline resources, while effectively ensuring the operational efficiency and production safety of wharves.

Case: 5G + BeiDou Smart Container Trucks at the Port of Ningbo Zhoushan
The Port of Ningbo Zhoushan has built a 5G-enabled backbone network, with 612 public trunk navigation marks upgraded to support the BeiDou satellite navigation system. 5G enables concurrent operations of unmanned smart container trucks, thanks to its high data rate, low latency, and large connection

characteristics. 5G helps smart container trucks to give full play to the functions of a "super AI brain." After containers are secured, smart trucks will automatically begin transporting containers and can accurately identify nearby containers, machinery, lighthouses, and other objects. Smart trucks can also drive to the position specified for RTG crane operation along the optimal route provided by the intelligent dispatch system. In the event of an emergency, smart trucks can also automatically make decisions, such as decelerating, braking, turning, bypassing, and parking. With these capabilities, smart trucks are able to satisfy the requirements of horizontal transportation in the enclosed area of the port.

3. 5G + VR/AR + MEC

VR/AR technologies enable real-time remote monitoring through the use of 5G virtual private networks and IoT. Port safety includes safety management of berths, container yards, buffer zones, auxiliary construction areas, gates, buildings at wharves, and roads. Thanks to its high data rate and massive connections, 5G allows personnel to use mobile or portable terminals to monitor the production process and management systems and learn about the running status of the visual monitoring system without having to visit workshops in person. In addition, AI technologies like CNNs can be integrated to detect unsafe behaviors and events in real time, such as wrong-way driving, perimeter intrusion, and personnel not wearing safety helmets. This considerably improves monitoring efficiency and ensures production safety.

Case: AR Real-Scene Command Platform at the Port of Fuzhou

The Jiangyin port area of Fuzhou Port Group has rolled out the first 5G smart port platform in Fujian Province. By building a cutting-edge AR command platform, the port area is able to implement large-scale 3D monitoring. AR panoramic cameras can be used to remotely obtain panoramic video streams of the port area in real time, which helps production dispatch personnel control operation lines and adjust operation modes in real time. This has become an advanced means of port operation command. The HD surveillance camera, installed in the cab of a quay crane, rapidly backhauls the collected real-time video images to the MEC platform via 5G for intelligent analysis of the driver's facial expressions and driving status. If an abnormality such as fatigue or drowsiness is detected, a warning is immediately generated. By leveraging the power of 5G, the platform resolves issues related to insufficient bandwidth and high latency in 4K ultra-high-definition (UHD) video surveillance scenarios and provides clearer video images, which ensure more efficient and responsive intelligent analysis. These features of the platform effectively help reduce accident rates at ports and enhance the overall safety of port operations and personnel.

13.9.5 Typical Solutions for Digitalization and Intelligent Development in Ports

1. 5G + Smart port solution at the Port of Tianjin

This solution adopts the framework of "one network, two clouds, and N applications." It builds a 5G-based ubiquitous IoT, achieving full coverage of major areas at ports. The MEC edge cloud is deployed closer to the network edge for local data steering, and center and edge clouds of the smart port are constructed. In addition, the solution enables a diverse array of application scenarios, such as remote control of portal slewing cranes, excavator-based remote hold cleaning, intelligent tallying of bulk cargo, BeiDou-powered ship positioning, and digital twins of container yards. Figure 13.21 shows the 5G + smart port solution for the Port of Tianjin.

The solution focuses on intelligent reconstruction in five key production scenarios—berthing, loading and unloading, hold cleaning, bulk cargo tallying, and container yard management at wharves for bulk cargo—to implement smart port operation. In terms of remote loading and unloading, a remote control solution is designed for 5G portal slewing cranes (for loading and unloading bulk cargo at wharves). In this scenario, a portal slewing crane is deployed with two 5G CPEs, which carry HD video signals and PLC control signals, respectively, via different channels, thus keeping the latency of control services below a certain level. In addition, this scenario integrates the portal slewing crane's power generation system functions, such as monitoring, metering, intelligent lubrication, and energy consumption management, into a unified platform, thus achieving full-lifecycle equipment management. With regard to hold cleaning, 5G is used for remote excavator control. The portal slewing crane hoists the excavator into the hold for cleaning. A simu-

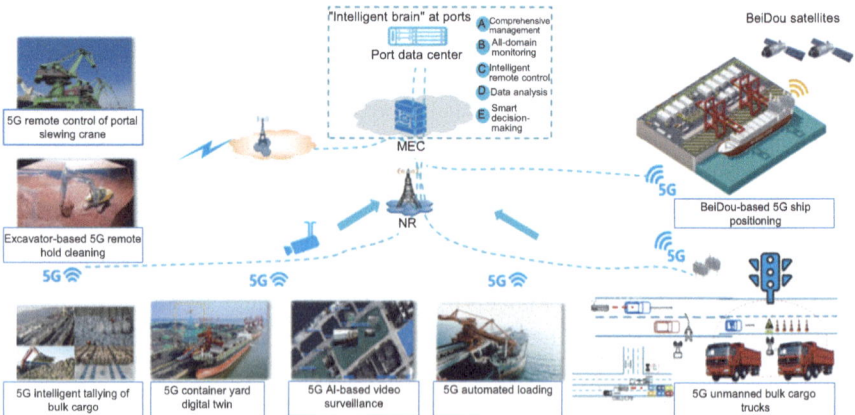

Fig. 13.21 5G + smart port solution at the Port of Tianjin

lated remote operation console is set up in the control room, with operational data and images sent back in real time via the 5G network, thus enabling remote excavator control and cargo hold cleaning operations. This effectively improves operational efficiency and prevents the risk of injury to personnel [16].

In terms of intelligent horizontal transportation, the Port of Tianjin cooperates with Huawei to build a 5G + L4 autonomous driving smart port where 76 IGVs have been in full operation for more than 12 months. This has helped significantly relieve the burden of recruiting drivers and effectively improved operational efficiency. The port has rolled out an intelligent horizontal transportation solution, which relies on vehicle-cloud synergy, to provide precise positioning, path planning, and obstacle avoidance for large trucks based on multiple sensors and algorithms. With this solution in place, unmanned large trucks can automatically adjust their route and speed based on real-time goods requirements and traffic conditions, while exchanging information and collaborating with other vehicles and equipment. In 2022, the highest average ship operation efficiency in section C reached 36 moves/h, with a 20% increase in the average operation efficiency of a single bridge crane, and a 20% decrease in the overall energy consumption of a single container.

2. 5G + BeiDou smart port solution at the Port of Tangshan

The Port of Tangshan's 5G + BeiDou smart port solution provides real-time centimeter-level positioning using 5G networks and the MEC platform. Figure 13.22 shows the 5G network architecture of this port. 5G virtual private industry networks are constructed according to a "full coverage" plan in order to provide seamless coverage in port operation areas. For the 4.9 GHz 5G network, a 3:2 slot configuration (an ultra-large uplink slot configuration) is configured to provide an uplink peak rate of 400 Mbit/s in order to meet the requirements of remote crane control and video backhaul at a port. The MEC

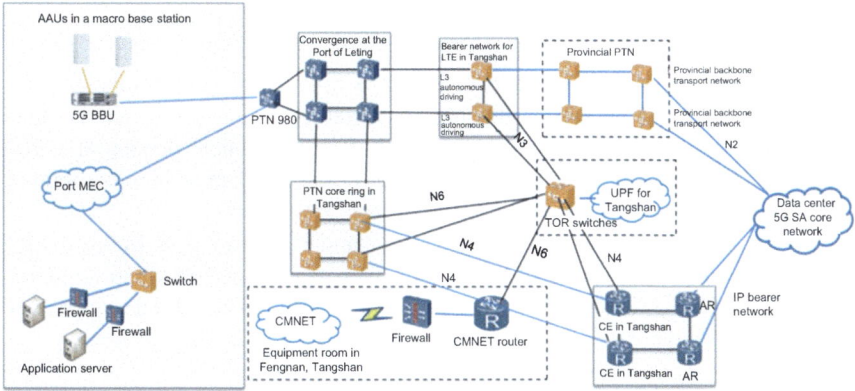

Fig. 13.22 5G network architecture of the Port of Tangshan

platform meets the 10 ms low-latency control requirements to allow edge computing data to be processed within the port and separates the production network from the public network. In addition, the platform is also deployed with port automation analysis and dispatch applications to improve user experience and data security.

The Port of Tangshan leverages 5G intelligent reconstruction to enable 5G port equipment remote control, 5G unmanned horizontal transportation, and 5G intelligent video analysis and achieve smart transformation and upgrade of horizontal transportation and vertical loading and unloading systems. For example, in 5G port equipment remote control scenarios, a smart dispatch center is built utilizing high-precision positioning, computer vision, and 5G to remotely control loading and unloading in the central control room. During 5G unmanned horizontal transportation, unmanned container trucks support centimeter-level precise parking at fixed points, container loading and unloading, automatic obstacle avoidance, and remote control based on 5G networks, differentiated services, high-precision maps, and lidar. In this way, the port is able to achieve full-scenario automatic operation of unmanned container trucks and unmanned trailers [16].

13.9.6 Path for Large-Scale Replication and Promotion

5G converged applications at ports will be developed in three phases.

Phase 1 (2020–2021): network replacement. In this phase, the manufacturing industry replaced original wireless or wired networks with 5G to give full play to the large connectivity of 5G. The replacement focused on inspection and monitoring services during port operation and management, such as 5G-enabled UHD video surveillance, UAV-based inspection, and environment information collection, to improve the overall safety at ports.

Phase 2 (2022–2024): converged technology application. This phase was characterized by the deepening integration of 5G with other technologies such as AI, big data, and cloud computing, achieving digital upgrade of port equipment and unmanned production. During this phase, converged applications such as intelligent tallying, equipment information collection, unmanned driving at ports, and remote control of quay cranes and gantry cranes began to be incorporated into core remote control and logistics systems.

Phase 3 (2025 and later): application integration and transformation. In this phase, 5G will comprehensively enable unmanned smart ports which integrate major application scenarios in the first two phases and implement mutual mapping of port data. The typical 5G application in this period will be digital twins.

13.10 Electric Power

13.10.1 *Overview of Digitalization and Intelligent Development in the Industry*

Electric power is crucial to national economies and people's livelihoods. In recent years, the power industry in China has undergone significant changes and faced numerous challenges as the country strives to achieve its "dual-carbon" goals. 5G is well suited for supporting smart electric power as it can be applied to support power generation, transmission, transformation, distribution, and consumption. It can be applied to a range of services, including control services, data collection services, mobile application services, and new power grid services like multi-site convergence [17]. Table 13.1 describes the requirements of power communications for 5G networks. When applied to control services, 5G can optimize energy configurations to prevent large-scale power outages. It can also aid in the online monitoring of real-time data on power distribution networks. When applied to collection services, 5G makes it easier to collect and provide raw power consumption data for the entire system. When applied to mobile application services, 5G helps prevent safety accidents and environmental pollution, reduces the need for manual inspections, and assists workers in remote live-line work. And when applied to multi-site convergence services, 5G helps enterprises become a platform sharing information with others.

Many regions in China have proposed smart grid construction plans under national policies such as the *Notice on Organizing the Implementation of New*

Table 13.1 Requirements of electric power communications for 5G networks

Network requirement	5G advantage	Description
Reliable operations	High reliability	Secure and reliable operations are basic requirements of the power system. The high reliability of 5G can enhance the reliability of the power grid
Flexible responses and precise controls	Low latency	The power system must be able to respond to changes flexibly, and certain services cannot be interrupted. The millisecond-level latency of 5G can fulfill the real-time communication needs of the power grid
Massive data transmission	High speed	Power grid IoT applications are put into large-scale use, leading to a large amount of real-time measurement data and video data. The high-speed capabilities of 5G can provide robust support
Internet of everything	Wide connectivity	The wide connectivity of 5G can satisfy the connection requirements of ultra-large-scale smart terminals on the power grid
Battery life assurance for devices	Low energy consumption	5G has optimized hardware communications protocols that extend the lifespan of power grid devices

Infrastructure Construction Projects (Broadband Networks and 5G) in 2020 and *5G Application Implementation Solution in the Energy Field*. Regions like Xiong'an New Area, Inner Mongolia, Yunnan, and Hainan have already started their smart grid construction. For example, Xiong'an New Area is integrating 5G into power grid construction. It has verified a pilot project for 5G-based power services, testing the performance of power distribution automation and power consumption information collection. Xiong'an New Area additionally launched China's first 5G + MEC protective relay IoT project based on the SA architecture in October 2020, with cutting-edge technologies employed.

Power grid companies are at the forefront of 5G smart grid technology breakthroughs and engineering practices. The State Grid Corporation of China has conducted extensive research into some 5G services, which have already been implemented in the fields of smart grid construction, control services (such as differential protection for power distribution networks), and mobile inspection services (such as video interaction). The first phase of the Qingdao 5G Smart Grid Project, for example, which was jointly developed by State Grid Qingdao Power Supply Company, China Telecom Qingdao Branch, and Huawei entered production in July 2020. According to new reports, the project can automatically detect and isolate faults in power distribution lines within a few milliseconds. Additionally, it has reduced the power consumption per 5G base station by 20% by utilizing peak-valley pricing, which addresses rising concerns about the high power consumption of 5G operations. China Southern Power Grid has also carried out pilot projects and cooperation in the field of 5G smart grid control services, including differential protection for power distribution networks. The company partnered with China Mobile to establish China's largest 5G smart grid application demonstration area in Guangzhou's Mingzhu Bay. This project boasts a high number of service scenarios and has made significant progress in verification, ranking among the top in China.

At the same time, operators have accelerated cooperation on 5G with the electric power industry and conducted a series of 5G-enabled projects, exploring control services (such as precise load control and differential protection for power distribution networks), collection services (such as power consumption information collection), and mobile inspection services. Additionally, some power equipment enterprises are preparing to engage in extensive partnerships with communications equipment vendors.

13.10.2 Trends of Digitalization and Intelligent Development in the Industry

Electric power system will play an important role in making energy supplies greener, more secure, more efficient, and more user-friendly thanks to electric power digitalization.

13.10 Electric Power

1. Power grid digitalization

    Power grid digitalization is when a digital twin of a physical power grid is established. Multiple operations implemented on the digital twin can then be applied to the physical power grids to achieve bidirectional interaction, including standard reference data traceability, status awareness, online monitoring, behavior tracking, trend analysis, knowledge mining, and scientific decision-making. Digitalization enables a higher level of intelligence on the power grids, which makes power grid operations more secure, reliable, intelligent, and cost-effective. Advancements in digital technologies will stimulate further transformation and upgrade in power grids. This will help power grids adapt to external challenges such as the large-scale introduction of new energy sources, power market reform, and diversified user needs, while maintaining a balance between supply and demand. This will result in greener and more secure, efficient, and cost-effective power grids.

2. Electric power service digitalization

    Electric power service digitalization provides digital interaction, automatic services, and intelligent experience to customers. Power grid enterprises can modernize their power supply service systems by integrating digital technologies into their service provisioning process. The goal of this is to build an agile front end that can better serve customers and occupy markets; an efficient middle end that enables resource sharing and capability reuse; and a reliable back end capable of systematic support and comprehensive assurance. This allows enterprises to also extensively expand their customer resources to achieve seamless online and offline connectivity. Furthermore, they can develop application services that are easy to use, quick to respond, and flexibly customizable, to enhance service efficiency and customer satisfaction. By innovating their services, power grid enterprises can improve user experience, unleash customer potential, and meet customer requirements.

3. Energy ecosystem digitalization

    Energy ecosystem digitalization is the construction of a smart energy ecosystem based on a unified digital service platform. This platform must utilize digital technologies to guide the flow of energy, data, and services in an organized manner, resulting in a modern, efficient, cost-effective, and environmentally friendly energy ecosystem. Such platforms can engage all manner of industry players such as governments, upstream and downstream parties, and customers to allow for the free exchange of energy, data, and services. This promotes co-existence, sharing, integration, and mutually beneficial advancement for the entire ecosystem. Innovative transaction and interaction models can be used by all parties involved, reinforcing power grid enterprises' capabilities to integrate the entire energy industry value chain. This encourages power grid enterprises to become value chain integrators and energy ecosystem service providers.

13.10.3 Requirements for Digitalization and Intelligent Development in the Industry

1. Power inspection method innovation

   Power transformers and transmission lines are the basic infrastructure of power transmission. They require scheduled and periodic inspections to ensure power supply reliability and quality. Transmission lines crisscross China's countryside, and difficult terrain often makes power inspection difficult. Traditional manual power inspection requires a lot of manpower and material resources. It can also be dangerous, difficult to manage, and inefficient with poor real-time performance and high operation risks. This method cannot keep up with the secure operation requirements of rapidly developing modern power grids.

   Although UAVs and robots have been used to replace some manual inspection, there are still issues that need to be addressed. One such issue is the lack of real-time communication between inspection devices and related personnel, which prevents immediate reporting of the inspection status or problems. In addition, fault evaluation currently relies heavily on individuals' experience, and inspection devices lack intelligent identification and analysis capabilities. Emerging technologies such as 5G, AI, AR, and satellite Internet can enable new functions like high-precision locating, fault warning and analysis, and remote real-time guidance during power inspection. New intelligent inspection methods are required in the electric power industry to reduce labor intensity, improve inspection efficiency, expand the scope of inspections, and make inspection results digitally accessible. This will ultimately increase the safety, stability, and efficiency of power grid operations.

2. Security control for power distribution networks

   As new distributed energy sources become more prevalent, the power distribution network will change from a radiation network to an active network where the fault current flows bidirectionally and fault characteristics change frequently. The traditional three-stage overcurrent protection method used by power distribution networks will not be able to adapt to new energy sources. In contrast, current differential protection is highly precise when locating faults, very sensitive, and does not rely on voltage information. This makes it a great fit for updated distribution network structures. It is able to quickly locate and isolate faults on distribution networks by comparing the current differences of differential protection terminals. To do this, two or more associated differential protection terminals must be time-synchronized with a precision of less than 10 μs, and the maximum transmission delay on one side should not exceed 12 ms for E2E interaction.

   Current differential protection using optical fiber communication is commonly used as the primary protection for high-voltage transmission lines [18]. However, distribution networks have limited optical fiber coverage and involve many widely dispersed terminals. Implementing current differential protection on distribution networks would require a lot of optical fibers to be deployed,

13.10 Electric Power

which is both expensive and difficult to achieve. This makes 5G critical if we want to meet the low-latency, high-reliability, and high-precision service requirements of differential protection. In addition, satellite communications systems such as BeiDou and GPS can be used to provide high-precision timing services for differential protection on distribution networks, implement multi-end information exchange, and ensure secure and stable operations on distribution networks [19].

3. Refined power load management

The factors that cause power grid frequency fluctuations will continue to increase as power transmission shifts to ultra-high voltage alternating/direct current (UHV AC/DC) transmission and long-distance cross-region transmission. As part of the UHV AC/DC power grid system protection, precise load control systems have many advantages such as multiple-point and wide-area coverage, strong selectivity, quick responses, and minimal impact on users' power consumption. If UHV DC systems experience continuous commutation failures, DC lockout faults, and receiver grid power loss exceeding a certain limit, the power grid frequency will drop sharply or even experience a system frequency collapse. To prevent large-scale power outages, a precise load control system can utilize the interruptible load within the production system as a control object, promoting friendly interaction throughout the power grid, power supply, and load.

In such cases, to ensure that the power grid frequency is restored to normal quickly, the load control system requires minimal communication transmission latency between different layers. The latency between a master station (or substation) and a terminal should be less than 50 ms. Currently, optical fiber communication has been established between the centralized coordination station, the precise load control master station, and substations to facilitate load control instruction transmission among them. However, the optical fiber coverage between substations and terminals is still uncommon. This is due to how widely large number of terminals are often dispersed, making optical fiber deployment expensive and challenging. Newer technologies are needed to meet the low-latency and high-reliability communications requirement between precise load control substations and terminals.

13.10.4 5G + AI Technology Convergence Analysis

1. 5G + Satellite

Satellite technologies have found widespread acceptance in China's electric power sector, where new technologies are transforming conventional systems for power generation, transmission, transformation, distribution, and consumption. Table 13.2 gives an overview of satellite technology applications in major electric power services. Satellite technologies can provide high-precision services down to the centimeter-level for real-time positioning and navigation and even

Table 13.2 Satellite technology applications in major electric power services

No.	Service	Typical scenario	Maturity
1	Infrastructure construction	Smart construction site	★★★★
2		Logistics (large devices)	★★★★
3		Field operation risk control	★★★
4	Operation and inspection	Geological hazard monitoring	★★★★★
5		Pole and tower tilt monitoring	★★★★★
6		Substation foundation settlement monitoring	★★★★
7		UAV intelligent inspection	★★★★★
8		Line fault location	★★★
9		Personnel safety in substations	★★★
10		Power line maintenance	★★★
11	Marketing	Power consumption data collection	★★★★★
12		Terminals for marketing operations	★★★
13		Electricity theft protection	★★★
14		High-precision positioning for marketing operations	★★★
15	Scheduling	Substation timing services	★★★★
16		Blind scheduling for small hydropower stations	★★★★★
17	Supportive services	Emergency communications	★★★★
18		Vehicle management	★★★★

down to millimeters for post-processing operations in scenarios such as power inspection, settlement detection of transmission tower foundation, and geological hazard monitoring of line corridors. Moreover, satellite technologies can provide nanometer-level timing for services such as power scheduling, device status analysis, and connection of new energy sources to the grid. It can also provide emergency communications for field operation personnel. Integrating satellite technologies in the electric power sector can enhance the development of services including infrastructure construction, operation, inspection, marketing, and scheduling in the sector.

5G can improve satellites' positioning and timing capabilities. Satellites can be used to build a unified time-frequency network with nanosecond time synchronization. When 5G, with its high reliability and low latency, is applied on such a network, real-time power scheduling control and online payment can be implemented. In addition, 5G significantly reduces the startup time for high-precision satellite positioning, improves positioning accuracy and reliability, and allows for interconnection and smart management of power equipment. To date, 5G + satellite deployment has been tested in power grids in China to improve operations like inspection, power supply, power consumption information collection in remote areas, and substation foundation settlement monitoring [20].

13.10 Electric Power

Case: State Grid Qingdao Power Supply Company Deploys 5G + BeiDou for Intelligent Inspection

In February 2021, the State Grid of China tested its first 5G + BeiDou UAV power line inspection system in Qingdao. This system, developed in collaboration with China Telecom and Huawei, marks a significant milestone in the application of advanced technologies in power grids. It uses 5G, self-developed Chinese chips, the BeiDou navigation system, and AI technologies to digitize the entire process of unmanned power line inspection, covering route planning, real-time monitoring, and image identification to defect summary and reporting. The system greatly simplifies operation, backhaul, and analysis. For instance, to tackle operation challenges, State Grid Qingdao Power Supply Company proposed a BeiDou-based autonomous UAV inspection solution that leverages BeiDou's centimeter-level intelligent spatiotemporal services and 3D laser point cloud data. This enables the UAVs to autonomously plan their routes, start with one click, automatically complete inspection tasks, and return to a specific area, without the need of manual intervention.

2. 5G + AI

AI is catalyzing next-generation intelligent electric power systems. AI technologies like computer vision, natural language processing, and speech recognition have upgraded the capabilities of UAV inspection, intelligent substation monitoring, power generation, and load forecast systems. Table 13.3 describes the AI applications in major electric power services. Intelligent analysis assists with large-scale situations and improves lean grid operations, while helping

Table 13.3 Application of AI in major electric power services

No.	Electric power service	Application scenario
1	Forecast	Load forecast, new energy power generation forecast, and electricity price fluctuation forecast
2	Overall control	Ultra-short-term load forecast, training of dispatchers, intelligent risk identification, intelligent handling of accident policies, and comprehensive energy system control
3	Simulation	Situation awareness, ultra-real-time deduction, and intelligent prediction of dynamic processes
4	Overhaul	Inspection and intelligent analysis using UAVs and robots, equipment defect monitoring, security evaluation, and preventive maintenance
5	Field operations	Facial recognition, behavior recognition, health monitoring, and intelligent wearables
6	Customer services	Business assistance, intelligent customer service, and power resource coordination
7	Marketing	User profiling, precise marketing, and differentiated services
8	Office work	File processing, job match, and conferences

reduce costs and improve efficiency. In the upcoming years, we will see more AI deployed across every facet of electric power services, covering everything from power generation to end-user management.

5G + AI support the digital and intelligent development of the electric power industry. For example, AI technologies like image and sound recognition can significantly improve the efficiency and accuracy of inspection. Large-bandwidth and low-latency 5G networks enable these technologies to instantly detect faulty devices and provide real-time online guidance for onsite operations, facilitating swift fault rectification and ensuring service continuity. The project of China Southern Power Grid shows the success of 5G and AI for intelligent inspection in power transmission and transformation, with a reported 80-fold increase in efficiency.

Case: Shenzhen Power Supply Bureau Releases a Pre-trained AI Model
On February 15, 2022, the Shenzhen Power Supply Bureau of China Southern Power Grid joined Huawei to announce their latest advancements in AI + electric power. These include the first pre-trained AI model developed for the electric power industry based on the Ascend ecosystem and China-developed full-stack AI using the same ecosystem. To address common issues that affect power supply, like downtime caused by airborne debris that has become entangled in power lines, the intelligent inspection system empowered by 5G and AI technologies enables employees to monitor the airborne debris in real time from inside their office. As recognition tasks account for more than 80% of AI application scenarios in routine power supply work, Shenzhen Power Supply Bureau developed the industry's first pre-trained AI model using the Huawei Ascend ecosystem. This model has fueled a fivefold improvement in AI R&D efficiency and boosted the average recognition accuracy from 85% to 95%. This means that operations such as device risk detection and fault locating are more efficient, accurate, and intelligent. Currently, the pre-trained model has been used in 12 types of operations, including UAV refined inspection.

3. 5G + Edge computing

Unlike traditional big data processing, edge computing leverages capabilities from edge-cloud synergy, edge-edge synergy, and edge intelligence to handle challenges facing the electric power industry such as high real-time performance requirement, short data period, and complex tasks. Edge computing provides effective support for data collection services like smart metering, forecast services like power consumption forecast, and inspection services like electric power inspection. 5G and edge computing form a new computing mode, where the unique capabilities of 5G are accessible through edge nodes while edge computing experiences a shorter latency on 5G networks. This combination has a broad prospect in the electric power industry and can be applied in connection of new distributed energy sources to the grid, distribution automation, smart metering, and inspection. Although the use of 5G + edge computing in the power grid is still in its early stages, pilot projects such as 5G + edge computing smart substations have been implemented to explore a new mode of power system based on edge-cloud synergy and multi-site convergence.

Case: Precise Load Control Based on 5G + Edge Computing
In December 2020, State Grid Qingdao Power Supply Company, China Telecom Qingdao Branch, and Huawei conducted a test on millisecond-level precise load control using edge computing and 5G E2E slicing for the first time. This test involved uploading load data from precise control devices and transmitting it across the device group in milliseconds through 5G channels. Following the success of the test, the State Grid has now put its first millisecond-level precise load control devices, covered by 5G slices on a public network, into trial operation at Qingdao Power Supply Company. Precise load control is a control zone service that has strict requirements for network and data security. 5G E2E slicing and edge computing can flexibly match service demands with network resources. Physical network resources are fully utilized to shape different 5G slices, meeting varied requirements in different scenarios.

4. 5G + AR

5G networks provide better and more stable experience for AR applications than Wi-Fi and LTE networks. In the electric power sector, 5G + AR has been used in fields such as power inspection and field operations. For instance, 5G-based AR smart wearables have been used for substation inspection, empowering field operators to detect, collect, and store real-time device information like temperature, video, and audio. This helps accelerate fault location and record the entire O&M process, releasing more resources to be used in other operations. If the staff cannot handle the fault on site, they can start a video call to seek remote assistance from experts, where relevant data is sent to experts in real time for analysis and handling.

Case: 5G + AR Remote Collaboration Drives an Intelligent Futuer for CGN New Energy
China General Nuclear Power Corporation (CGN) New Energy uses a 5G + AR cloud review solution to enhance their supply chain management with intelligence and meet sustainability goals in the industry. The online review solution combines the cloud platform, Internet, and intelligent AR devices to enable remote multimedia information communication between

supplier factories and the reviewer. Compared with traditional onsite review, the solution provides a complete set of functions to evaluate files, plant conditions, and workshop operations online, without the restrictions on time and location. This ensures reliable review quality and meets project construction requirements. The reviewer can examine the suppliers' files, verify the authenticity and standardization of the files, and interact with suppliers online and in real time. The cloud review uses a closed-loop design, so that all reviews combine information from issue identification, reporting, analysis, handling, tracking, acceptance, to close. For CGN New Energy, this solution gives a unified platform with which to connect experts from all over the country and achieve flexible cross-region qualification and quality assurance monitoring.

13.10.5 Typical Solutions for Digitalization and Intelligent Development in Electric Power

1. 5G + Smart grid solution of the State Grid

    A new electric power system has been proposed by the State Grid of China using the 5G + smart grid solution (see Fig. 13.23). This solution involves three infrastructure layers: device, pipe, and cloud. It runs a production control network and a management information network and covers power generation, transmission, transformation, distribution, and consumption. Typical application cases include emergency communications in inspection, intelligent inspection of transmission lines, pipeline tunnels, and substations, and energy storage of 5G base stations.

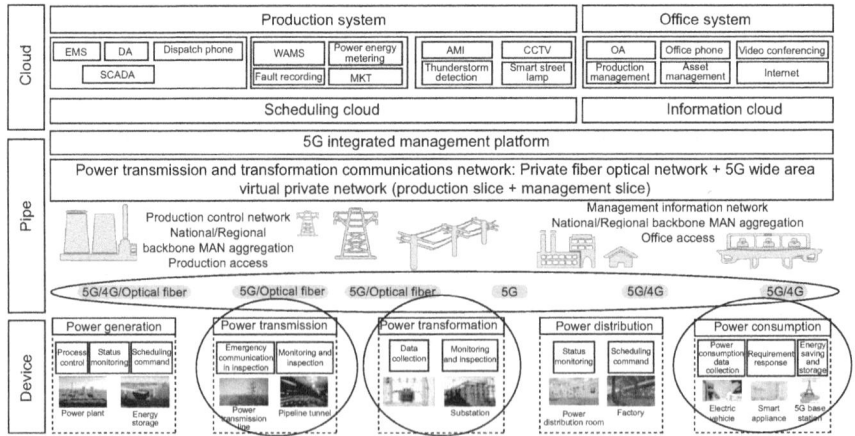

Fig. 13.23 5G + smart grid solution of State Grid

13.10 Electric Power

The solution has five major application scenarios. First is a 4D emergency communications system, which consists of a communications system in a backpack that uses satellite links as backhaul links in remote areas, and a UAV-mounted base station that provides instant ground coverage. Second is the full 5G coverage of power transmission lines from 700 MHz base stations, each covering the same area as that of 10 high-frequency base stations, greatly reducing site investment. Third, full 5G coverage of power tunnels enables inspection personnel with immediate communications in case of an emergency. Fourth, 5G intelligent inspection for substations is now possible in just 1 h, a huge improvement on 3 days typical with manual inspection. The fifth deployment is a smart carbon chain solution that operates under the analytics as a service (AaaS) model. In this solution, base station batteries implement distributed digital energy storage over real-time 5G backhaul networks. Data is aggregated to the big data cloud platform and analyzed using China Mobile's Jiutian AI model to improve the selection of base station and time ranges for charging and discharging based on the peak-valley pricing and energy storage policies. This effectively reduces operators' electricity costs, while all relevant information is securely stored on the blockchain platform.

2. 5G + Smart nuclear power solution of Qinshan Nuclear Power Plant

Qinshan Nuclear Power Plant has deployed a 5G virtual private network (see Fig. 13.24) for full 5G coverage in its production area and plant front area. A customized design of deploying the entire 5G core network on the nuclear power campus is adopted to build an efficient, secure, and stable physical 5G private network. The network supports various applications such as group video conference, video collection, positioning, and mobile office. Further, the network devices meet nuclear power standards in terms of electromagnetic compatibility, radiation resistance, and nuclear power information security.

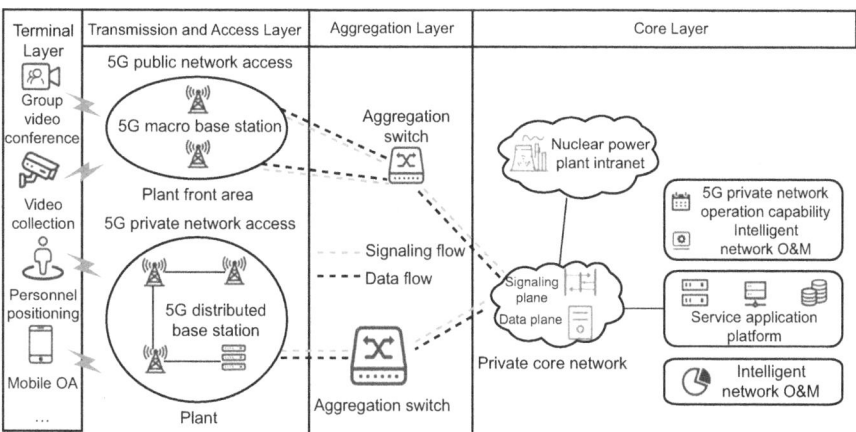

Fig. 13.24 Overall architecture of the 5G virtual private network for Qinshan Nuclear Power Plant

Qinshan Nuclear Power Plant integrates abundant service applications on the 5G virtual private network, including production control, collection, mobile IoT, and video surveillance. Among them, 5G visualized commanding and dispatching and 5G high-precision positioning have been put into use. In 5G visualized commanding and dispatching, 5G technologies are used to enable applications such as multi-point video conferencing, collaboration, and remote online guidance. These applications realize multi-point HD E2E communications within the nuclear power plant, efficient collaboration with internal and external personnel, visualized inspection and remote fault diagnosis by experts, and mobile visualized operations, thereby improving O&M efficiency. In 5G high-precision positioning, 5G base stations using Bluetooth for positioning are deployed to support positioning, navigation, and warning functions. In this way, personnel and vehicles can be positioned and managed, fulfilling the security, routine O&M, and overhaul requirements of nuclear power plants and allowing for a versatile network that can serve multiple purposes.

13.10.6 Path for Large-Scale Replication and Promotion

The widespread adoption of 5G in trial has been met with critical acclaim. As ubiquitous power IoT develops, 5G will be able to continuously meet the demands of evolved electric power services. Figure 13.25 shows the roadmap for 5G in this sector.

Phase 1 (2020–2021): 5G gradually replaced existing wireless and wired systems thanks to its large connectivity and bandwidth, which made it ideal for information collection and mobile inspection. The main application scenarios in this

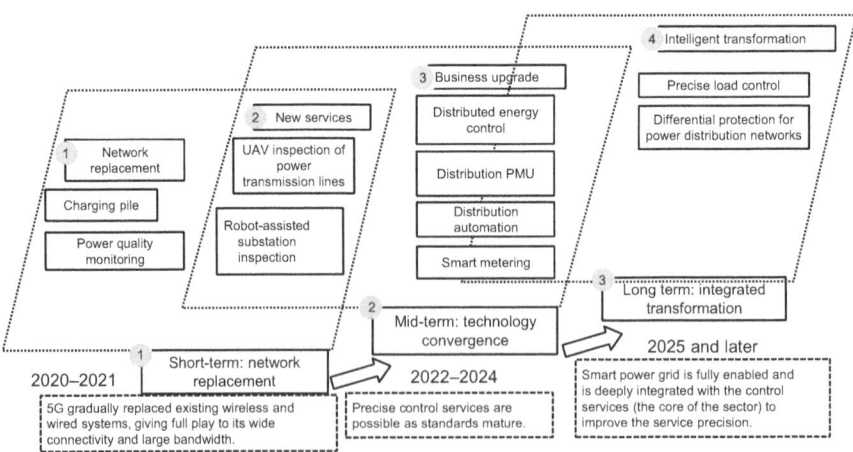

Fig. 13.25 Phases of large-scale 5G application in electric power

phase included charging piles, power quality monitoring, UAV inspection of power transmission lines, and robot-assisted substation inspection.

Phase 2 (2022–2024): As related standards mature, 5G is deployed alongside with emerging technologies like AI, big data, and cloud computing to implement real-time data collection at any weather and preliminary precise control. The main application scenarios include distributed energy control, distribution phasor measurement unit (PMU), distribution automation, and smart metering.

Phase 3 (2025 and later): 5G fully enables smart grids, where 5G applications are extensively used throughout the electric power industry and deeply integrated with the control services (the core of the sector) to improve service timeliness and precision. The main application scenarios during this phase include precise load control and differential protection for power distribution networks.

References

1. China Academy of Information and Communications Technology (CAICT). Research on the path of development and policies to promote 5G applications [R] (in Chinese). 2021.
2. CAICT. Research on the methods of industry digital transformation [R] (in Chinese). 2020.
3. Cyberspace Administration of China. Digital China Development Report (2022) [R]. 2022.
4. Global Public Sector, Enterprise BG, Huawei. White Paper on Architecture for Intelligent Transformation of Public Services [R]. 2023.
5. Tencent Research Institute. Report on the status quo and development of smart emergency response in China [R] (in Chinese). 2022.
6. ZHANG Z J, LI J Y, ZENG Y, et al. Progress update on the research on the application of 5G in China's meteorological industry [J] (in Chinese). Guangdong Meteorology, 2023, 45(1): 63–66.
7. Huawei. Accelerating Intelligent Transformation White Paper [R]. 2023.
8. WEN F A. The digital transformation and development of agriculture: its significance, problems, and the implementation path [J] (in Chinese). Social Sciences in Chinese Higher Education Institutions, 2023(3): 111–120.
9. CAICT. Research on the development of 5G+tourism applications [R] (in Chinese). 2021.
10. CAICT. Research on key issues in the development of 5G+smart education applications [R] (in Chinese). 2022.
11. China Unicom. 5G Campus Private Network and Application White Paper [R]. 2022.
12. CAICT. White paper on the innovation and development of 5G applications [R] (in Chinese). 2022.
13. Telecommunication Development Industry Alliance (TDIA). White paper on the development of the 5G+industrial Internet industry [R] (in Chinese). 2022.
14. 5G Deterministic Networking Alliance (5GDNA). White paper on how 5G industrial interconnection enables 5G fully-connected factories [R] (in Chinese). 2022.
15. CAICT. Research on the ways in which the industrial Internet can promote the transformation of industry digitalization [R] (in Chinese). 2021.
16. Ministry of Industry and Information Technology (MIIT) of the People's Republic of China. A compilation of typical cases from the 5th (2022) Zhanfang Cup 5G Application Competition [R] (in Chinese). 2022.

17. Deloitte, Global Energy Interconnection Research Institute Co., Ltd. 5G Empowers the Future of Electricity [R]. 2021.
18. JIANG S, SHEN B, LI Z Q, et al. Application of 5G communication technology in distribution network protection [J]. Electric Power Information and Communication Technology, 2021, 19 (5): 39–44.
19. GAO H L, XU B, XIANG M J, et al. Research and application of self-synchronized differential protection for distribution networks using 5G as the communication channel [J]. Power System Protection and Control, 2021, 49(7): 1–9.
20. MIIT of the People's Republic of China. A compilation of typical cases of 5G application in the energy field from 2022 [R] (in Chinese). 2022.

Chapter 14
Trends and Prospects

Digital technology is driving widespread transformation. New network technologies represented by 5G are ushering in a new era of Internet of Everything (IoE), where improved device access and information transmission capabilities are fueling explosive growth in edge traffic and industry traffic. New analysis technologies, such as artificial intelligence (AI) and big data, have kicked off a profound transformation of decision-making processes and are pushing the boundaries of what is possible well beyond human capabilities. New mutual trust technologies such as blockchain are enabling trusted service collaboration in untrusted environments, making data tamper-proof, and ensuring network-wide consistency for multi-party data maintenance and cross-verification. And this is just the start of what digital transformation promises to enable in the future.

14.1 NaaS in 5.5G

5G and AI convergence is expected to continue deepening and scaling up for applications refined in more fields. 3GPP officially named the next evolution of 5G as 5G-Advanced (5G-A) (hereinafter referred to as 5.5G) in April 2021. They announced that 5.5G would be rolled out in three phases through Release 18 (Rel-18), Release 19 (Rel-19), and Release 20 (Rel-20). 5.5G defines new goals and capabilities beyond 5G to provide users with better services and enable 5G to create greater social and economic value.

5.5G standards focus on six technological capabilities: seamless 10 Gbit/s, integrated sensing and communication (ISAC), universal intelligence, deterministic capability, massive Internet of Things (IoT), and ubiquitous connectivity (see Fig. 14.1). 5.5G provides a tenfold increase in network speeds, delivering 100 Gbit/s to support applications with higher requirements, such as 4K/8K ultra-HD video, augmented reality (AR), virtual reality (VR), and real-time big data transmission.

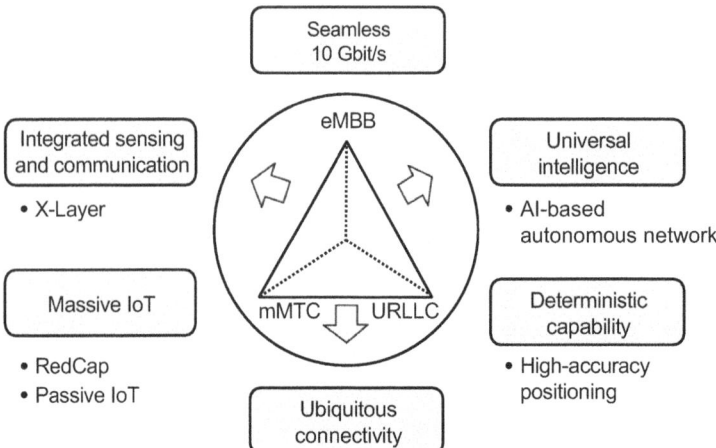

Fig. 14.1 5.5G network capabilities

5.5G also utilizes more advanced signal processing technologies and optimization algorithms to prolong device battery life and reduce energy consumption. In addition, 5.5G introduces higher-level modulation and demodulation technologies as well as error correction algorithms to improve data transmission reliability and ensure that important applications can operate smoothly. It utilizes 5G Reduced Capability (RedCap) to provide upgraded connection capabilities for medium- and high-speed IoT applications, delivering high transmission rates, low power consumption, low device complexity, and connectivity for massive devices. Passive IoT technologies also provide innovative approaches to reduce node power consumption and make up for the disadvantages of radio frequency identification (RFID).

5.5G technology evolution focuses on achieving four upgrades: enhancing broadband service capabilities, improving network operation efficiency, defining new use cases, and fostering network intelligence. 5.5G is built upon the "5G triangle" and serves as a half-way point between 5G and 6G (see Fig. 14.2). It is intended to help guide the continuous enhancement of broadband capabilities, the development of refined solutions for vertical industries, and the exploration of AI convergence technologies and new ISAC services, which will be needed for 6G. 5.5G evolution will continue to empower vertical industries in multiple ways as it gradually shifts its focus from requirement and scenario definition to innovative service content design. In 2024, based on Rel-18, 5.5G is expected to enter commercial use and provide better on-demand networks and a true network as a service (NaaS) for industry users.

5.5G enables immersive real-time experiences. 5.5G can meet higher application requirements, especially for immersive experiences, thanks to the 10 times higher peak rates it can achieve over 5G, along with its other performance enhancements and scenario expansions. Internet of People (IoP) services can now deliver immersive 3D experiences, with recent breakthroughs in 3D technologies, terminals, and

14.1 NaaS in 5.5G

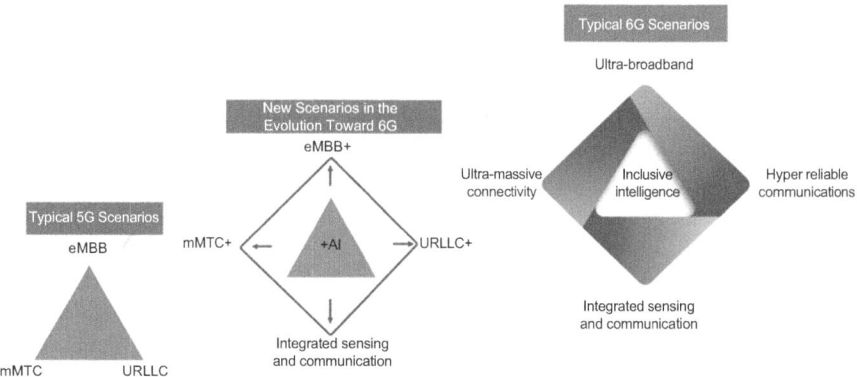

Fig. 14.2 5G-to-6G evolution roadmap

content. 5.5G also uses intelligent service identification, intelligent scheduling, intelligent optimization, and other technologies to make immersive experiences visible, controllable, and maintainable. Artificial intelligence generated content (AIGC) is also evolving, first from text to text, then to video, and finally to 3D content. For example, the 5.5G networks deployed by China Mobile and its industry partners have been used to create immersive 3D experiences at the Hangzhou Asian Games, thanks to various 5.5G applications such as cloud extended reality (XR) and naked-eye 3D displays. The 5.5G networks used in those projects offer high bandwidth and low latency based on intelligent service awareness [1]. 5.5G is expected to further extend AR, VR, and XR applications and enable metaverse applications that will bring all-sensing, interactive, and immersive experiences into life.

5.5G is making intelligent connectivity a reality. Global IoT connections are rapidly increasing. According to the Ministry of Industry and Information Technology (MIIT) of the People's Republic of China (PRC), by the end of February 2022, the country's three tier-1 basic telecommunications companies—China Telecom, China Mobile, and China Unicom—served 2.364 billion cellular IoT terminal users, who account for 57.5% of the mobile network terminal connections in China. 5.5G is also critical for IoT application thanks to its ability to lower costs, lower power consumption, and prolong standby time. More IoT modules will emerge, supporting everything from industrial-grade high-speed connections to RedCap and passive IoT and delivering speeds anywhere from Gbit/s to kbit/s. Specifically, RedCap provides simplified functions that lower power consumption and reduce the cost of IoT applications, which will help the IoT market grow. As 5.5G commercialization progresses, RedCap will evolve to support medium-rate Cat.1 scenarios (LTE UE-Category 1). Passive Internet, on the other hand, will allow for hundreds of billions of concurrent IoT connections with lower speeds and almost zero power consumption [2].

5.5G unleashes value through ubiquitous sensing. 5G is already capable of delivering positioning accurate to 1 m in outdoor environments, and the advantages of mobile communications networks over satellite network systems like BeiDou and GPS in indoor environments are also clear. As 5.5G is even faster and more accurate than 5G, it will be able to deliver centimeter-level positioning by combining existing positioning technologies and beamforming with integrated sensing and communication. Integrated sensing and communication, typically, plays a pivotal role in low-cost networks and delivers submeter-level accuracy and seamless and ubiquitous sensing. This novel technology meets the ubiquitous sensing demands of various industries and has broad advantages in industrial production, Internet of Vehicles (IoV), and the low-altitude economy [3, 4]. For example, for low-altitude security in smart low-altitude scenarios, integrated sensing and communication can be deployed to monitor and control unmanned aerial vehicles (UAVs) and enable obstacle avoidance, intrusion detection, and flight path management services to ensure flight safety.

5.5G empowers intelligent, simplified, and converged networks. Network resource virtualization, service diversification, and the continuous rollout of new 5G capabilities, such as network slicing and edge computing, have already begun challenging the capabilities of 5G. Also on networks that have or are being upgraded to 5G, the legacy terminals, access modes, and transmission approaches still exist and reduce the versatility of those networks. They make new functions difficult and slow to iterate and increase equipment costs while slowing down technology development. 5.5G will support the convergence of different access modes and networks [5], and so can be used to create next-generation converged networks that accommodate multiple industries and protocols, connect air and ground resources, and support industrial IoT (IIoT) applications [6].

14.2 Upgrade from Cloud-Network Convergence to Computing-Network Convergence

As digital transformation deepens, various digital scenarios are posing increasingly high requirements on dedicated, elastic, ubiquitous, and collaborative ICT infrastructure (which refers to information and communications technology infrastructure). This presents challenges for traditional computing networks and makes it necessary to combine different forms of computing power to meet computing power requirements (see Fig. 14.3). Computing-network convergence is the latest way to improve the computing-network service model after cloud-network synergy and cloud-network convergence. It is a pioneering step taken by China in the computing-network field and is of great significance in promoting the development of digital economy.

Computing-network convergence centers on computing power. Intelligent network connections identify the distribution of computing resources, and compute-aware routers route user tasks to suitable computing resources. Figure 14.4 shows how computing-network convergence will evolve. In general, it will integrate more

14.2 Upgrade from Cloud-Network Convergence to Computing-Network Convergence

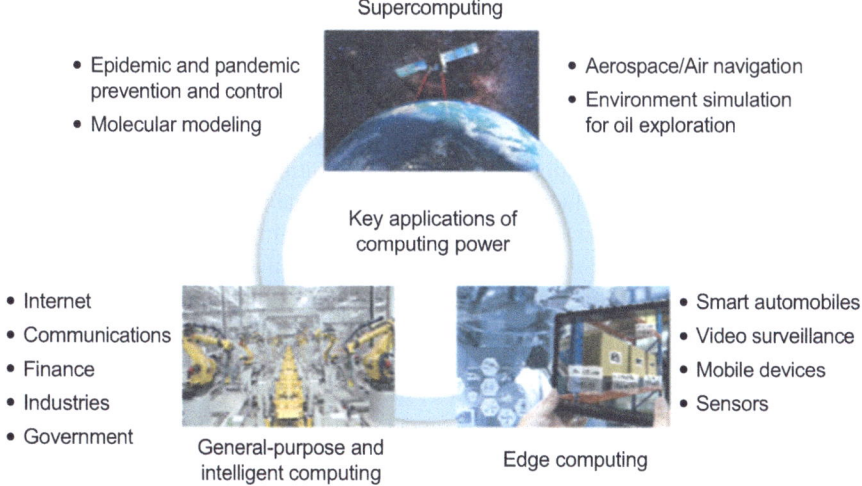

Fig. 14.3 Diversified computing power requirements

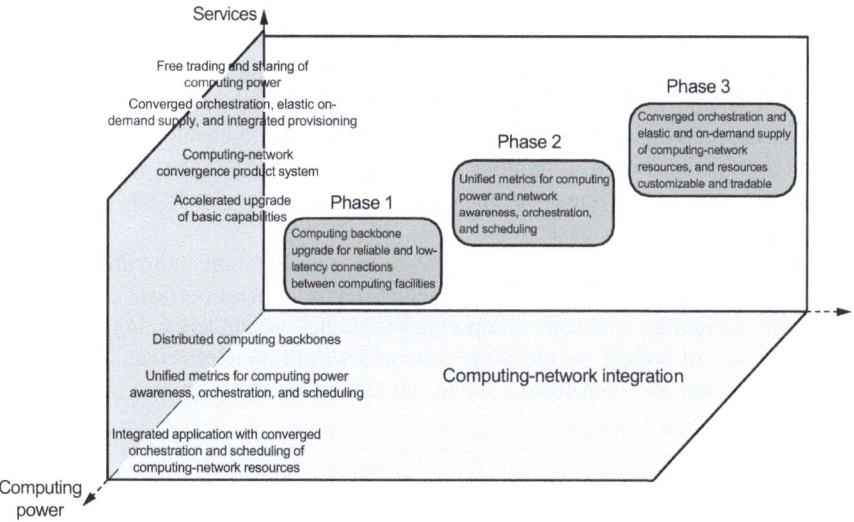

Fig. 14.4 Computing-network convergence capability evolution

elements and resources (go wide), provide computing-power-based integrated services (go deep), and evolve to meet long-term stretch targets (go continuous).

Computing-network convergence is in the process of building a computing-network integrated system to enable ubiquitous connectivity and fast access to and on-demand supply of computing resources. This process is mainly being driven by three major scenarios, including "east data, west computing," computing power interconnection, and cloud-edge-device synergy. "East data, west computing" is a major strategic project launched by China to channel data from eastern regions to computing nodes in western regions. This project cannot be completed using traditional computing-network services because these network services are not able to work together to ensure timely and secure long-distance transmissions and they do not support on-demand scheduling. Computing-network convergence then comes into play to construct a national integrated computing power network where upgraded computing power facilities are deployed to enable cross-region and long-distance scheduling of demands and data, thereby unlocking the value of data.

Computing power interconnection is carried out by China's three tier-1 operators and cloud vendors, which aims to achieve multi-cloud collaboration and improve overall service capabilities. As the realization of Moore's Law is slowing down and process enhancement, at an ever-increasing cost, is approaching its limits in improving chip performance, computing power is facing bottlenecks in its development. Computing-network convergence—the process of building an innovative new infrastructure system that integrates computing power and networks—is the key to overcoming these bottlenecks and mobilizing computing power resources for large-scale supply in the post-Moore's Law era.

Cloud-edge-device synergy connects massive computing resources on the clouds and real-time computing resources at the edges to support service applications. It can be used for video consultations, smart factories, and autonomous driving, among other things. Two major requirements need to be met for cloud-edge-device synergy. The first is that at the network level, efficient interconnection must be achieved between cloud-edge-device computing facilities to enable massive terminals to have quick access to computing services. The second is that at the computing power level, computing power resources must be more accurately and elastically distributed to heterogeneous devices.

In the long run, computing-network convergence will become more intelligent to enable comprehensive perception. Cloud-edge-device general-purpose computing, intelligent computing, and supercomputing backbones are already being deployed. Deterministic, all-optical, and lossless networks will provide effective support for data transmission and help form a green, intelligent, secure, and free computing-network convergence system.

14.3　New Opportunities and Possibilities: Using Data to Create Value

Data has emerged as a new factor of production and is quickly being integrated into production, distribution, circulation, consumption, and social service management processes. It has become a key driving force of change in production, lifestyle, and governance. While digital technology is leading the development of the data industry in fields such as data collection, data processing, and data analysis, value is created from scattered data, promoting innovation and accelerating industry upgrades.

14.3 New Opportunities and Possibilities: Using Data to Create Value

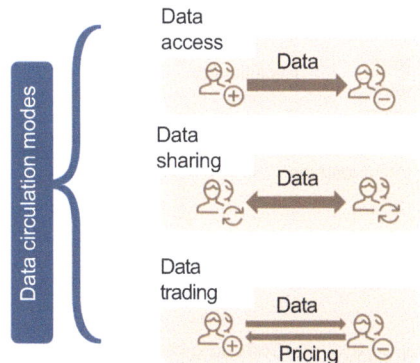

Fig. 14.5 Major data circulation modes

Data has a multiplier effect on other factors of production. It will help equilibrate supply and demand, enable the innovation value chain, and amplify the value of factors such as labor and capital in various industries. Figure 14.5 shows the major data circulation modes.

Public data utilization will be a breakthrough for industry development. According to the guidelines of the State Council of the PRC on strengthening the construction of digital government, business and industries must make efforts to improve their abilities to use public data and promote economic and social development. By the end of 2023, 25 provinces, cities, and autonomous regions in China had released related regulations or drafts to provide policy assurance for market-oriented data circulation, so as to promote data utilization and industry development. China has already built 20 provincial data sharing platforms on which public data plays a strategic and key role. Public data can be directly used to build up the digital economy, digital government, and digital society, and this will create immeasurable economic and social value and drive the integration, sharing, development, and application of other data resources such as enterprise data and social data. Making public data available and accessible to the general population may not generate many popular applications in the short term. However, it can champion fair competition between enterprises, individuals, and social organizations and meet the needs of all members of society.

The idea that "data is available but invisible" represents the industry development path for factors such as circulation requirements, security threats, the lack of rules, and supervision (see Fig. 14.6 for trends in the application of data in industries). Privacy computation is a technology that makes data available but invisible, which addresses the long-standing privacy concerns raised with regard to data circulation. It encrypts data before it is shared, restricts data use based on purpose, and ensures that data is not exposed while being used. Decentralized blockchain has also contributed to data security. It enables a unique digital digest to be assigned to particular data for data rights confirmation. Available but invisible data will help organizations use data and train their machine learning models more efficiently in

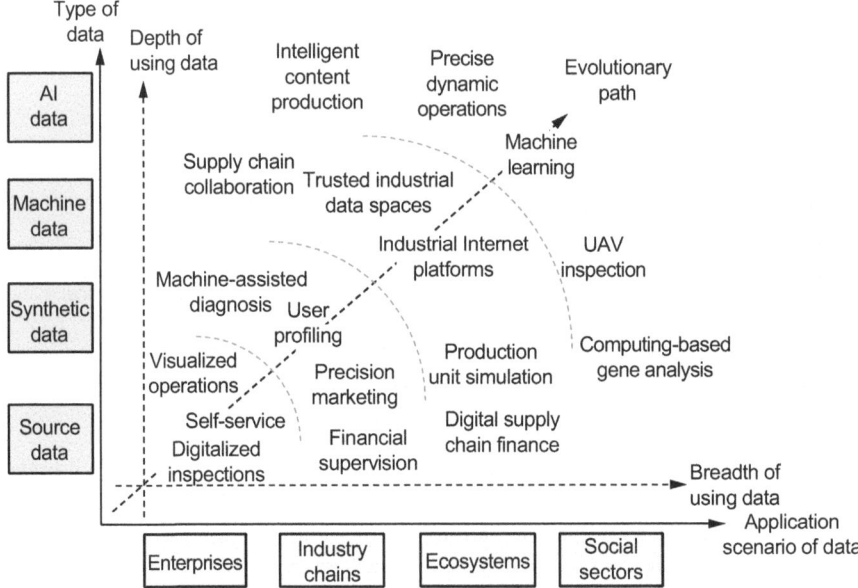

Fig. 14.6 Trends in the application of data in industries

line with government regulations while protecting user privacy and ensuring data security. In the future, a comprehensive technical solution will be explored to cope with scenario-specific issues concerning trusted certificate storage during data trading and circulation.

Various new forms of business centered on the use of data are emerging. China's data ecosystem industry is developing rapidly as the data market continues to expand and grow. According to the *China Data Ecosystem Industry Development Report (2023)*, from 2013 to 2023, the number of data vendors in China surged from about 110,000 to about two million, which represents a compound annual growth rate (CAGR) of over 30%. Technical, service, and application data vendors have all been developing to build a prosperous industry ecosystem and enrich the value-driven data application scenarios [7]. The *2023 China Data Transaction Market Research and Analysis Report* showed that China had plentiful data resource application scenarios. The finance and Internet industries had the highest data demands, accounting for 35% and 24% [8], respectively. Other industries, such as communications, manufacturing, healthcare, transportation, and education, also showed an increasing demand for data products. There are many other industries that also have the potential to leverage data applications.

Data will be used more broadly and more deeply, and the flow of data will continue to drive the data industry forwards. On the one hand, the breadth of data utilization is growing. As public data becomes more available and as we continue to share, trade, and circulate data, it will create more value. Enterprises will be the first to benefit, followed by the industry ecosystem, and finally various social sectors. On the other hand, the depth of data utilization is also increasing, leading to a shift of data application from data analysis with single and scattered data sources to large-scale, converged, and industrialized application development. In the future, the data market is likely to undergo a reshuffle, and technology and industry leading companies may undertake joint ventures to compete with tech giants like Alibaba Cloud and Huawei.

14.4 In-Depth Development of Innovative Digital Applications for Multiple Fields

5G converged applications are maintaining their development momentum in both vertical industries and consumer markets. They are evolving from single applications to systematic applications, from pilot programs to large-scale commercial use, and from unclear business models to new multi-form models.

Operators are exploring new products and services for the mass market. Many basic telecommunications and Internet enterprises have stepped up exploration efforts in consumer markets such as games and entertainment, sports broadcasting, home services, as well as culture and tourism, and many have launched new 5G packages and personal applications such as 5G messaging, 5G new calls, AR/VR, 5G cloud games, and digital humans. For example, China Mobile is working with terminal vendors, equipment vendors, and other enterprises to develop new call services. Migu Video, a company in China, has innovated and released multiple digital products such as 5G cloud VR and 5G cloud gaming. Internet enterprises have also started exploring 5G capabilities to find new ways of applying ultra-HD displays and XR to enhance everyday life and further improve user experiences. However, there has not been any large-scale promotion and only some of these services have been piloted so far.

In vertical industries, the number and variety of digital products and services have increased rapidly. 5G-enabled industry convergence fields, such as the industrial Internet, smart mining, smart healthcare, and smart ports, are accelerating large-scale application rollout for some scenarios. 5G has enabled significant breakthroughs and continues to enable applications both in the aforementioned fields and in other fields such as manufacturing and fully connected plants. By the end of 2023, more than 29,000 virtual private 5G networks had been built for industries in China, and more than 94,000 5G applications had been integrated into 71 of the 97 national economic categories.

Digital applications are being explored to better serve the public in different scenarios. Digital technology is inclusive, convenient, open, and shareable. It can be leveraged to improve people's lives (in terms of basic necessities like clothing, housing, food, and transportation) and to make public services (such as education, healthcare, and assisted living) more convenient, inclusive, and accessible. Traditional service businesses on digital platforms are developing new and easy ways to provide high-quality public services to remote areas to promote equal access to public services. Enterprises are also using digital technologies to increase their competitiveness and innovation and minimize risks in intelligent production and operation, digital product innovation, and agile user services. Preliminary 5G + AI use cases that warrant piloting and further exploration have already emerged in healthcare, education, culture and tourism, and smart cities, and more applications will emerge in the future.

Industry enterprises are actively participating in the industry ecosystem and this is injecting momentum into the innovation of products, services, and business models. Certain basic telecommunications enterprises, manufacturing enterprises, Internet enterprises, application development enterprises, universities, and research institutes have already proactively established more than 32 5G innovation centers which aim to develop technologies, industry services, and a generic technology platform focusing on the innovation of 5G applications. Some basic telecommunications enterprises, Internet enterprises, industry integrators, and industry enterprises are also leveraging their individual competitive advantages to improve their provision of 5G application solutions. Currently, there are almost 200 5G application solution providers working in more than ten sectors, including the manufacturing and energy sectors.

In the future, digital productivity will lead systematic innovation in technology, management, modeling, business, and mechanism development, and this will blur the boundaries between industries and incubate multiple new forms of business that will drive social development. In addition to smart transportation, smart healthcare, and smart culture and tourism, cutting-edge digital technologies, such as digital twins, the metaverse, and digital humans, will also lead to new opportunities and significant improvements [9, 10].

14.5 AI Big Models: Driving the Emergence of New Business Forms

Large models have powerful natural language and multi-modal information processing capabilities which enable them to cope with tasks at different semantic granularities and perform complex logical reasoning. Transfer learning and few-shot learning are also powerful techniques that enable large models to quickly master new tasks and adapt to different domains and data modes. In the future, with further improvement in model capabilities and in-depth knowledge integration, large models will likely become basic production tools for various industries.

Task-specific large models with "emergent abilities" are already being used in knowledge-intensive fields such as astronomy, materials, biomedicine, and physics to facilitate the development of innovative and valuable applications in areas such as meteorological research, medical R&D, and physical law discovery. For example, researchers from Harvard Medical School and Oxford University jointly developed an AI model called "EVE," which can make accurate predictions about the meaning of variations in human genes. This model has analyzed 36 million gene variants for more than 3200 disease-associated genes and reclassified 266,000 variants as either "benign" or "disease-causing." In the future, this AI model can serve as a tool to help geneticists and doctors improve the accuracy of diagnoses and prognoses and develop better treatment plans.

Industry-specific large models enable the intelligent transformation of industries, and industry applications unleash the long-term value of large models. Industry users cannot directly apply the existing general-purpose large models, so industry-specific large models have been designed to meet industry needs. For example, in the information retrieval field, a large model can recognize what a user needs based on their queries and can further refine these queries to retrieve the most relevant data. Another example is in media and broadcasting, where a large model can write entire articles or just titles, abstracts, and paragraphs based on a user's requests. Emerging applications such as smart cities and smart transportation are relying more on large models to enable unified perception, association analysis, and situational forecasting for core city services in order to improve decision-making and city governance.

Large models also boost AIGC applications. The capabilities that large models have in terms of natural language processing, computer vision, and cross-modal technologies support and provide new ways to improve content generation technologies. With its formidable generation capabilities and extensive knowledge, generative AI can complete certain basic mechanical tasks such as information mining, material invocation, and copy-based editing, which will enable personalized content to be efficiently generated on a massive scale at a lower marginal cost. It will revolutionize content production by introducing new processes and paradigms, generate more imaginative and engaging content, and develop more diverse ways of transmitting information. Generative AI and its innovative solutions are already being widely used. Multi-modal and multi-scenario large models have been integrated into various industry processes, including design, modeling, and detection in the industrial field, drug discovery, diagnosis, and treatment in the medical field, as well as training and intelligent teaching assistant in the education field [11, 12].

References

1. China Mobile. 5G-Advanced New Capability and Industrial Development Whitepaper [R]. 2022.
2. China Mobile, China Telecom, China Unicom, et al. 5G-Advanced Technology Evolution from a Network Perspective 2.0(2022) [R]. 2022.
3. China Unicom. China Unicom 5G-A Technical White Paper: Convergence of Communications, Sensing, and Computing [R]. 2022.
4. DUAN X Y, YANG L, XIA S Q, et al. Technology development mode of communication/sensing/computing/intelligence integration [J]. Telecommunications Science, 2022, 38(3): 37–48.

5. LI Q, LI W Y, SUN X W, et al. Thinking of native artificial intelligence in 6G networks [J]. Telecommunications Science, 2021, 37(9): 20–29.
6. XIA X, QI W, WANG H, et al. Discussion on 5G-Advanced Network and Service Evolution Requirements [J]. Mobile Communications, 2022, 46(1): 15–19.
7. Shanghai Data Exchange. China Data Ecosystem Industry Development Report [R]. 2023.
8. Shanghai Data Exchange. 2023 China Data Transaction Market Research and Analysis Report [R]. 2023.
9. ZHONG J, TANG X Y, ZHU L, et al. Evolution and industry trend of 5G key technologies [J]. Telecommunications Science, 2022, 38(5): 124–135.
10. China Mobile Intelligence, GSM Association (GSMA) Intelligence, Global TD-LTE Initiative (GTI). Unleashing New Value with New 5G Technology [R]. 2023.
11. Chinese Association for Artificial Intelligence. China artificial intelligence white paper series — Large models (2023) [R] (in Chinese). 2023.
12. Tencent Research Institute, Tongji University, et al. Man-machine symbiosis — The top ten trends in AI development in the large model era [R] (in Chinese). 2023.

The manufacturer's authorised representative in the EU is Springer Nature Customer Service Centre GmbH, Europaplatz 3, 69115 Heidelberg, Germany. If you have any concerns regarding our products, please contact ProductSafety@springernature.com

Printed and bound by CPI Group (UK) Ltd, Croydon, CR0 4YY

26/03/2026

02078969-0004